Blue-Collar Empire

Blue-Collar Empire

The Untold Story of US Labor's Global
Anticommunist Crusade

Jeff Schuhrke

VERSO

London • New York

First published by Verso 2024
© Jeff Schuhrke 2024

The moral rights of the author have been asserted

1 3 5 7 9 10 8 6 4 2

Verso
UK: 6 Meard Street, London W1F 0EG
US: 388 Atlantic Avenue, Brooklyn, NY 11217
versobooks.com

Verso is the imprint of New Left Books

ISBN-13: 978-1-83976-905-4
ISBN-13: 978-1-83976-908-5 (US EBK)
ISBN-13: 978-1-83976-907-8 (UK EBK)

British Library Cataloguing in Publication Data
A catalogue record for this book is available from the British Library

Library of Congress Cataloging-in-Publication Data

Names: Schuhrke, Jeff, author.
Title: Blue-collar empire : labor internationalism, the global cold war,
    and the untold history of the AFL-CIA" / Jeff Schuhrke.
Description: London ; New York : Verso Books, [2024] | Includes
    bibliographical references and index.
Identifiers: LCCN 2024003292 (print) | LCCN 2024003293 (ebook) | ISBN
    9781839769054 (paperback) | ISBN 9781839769085 (ebk)
Subjects: LCSH: AFL-CIO —History. | AFL-CIO —Corrupt practices. | Labor
    unions —Political activity —United States —History. | United
    States —Foreign relations. | Anti-communist movements —United States. |
    Anti-communist movements. | Labor movement. | Class consciousness.
Classification: LCC HD8055.A5 S335 2024 (print) | LCC HD8055.A5 (ebook) |
    DDC 331.880973 —dc23/eng/20240325
LC record available at https://lccn.loc.gov/2024003292
LC ebook record available at https://lccn.loc.gov/2024003293

Typeset in Minion by Hewer Text UK Ltd, Edinburgh
Printed and bound by CPI Group (UK) Ltd, Croydon, CR0 4YY

Contents

Abbreviations

AAFLI	Asian American Free Labor Institute
AALC	African American Labor Center
AATUF	All-African Trade Union Federation
ACTWU	Amalgamated Clothing and Textile Workers Union
AFL-CIO	American Federation of Labor and Congress of Industrial Organizations
AFSCME	American Federation of State, County, and Municipal Employees
AFT	American Federation of Teachers
AIFLD	American Institute for Free Labor Development
BGTUC	British Guiana Trade Union Council
CGIL	Italian General Confederation of Labor
CGT	General Confederation of Workers (France and Argentina)
CIA	Central Intelligence Agency
CIT	Inter-American Confederation of Workers
CONATRAL	National Confederation of Free Workers (Dominican Republic)
COSATU	Congress of South African Trade Unions
CPUSA	Communist Party USA
CROM	Regional Confederation of Mexican Workers
CTAL	Confederation of Latin American Workers
CTM	Confederation of Mexican Workers

CUT	Unitary Central of Workers (Chile)
CVTC	Vietnamese Confederation of Christian Workers
CVT	Vietnamese Confederation of Workers
CWA	Communications Workers of America
ERP	European Recovery Program (Marshall Plan)
FMLN	Farabundo Martí National Liberation Front (El Salvador)
FOUPSA-CESITRADO (FC)	United Front for Autonomous Unions-Central Union of Dominican Workers
FTUC	Free Trade Union Committee
FTUI	Free Trade Union Institute
ICFTU	International Confederation of Free Trade Unions
ILGWU	International Ladies' Garment Workers' Union
ILO	International Labor Organization
ILWU	International Longshore and Warehouse Union
KFL	Kenya Federation of Labor
KMU	May First Movement (Philippines)
LID	League for Industrial Democracy
NAFTA	North American Free Trade Agreement
NED	National Endowment for Democracy
NLC	National Labor Committee in Support of Democracy and Human Rights in El Salvador
ORIT	Inter-American Regional Organization of Workers
OSS	Office of Strategic Services
PAFL	Pan-American Federation of Labor
SDUSA	Social Democrats, USA
SOBSI	Central Organization of All Indonesian Trade Unions
TUCP	Trade Union Congress of the Philippines
TUEL	Trade Union Educational League
UAW	United Auto Workers
UCS	Salvadoran Communal Union
UE	United Electrical Workers
UMW	United Mine Workers
UPD	Democratic Popular Unity (El Salvador)
USAID	United States Agency for International Development
WFTU	World Federation of Trade Unions

Introduction

It is extremely rare for the president of a major national union to be ousted by a rival in a contested election, but in April 1964, that is precisely what happened to Arnold Zander. Longtime president of the American Federation of State, County, and Municipal Employees (AFSCME), Zander lost his bid for re-election at the union's annual convention by a mere twenty-one votes to progressive reformer Jerry Wurf.

An energetic leader, Wurf would transform AFSCME from a corrupt and lethargic bureaucracy into the nation's fastest-growing union and a vehicle for civil rights activism. In a matter of years, the union under Wurf's stewardship would organize hundreds of thousands of public sector employees—many of them African Americans who had traditionally been excluded from organized labor—including municipal garbage workers, hospital orderlies, janitors, social workers, office workers, school staff and many others. Most famously, Wurf would stand shoulder-to-shoulder with Martin Luther King Jr. during the civil rights icon's final campaign: the 1968 Memphis sanitation workers' strike.

But on taking office as AFSCME's new president in 1964, Wurf found himself in the bizarre position of having to rebuff overtures from the Central Intelligence Agency. The trouble began almost immediately after he moved into the union's Washington headquarters from his home base in New York. There he discovered a mysterious group of men, with no apparent ties to the union, working out of the building's fourth floor in the "International Relations Department." Wurf made inquiries and learned the men were, in fact, CIA operatives. With Zander's approval, they had been covertly organizing and financing anticommunist, pro–United States trade unions in Latin America since at least 1958.

Apparently having no prior awareness of this arrangement, and believing it was not in the union's best interest to continue it, Wurf shut down AFSCME's International Relations Department, fired the men on the fourth floor, and thus cut the union's ties with the spy agency. A few weeks later, he got a call from a White House official asking him to reconsider, and was then driven out to a private home in Maryland where high-ranking CIA officers tried to talk him into continuing the old arrangement that had existed under Zander. Not wanting his union to be an arm of the US foreign policy apparatus, Wurf refused. But he promised never to publicly disclose the identities of the officials he spoke with or any details about the operation he had discontinued—a promise he kept.

While Wurf remained quiet about the AFSCME-CIA relationship that he ended, three years later, investigative reporters from the *New York Times* and *Washington Post* brought the story to the public's attention amid a series of exposés of various organizations the Agency had secretly bankrolled over the years. The most significant and shocking revelation was that in 1963, just a year before Wurf became AFSCME president, the union disbursed as much as $1 million in CIA funds to support an eighty-day general strike in a tiny South American country with the aim of destabilizing its democratically elected government. Later dubbed "the world's longest general strike" by a pair of historians, the work stoppage took place in Guyana, which was then a colony of the United Kingdom called British Guiana. The strike's purpose was to undermine the colony's chief minister, Cheddi Jagan, whose government operated semi-autonomously from the British.

An open Marxist and staunch democrat, Jagan sought to lead the colony through its planned transition to full independence and implement socialist reforms like nationalizing the sugar industry. Unwilling to tolerate another explicitly leftist government in the Western Hemisphere after Cuba's Fidel Castro declared himself a communist, President John F. Kennedy was determined to see Jagan removed from power before British Guiana became independent. The US State Department and CIA got to work on a covert plan to destabilize Jagan's government, which involved wooing and financing some of the colony's trade unions—those affiliated with the domestic political opposition.

In April 1963, with Washington's backing, the anti-Jagan unions launched a general strike, ostensibly to protest a labor reform bill the chief minister had proposed. The work stoppage brought British Guiana's economy to a standstill, leading to shortages of food and fuel, while scaring away potential foreign investors. It also exacerbated racial tensions in the colony, which was divided between Indo-Guyanese (who mostly supported Jagan, who was of East Indian descent) and Afro-Guyanese (who generally supported Jagan's Black political rival). As Jagan supporters refused to participate in the strike—which they recognized as a foreign-backed, politically motivated effort—they were physically attacked by strikers, whom they then attacked in return. Violent race riots soon broke out.

With British Guiana's economy and social fabric in tatters, a defeated Jagan shelved his labor reform bill in July. Declaring victory, the political opposition called an end to the general strike. The following year, in an election rife with US meddling, Jagan and his leftist political party were voted out of power.

While general strikes around the world usually last for a matter of days or weeks, the one in British Guiana lasted nearly three months. It was sustained only thanks to the infusion of US cash that allowed the approximately 50,000 strikers to feed their families and maintain a roof over their heads while they went without pay. Originating with the CIA, the money was transmitted to the local unions primarily by AFSCME's International Relations Department, the same department Jerry Wurf would shutter a year later.[1]

AFSCME, the union that famously empowered hundreds of thousands of long-exploited public sector workers in the United States and partnered with Martin Luther King Jr. in the heroic 1968 Memphis sanitation workers' strike, had also—only a few years earlier—helped to sabotage a progressive and democratic government in a small, impoverished colony by crippling its economy and stoking racial violence.

On a broader scale, the same twentieth-century American labor movement that brought a measure of economic security and personal dignity to millions of working people also participated in some of the most shameful and destructive episodes in the history of US imperialism. For decades, trade unionists in the United States have struggled to make sense of this, reluctant to discuss or even think about it. But with the US labor movement now undergoing a youth-led renaissance, and with renewed "great power" rivalries threatening billions of lives amid a host of other planetary crises, it is long past time for a thorough reckoning.

There is power in a union. Not only the power to secure pay raises and employee benefits, but also—as the 1963 general strike in British Guiana demonstrates—the power to bring economies to a halt and overthrow governments. In the latter half of the twentieth century, the American foreign policy establishment wholly recognized this power. US officials particularly understood that labor movements abroad would play a decisive role in determining the outcome of the Cold War contest for worldwide ideological, geopolitical, and economic supremacy.

Coming out of the crises of the Great Depression and World War II, and fearing the growing influence of communism, Washington planners built what was intended to be a well-managed international capitalist system backed by US economic and military strength. This system would be protected and expanded through what many scholars call an "informal empire," based not on outright territorial conquest, but on political, economic, and cultural dominance. In administering such an informal empire, where indirect influence rather than explicit control was often (though hardly always) the modus operandi, the American state would exert power through numerous nongovernment subsidiaries. These included financial institutions, business associations, scholarly societies, news outlets, publishing houses, political parties, private charities, student organizations—and, importantly, trade unions.

As enemies, foreign unions could seriously upset US imperial designs. But as allies, they could be invaluable assets for maintaining and expanding capitalism, while also stymieing the spread of communism. Labor movements abroad therefore became a crucial target of US imperial intervention: rather than allow them to risk the ongoing accumulation of capital by radicalizing workers and fueling leftist political movements like the one led by Cheddi Jagan, unions would need to be turned into instruments for containing the global working class and its disruptive potential.

To subvert overseas unions for their own imperial ends, Washington officials found an enthusiastic partner in the American Federation of

Labor and Congress of Industrial Organizations—the national labor federation that comprised most of the country's unions, including AFSCME. Anticommunism was not new to AFL-CIO leaders, who already had a history of fighting communists and other leftists for control of their unions that long predated the Cold War. Strategically positioning themselves as the dependable opponents of radicals, AFL-CIO officials eschewed ideas of class conflict and toppling capitalism. They adhered to the durable notion that class collaboration and limited workplace bargaining over "bread and butter" issues would bring workers all the prosperity they needed. Further, they believed free trade and the extension of American capital into foreign markets would benefit workers both at home and abroad by raising wages and living standards.

This book tells the story of US labor officialdom's quest to control the workers' movements of Europe, Latin America, Africa, and Asia between the 1940s and 1990s—and the bitter conflicts exacerbated along the way. When thinking about labor's role in the Cold War, it is important to understand that "the Cold War" was not only an East-West struggle between rival superpowers, but also a series of imperial, often grotesquely violent intrusions by the Global North into the Global South. Like a roving picket marching from country to country, the AFL-CIO's international agents carried out their own imperial intrusions, expending incredible energy and resources to block revolutionary ideologies and militant class consciousness from taking hold in foreign labor movements.

In practice, this meant meddling in the internal processes of other countries' unions, stoking internecine rivalries, creating and financially propping up splinter labor organizations, grooming cadres of conservative unionists, and occasionally using the power of the strike to sabotage left-wing governments. American labor officials usually carried out such activities without the full knowledge or approval of the rank-and-file union members they purported to represent. In the few instances where US unionists became aware of what their national leaders were up to in foreign lands, they forcefully protested.

Union activists, journalists, and scholars first began documenting US labor's Cold War intrigues in the late 1960s, the same period when AFSCME's partnership with the CIA in British Guiana came to light. Early studies and exposés characterized the AFL-CIO as being little more than a puppet of the US government. The spotlight was especially shone on labor's shadowy ties to the CIA. Many assumed the spy agency was corrupting hapless union leaders, while many others mockingly called the labor federation the "AFL-CIA."[2] More recent studies have demonstrated how the CIA was only the most notorious government entity that organized labor partnered with. In reality, the AFL-CIO became closely allied with almost the entire US foreign policy apparatus—not only the CIA, but also the State Department, Agency for International Development, and National Endowment for Democracy.

Scholars in the early twenty-first century rightly contend that American labor leaders were not just dupes of the government, but were instead aggressive cold warriors in their own right. Labor officials—many of whom spent their early years maneuvering to expel radicals from their own unions—did not need to be corrupted by the CIA, since they were willing to wage the Cold War with or without the government's cooperation, and were already waging it before the CIA had come into formal existence. Because of their firsthand experience battling leftists in their union ranks, many labor officials even saw themselves as more committed and effective anticommunists than their government counterparts, leading to an occasionally contentious relationship. What's more, recent studies show how unionists in the countries on the receiving end of US labor's interventions had their own agendas, which they often advanced by using the substantial resources the AFL-CIO could provide.[3]

The present study builds on this existing scholarship and journalism, while also incorporating original archival research, to provide a comprehensive history of US labor's global reach in the latter half of the twentieth century. The main characters are the high-ranking AFL-CIO officials—nearly all white men—who shaped and implemented labor's international policy. Foreign labor leaders and union dissenters at home also figure prominently in this story.

When we examine top labor officials' actions in the realm of foreign policy, it becomes clearer how the global Cold War directly contributed to US labor's decline in the latter half of the twentieth century. In 1947, the year the Cold War began in earnest, approximately 35 percent of US private sector workers were union members—a historic high point. But by the time the conflict ended with the dissolution of the Soviet Union in 1991, that number had plummeted to only about 11 percent. This was not a coincidence.

With a greater share of American workers belonging to unions in the mid-1900s than ever before or since, for a brief period, the labor movement enjoyed unprecedented political clout and economic muscle. One out of every three nonagricultural workers was in a union. Unions were strongest in the mass production industries at the center of the national (and global) economy. With the genuine strength unions brought to bear, labor disputes were often front-page news, and many national labor officials were household names.

AFL-CIO leaders might have used this influence to advance the long-term well-being and security of the working class by advocating for a robust welfare state, organizing the unorganized, and hindering militarism and war. Besides a few exceptions like Jerry Wurf, they did not pursue such goals. Instead, with the Cold War looming over virtually every decision they made, they chose to direct much of their energies toward waging a global anticommunist crusade.

In practice, "anticommunism" did not only mean opposition to actual communists, but also an intolerance—sometimes a violent hatred—for almost any progressive, left-leaning ideas challenging the capitalist status quo and for the people or groups advocating them. Shunning some of the most dedicated and militant unionists due to their political affiliations, cozying up to Corporate America in the name of patriotism, and devoting so much attention and so many resources to interfering in foreign unions, AFL-CIO leadership unwittingly helped lay the groundwork for organized labor's near decimation at the end of the century.

To justify their overseas interventions, top labor officials insisted they were promoting "free" and "democratic" unionism around the world. In fact, their anticommunist fixation tended to only make unions more autocratic, both at home and abroad. In the United States and in other countries, worker organizations frequently had large numbers of communists or other leftists. Union democracy allowed such radicals to win leadership positions and gain influence over labor movements. For anticommunists, this was intolerable, and genuine union democracy was therefore unacceptable to them.

In a process that first unfolded in the United States and was then replicated in many other countries with the AFL-CIO's support, leftists were systematically driven out of organized labor, and union constitutions and procedures were violated or unilaterally changed to ensure anticommunists could maintain an iron grip over worker organizations. This was analogous to how, in order to supposedly safeguard freedom, many anticommunist governments around the world became brutally authoritarian during the Cold War, usually with US support.

Similarly, in the name of opposing "totalitarianism"—especially state domination of unions—American labor frequently sponsored foreign unions that were ironically under tight state control. In the Global South, or Third World as it was then called, this was often connected to what was thought to be the requirements of development. Desperate to rapidly grow their economies, governments in poorer countries demanded that unions temper workers' expectations rather than make forceful demands. In these situations, where it was feared the failure to achieve economic development might open the door to communist revolution, the AFL-CIO would rather unions be extensions of the state than authentic organs of worker discontent.

This would ultimately prove to be an act of self-sabotage. Bolstering conservative, procapitalist unions in the Third World at the expense of more independent and militant labor movements partly paved the way for US multinationals to move production offshore and drive down global labor standards in the "race to the bottom" at century's end. With unions around the world rendered docile and undemocratic, and with labor movements divided and weakened, it became far easier for capital to exploit workers both in the United States and overseas.

Additionally, while touting the virtues of autonomous unionism free from state control, the AFL-CIO itself took millions of dollars from Washington to bankroll its foreign programs, while closely collaborating with US government agencies across the globe. American labor leaders saw nothing hypocritical in this, since their arrangement with Washington was, in their view, simply a function of a pluralistic society in which different groups freely work together. Besides, "free" trade unionism was ultimately only a euphemism for anticommunist trade unionism, because in their view, everything communists touched was inherently "totalitarian."

The world we inhabit today—one in which capital flows effortlessly across nations and multibillionaires take joyrides into outer space while a subjugated global working class remains bounded by militarized borders on an ecologically degraded planet—was shaped most decisively by the US government's actions during the Cold War. The American labor movement was perhaps the only organized force that could have exerted the necessary outside pressure to alter Washington's calculus, and thus alter the fate of the world. Instead, AFL-CIO officials, without consulting the millions of workers they represented, chose to be partners in the making of an unequal international order dominated by capital.

Understanding why and how this happened is essential for all those who want to build the kind of multiracial, inclusive, international working-class movement that is necessary in the twenty-first century to overcome oppression, militarism, and exploitation around the world. Reckoning with this history is therefore the responsibility of every serious trade unionist and labor advocate in the United States.

The Early Labor Movement

To begin making sense of the AFL-CIO's support for US imperialism, and particularly its embrace of Washington's worldwide anticommunist campaign during the Cold War, we need to briefly review the earlier history of the American labor movement.

From the time of chattel slavery and indentured servitude to the era of precarity and "McJobs," the United States has always been one of the most anti-worker countries in the world. Independent producers and entrepreneurs have been idealized and celebrated, while those either physically or economically coerced into toiling for others have traditionally been shamed and scorned. In the nineteenth century, workers who tried to build collective power to resist exploitation were met with unremitting hostility by both employers and the state. The courts ruled that the nation's earliest unions were illegal conspiracies threatening employers' sacred rights to hold private property and make profits.

The development of a unified and cohesive working-class consciousness in the nineteenth-century United States was thwarted by various historical particularities. These included uneven industrialization and proletarianization thanks to the nation's ever-expanding frontier, religious and ethnic divisions between native-born and immigrant workers, and especially anti-Black racism on the part of whites. From early in the nation's history, US workers were segmented and stratified, with higher-skilled, professional, white, native-born male workers enjoying greater social, political, and economic privileges than the less skilled, immigrants, workers of color, and women workers.[4]

In the decades after the Civil War, for the first time, a majority of Americans and newly arriving immigrants were pushed into the ranks of dependent wage workers thanks to rapid industrialization. Those who went on strike and challenged the dominance of capital in this period faced brutal repression at the hands of state militias, the army, recently created urban police forces, and private security firms like the notorious Pinkertons.

The US labor movement of the late nineteenth century was populated by socialists, anarchists, and reformers of various stripes aiming to achieve radical social transformation, particularly seeking the abolition of the wage system, not unlike how slavery had recently been abolished. The working-class reformism of this era came to be epitomized by the Knights of Labor. Founded in 1869 as a secret society due to the traditional repression of unions, the Knights began organizing out in the open in the 1880s in the midst of growing working-class unrest. Seeking to unite all "toilers" regardless of craft or skill, and calling for the establishment of a more egalitarian society, it grew to over 700,000 members by 1886, making it the country's largest-ever workers' organization up to that point. While the Knights' membership included many union militants and radicals, national leaders like Terence Powderly were notably opposed to strike action, instead favoring the promotion of cooperatives in order to remake the economy.

Some skilled craftsmen—including cigarmakers, printers, iron molders, and carpenters—grew alienated by Powderly's aversion to strikes and his fascination with what seemed to them like utopian goals. In 1881, they founded the Federation of Organized Trades and Labor Unions (FOTLU), which prioritized organizing along strict craft lines and going on strike to achieve immediate workplace gains.

The FOTLU famously called for nationwide work stoppages on May 1, 1886, to demand the eight-hour workday, a cause enthusiastically taken up by many Knights members and labor anarchists. In Chicago, this campaign culminated in a bomb being hurled into a column of police officers in Haymarket Square, an act used to justify a government crackdown on union radicals (including the hanging of four Chicago anarchists who had nothing to do with the bomb), and helped precipitate the decline of the Knights of Labor. Seven months after the

Haymarket bombing, the FOTLU was reconstituted as the American Federation of Labor (AFL).

Having witnessed the limitations of the Knights and the harsh repression of radicals, the AFL would gradually distance itself from revolutionary theories and broad reform movements, instead demanding a better deal for skilled white workers within the confines of industrial capitalism. By the mid-1890s, the Federation's leaders—mostly craftsmen of Northern European origin—believed that capitalism was here to stay and there would be no revolution. Eventually rejecting notions of class consciousness, they came to champion "job consciousness," calling for higher pay and shorter hours while signaling their allegiance to the established social and economic order. They referred to their philosophy as "trade unionism, pure and simple," but it would later be better known as "business unionism."

Experiencing the anti-labor repression of the Gilded Age firsthand, and understanding just how deeply capitalism was ingrained in the national psyche, AFL leaders were convinced that their more conservative vision was the only practical way forward for the US labor movement. Still, the Federation and its affiliated craft unions were hardly models of docility, as they often wielded a high degree of workplace militancy to win more control over their labor. As a less ideologically threatening and ostensibly more pragmatic alternative, in the 1890s the AFL surpassed the Knights in terms of influence, respectability, and membership numbers.

The chief spokesperson for business unionism was Samuel Gompers, who served as AFL president from its founding in 1886 to his death in 1924 (with the exception of one year). Born in London to Dutch Jewish parents, Gompers emigrated to the United States as a teenager. He was initially drawn to socialism as a young cigarmaker in New York City, but gradually came to believe that "pure-and-simple" unionism was more practical and effective than radical theories.

In his lengthy career as the AFL's top official, Gompers was consistently preoccupied with achieving recognition for organized labor as the legitimate partner of business and government in the maintenance of the capitalist order. He and other business unionists contended that what was good for the US economy—in other words, what was good for capitalism—was good for American workers, as long as they could have a seat at the table.

In striving for respectability and legitimacy, over the years Gompers frequently found himself at odds with radicals both within and outside the AFL, making him and his lieutenants increasingly defensive against leftist influence in the labor movement. This led to bruising internal union conflicts that helped shape the intense anticommunism of many twentieth-century US labor officials.[5]

Labor Internationalism

Since at least 1848, when Karl Marx and Friedrich Engels published *The Communist Manifesto* in Europe, many in the emerging industrial working class understood the need to organize across national boundaries to effectively challenge the power of capital and avoid being pitted against one another. In the 1860s, radicals from a number of European countries attempted to unite the workers of the world by founding the International Workingmen's Association, later known as the First International. In the United States, socialist workers organized over thirty chapters of the First International in the years immediately following the Civil War, but amid factionalism the International fell apart in 1876.

In the 1880s, the Knights of Labor also developed an internationalist vision, dispatching organizers abroad to connect workers of the same trades in different countries. Eventually, the Knights established assemblies in Canada, Britain, Ireland, France, Belgium, Italy, South Africa, Australia, and New Zealand.

When European socialists met in Paris to found the Second International in 1889, the AFL sent a representative seeking their support in calling for worldwide demonstrations on May 1, 1890, to demand a universal eight-hour workday—a revival of the earlier campaign that had been stopped by the Haymarket Affair. The Second International agreed, declaring May 1 (May Day) to be International Workers' Day, a tradition that has lasted for well over a century. But the AFL's relationship with the Second International cooled in the 1890s as Gompers became ever more alienated from socialists and socialism. The Federation soon distanced itself from May Day and its radical associations, instead only observing Labor Day in the United States on the first Monday of September.[6]

In the aftermath of the 1898 Spanish-American War, the US military occupied Cuba while also taking possession of the former Spanish colonies of Puerto Rico, Guam, and the Philippines. The same year, the United States also annexed the Hawaiian Islands. This sudden overseas territorial expansion disturbed many Americans, who feared the country was acquiring an overseas empire much like the European colonial powers.

The drive for imperialism came in part from the monopoly trusts seeking new markets for US manufactured goods and new sources of raw materials and agricultural commodities, particularly after crises of overproduction had led to economic depressions in both the 1870s and 1890s. Gompers spoke for the majority of US unionists when he came out against the annexations of 1898, especially due to fears that so-called "savage" and "barbarian" Latinos and Asians in the newly acquired territories would become a source of cheap, exploitable labor and drive down standards for white workers. Such racism and xenophobia were widespread in the AFL, which for decades was prominent in movements to restrict immigration, while also tolerating the exclusion or segregation of Black workers in its affiliated unions.

Gompers became a vice president of the Anti-Imperialist League, a national organization whose members included high-profile industrialists and politicians like philanthropic steel magnate Andrew Carnegie and former US president Grover Cleveland. For Gompers, being part of the Anti-Imperialist League was an opportunity to showcase the AFL's ability to work in partnership with powerful figures from the worlds of business and government. The fact that Carnegie and Cleveland had respectively worked to smash organized labor during the famous Homestead and Pullman strikes a few years earlier apparently did not bother him.

Within only a few years, Gompers and the AFL accepted the new realities of US empire, backing the formation of unions in newly acquired territories, especially in Puerto Rico. In the early 1900s, the Federation supported the construction of the Panama Canal and made no protest when the United States invaded and occupied Haiti, the Dominican Republic, and Nicaragua. Meanwhile, as US capital spread into Canada, several local unions in that country began joining AFL affiliates, leading to US unions often being called "international" unions.[7]

Labor and the State: World War I

While the AFL's acceptance of capitalism may have been expedient for avoiding outright repression, in the long run it proved to make organized labor dependent on the benevolence of the state. As long as the strategy hinged on not merely surviving, but thriving within the existing political and economic system, then American labor would need the state to recognize its legitimacy and provide it some measure of access to decision-making. In the twentieth century, labor officials would therefore establish alliances with the federal government that eventually took the form of the AFL-CIO's full-scale complicity with imperialism during the Cold War.

One might imagine that the national labor-state partnership began in order to address domestic issues like social welfare or workplace safety, but in fact it was first forged in the realm of foreign policy. To union leaders and rank-and-file members overwhelmingly concerned with how to deal with employers and improve workplace standards, questions of foreign policy could seem extraneous. Because it was so remote to their day-to-day interests, internationalism was one area where many unionists in the early twentieth century were willing to allow a federated, national body like the AFL to take the lead. As a result, Gompers increasingly involved himself in foreign affairs, especially since he saw this as an avenue for the Federation to gain legitimacy in the eyes of the political and business establishments.

This was most evident during the presidency of Woodrow Wilson in the 1910s. As Wilson weighed to what degree the United States should intervene in the Mexican Revolution, Gompers eagerly offered the AFL's services, providing advice and information based on the Federation's contacts with Mexican unions. The AFL partnered with the Wilson administration to try taming the more radical impulses of the Mexican Revolution by organizing a Pan-American labor organization founded on the principles of business unionism.[8]

But Gompers grew even closer to Wilson during World War I. As Wilson prepared to bring the United States into the conflict, he faced a major hurdle in the form of left-wing, antiwar elements in the labor movement. These included not only the Industrial Workers of the World (IWW)—an anticapitalist, syndicalist alternative to the AFL founded in 1905—but also many socialists and anti-British immigrants within AFL-affiliated unions.

The presence of unions in key production industries like mining, steel, meatpacking, and shipbuilding meant that organized labor was well positioned to hamper the US war effort. Recognizing this, Wilson enlisted the aid of Gompers, appointing him to the prestigious Council on National Defense in order to win labor's support for the war. Gompers was, of course, eager to convince government and business leaders that the AFL and its affiliated unions could be valuable allies when it came to boosting wartime production.

In the short term, this calculation paid off for the AFL. Through the War Labor Board—a federal agency created by the Wilson administration to arbitrate industrial disputes and keep production running smoothly—workers in many industries achieved vast improvements in pay, hours, and conditions, while unions greatly increased their memberships. Still, despite Gompers's calls for industrial peace during the war, many AFL-affiliated unionists remained militant and used the wartime emergency to force concessions from employers. Of all the strikes in the United States during World War I, 95 percent were led by AFL-affiliated unions, compared to only one in six led by the more radical but numerically smaller IWW.

Gompers became such a trusted ally of Wilson that at the war's end he played a key role in executing the president's vision of liberal internationalism, traveling to Paris to chair the Commission on International Labor Legislation. The commission created the International Labor Organization (ILO), which became part of the new League of Nations and aimed to bring workers, employers, and governments together in the name of economic equity and social stability. Ironically, the United States refused to ever join the League of Nations due to both right-wing isolationism and left-wing critiques of the League's undemocratic structure, and only finally joined the ILO in 1934.[9]

The gains achieved by AFL-affiliated unions during World War I were quickly lost after the war ended, as employers forcefully reasserted their dominance over workers and a union-busting "open shop" campaign swept the nation during the 1920s—illustrating that labor's strategic bargain with the state did not pay off in the long term. Labor officials would not learn from this experience. A similar dynamic would play out repeatedly in the twentieth century, as the labor movement's support for World War II and the Cold War also achieved temporary advantages for industrial workers that the government would then

callously allow Corporate America to undo once organized labor's
assistance was no longer needed.

AFL vs. Communists

Business unionists presented themselves to employers and the state as a
bulwark against worker radicalism. After numerous battles for control
of the labor movement, Gompers and other conservative AFL leaders
eventually came to despise leftists, viewing them as the principal obstacle in their path to gaining legitimacy and material gains for workers.
An ideology of revolutionary class consciousness was in direct opposition to everything business unionists stood for. Anarchism, socialism,
and communism therefore became natural enemies of the AFL
bureaucracy.

Though sympathetic to Marxism in his youth, for most of his career
as a labor leader Gompers was hostile toward socialists, describing them
as "men whose minds have been warped by a great failure or who found
it absolutely impossible to understand fundamentals necessary to developing practical plans for industrial betterment."

In his position on the Council on National Defense during World
War I, Gompers stood by as the government targeted IWW radicals
who opposed the war, imprisoning or deporting many of their key
leaders and thus eliminating many of the business unionists' rivals.
After Russia's Bolshevik Revolution in 1917, he opposed US recognition of the Soviet Union, calling the Bolsheviks "pirates" who had
raised "the black flag over helpless Russia and declared war upon the
established order about which the fabric of civilized life had been
woven." Writing shortly before his death in 1924, the longtime AFL
president concluded that "the Soviets have demonstrated beyond
question that Socialism is economically unsound, socially wrong, and
industrially impossible."[10]

In the aftermath of World War I, young American radicals inspired by
the Bolshevik Revolution founded the Communist Party USA. In the face
of the anti-labor onslaught of the 1920s, communist activist and veteran
union organizer William Z. Foster ambitiously hoped to transform the
AFL into a class-conscious, anticapitalist body through the Trade Union
Educational League (TUEL). A network of worker radicals who formed

rank-and-file committees inside AFL affiliates, the Communist Party–backed TUEL built alliances with noncommunist progressives, spread left-wing ideas, called for the organizing of the unorganized, and encouraged craft unions within the same industries to "amalgamate" (merge together) in order to maximize their strength. TUEL activists ran for union office—often winning—and brought their politics and organizing strategies up for debate at union meetings and conventions.

The conservative leaders of the AFL and its affiliates were outraged by this "boring from within" strategy, correctly viewing it as a threat to the philosophy and practice of craft-oriented business unionism. It was all the more infuriating to them because it seemed to be sowing internal division at the precise moment when unions were under employer attack and membership was declining. AFL leadership therefore used heavy-handed methods to isolate and drive out the communists and their sympathizers, including cutting off subsidies to and threatening to revoke the charters of local bodies where the TUEL was making inroads, like the Chicago Federation of Labor and Seattle Central Labor Council. The top officers of AFL affiliates—including the United Mine Workers and International Ladies' Garment Workers' Union—similarly expelled pro-TUEL activists from their own unions through undemocratic means.

For having dared to try changing the AFL's political orientation and organizing strategy from within, communists became even more hated by the business unionists—explaining why many labor officials were arguably more staunchly anticommunist than even the US government during the Cold War.

Meanwhile on the European labor scene, a rift emerged between socialist and communist unionists in the early 1920s that would also later prove consequential in the Cold War. In the period around World War I, most trade unions in Western Europe were closely tied to Socialist and Social Democratic parties. In 1919, these unions banded together to form the International Federation of Trade Unions, also known as the "Amsterdam International" after the city where it was headquartered. Gompers participated in the International's founding during his post-war sojourn in Europe, but ultimately kept the AFL out of it due to its socialist orientation.

Although the social democratic unionists of Western Europe initially celebrated the Russian Revolution, they hesitated to answer the Bolsheviks' calls for proletarian revolution in their own countries. The Bolsheviks then attacked them for being too cozy with capitalists and established the Red International of Labor Unions, or Profintern, to rival the Amsterdam International. For their part, the social democratic unionists accused the new Soviet government of deceiving and oppressing the Russian working class.

This mutual animosity would only grow, but was importantly put on hold in the late 1930s and early 1940s amid the threat of fascism. In later years, social democratic laborites in Western Europe would form an uneasy alliance with the more conservative American unionists to fight the Cold War.

Labor and the State: The Depression and World War II

The economic emergency of the Great Depression brought questions of labor to the forefront of US politics in the 1930s. With capitalism in crisis and millions of unemployed or underpaid workers growing restless, government officials looked for ways to simultaneously revitalize the economy and stabilize labor relations.

Although AFL leaders had long sought the government's respect and were happy to partner with Washington during World War I, the Federation was generally not in favor of the state's direct involvement in industrial relations. The AFL instead preferred negotiations between unions and employers with minimal state intervention—a system generally referred to as voluntarism, but perhaps better understood as "collective laissez-faire."[11] This was in part because the state had traditionally intervened on the side of employers in labor conflicts, using court injunctions or outright violence to repress workers who went on strike. It also reflected the fact that the AFL unions represented craftsmen whose skills made them difficult to replace, thus giving them a high degree of bargaining power and, in their view, rendering government meddling unnecessary and undesirable. Having the state serve as a compulsory arbiter between employers and employees in the hope of securing fairer labor relations was far more appealing to less skilled, more easily replaceable workers in the growing mass industries of the early twentieth century, particularly women and immigrants.

With the passage of the 1932 Norris-LaGuardia Act, the AFL craft unions got what they had long desired: the right to negotiate with employers free from government interference. But for non-unionized industrial workers, both the state and organized labor needed to do more. Starting in 1933, a militant wave of strikes, led and encouraged by radicals, erupted among industrial workers across the country. Dissident AFL union presidents soon founded the Committee for Industrial Organization (CIO, later renamed the Congress of Industrial Organizations after it broke with the AFL completely) to take advantage of this upsurge and organize the unorganized within entire industries, instead of only along craft lines.

In 1935, the US government assumed a new, more robust role in employment relations with the passage of the National Labor Relations Act. This landmark piece of New Deal legislation set a legal path for unionization and established a series of rules and regulations governing collective bargaining. While AFL leaders initially frowned upon this unprecedented intrusion by the federal government, the CIO took advantage of the National Labor Relations Act to rapidly unionize workers of all crafts and skill levels in the steel, auto, rubber, electrical, and other mass production industries.[12]

Much to the chagrin of the AFL's conservative leaders, the CIO's affiliated unions welcomed in communist organizers because of their effectiveness and dedication. Further, the CIO popularized militant shop-floor tactics like the sit-down strike to win union recognition and contest the day-to-day power of managers, while also supporting social reform goals like racial justice and women's rights. But despite the CIO's rapid growth, the AFL remained the larger labor federation.

During World War II, the state took on an even greater role in labor relations. New wartime federal agencies were created to manage production and control wages and prices, with many CIO and AFL officials serving in them. As it had during World War I, the US government established a National War Labor Board that could use binding arbitration in disputes between unions and employers to ensure continuous production of essential war materiel without the interruption of strikes and lockouts.

Organized labor once again made a strategic wager with the state to secure gains amid a world war. In exchange for submitting to the wartime bureaucracy and promising not to strike, unions received extraordinary security thanks to new government protections, with national union membership skyrocketing from about 9 million in 1940 to nearly 15 million by 1946.

But as labor historian Nelson Lichtenstein has noted, for the CIO particularly, this strategic wager amounted to a Faustian bargain. Under the wartime labor regime, militant tactics like sit-down strikes and slowdowns, which had won industrial workers newfound shopfloor strength in the late 1930s, were suddenly derided as unpatriotic or as the machinations of traitorous communists. Key CIO officials like Walter Reuther of the United Auto Workers became convinced that the main arena of labor struggle had shifted from the factory floor to the halls of Washington, where they expected to participate in economic planning alongside government bureaucrats and corporate managers.[13]

Becoming more reliant on the US government went hand in hand with surrendering collective power at the workplace. Labor officials therefore came out of World War II believing that maintaining the state's favor, in part by demonstrating intense patriotism and hatred for foreign enemies, was crucial to the continued growth of their unions.

By the mid-1940s, then, the US labor movement had become ever more entwined with the American state through the experiences of the Great Depression and two world wars. What's more, the nation's dominant labor federation, the AFL, continued to fundamentally reject radicalism and resent leftist attempts to gain a foothold in unions, while the upstart CIO would begin abandoning its earlier tolerance for communists and commitment to shopfloor struggle as the political environment shifted rightward. All of this helped set the stage for US labor's eager participation in the global Cold War.

PART I

Free Trade Unionism: 1945–1960

1

The Free Trade Union Committee

On a spring evening in 1945, New York City's Central Labor Council held a ceremony to dedicate its new meeting hall on East 17th Street. The event's special guest speaker was George Meany, the second-highest-ranking official in the American Federation of Labor.

It was April 5. Overseas, World War II was nearing its end. Two months earlier, President Franklin D. Roosevelt had met with Soviet leader Joseph Stalin and British prime minister Winston Churchill at Yalta to begin planning the postwar peace. In three weeks, delegates from fifty Allied countries were due to meet in San Francisco for the founding conference of the United Nations. In international trade union circles, plans were in place to form a kind of United Nations for organized labor to bring together the national union centers of the Allied countries, particularly those of the Soviet Union, Britain, and United States.

But addressing New York's body of AFL affiliates that night, Meany announced that the Federation would boycott any attempt at international labor unity that involved Soviet trade unions. They were not unions at all, Meany insisted, but merely "creatures of the state" that subordinated the needs and rights of workers to the policies of the Politburo. Our Soviet allies, he contended, were no better than our Nazi enemies, since both were "totalitarian" governments enslaving their peoples. The Federation would no more associate with a communist worker organization than with a fascist labor front. "What could we talk about?" Meany asked rhetorically. "The latest innovations being used by the secret police to ensnare those who think in opposition to the group in power? Or, perhaps, bigger and better concentration camps for political prisoners?"[1]

What stands out about Meany's anti-Soviet speech was its timing. While the United States and the Union of Soviet Socialist Republics had been enemies in the past and would soon be enemies again, in April 1945 they were still allies. Their common enemy, Hitler, was still alive, the Third Reich was still (barely) standing, and victory in Europe was still a month away. The US government strongly discouraged high-profile Americans like Meany from publicly denouncing the USSR. It would be another ten months before diplomat George Kennan sent his "long telegram" to the State Department warning of Soviet expansionism, and eleven months before Churchill famously declared that an "Iron Curtain" had descended across Europe—two moments that historians often consider the earliest indicators of the Cold War.

Meany's speech in New York that night, which would not have gone unnoticed by communists in both the United States and USSR, was arguably the opening salvo in the superpower conflict that would shape geopolitics for the next half century.

George Meany and the AFL's Anticommunism

Raised in the Bronx, Meany followed his father into the plumbing trade in 1910 at the age of sixteen. After twelve years on the job, he put down his tools for good and became a full-time business agent for his union, Local 463 of the United Association of Journeymen Plumbers.[2]

By the 1930s, Meany had risen through the ranks of labor officialdom to become president of the New York State Federation of Labor, a prominent position that eventually landed him the job of AFL secretary-treasurer. He would become president of the AFL in 1951, then president of the merged AFL-CIO in 1955. Unafraid to exercise his authority and never shy about speaking his mind, Meany would be the most powerful figure in the US labor movement from the early 1950s to the late 1970s.

As a devout Catholic schooled in the traditionally conservative building trades, anticommunism came naturally to Meany. When asked by his biographer if there was any single event that shaped his anticommunism, he answered vaguely, "Nothing except my feeling that I don't like to get kicked around . . . When I saw workers being kicked around by Communists, I immediately became an anti-Communist."

Though many of his contemporary business unionists in the 1920s and 1930s battled with communists over control of their organizations, Meany did not have this problem. As he explained later in life, there were only "a couple of Commies" in his plumbers' union local, who "would come to the meeting week after week and talk against capitalism and all that stuff," but were generally ignored and "never were a threat to our union."[3] Nevertheless, Meany came of age as a unionist at a time of great internal conflict within labor's ranks between communists and noncommunists, and he also was greatly influenced by the AFL's conservative style of trade unionism.

Since shortly after its establishment in 1886, the AFL had striven to be the moderate alternative to radical Marxist and anarchist labor agitators. It is no surprise, then, that the Federation opposed the USSR from the moment the 1917 October Revolution brought the Russian Bolsheviks to power. The Communist Party USA (CPUSA) was founded in 1919, looking to the Communist International (Comintern) in Moscow for guidance. The CPUSA believed workers should be organized by industry instead of by craft. Industrial unionism meant all workers in a given industry, regardless of their particular job or skill level, should belong to the same union to increase their collective strength. The AFL, however, clung to a tradition of organizing workers according to their specific craft, a policy that favored more skilled, less replaceable workers, who tended to be white, male, and of Northern European origin.

Through the Trade Union Educational League (TUEL), in the 1920s the CPUSA endeavored to organize workers from inside the existing AFL-affiliated unions, a strategy known as "boring from within." Conservative business unionists, as well as many socialist unionists, feared that communists in union leadership positions would put the party's (and thus Moscow's) ideological and political aspirations above the more immediate interests of the union membership. Hoping to bring about proletarian revolution, communists naturally thought organized labor's objectives should be aligned with those of the party, but these ambitions did not prevent them from being honest and practical trade unionists. Top AFL officials fiercely resisted and deeply resented communist efforts to democratically gain control over existing unions.

With the Comintern believing the world ripe for working-class revolution, in 1929 the Communist Party USA abandoned "boring from within" to practice "dual unionism"—organizing its own, parallel unions outside the established ones. As a result, CPUSA organizers transformed the TUEL into the Trade Union Unity League to compete with the AFL. Though happy that communists were no longer "infiltrating" their affiliated unions, AFL leaders like Meany scorned this effort to form parallel organizations that threatened to draw workers away from the Federation and divide the labor movement.

In the early years of the Great Depression, the communist–led Trade Union Unity League organized some of the most marginalized members of the US working class, including Black and Latino agricultural workers. But in 1935, it was disbanded after the Comintern directed communists around the world to unite with other progressive forces as part of a "Popular Front" to oppose the growing menace of fascism. Many ex–Trade Union Unity League organizers now made their way into the Committee for Industrial Organization, cofounded that same year by John L. Lewis.

Autocratic president of the United Mine Workers, Lewis was a forceful presence within the AFL. He had been pressuring the Federation's leaders to take full advantage of President Roosevelt's New Deal—which offered newfound legal protections for union organizing and collective bargaining—to quickly unionize the millions of unorganized workers in mass production industries like steel and auto. The only way to do this would be to abandon craft unionism and to organize workers on an industrial basis, something the AFL's craft unionists were loath to do.

In response to the AFL's refusal to act, Lewis and a handful of other national union presidents formed the CIO in late 1935 to unionize the mass industries, without the Federation's blessing. The following year, AFL president William Green suspended the ten unions that comprised the CIO for their unruliness.

Now operating as an independent labor organization, within only a few years the CIO successfully unionized some of the largest industrial companies in the nation, including US Steel and General Motors. At its best, the CIO consciously strove to be a people's movement, uniting workers of all races, genders, ethnicities, religions, political persuasions, and trades. Much of the CIO's rapid success was thanks to the tireless organizing of communist unionists, who were welcomed into its ranks—though they typically did not announce their party membership.

Lewis, a Republican who only briefly supported Franklin Roosevelt, was certainly no radical, and in fact had expelled communists from the United Mine Workers in the 1920s for daring to challenge his undemocratic stranglehold over the union. Yet he tolerated "reds" in the CIO because he recognized their organizing acumen. Even Meany admitted that the communists were "very, very good organizers."[4] But Lewis was also careful to use his control over the CIO to ensure that the Communist Party would not gain too much power within its affiliated unions. "Who gets the bird," Lewis once rhetorically asked in response to concerns about his unlikely allies, "the hunter or the dog?"[5]

Still, by the 1940s, several CIO unions were led or heavily influenced by communists, including the United Electrical Workers; the International Longshore and Warehouse Union; and the International Union of Mine, Mill and Smelter Workers. Other unions also had notable red factions, including the Detroit-based United Auto Workers (UAW), the CIO's largest affiliate.[6]

Thanks to the unifying politics of the antifascist Popular Front, by World War II's end, communists were prevalent and influential in the US labor movement (namely, the CIO), as well as in other countries' labor movements. It was exactly this tolerance of communist unionists that Meany, serving as AFL secretary-treasurer, hoped to end as the war came to a close.

In October 1945, representatives from the Allied nations' trade union centers met in Paris to found the World Federation of Trade Unions (WFTU). The WFTU's mission was to continue the wartime alliance between communist and noncommunist labor organizations and to promote a postwar world premised on peace and justice for all workers.

As promised, the AFL boycotted the Paris meeting and refused to have anything to do with the WFTU. Nevertheless, US workers were represented thanks to the participation of the CIO, which joined the new international body. But under the stewardship of Meany and other

stalwart labor anticommunists, the AFL was already working to undermine the new WFTU.

Woll, Dubinsky, and the FTUC

The shape of the postwar international union movement was on the
minds of the delegates at the AFL convention in New Orleans in
November 1944. British, Soviet, and CIO unionists were already making
plans to establish the World Federation of Trade Unions, much to the
chagrin of AFL officials, who did not recognize the legitimacy of Soviet
trade unions and who considered the CIO to be a procommunist rival.

To begin building a countermovement to Popular Front–style labor
internationalism, the delegates at the 1944 AFL convention voted to
establish what they called the Free Trade Union Committee (FTUC), a
body that would soon function as the Federation's primary weapon for
waging the coming Cold War.[7]

As its name implied, the FTUC's purpose was to aid "free" trade
unions overseas, particularly in war-ravaged Europe. The term "free
trade unionism" had come into popular usage by AFL leaders in the
1930s. It initially referred to bona fide, autonomous unions free
from employer dominance—a rebuke to the phony company unions
that proliferated in the 1920s and early 1930s. But by 1944, the term
was specifically used to denounce fascism and communism, both
considered "totalitarian" systems where unions were dominated by
the state.

The FTUC included three key AFL officials: Meany, Matthew Woll,
and David Dubinsky. Since becoming AFL secretary-treasurer in 1941—
making him second only to Green in the Federation's organizational
hierarchy—Meany had wanted to make his mark without appearing to
compete with the AFL president. Foreign policy was the perfect avenue.
Green was largely uninvolved in international affairs, creating a vacuum
Meany could fill.[8] This ambition, along with his anticommunist convictions, compelled the former plumber to become the liaison between the
Free Trade Union Committee and the AFL's Executive Council.

Serving as the FTUC's chairman was Woll, the former president of
the International Photo-Engravers Union. In his mid-sixties at the time
of the FTUC's founding, Woll had been an AFL vice president for

decades. He had therefore been on the front lines in the struggles against the communist "boring-from-within" strategy of the 1920s, at one point even publicly chastising the New York police for not taking harsher action against picketers in a communist-led furriers' strike.[9] He was once considered the heir apparent to Samuel Gompers, but lost his bid for the AFL's presidency to Green after Gompers's death in 1924.

Known as an "arch conservative" and "labor's fiercest champion of capitalism," Woll was "violently anti-Communist," a position shaped and hardened by his years battling the labor-left for control of the Federation and its affiliated unions. As the longtime chair of the AFL's International Labor Relations Committee, he occasionally attended overseas conferences and made sure the Federation's international-themed resolutions were reprinted in pamphlet form, but did little else on the foreign affairs scene prior to World War II. With his veteran status as an AFL leader, Woll was a sensible choice to serve as the FTUC's public face.[10]

Dubinsky was in many ways the real driving force behind the Free Trade Union Committee. President of the New York–headquartered International Ladies' Garment Workers' Union, he was one of the labor movement's more energetic and visionary leaders. Born David Dobnievski in the Russian Empire, as a teen in Poland Dubinsky was a bakery union activist and political prisoner before emigrating to the United States in 1911 at age nineteen. He joined the Socialist Party and went to work in New York's clothing industry, becoming an ILGWU member. It was perhaps the most diverse union in the nation, with a membership composed of Jews, Poles, Italians, and other European immigrants, as well as African Americans who were part of the World War I–era Great Migration from the South and Puerto Ricans beginning to migrate to the mainland.

In the 1920s, the ILGWU was wracked by a civil war between communists on the one hand and a coalition of conservatives and anticommunist socialists on the other. Riding a wave of rank-and-file, women-led frustration over the union's traditionally undemocratic structure, reds were elected to leadership positions in several large locals. Eager to hold on to their power, the ILGWU's conservative top officials made various repressive attempts to prevent communists from becoming an influential bloc within the union, such as unseating them at national conventions or suspending them from local office.

But the communists continuously defied these efforts, and in 1926 they led a strike of 40,000 New York City cloak makers. The ILGWU's communists and anticommunists were at odds throughout the work stoppage, which dragged on for twenty-eight weeks and nearly bankrupted the union. A settlement was ultimately reached that was less favorable than what the cloak makers had been initially offered before the strike. The union's left and right mutually blamed each other for the debacle.[11]

As this internal conflict played out within the ILGWU, the socialist Dubinsky rose through the union's ranks, allying with the old-guard bureaucrats to oppose the communist upstarts. Since his time as a teenage socialist in the Russian Empire, Dubinsky had favored the comparatively moderate Mensheviks over the more radical Bolsheviks. In the aftermath of the October Revolution, which saw the Bolsheviks come to power, he was dismayed to watch his Socialist Party of America be torn apart by fierce disagreements over whether to back the emerging Soviet Union. Convinced the ILGWU's reds would either inadvertently destroy the union or make it subservient to Moscow, Dubinsky vigorously supported undemocratic methods to silence, marginalize, or expel them.[12]

After the communists had either been chased out of the ILGWU or voluntarily exited to pursue the Comintern's new "dual union" strategy, Dubinsky became the garment worker union's national president in 1932. Abandoning socialism to embrace New Deal liberalism, he led successful mass organizing campaigns to rebuild the union after years of internal strife. Between 1935 and 1938, Dubinsky—and the ILGWU by extension—was a somewhat reluctant member of the CIO. While he supported industrial unionism, he was also cautious about alienating the AFL and sowing labor disunity, and was greatly displeased by John L. Lewis's toleration of communists (it was Dubinsky whom Lewis rhetorically asked, "Who gets the bird?"). After the CIO changed from the seemingly ad hoc Committee for Industrial Organization into the more permanent Congress of Industrial Organizations in 1938, Dubinsky pulled the ILGWU out and was welcomed back into the AFL fold two years later.[13]

During World War II, Woll and Dubinsky teamed up to form the Labor League for Human Rights, a humanitarian organization that aided European unionists displaced by the war or persecuted by the Nazis. When the AFL established the Free Trade Union Committee in

1944, it was initially placed under the auspices of the Labor League, receiving most of its funding from Dubinsky's ILGWU.[14] Woll, Dubinsky, and Meany were the officers presiding over the new FTUC, but they needed someone to run it full time. Dubinsky had just the man for the job: Jay Lovestone.

From Communist to Anticommunist: Jay Lovestone

One of the most fascinating and unsavory characters in the history of US labor, Lovestone would come to be identified with the AFL's Cold War foreign intrigues more than any other individual. Born Jacob Liebstein, at the age of nine Lovestone moved with his family from their home in czarist Lithuania to New York City in 1907. The son of a rabbi, he was drawn to intellectual pursuits, studying accounting at the City College of New York and briefly attending law school at New York University. Lovestone became involved in radical politics during his student years, serving as the president of the City College's chapter of the Intercollegiate Socialist Society, the student wing of the Socialist Party. Electrified by the Bolshevik Revolution, at twenty years old he dropped out of law school and helped found the Communist Party USA in 1919. He became one of the party's chief propagandists as editor of its official newspaper.

With the CPUSA often operating underground in the 1920s due to government repression, and with the party roiled by constant infighting, Lovestone became adept at engaging in covert activities, corresponding in code, and both hatching and unravelling conspiratorial plots.[15] In the words of historian Irving Bernstein, Lovestone was "a formidable hater, [who] enjoyed vituperation and denunciation, and held both his enemies and his intellectual inferiors in contempt."[16]

With the help of key allies in the Comintern, Lovestone maneuvered his way into becoming the CPUSA's executive secretary in 1927. But on a delegation to Moscow two years later, he was stripped of his authority and excommunicated from the party by Stalin himself. Lovestone's alliance with Stalin's Politburo rival, Nikolai Bukharin, along with his belief that there must be a unique revolutionary strategy for the United States—a heresy called "American exceptionalism"—had alienated the Soviet leader.

Calling Lovestone "an adroit and talented factional wire puller," Stalin said he doubted "very much at this stage that Comrade Lovestone can be a party leader."[17] After reprimanding Lovestone, the Comintern ominously ordered him to stay in Moscow and confiscated his passport. With the help of friends, he managed to sneak out of the USSR, returning home to New York to find himself blacklisted from the CPUSA. Ostensibly still a believer in the revolutionary cause, but now a decided enemy of the official party, Lovestone and his loyalists formed the Communist Party (Opposition), better known as the "Lovestoneites."[18]

In 1933, a group of Lovestoneites led by Charles "Sasha" Zimmerman was elected to the leadership of Local 22 of the ILGWU in New York. Zimmerman had previously held union office within the ILGWU in the 1920s before being involuntarily relieved from his responsibilities as punishment for his Communist Party membership. But after joining Lovestone's anti-Stalin opposition group, by April 1933 he had been forgiven by Dubinsky and allowed to once again run for ILGWU office, winning the presidency of Local 22. With Lovestone's help, Zimmerman led the local on a successful strike that August, which so impressed Dubinsky that he invited Lovestone to speak at the union's national convention the following year—marking the latter's entrance into "good standing" in the labor movement.[19]

Through Dubinsky, Lovestone was introduced to United Auto Workers president Homer Martin in 1937. At the time, both the UAW and ILGWU were in the CIO, and the nascent auto union was in the midst of a bitter internal dispute. On one side was Martin, a temperamental Baptist preacher whose gift for oratory had propelled him to the UAW presidency the year before. On the other side were the UAW's leftists, a tenuous alliance between members of the Socialist Party and the CPUSA.

The UAW socialists were led by the youthful and ambitious Walter Reuther, president of the large Local 174 on Detroit's West Side. The union's communists were led by a group of respected veteran organizers who had built the UAW from the ground up. Fearful of the strong presence of radicals within the union's leadership and what it meant for his own hold on power, Martin sought to neutralize the socialists and communists. With his intimate knowledge of the Left, Lovestone, the "factional wire puller," was brought into this explosive mix to advise Martin.

About a dozen Lovestoneites were sent to the Midwest to serve as UAW staffers who would be loyal to Martin, while Lovestone himself stayed behind in New York and counseled the union president from afar. Among the Lovestoneites deployed to the UAW was twenty-five-year-old Irving Brown, whom Martin hired as an organizer—and who was destined to become Lovestone's most trusted international agent in later years.

Between 1937 and early 1939, Martin repeatedly tried to push the UAW leftists out of the union by firing or transferring staffers and suspending several of the union's executive officers. Lovestone was revealed as the architect of these hostile moves, leading Victor Reuther, Walter's younger brother and close confidant, to call him one of the "most Machiavellian union-splitters ever to prey on the American labor movement."[20]

As part of this constant maneuvering and backstabbing, Walter Reuther's alliance with the reds became increasingly frayed, as did his longstanding ties with the Socialist Party, from which he resigned. Reuther soon formed his own caucus and put himself on a path that would eventually lead him to the union's presidency several years later.

In the meantime, the CIO intervened and ended the UAW infighting in early 1939, sending Martin and the Lovestoneites packing, as well as reducing the influence of the union's communist faction. Thanks to his role in nearly destroying the UAW during the internal feud, Lovestone had made lifelong enemies in Walter and Victor Reuther.[21]

In the late 1930s, following the execution of his old ally Bukharin in the Soviet Union, as well as the signing of the short-lived nonaggression pact between Hitler and Stalin, Lovestone finally renounced radical politics altogether, completing his decade-long transformation from communist to full-fledged anticommunist. He disbanded his communist opposition group at the end of 1940 and went to work for the ILGWU's International Relations Department.

Once the United States entered World War II, Lovestone tried to do his part by seeking a job with the Office of Strategic Services (OSS), the military's wartime intelligence agency, but was rejected because of his high-profile communist past. In 1943, the OSS established a Labor Desk in Europe to assist underground unionists in coordinating antifascist resistance efforts, headed up by labor lawyer Arthur Goldberg. Wanting to prove his usefulness, Lovestone voluntarily supplied Goldberg with letters of introduction to over thirty European labor leaders he knew from his years as an influential leftist. From that point on, he became increasingly enmeshed the world of US intelligence.[22]

After the AFL formed the Free Trade Union Committee in 1944, Dubinsky tapped Lovestone to manage its day-to-day operations. He was the perfect choice. The new FTUC's mission would be combating the growth of communist influence in the international labor movement, and few people knew the inner workings of world communism better than Lovestone. "Jay had been on both sides of the fence, his mind was like a road map, he knew the place names on the other side, he knew who was pulling the strings," explained Ernest Lee, Meany's son-in-law, who would later work with Lovestone in the 1960s. "He saw plots everywhere. If you argued with him, he'd say 'I know them, I know how they operate.' And 90 percent of the time he'd be right."[23]

Meany and Woll came to see the value in having an ex-red on their side. While their own anticommunism was blunt and visceral, Lovestone had the ability to articulate anticommunism more intellectually, employing "elaborate left-wing political verbiage."[24] Meany later recounted his initial hesitance about partnering with Lovestone and how he was eventually swayed:

> The Communists hated him, and the anti-Communists wanted no part of him. Me, I wouldn't be seen on the same side of the street with him. But Dubinsky worked with him about five years, then told me, "The son of a bitch is OK, he's been converted." On Dubinsky's say-so, I accepted him.[25]

Irving Brown's Mission to France

Through much of 1945, the AFL's fledgling Free Trade Union Committee slowly raised funds from AFL-affiliated unions to become operational. While the FTUC's original fundraising goal was $1 million, it had collected only about $200,000 by the end of the year.[26]

In the meantime, the war in Europe came to an end that May with Germany's surrender. Among the Allied powers, the Soviet Union had shed the most blood to attain this victory, losing more than 27 million people over the course of the war. The Red Army had faced the full brunt of the German war machine, expelling the Nazis from Eastern Europe, while the United States and Britain had opened a second front with the invasion of France in June 1944. At the war's end, Stalin was determined to secure the USSR's borders above all else, a goal that required remaining in control of Eastern Europe.

The US government—unexpectedly led by President Harry Truman after Roosevelt's death in April—was willing to grant such territorial concessions, but was determined to prevent Western Europe from being absorbed into the Soviet sphere of influence as well. That was a real possibility in 1945, since, thanks to the leading role they had played in the wartime antifascist resistance, the Communist parties of Western Europe were remarkably strong and popular.

While there was already a worrying amount of latent distrust between the United States and USSR, the Cold War was not yet an explicit reality in 1945. This was evident in the growing unity between communist and noncommunist national trade union centers, manifested in the establishment of the World Federation of Trade Unions. But for the vehemently anticommunist AFL, the Cold War was already on, and its FTUC was ready to spread "free" trade unionism abroad.

While "free" trade unionism initially referred to unions being free from employer or state domination, by 1945 the term was being used by the AFL as a synonym for anticommunist unionism. In other words, even if a union were autonomous and democratic, the AFL would still consider it illegitimate and "unfree" if it happened to be led or influenced by communists.

In the eyes of "free" trade unionists, reds could never truly attain union leadership through democratic methods or with rank-and-file support—they could only do so through some kind of illicit conspiracy. Because they followed the "totalitarian" Soviet Union, everything communists did, and every organization they touched, was "totalitarian" by extension. As historian James Prickett demonstrated, commonplace political activity within unions would be characterized as nefarious when undertaken by communists. "Non-Communists win union elections, but Communists 'capture' a union," Prickett wrote. "Non-Communists join unions; Communists 'infiltrate' or 'invade' them. A non-Communist states his or her position; a Communist

'peddles the straight party line.' Non-Communists influence or lead
groups; Communists dominate them."[27]

Ironically, to bring foreign labor movements over to their brand of
unionism, the AFL's "free" trade unionists would willfully engage in
exactly the kind of underhanded, intrusive, and undemocratic methods
they routinely ascribed to their communist foes.

Meany, Woll, Dubinsky, and Lovestone reckoned the first order of business upon the war's end would be appointing a field representative to
visit Europe on behalf of their Free Trade Union Committee to assess
the labor situation firsthand and begin the work of bolstering anticommunist union factions. Lovestone chose his trusted associate Irving
Brown for the job.

Brown had been one of the Lovestoneites hired by Homer Martin
during the UAW's internal feud in 1937–38. A Bronx native, Brown first
met Lovestone as a student at New York University in the early 1930s. As
the story goes, Brown—serving as president of the socialist-affiliated
Social Problems Club—cast the tie-breaking vote in a controversial
decision to invite the former Communist Party leader to come speak on
campus. The two men struck up an immediate friendship, with Lovestone
becoming a mentor to Brown.

After Brown graduated in 1932, Lovestone helped him get a job as a
researcher for ILGWU Local 22. Brown also married Lovestone's secretary, Lillie Smith. As a pro-Martin UAW staffer in the late 1930s, he
organized Ford workers in Chicago, establishing his union bona fides.
Between April and September 1945, Brown worked as a labor advisor to
the US Foreign Economic Administration, which was then setting
economic policy for occupied Germany. During this stint, he first visited
Europe and likely developed contacts with the OSS.[28]

Brown arrived in Paris as the Free Trade Union Committee's new
field representative in November 1945, one month after the World
Federation of Trade Unions' founding conference had been held in
the same city. Because the FTUC was not on firm financial footing,
Brown's position was initially temporary.[29] This financial weakness,
combined with his own ignorance of French, might have served to
undermine Brown's mission, but the FTUC representative was
uncannily motivated and resourceful. With some help from the US
Embassy and OSS, but mostly on his own initiative, he quickly

established allies among French trade unionists and assessed the national labor scene.

After two weeks in Paris, he reached the conclusion that France was "the number one country in Europe from the point of view of saving the western labor movement from totalitarian control."[30] Comprising unions representing a total of 5 million workers, the CGT (General Confederation of Labor) was France's primary national union center and a founding member of the World Federation of Trade Unions. In late 1945, nearly two-thirds of the CGT's affiliates were led by unionists from the French Communist Party. The French communists had been at the heart of the underground resistance movement during the Nazi occupation, and they now shared power alongside the Socialist and Christian Democratic parties in France's postwar tripartite government. They were keen to consolidate their control over the CGT to further bolster their position in both the government and in newly nationalized industries like electricity, banking, insurance, and coal.

Brown forged relationships with the CGT's secretary general, the elderly socialist Léon Jouhaux, and his younger second-in-command, Robert Bothereau. Jouhaux was not fond of the reds, but was willing to tolerate them in the name of trade union unity. Bothereau, on the other hand, was a determined anticommunist and headed up a faction called Resistance Ouvrière (Workers' Resistance), made up of CGT dissidents who were unhappy with the growing strength of the communist unionists.

Looking ahead to the CGT's April 1946 convention, in which the reds planned a vote on restructuring the confederation's executive committee to reinforce their majority, Brown encouraged Resistance Ouvrière to pose a challenge and whip up "no" votes. "There is no great hope that the [communists] will be defeated," he wrote to Woll, "but a crystallization and consolidation of the *true* trade union forces can begin."

Brown had his work cut out for him. Bothereau's faction was nowhere near as organized or well financed as the communists, who were receiving support from the Soviet Union. At the same time, France was facing economic ruin in the wake of the war, and the CGT's working-class members were more preoccupied with daily survival than trade union politics.

In December 1945, with five months to go until the CGT convention, Brown wrote to Dubinsky and Woll requesting $100,000 to support

Resistance Ouvrière. It was a "desperate situation," he explained, "but the stakes are high and worth the fight for free trade unionism."[31] But by March, Brown had received only $3,000—a thousand to assist Resistance Ouvrière in expanding its ranks and sending delegates to the convention, the rest for his own personal expenses. In part this was because the FTUC was struggling to get donations from AFL-affiliated unions, but it was also because Woll and Dubinsky were not entirely convinced Brown's longshot gambit merited much investment.[32]

Still, Brown did his best to stir up internal strife within the French labor movement. To address the postwar economic crisis, communists in the CGT were advancing the tripartite coalition government's policy of prioritizing increased industrial productivity over raising wages, which Brown used as a point of criticism as he spoke at union meetings around the country in early 1946. He privately admitted that sowing discord as an outsider was "not a nice way of doing business," but reasoned it was "necessary" work.[33]

Without much material aid from the AFL, Resistance Ouvrière failed to make a splash at the CGT's April 1946 convention. The communists' measure to restructure the CGT's executive committee to their advantage was approved by a majority of delegates. Brown called it a "catastrophic defeat" and encouraged members of the losing anticommunist faction to reject the democratic decision and refuse to fall in line under a "false banner of unity." Arguing that the CGT was now beyond saving, he called on the Bothereau group to break away and form a new, rival trade union center—the kind of "dual unionism" the Comintern had once promoted, but now being advocated by its opponents.

Brown knew that consciously dividing French labor would be a sensitive mission, explaining that the "free" trade union forces would have to "handle this issue with great care and preparation so that the split becomes a logical necessity in the eyes of the workers and not something which they fear will reinforce the interests of the employers."[34]

Splitting French Labor

After a year in Europe, Irving Brown returned to the United States in October 1946 to attend the AFL convention in Chicago. The previous twelve months had witnessed the largest strike wave in US history, with 5 million workers from both the AFL and CIO hitting picket lines to demand higher wages amid rising inflation and safeguard their jobs in the conversion from a wartime to a peacetime economy.

Even with this massive labor unrest, and perhaps because of it, a major theme of the AFL convention was anticommunism, with multiple resolutions denouncing the CIO for its tolerance of communists.[35] By the time of the AFL convention, the Cold War was coming into sharper focus. The fragile wartime alliance between Washington and Moscow was rapidly eroding. It was clear that the United States and its Western allies were heading into a standoff with the Soviet Union and its new satellites over the political and economic future of Europe. In this context, AFL leaders and convention delegates were committed to beefing up the Federation's foreign presence, particularly through the Free Trade Union Committee.

In his report to the convention, Brown blamed the WFTU—which "was conceived by the Russian dictatorship"—for slowing the growth of "free" trade unions in Western Europe.[36] The delegates voted to give Brown a permanent office in Europe, as well as to create a new International Affairs Department for the AFL.

A couple months later, Dubinsky and Woll's Labor League for Human Rights was shut down, since its wartime humanitarian mission was now considered over. The FTUC, which had been an auxiliary of the Labor League, became a standalone entity with more committed funding from the AFL. This meant Lovestone could assert much more authority over the FTUC than he had during the previous two years, with Brown now reporting directly to him. Ever the propagandist, one of Lovestone's first priorities was to begin publishing an international newsletter—the *Free Trade Union News*—translated into multiple languages and spreading the gospel of anticommunist, "free" trade unionism.[37]

Brown returned to Europe in the spring of 1947, setting up his permanent office in Brussels (though within a few years he would establish his base in Paris). With him were his wife, Lillie, and their young son. The FTUC soon scored one of its earliest victories.

The French Communist Party and the CGT continued prioritizing increased production over wage raises until April 1947, when workers at the nationalized Renault auto factory in a Paris suburb went on strike demanding a 10 percent pay increase. The CGT and French Communist

Party now reversed their former policy by throwing their support behind the strikers, much to the consternation of Paul Ramadier, the socialist head of France's coalition government. Acting on Washington's wishes, Ramadier dismissed the communist members of the government in May, citing their backing of the disruptive Renault strike as the reason.

The following month, newly appointed US secretary of state George Marshall publicly proposed a robust program to rebuild Europe's war-shattered economies through American aid, loans, and exports—helping establish a revitalized international capitalist system managed and protected by the United States. The proposal, which the French communists correctly regarded as an attempt to further shunt them aside politically and render their anticapitalist vision obsolete, was embraced by the Ramadier government.

Feeling backed into a corner, communists in the CGT called a series of tumultuous strikes that rocked the nation for much of the rest of the year. The French economy had already been devastated by the war, and the mass work stoppages of 1947 only seemed to be making things worse. While the strikes served to articulate the economic suffering of French workers, they notably also functioned as a political protest by the communists against Marshall's proposal. The anticommunist minority on the CGT's executive committee, including Robert Bothereau, as well as thousands of noncommunist rank-and-filers, became ever more frustrated by the militant actions called by the confederation's communist majority.[38]

Brown remained determined to assist Bothereau's Resistance Ouvrière faction, which by now had changed its name to Force Ouvrière (Workers' Force). Bothereau, his union allies, and Brown had long believed that a break from the CGT was inevitable, and a split now appeared imminent. Brown mailed out 24,000 copies of the *Free Trade Union News* in French to noncommunist unionists around the country. The FTUC had allocated $6,000 for his activities in France, but over the course of 1947 he asked for nearly $12,000 more to aid in organizing the CGT's dissidents.

"In spite of what may happen in any other part of Europe, for the moment the best of American plans will go for naught if this French situation is not broken," Brown wrote to Lovestone in August. "Whatever may be the long run answer to Europe's problems, it is still France that must be cracked or else every move we make will be paralyzed in advance."[39] That November, amid all the chaotic strike activity, the dissident faction made plans to break away from the CGT. The veteran socialist labor leader Léon Jouhaux was not personally in favor of a schism, but followed the lead of Bothereau and other younger activists.

The next month, the Force Ouvrière faction—which included white-collar civil service unions—formally pulled out of the CGT, becoming its own national trade union center at a founding congress the following April.[40] "Our work and our propaganda of the last two years in spite of all inadequacies have had their effect," a jubilant Brown wrote to Lovestone as the French labor movement was torn apart.[41]

The strikes of 1947 transformed both the French Communist Party and CGT from mainstream institutions in the country's political and economic life into overnight pariahs. Although the CGT remained the nation's largest trade union center after Force Ouvrière's exit, much of the French public now regarded it more as a front for the recently ostracized communists instead of the legitimate, unified voice of labor.

The Cold War–inspired factionalism in the French labor movement weakened the power of the country's unions overall. Throughout the 1950s, as the nation's economy grew thanks to US aid, the now avowedly anticommunist French government granted wage increases primarily to keep workers from wanting to join the CGT. This, combined with the existence of an alternative in Force Ouvrière, meant the CGT lost half its membership between 1949 and 1958.[42]

Though the AFL's Free Trade Union Committee helped organize Force Ouvrière, as historian Anthony Carew notes, a rupture in the French labor movement might well have happened anyway because CGT dissidents like Robert Bothereau were wary of their communist counterparts from the start. The FTUC's real contribution would come *after* the split, when it was instrumental in keeping Force Ouvrière financially afloat, allowing it to remain a competitive rival to the much larger and better-funded CGT.[43]

The fracturing of the CGT and related shunning of communists from French politics—which would allow for Marshall aid to mold an interdependent economic relationship between France and the United States—served as a framework for waging the early Cold War in other European countries like Italy and West Germany.[44] The AFL's internationalists hoped the kind of division they had promoted in the French labor movement could be replicated on a larger scale within the World Federation of Trade Unions, with the goal of establishing a new international body of anticommunist "free" trade unions.

Despite the Free Trade Union Committee's overwhelming focus on Europe, the first significant defeat for the WFTU's Popular Front–style labor internationalism would occur in Latin America.

2

Good Neighbors

The Pan-American Federation of Labor

In the late nineteenth and early twentieth centuries, unions in Central America, South America, and the Caribbean followed revolutionary anarchist tendencies similar to workers' movements in Spain and Italy. Latin American workers toiled in plantations, railroads, mines, mills, oilfields, and refineries that were often owned by wealthy financiers and industrialists in the United States. At the urging of US capitalists, Washington repeatedly intervened in the social and political affairs of Latin American nations to safeguard their investments. This usually meant sending in troops for both short and long periods, and sometimes meant, as in the aftermath of the Spanish-American War in 1898, formally annexing territory.[1]

Though he opposed territorial expansionism and feared that exploited labor from so-called savages in newly annexed regions would drive down wages for white workers, AFL cofounder and president Samuel Gompers generally accepted US supremacy in Latin America and beyond. Controlling the world's markets would strengthen the US economy, and that control, he and others reasoned, would benefit North America's skilled workers.[2]

During the Mexican Revolution in the 1910s, which was essentially a rebellion against years of despoliation by foreign capital, Gompers advised President Woodrow Wilson to support imposing the AFL's model of conservative business unionism onto Mexican labor to temper the radicalism playing out on the United States' doorstep. This seemed especially urgent, since the syndicalist Industrial Workers of the World was already influential among many of the revolutionaries after years of organizing Mexican workers—and even more urgent after Russia's Bolshevik Revolution in 1917 set a potential example for Mexicans to follow.[3]

Similarly wanting to bring Mexican labor under control, and hoping to keep Wilson in his good graces, the moderate revolutionary leader Venustiano Carranza called for the creation of an AFL-style national trade union center that would support his own Constitutionalist faction. The result was the formation of the CROM (Regional Confederation of Mexican Workers) in May 1918. Led by Carranza ally Luis N. Morones, the CROM represented a break from the Latin American labor movement's traditional adherence to anarchism.

At Gompers's urging, a "Pan-American" labor conference was held in the border town of Laredo, Texas, only six months after the CROM's founding. Seventy-one delegates attended, mostly from the AFL and CROM, but also one delegate each from Guatemala, El Salvador, Costa Rica, and Colombia. As the AFL and Wilson administration hoped, the gathering resulted in the creation of the Pan-American Federation of Labor (PAFL). Although unions from other Latin American countries were involved, the PAFL was to be primarily a partnership between the AFL and the CROM—with the latter in a subordinate role.[4]

Gompers was elected the PAFL's president at its founding meeting in Laredo. The new international union organization called for higher wages, better working conditions, and civil liberties for all workers of the Western Hemisphere, but its central purpose was to counteract radical tendencies in the labor movements of Latin America, especially in Mexico. Santiago Iglesias, the AFL's main representative in Puerto Rico and a driving force behind the PAFL, explained that the Pan-American labor organization was meant to be the "instrumentality through which constructive trade unionism can gain the ascendancy in Latin America, thus saving the [US] trade union movement from a continuing battle at its back door with a most destructive and revolutionary labor movement."[5] In many ways, then, the PAFL embodied international "free" trade unionism *avant la lettre*.

In 1924, Gompers died of heart failure in San Antonio, Texas, on his way back from a PAFL meeting in Mexico City, where he had just been re-elected the organization's president. With no succession plan laid out in the PAFL's constitution, its leadership fell to the new AFL president, William Green, who did not share his predecessor's interest in international affairs.[6]

Lombardo's Internationalism

After Gompers's death, the Pan-American Federation of Labor went into decline, and by the 1930s it was inactive. In Mexico, Morones's CROM was supplanted by a new, more dynamic trade union center: the CTM (Confederation of Mexican Workers), established in 1936 by Vicente Lombardo Toledano.

A Marxist intellectual, educator, and former CROM officer, Lombardo founded the CTM to unite communist and progressive noncommunist unionists to fight for the economic independence of Mexico. Though never a member of the Mexican Communist Party, he was an open admirer of the Soviet Union, which he visited in 1935.[7] Soon after its creation, the CTM allied with the nation's president, Lázaro Cárdenas, who shared much of Lombardo's vision for social and economic justice. Thanks to the pressure brought to bear by workers in CTM-affiliated unions, Cárdenas took the bold step of nationalizing Mexico's railroad and oil industries in 1937 and 1938, respectively.

Like the agricultural lands the Cárdenas administration was busily redistributing to campesinos, the railroad and oil industries were largely owned by foreign capitalists. The government's expropriations, along with the CTM's organizing, angered international business interests, prompting Lombardo and Cárdenas to seek broader support through the creation of a new Latin America–wide labor confederation.[8]

On the CTM's invitation, worker organizations from thirteen Latin American countries convened in Mexico City in September 1938 for the founding congress of the CTAL (Confederation of Latin American Workers). The CTAL followed the Popular Front spirit of unity between communist and noncommunist unions, while also explicitly denouncing fascism. The new organization adhered to Lombardo's belief that the fight against capitalism was inextricably linked to the fight against US empire. It called for an end to both labor exploitation and economic imperialism, adopting the motto "For the Emancipation of Latin America."

Unlike the AFL-dominated Pan-American Federation of Labor, the CTAL would be of, by, and for Latin Americans. Still, unionists from outside the region were invited to the founding congress in Mexico City to be fraternal observers. Léon Jouhaux of the French CGT attended, as did the CIO's John L. Lewis. The AFL was also invited, but—just as it would do at the founding of the World Federation of Trade Unions seven years later—refused to participate on grounds that the CTAL welcomed communists into its ranks.[9]

AFL leaders were disturbed by the CTAL's formation, convinced that Lombardo's brand of anti-imperialism would strengthen Soviet influence in Latin America at the expense of the United States. Unfortunately for the Federation, Washington was not inclined to do anything about the CTAL. In accordance with President Franklin Roosevelt's "Good Neighbor" policy, the United States in the 1930s temporarily broke from its pattern of interventions in Latin America and was generally more respectful of national sovereignty in the region.

Cárdenas was succeeded as Mexico's president in 1940 by the moderate Manuel Ávila Camacho. In this new political atmosphere, many of the CTM's top officials grew uncomfortable with Lombardo's radicalism. When his term as the CTM's general secretary came to an end in 1941, the Marxist labor leader stepped down rather than seek a second term, remarking, "I leave office a rich man—rich in the hatred of the bourgeoisie."[10] Nevertheless, Lombardo remained president of the CTAL.

The early to mid-1940s was a period of democratic openings and mass political participation across Latin America. Washington provided ample economic aid to the region to bolster industrial production for the Allied war effort, leading to economic growth and an expansion in Latin America's urban working class. Populist, liberal, and social democratic political parties came to power, the traditional bans on communist parties were lifted in many countries, and unions were allowed to operate more independently.

But immediately after the war, Washington abandoned the Good Neighbor policy and moved to return Latin America to its former dependent status as an exporter of raw materials. Economic aid from Washington significantly decreased and the United States flooded Latin American markets with its own manufactured goods. In this changing context, Latin American politics moved sharply to the right. Now more reliant on attracting private capital from abroad, economic and military elites cracked down on the popular movements that had grown in the previous years, attempting to rein in unions and present a docile labor force to foreign investors. As an anti-imperialist and anticapitalist, Lombardo was determined to resist this trend, making him dangerous in the eyes of the State Department.[11]

In 1945, Lombardo brought the 3.3 million–member Confederation of Latin American Workers into the new World Federation of Trade Unions. From the moment of the CTAL's creation, the AFL had been weakly trying to resurrect the Pan-American Federation of Labor, to no avail. Now, with the CTAL joining the WFTU and thus formally partnering with the Soviets, the "free" trade unionists in the North became even more determined to create a rival to Lombardo's organization—one that would be more tolerant of US dominance.

To accomplish this, the AFL needed a full-time ambassador to the region, which it would get in early 1946 with the recruitment of an Italian émigré named Serafino Romualdi.

Serafino Romualdi's Travels

From the mid-1940s to the mid-1960s, Romualdi was considered "the principal personification" of US labor's interests in Latin America and the Caribbean.[12] He was born and raised in central Italy. As a young schoolteacher in 1920, Romualdi joined the Italian Socialist Party, which was then in turmoil. The party's members were frequent targets of violent attacks by Benito Mussolini's Fascist Party, while division was brewing within its own ranks over the question of supporting the Russian Bolsheviks. The party split in 1921, with the left wing forming the Communist Party of Italy.

Romualdi blamed the communists for the internal division and stuck with the socialists, becoming editor of the party newspaper, *Il Progresso*. In October 1922, not long after Romualdi was beaten in the street by a fascist gang, Mussolini became Italy's prime minister. Convinced it was unsafe for him to remain in the country, the twenty-two-year-old socialist fled to the United States.

Eventually settling in New York, Romualdi worked for a decade as an editor for pro-union, antifascist Italian-language newspapers, reaching a wide readership of working-class Italian immigrants. In 1933, he was hired by David Dubinsky's International Ladies' Garment Workers' Union—which had thousands of Italian American members—to do editorial and public relations work. Associating with Dubinsky, who shared Romualdi's antifascist and anticommunist convictions, gave the Italian immigrant clout in the world of trade union politics.[13]

With the outbreak of World War II, Romualdi became active in the Mazzini Society, an organization of antifascist Italian Americans urging support for the Allies. The Mazzini Society was troubled by reports of Italian immigrant communities in South America expressing pro-Mussolini sympathies, and therefore dispatched Romualdi to Argentina, Brazil, and Uruguay in 1940 on a six-month antifascist propaganda mission.

Romualdi's efforts attracted the attention of the recently formed US Office of the Coordinator of Inter-American Affairs. Run by Nelson Rockefeller, whose powerful family had considerable investments in the region, the office's main purpose was to counter fascist influence in Latin America and keep the Western Hemisphere firmly in the Allied camp. In 1942 and 1943, Romualdi again traveled to South America, this time as a representative of Rockefeller's agency, where he continued doing propaganda work and establishing contacts across the region.[14]

Romualdi came home to the United States in September 1943, just after the fall of Mussolini in Italy. He was eager to return to his native country on behalf of his adopted one, with an eye toward aiding the reorganization of the Italian labor movement, which had been dominated by the fascist regime for two decades. The Allies planned to shepherd an agreement between the country's three major antifascist political parties—the Socialists, Communists, and Christian Democrats—to share leadership of Italy's labor movement.

Due to his years of involvement in anticommunist socialist circles, as well as his years working for Dubinsky's ILGWU, Romualdi was a dedicated "free" trade unionist. This ironically made him skeptical of trade union freedom if it meant allowing communists to gain influence. Using the connections that he had made while representing the US government in Latin America, Romualdi reached out to Assistant Secretary of State Adolph Berle, warning that the Italian communists "would take advantage of the freedom to organize . . . to seek control of the labor movement for their exclusive political interests and designs." He recommended that the "democratic elements" of Italian labor—code for the anticommunists—be "organized, advised, and, if necessary, *led* to take a more militant stand" against the reds. Impressed with Romualdi's advice, Berle sent him to Italy as a newly minted officer in the Office of Strategic Services, the wartime US intelligence agency.[15]

Romualdi operated in Italy from July 1944 to April 1945. "My OSS assignment was not of the cloak-and-dagger nature generally attributed to anyone who worked in that outfit," he would explain in his memoir. "I operated completely in the open." Shortly before his arrival, the Italian Socialist, Communist, and Christian Democratic parties had jointly formed a new national trade union center, the CGIL (Italian General Confederation of Labor). Convinced that the communists held the upper hand and would eventually take full control of the CGIL, Romualdi spent most of his OSS mission trying to persuade the Allied military command to split the new confederation by pushing for the communists' exclusion.

To Romualdi's disappointment, the three political camps remained united within the CGIL, and the US military government treated the communists as legitimate actors. By the spring of 1945, he "came to the conclusion that it was useless to stay in Italy" and formally left the OSS, though he would remain close to the US intelligence community. He returned to Rockefeller's Inter-American Affairs Office, which sent him on another tour of Latin America later that year.[16]

Following Japanese surrender and the end of the war, Romualdi went back to his old job at the ILGWU's communications department in New York, but Dubinsky and the AFL had bigger plans for him. With his anticommunist credentials, experience in intelligence and propaganda, and numerous contacts in Latin America, Romualdi was just the man to bring the AFL's "free" trade union crusade south of the border.

Romualdi writes in his memoir that he was approached by two South American labor leaders in December 1945—Bernardo Ibáñez of Chile and Arturo Sabroso of Peru—who were briefly in New York on their way home from attending an International Labor Organization (ILO) conference in Paris. Ibáñez, a socialist, was president of the Chilean Confederation of Workers. Sabroso, a member of Peru's social democratic American Popular Revolutionary Alliance, was president of the Peruvian Confederation of Workers.

Both the Chilean and Peruvian labor confederations were affiliates of Lombardo's CTAL. As Romualdi tells it, Ibáñez and Sabroso were becoming wary of their connection to the communist-friendly CTAL, especially after it joined the Soviet-linked WFTU. They could see which way the geopolitical winds were blowing and wagered that their organizations would be safer taking a more pro-US, anti-Soviet position. Romualdi quickly arranged for the two men to meet with Matthew Woll, chair of the AFL's Free Trade Union Committee. Woll, Romualdi, Ibáñez, and Sabroso concocted a plan to convince Latin American trade union centers to pull out of the CTAL and establish a new inter-American labor body dedicated to anticommunist "free" trade unionism. The AFL's Cold War was now on its way to Latin America.[17]

"Free" Trade Unionism in Latin America

In January 1946, the AFL hired Romualdi for the newly created position of inter-American representative. At the time of his appointment, the Federation publicly announced that his assignment would be to organize a new hemispheric labor confederation to rival the CTAL. Unlike the CTAL, the proposed international body would include North American unions in the tradition of the old Pan-American Federation of Labor.

Lombardo called this news the "equivalent to a declaration of war," denouncing Romualdi as an "agent provocateur." Alongside George Meany, the AFL's new inter-American representative attended an ILO hemispheric conference in Mexico that February "to win converts to our project," successfully convincing Venezuelan and Canadian unionists to get on board. In mid-1946, Romualdi went on a twelve-week tour of Latin America to gain more "converts."[18]

Because Latin American unions were closely linked to political parties, during this trip he established relationships with some of the region's most prominent social democratic and populist politicians. These included Costa Rica's José Figueres, Venezuela's Rómulo Betancourt, and Peru's Víctor Raúl Haya de la Torre. Figueres would become the Costa Rican president in 1948 and hold office for most of the 1950s, while Betancourt was the president of Venezuela from 1945 to 1948 and would serve a second term in the early 1960s.

In addition to being pro-labor social reformers, such political figures were also staunch anticommunists and antifascists, making them natural allies of the AFL's "free" trade union movement. Figueres's Social Democratic Party was allied with the Catholic-oriented Costa Rican Confederation of Workers, de la Torre's American Popular Revolutionary Alliance led the Peruvian Confederation of Workers, and Betancourt's Democratic Action Party would facilitate the formation of the Venezuelan Confederation of Workers in 1947. Each of these national trade union centers, along with the Chilean Confederation of Workers, embraced "free" trade union ideals and would serve as the foundation for the AFL's proposed new hemispheric labor organization.[19]

By the end of his 1946 trip, Romualdi had convinced fifteen union leaders from eight Latin American countries to attend the AFL convention in Chicago that October. It was the same convention that saw Irving Brown report back on his activities in Western Europe and the Federation cement its commitment to battling communism at home and abroad. In recognition of the Latin American delegation, a special "Pan-American Day" ceremony was held during the gathering. AFL officials and their Latin American counterparts pledged their mutual cooperation to turn "the western hemisphere into a fortress for world peace and freedom," receiving thunderous applause from the convention floor. "The most extensive and intensive cooperation among the *democratic* ranks of organized labor thruout [sic] the Americas is the very first prerequisite for sound and effective unity of the peoples of the western hemisphere," asserted a report prepared for the ceremony by Romualdi and Woll. The report alleged, without specifics, that "the Communists in Latin America" were waging a "campaign of vilification against democratic ideals," but vowed that the AFL stood ready to defend democracy against all "breeds" of "totalitarian tyranny."[20]

A high point of the Pan-American Day celebration came when Meany delivered an address explaining the AFL's vision for hemispheric solidarity, which was rhetorically in the same vein as Roosevelt's Good Neighbor policy. Aware that Latin American leftists like Lombardo linked labor exploitation to US imperialism, Meany confronted the issue head-on in his speech. "We hear a great deal of talk on the part of Communist leaders in Latin America about Yankee imperialism," the AFL secretary-treasurer said. "I think we should let these Latin American brothers here today know that we are keenly conscious of the sorry spectacle that some American capitalists have made of themselves in Latin America." But, he continued, as a labor federation ostensibly representing the interests of the working class, the AFL was not an instrument of capitalist imperialism.

"We are just as much opposed to American capital exploiting Latin American labor as we are to American capital exploiting American labor," Meany insisted. "We would like to see the development of Latin America pressed forward with the assistance of American capital, but any capital that goes into Latin America should go in the spirit that capital could be a blessing and should not under any circumstances be a curse."[21]

Despite such assurances, in later years US labor officials would forge formal partnerships with US capitalists in attempts to change the anti-imperialist views of Latin American workers. In the meantime, the AFL was already beginning to partner with the US foreign policy establishment to divide the Latin American labor movement.

Washington formally caught up with the AFL on the Cold War in early 1947. With the USSR pressuring Turkey to allow Soviet ships to pass freely through the Turkish Straits, and with Greece convulsed by a civil war between British-backed royalist forces and the same communist guerillas who had resisted Nazi occupation, the Truman administration feared the Soviets were attempting to extend their sphere of influence into the Mediterranean and Middle East.

In March 1947, President Truman went before Congress and announced what later became known as the Truman Doctrine. Promising financial and military assistance to Greece and Turkey, he declared that at "the present moment in world history, every nation must choose between [two] alternative ways of life." One way of life was based on freedom, the other on oppression. While not explicitly calling out the Soviet Union or communism, it was clear what Truman meant by this statement, especially when he noted that the countries of Eastern Europe had "recently had totalitarian regimes forced upon them."

In Truman's schema, then, there was a "free world," led by the United States, and a totalitarian world, led by the Soviets. He contended that henceforward it "must be the policy of the United States to support free peoples who are resisting subjugation by armed minorities or by outside pressures." In practical terms, this meant the "containment" of communism would now be the overarching objective of US foreign policy.[22]

Three weeks after the Truman Doctrine was announced, Romualdi and Ibáñez of Chile met with State Department official Spruille Braden. A former ambassador to several Latin American countries and an ardent anticommunist, Braden was serving as assistant secretary of state for American republic affairs. Braden had been calling on the United States to abandon the Good Neighbor Policy since the end of World War II, arguing that "careless tolerance of evil institutions" was endangering "our future self-preservation."[23] Romualdi and Ibáñez told him of their concerns that "totalitarian" organizations like the CTAL threatened to overrun Latin American unions, and explained their effort to organize a new hemispheric labor confederation.

With combating communism abroad now official US policy, Braden promised the men that "from now on" the State Department would "be not only sympathetic but cooperative" in the AFL's mission to spread "free" trade unionism in the hemisphere. He instructed the State Department's emerging corps of labor attachés, posted at US embassies across the region, to assist Romualdi.

The labor attaché program originated as an experiment in the middle of World War II. Already planning its postwar foreign policy and knowing that the cooperation of organized labor would be vital in the reconstruction of Europe, the Roosevelt administration began developing a cadre of union specialists for the State Department's Foreign Service in 1943. Their job would be to establish contacts with representatives of labor movements abroad and provide information about them to the US government. Officials chose Latin America as a testing ground since "it was the only area of the world where one had both a normal, that is a non-war, situation, as well as several countries with important trade union movements and political parties of the Left influenced by labor."[24]

Romualdi also had the backing of one of his old colleagues at the Office of Inter-American Affairs, John Herling, chief of the office's Labor Division.[25] Herling was a longtime member of the Socialist Party of America and a former assistant to the party's leader, Norman Thomas. Thanks in part to Herling's influence, Thomas embraced the cause of spreading "free" trade unionism in Latin America.

A Presbyterian minister by training, Thomas came to the Socialist Party through his advocacy on behalf of conscientious objectors during

World War I. Never a Marxist, Thomas was a reformer who championed civil liberties, civil rights, pacifism, and economic justice. He became head of the Socialist Party in the 1920s when it was plagued by infighting and reeling from the death of its legendary standard-bearer, Eugene Debs. Between 1928 and 1948, Thomas ran for president six times, giving a "respectable," middle-class, Anglo-Saxon face to the US socialist movement. After World War II, he became an increasingly vocal anticommunist. He framed his opposition to the reds as a defense of democracy against totalitarianism, much like officials in the AFL and US government, though Thomas was more critical of capitalism.

Thomas was just one of many leading socialists and social democrats in the United States and around the world who constituted what the US foreign policy establishment began referring to as the "Democratic Left" or "Noncommunist Left." Government officials saw this international political bloc as a crucial ally for combating communism in the early years of the Cold War, because its representatives had access to and influence over the people who often formed the base of communist parties: workers and progressive intellectuals.

Argentina

As a former OSS officer and friend to the State Department, Romualdi was considered by some in Latin America to be more an agent of Washington than an ambassador of the US labor movement. As he traveled the region classifying worker organizations into those he determined to be "free" and those he judged were "unfree," Romualdi was inevitably met with suspicion and hostility in some countries—and nowhere more so than Argentina.

The trouble began in late 1945, when Colonel Juan Perón became the country's de facto head of state. Argentina had been ruled by the military since 1943, and as minister of labor, Perón built a massive base of popular support by establishing a social welfare system, enforcing workplace rights, strengthening unions, and siding with workers in industrial disputes. In particular, he helped reorganize the country's national trade union center, the Argentine CGT (General Confederation of Labor—not to be confused with the French CGT) into the largest and most powerful labor organization in South America. Having earned the loyalty of the Argentine working class, Perón was able to sideline his rivals in the military regime and attain power in October 1945, though he would not formally assume the nation's presidency until the following June.

With Perón championing economic nationalism and instituting radical social reforms at the same moment the United States was deserting the Good Neighbor policy in Latin America and curtailing the New Deal at home, US diplomats like Spruille Braden sounded the alarm about the new Argentine president. Perón, Braden argued, was a potential obstacle to the postwar hemispheric order Washington was intent on shaping.[26]

For his part, Romualdi regarded the Argentine leader as another Mussolini. Like the Italian strongman, Perón believed in using the power of the state to manage class conflict and direct economic growth. This meant trade unions would be controlled by the government. Fresh back from his final Latin America tour on behalf of the Office of Inter-American Affairs in late 1945, Romualdi wrote an article in the AFL's official newspaper warning that Perón was a "dictator" and charging that the Argentine CGT was a "fake" labor body.

After seeing the article, offended CGT officers wrote to AFL president Green, refuting Romualdi's claims and inviting an AFL delegation to Argentina to learn the truth. During his twelve-week trip to Latin America in mid-1946, Romualdi made a stop in Argentina attempting to patch things up. He had a cordial meeting with CGT officials, who insisted they were free from government domination. The visit went so well that three CGT leaders came to the AFL's convention in Chicago that October to participate in the Pan-American Day ceremony.[27]

This cordiality was to be short-lived. By 1947, Braden and others in the State Department were advocating for the United States do everything possible to isolate and weaken *Peronismo*. Under Perón's leadership, the Argentine economy was rapidly growing through import substitution industrialization, which replaced reliance on foreign suppliers with state-funded domestic production. Peronismo was therefore gaining widespread support across Latin America, threatening both US exports and geopolitical influence.

In January and February 1947, Romualdi led a delegation of nine AFL officials to Argentina, ostensibly to secure the CGT's participation in the proposed new inter-American body of "free" trade unions. The State Department's noted hostility toward Peronismo, combined with Romualdi's known ties to the US foreign policy establishment, made Perón highly suspicious of the AFL delegation's true intentions. Perón was especially disturbed that the delegation's stated purpose was to "investigate" the CGT, as opposed to simply having fraternal meetings with fellow unionists.

Upon the AFL delegation's arrival in Buenos Aires, CGT secretary-general Luis Gay allegedly held a private meeting with Romualdi. In response, Perón accused Gay of entering into a conspiracy with Braden and Romualdi to try to "deprive" the president of "the workers' support." This could have been paranoia on Perón's part, though it would not have been out of the ordinary for the AFL to be plotting some kind of split in the Argentine labor movement. After all, at this same time Irving Brown was busily encouraging just that in France.[28]

Following the initial meeting with Gay, the AFL officials were stopped from meeting Argentine labor representatives for the remainder of their visit. The executive committee of the CGT backed Perón's allegation against Gay, forcing him to resign for being a "traitor." At the same time, Perón verbally attacked Romualdi at public gatherings and accused him in the national press of being sent by Washington to stir up trouble. Romualdi's delegation returned to the United States and issued a scathing report—made available to the public—which concluded that the Argentine CGT was "wholly and completely dominated by the Perón government." The AFL then formally struck the CGT from its list of "free" trade union centers and accordingly broke off all relations. As Braden and others in the State Department had wanted, Peronismo was being shunned, though AFL leaders insisted they had arrived at this position independently.[29]

The Lima Conference

With noncommunist, center-left political parties and US diplomats across the region rallying around the cause of "free" trade unionism, driven by the general resurgence of conservative politics that accompanied the end of World War II, Latin American labor leaders knew they had to pick a side in the emerging Cold War.

Because of its affiliation with the World Federation of Trade Unions—which meant associating with the Soviets—the CTAL became unpopular among high-ranking union officials trying to cautiously navigate the evolving geopolitical climate. Several national trade union centers that had previously been led or strongly influenced by communist parties saw factional disputes that ended with anticommunist socialists and social democrats winning control.

The Chilean Workers Confederation, led by Ibáñez, and the Peruvian Workers Confederation, led by Sabroso, disaffiliated from the CTAL. The Cuban Workers Confederation also pulled out of the CTAL and expelled its own communist members. Meanwhile, Colombia and Costa Rica each saw the formation of new national union centers inspired by Catholic social doctrine and sympathetic to "free" trade unionism. The newly formed Venezuelan Confederation of Workers was, for the time being, still willing to work with reds despite the anticommunism of Betancourt's Democratic Action Party, but it was simultaneously interested in partnering with the AFL.

All of these national labor groups, along with several others of the Western Hemisphere, including the AFL and Canada's Trades and Labour Congress, agreed to send delegates to a conference in Lima in January 1948 to finally form the much-discussed new inter-American labor confederation.[30]

In the run-up to the Lima gathering, Norman Thomas penned a statement of support, which was translated into Spanish and published in a number of Latin American newspapers. The US socialist leader made it clear that countering the CTAL, and thus the WFTU, was a moral imperative, describing the latter as "the creature of a dictatorship and the apologist for slave labor." "Men have to act," Thomas declared, "and the formation of an inter-American . . . federation of free trade unions is the single best action that can immediately be taken."[31] The intended outcome of the meeting in Lima was thus to deliver the first blow to Popular Front unity in the realm of international labor politics, a Cold War maneuver aimed at weakening and isolating world communism.

The Inter-American Labor Congress in Lima was attended by over 130 delegates from thirteen countries. The vast majority were from the Peruvian and Chilean national trade union centers, which had helped spearhead the crusade to reorient the Latin American labor movement in an anticommunist direction.[32]

Romualdi was there to represent the AFL, as was Philip Hannah, secretary-treasurer of the Ohio Federation of Labor and a former assistant secretary of labor. Hannah assured his Latin American counterparts that the AFL wanted "democratic inter-Americanism without imperialism," though the US delegation did not approve of a strongly worded declaration from the conference's Economic Program Committee that condemned the "imperialist manifestation of the United States economic policy in Latin America." The same committee also wanted to advocate for planned economies, but Romualdi pushed back, arguing that such views should not be "imposed" upon labor organizations like the AFL that "did not believe in state socialism."

Despite the clear anti-imperialist concerns of the Latin American delegates, the congress ultimately left the espousal of "economic and social theories" to the communists and CTAL, and instead focused on "practical" measures to improve the lot of workers and, of course, to "defend and strengthen democracy and freedom."[33] While the founding principles of Lombardo's CTAL had emphasized raising class consciousness and promoting national economic independence, under the AFL's influence, the Lima conference was more fixated on battling "totalitarianism."

Aside from debates about economic policy, the biggest controversy in Lima was the absence of the Argentine CGT. Because the AFL considered it the arm of a dictatorial regime, the CGT was unsurprisingly not invited to this gathering meant for "free" trade unions. At the start of the conference, Luis N. Morones of Mexico's CROM objected to the Argentine labor federation not being invited.

Though he was an avowed anticommunist who had been a central figure in the now-defunct Pan-American Federation of Labor, Morones was a supporter of Peronismo and distrusted Romualdi. On the convention floor, he called Romualdi "an agent of the State Department" who had "bought" some of the assembled delegates. He accused Romualdi of having "rigged the conference" just as he had "rigged the AFL condemnation of Argentine labor a year ago." Receiving no sympathy from the rest of the delegates, Morones stormed out of the gathering and paid a visit to Buenos Aires, where he was welcomed as a hero.[34]

Despite this brief drama, the proceedings in Lima went smoothly. As expected, its end result was the creation of a rival to the CTAL: the Inter-American Confederation of Workers (CIT). Ibáñez was named president of the CIT, which would be headquartered in his home city of

Santiago de Chile. George Meany was one of several national labor officials given the mostly symbolic title of vice president.

Romualdi, meanwhile, was given the title of secretary of international relations. In this role, he successfully got the United Nations, the ILO, and other international institutions to recognize the CIT as the "legitimate" representative of Latin American labor—at the expense of the CTAL, which was cast aside. At the ILO conference in San Francisco that June, Ibáñez took the seat on the governing board that had been held by Lombardo.

The Marxist CTAL president was becoming ever more isolated not only on the international stage, but also in his home country. The same week as the Lima conference, he was expelled from his own Confederation of Mexican Workers by its reformist leaders, who were acting under pressure from the Mexican government because Lombardo was trying to establish a new, leftist political party that might pose a challenge to the ruling party. The Mexican labor confederation simultaneously withdrew from the CTAL, though it did not join the new CIT.[35]

Weakened by the anticommunist turn in Latin American labor politics, the CTAL lost much of its previous prestige and became financially dependent on the World Federation of Trade Unions and Soviet government. The organization was finally dissolved in January 1964.[36]

The CTAL's decline greatly emboldened the international "free" trade union movement. At the same ILO meeting in San Francisco at which Ibáñez replaced Lombardo, representatives of the new Inter-American Confederation of Workers spoke with labor leaders from other parts of the world about the prospects for forming a global workers' organization to take on the WFTU.[37] "We were indeed getting ambitious," Romualdi wrote in his memoirs, "first the Western Hemisphere, and then the whole free world!"[38]

3

A Larger Pie

The Marshall Plan

Because of the emerging exigencies of the Cold War in the late 1940s, the international labor movement was on the verge of being divided into two hostile camps. The issue that would spark an irrevocable split was the Marshall Plan.

Proposed in June 1947 by Secretary of State George Marshall and approved by Congress the following April, the plan—formally called the European Recovery Program (ERP)—would see Washington provide $13 billion in economic aid to sixteen Western European countries between 1948 and 1952.

Ostensibly a humanitarian effort to revitalize the region's war-shattered economies, the Marshall Plan was intended to undercut the political influence that communist parties enjoyed in Western Europe thanks to their prominent role in the antifascist resistance. Instead of looking to the Soviet Union as an example for how to reorganize their nations' postwar economies, the ERP would ensure that European workers looked to the United States—both for economic aid and for imports. The Marshall Plan was therefore vital to achieving the goal of containing communism as expressed by the Truman Doctrine.

But beyond simply undermining communist influence, the Marshall Plan was a crucial step toward establishing a new, postwar international capitalist order. Instead of the ruthless competition between rival imperial states that had led to two world wars and exacerbated a global depression, this new system would integrate the world's capitalist economies through free trade, capital mobility, and a fixed currency exchange rate.

This purportedly harmonious economic order would be carefully managed by the US government—whether directly through the Treasury and State Departments or indirectly through the newly created World Bank and International Monetary Fund—and US military might would ensure its security. Not coincidentally, the most powerful players in this international capitalist system would be US industrial corporations and Wall Street banks. Through American aid, loans, and exports, the Marshall Plan would integrate a revitalized Western Europe into the new, US-managed economic order.

The emergent international capitalist system would function under the auspices of an informal US empire. Instead of the United States acquiring new territory or holding outright dominion over foreign countries as would a traditional empire, in this informal empire, Washington would assert its economic, political, and cultural power over the world in service to the accumulation of capital.

It would usually do so indirectly, through a variety of subsidiaries such as financial institutions, business associations, news outlets, publishing houses, scholarly societies, student organizations, private charities, political groups, and—of course—trade unions. Whenever communists (or followers of any other political movement hostile to US empire) threatened to close off a country or region to capital accumulation, the American state stood ready to intervene—whether through direct military engagement, engagement by proxy forces, or covert meddling.[1] Washington already had decades of experience with this type of imperialism in Latin America and the Caribbean.

Naturally, the Soviet government and communist parties around the world immediately opposed the Marshall Plan, with Moscow calling it "the open door for American goods and capital, for Wall Street's unlimited control of the finances and economy of the European countries."[2]

Relieved that Washington was adopting a bold anticommunist policy in Europe, AFL leaders fully endorsed the Marshall Plan. Not only would the ERP be a blow to the reds, but it would also secure export markets for goods made in the United States, thus increasing domestic production and creating union jobs for American industrial workers.[3] Despite their greater toleration of communists, the CIO and British Trades Union Congress—both members of the World Federation of Trade Unions—were also in favor of the Marshall Plan, particularly because of its promised economic benefits.

Jay Lovestone and Irving Brown of the AFL's Free Trade Union Committee, who had been maneuvering to divide the WFTU since its inception, now saw an opportunity. As early as July 1947, they began calling for an international conference of European labor federations to formally endorse the Marshall Plan. Lovestone and Brown knew perfectly well that the communist-led unions in the WFTU would never go along with such an endorsement, forcing the CIO, British Trades Union Congress, and other pro–Marshall Plan union centers to break with the worldwide labor body. Following such a schism, a new international organization of "free" trade unions could be formed in direct opposition to the WFTU.[4]

By late 1947, a rift in the WFTU over opposing views on the Marshall Plan appeared unavoidable, but none of its affiliated union centers were eager to precipitate a split. From his office in Brussels, Brown incessantly made public calls for pro–Marshall Plan unions to pull out of the WFTU, much to the annoyance of British labor leaders, who did not appreciate being pressured by a foreign representative. Also annoyed by the machinations of the AFL's representative, WFTU general-secretary Louis Saillant expressed his hope that "a certain union movement in the United States—a union group that leans for support on monopoly capitalists—would not attempt to trouble the unity of the WFTU."[5]

Walter Reuther's Anticommunism

From its earliest days in the mid-1930s, the CIO counted members of the Communist Party USA among its most effective and dedicated organizers. About a dozen of its affiliated unions were either led by communists or had influential communist factions. But throughout the World War II years, as several CIO officials abandoned shopfloor militancy in favor of an alliance with the state, mistrust and bitterness between the CIO's reds and noncommunists festered, eventually leading to purges and raids. Nowhere was this more evident than in the CIO's largest affiliate, the United Auto Workers (UAW).

Walter Reuther emerged as the auto union's chief anticommunist during World War II. This appeared to be quite a transformation from the radical he had been a decade earlier. In the 1930s, Reuther had not only been willing to partner with reds in intra-union politics, but, more remarkably, he and his brother Victor had spent nearly two years living in the Soviet Union. From November 1933 to June 1935, the Reuther brothers worked at the Ford-inspired Gorky Automobile Factory east of Moscow, writing glowing reports back home about the "proletarian industrial democracy" they were witnessing and how it was "an inspiring contrast to what we know as Ford wage slaves in Detroit."[6]

But as a rising star in the UAW bureaucracy in the 1940s, Reuther took the position that the best path forward for his union and for organized labor more generally—not to mention for his own union career—was a Faustian bargain with the capitalist state, brokered by officials like himself. Instead of a constant struggle for control of the workplace through strikes, slowdowns, and similar militant tactics, Reuther held that unionized workers would gain far more by behaving themselves on the shopfloor and boosting production in exchange for getting to partner with government and industry in economic planning. "Reuther thought the bargain well worth it," historian Nelson Lichtenstein writes: "Labor-liberal influence in Washington might yet shift the balance of power between labor and management in Pittsburgh, Detroit, Los Angeles, and Dallas, ensuring the growth and security of the trade unions and their democratic participation in factory, mill, and office."[7] In this calculation, too much workplace militancy might alienate Washington and thus be detrimental to the survival and growth of organized labor.

In exchange for officially pledging not to strike for the duration of World War II and enthusiastically encouraging rapid production of war materiel, unions won unprecedented security through the National War Labor Board's "maintenance of membership" policy, which effectively required the millions of new workers flooding into wartime industries to become union members. National union membership skyrocketed from about 9 million in 1940 to nearly 15 million by 1946.

This success helped convince Reuther and other CIO officials that the continued growth of unions depended on them proving their ability to be reliable, responsible partners for the government. Unionists who insisted on continuing along the path of militant class struggle—typically considered communists (although the CIO's communists had in fact vigorously supported the wartime no-strike pledge in the name of defeating fascism)—were accused of being reckless, treasonous, and an obstacle to union success.

While workers made sacrifices during World War II for the sake of Allied victory, corporations reaped enormous profits. Determined to win higher wages amid rising inflation upon the war's end, 5 million unionized workers across the United States participated in the nation's largest-ever strike wave between 1945 and 1946. In the midst of this, the ever-ambitious Reuther—who himself led a 113-day strike at General Motors—was elected to the UAW presidency in March 1946. Though he had attained newfound power, he still had to contend with an influential group of communists and their allies within the union.

In November of that year, Republicans took control of Congress for the first time since before the New Deal, promising to rein in organized labor following the strike wave. The new Congress represented a right-wing turn away from the New Deal liberalism of the previous fifteen years. In line with the wishes of Corporate America, busting unions and inciting a national anticommunist panic were the Republicans' top priorities. Labor leaders began grappling with how best to ride out the coming storm. "We are living in a period in which there are going to be witch-hunts, hysteria and red-baiting by the most vicious group of congressmen that have gathered under the dome of the Capitol," Reuther warned his fellow UAW officers.[8]

In 1947, Congress passed the Taft-Hartley Act—a series of amendments to the earlier National Labor Relations Act, which had created a legal framework for unions to gain recognition and bargain with employers—over President Truman's veto. The new law placed several restrictions on union activity and was decried by both the AFL and CIO as a "slave labor bill." Among other measures, the legislation banned militant tactics like the sit-down strike, allowed states to adopt anti-union "right-to-work" laws, and required union officials to sign affidavits stating they were not affiliated with the Communist Party.

The latter measure was the product of a new Red Scare and growing panic about Soviet spies "infiltrating" US institutions, especially unions. The Red Scare was encouraged by corporate bosses looking for a justification to crack down on organized labor. As General Electric's CEO put it in 1946: "The problems of the United States can be captiously summed up in two words: Russia abroad, Labor at home."[9]

In this more conservative atmosphere, the CIO's reds became not only an irritation to anticommunists like Reuther—who had been relentlessly working to undermine Communist Party influence in the UAW throughout the 1940s—but a major political liability. It was feared their continued presence in the CIO would only confirm the right-wing canard that the labor movement was an "un-American" Soviet conspiracy and thus make continued union growth, which now hinged on staying in the government's good graces, impossible. Rather than resist the anticommunist hysteria in defense of their unions, many in the CIO enthusiastically joined in the red-baiting.

In the months following the passage of Taft-Hartley, Reuther successfully pushed all communists and their allies out of UAW leadership and staff positions, as well as any noncommunists who opposed him. What's more, Reuther oversaw the UAW's raiding of two communist-led CIO affiliates—the large United Electrical Workers (UE) and the smaller Farm Equipment Workers—blatantly attempting to steal their members because their officers refused to sign the Taft-Hartley Act's anticommunist affidavits.

To accomplish all this, Reuther made the UAW a much less democratic, more top-down union than it had previously been. The union's annual conventions were made biennial, dissenting views were not allowed in the union's press, and no organized opposition caucuses were allowed. Reuther was therefore able to maintain an iron grip over the UAW for decades to come. Ironically, he made these undemocratic moves in the name of protecting the union from communist "totalitarianism." In contrast, as sociologists Judith Stepan-Norris and Maurice Zeitlin have meticulously demonstrated, the CIO's communist-led unions were far more democratically run.[10]

The CIO's Break with Communists

The Communist Party USA and its allies made one last attempt to swing American politics leftward and stop the Cold War in its tracks by endorsing Henry Wallace's 1948 third-party presidential candidacy. A veteran

New Dealer and Roosevelt's vice president for most of World War II, Wallace was a critic of the Truman Doctrine and Marshall Plan. He instead encouraged peaceful coexistence with the Soviets through the United Nations.

While officers of some of the CIO's communist-led unions like the UE backed Wallace's longshot campaign, Reuther and CIO president Philip Murray (who had succeeded John L. Lewis in 1940) denounced the former vice president for allegedly playing into the Soviets' hands and called on CIO affiliates to endorse Truman.

The CIO leadership's newfound hard line against communists was met with approval by the AFL. The Free Trade Union Committee's Matthew Woll wrote to Murray congratulating him for opposing the Wallace candidacy, encouraging the CIO to also bolt from the communist-tied WFTU. "It is difficult to understand," Woll wrote, "how the CIO can continue its association with and membership in the so-called World Federation of Trade Unions, which has been under the domination of the world Communist party certainly no less than the Wallace setup in our own country."[11]

Truman, the champion of "containment," won a second term in the 1948 presidential election, while Wallace, the anti–cold warrior, failed to carry a single state. The latter's poor electoral showing exposed the isolation and weakness not only of the CPUSA, but also of noncommunist progressives who still embraced Popular Front–style politics. Reuther, Murray, and the CIO's other anticommunists figured the time was right for a final break with all communists both at home and abroad.

At the January 1949 meeting of the World Federation of Trade Unions in Paris, the CIO's representatives complained that the organization was following Moscow's commands on the question of supporting Washington's Marshall Plan. They and the British delegation called for the WFTU to suspend all activities until the communist parties of Europe ceased attempting to "dictate" trade union policy. WFTU general-secretary Louis Saillant unsurprisingly refused to bring this provocative motion to a vote.

Then, as they had already planned to do, the representatives of the CIO, British Trades Union Congress, and Dutch national trade union center walked out of the meeting, formally disaffiliating from the WFTU. With that, the dream of postwar international labor unity was dashed.

Soon after, talks began on forming a new, anticommunist labor confederation to rival the WFTU.[12] Meanwhile, the governments of Western Europe and North America signed the North Atlantic Treaty that April. The treaty facilitated the creation of NATO (the North Atlantic Treaty Organization), a permanent military alliance in opposition to the Soviet Union and its satellites in Eastern Europe. Then, in late August, the Soviets successfully tested their first atomic bomb, meaning the United States no longer had a monopoly on nuclear weapons. A month later, Mao Zedong's forces took control of China after a long civil war, establishing a communist government. The Cold War was kicking into high gear.

In the immediate aftermath of these events, the CIO held its national convention in Cleveland in the first week of November 1949. Reuther came to the gathering armed with a resolution to expel one of the CIO's largest affiliates: the UE, whose leaders had supported the failed Wallace campaign. Led by communists, the UE had very recently merged with the smaller, similarly leftist Farm Equipment Workers union. Over the previous four years, both unions had been repeatedly raided by UAW organizers trying to siphon off their members—part of Reuther's persistent strategy of destroying the CIO's communists.[13] Incensed that Murray did nothing to stop the raiding and was now allowing the expulsion resolution to move forward, the UE boycotted the convention, effectively withdrawing from the CIO.

Presenting his resolution in Cleveland, Reuther argued that by backing Wallace the previous year, CIO communists and their allies "scabbed against us at the ballot box." The reds, he said, were a "cancer" that needed to be excised to "save the body of the CIO."[14] The delegates voted in favor of the UAW president's resolution, and the new International Union of Electrical Workers was established on the spot to go out and begin stealing the UE's 500,000 members. Over the next ten years, the UE's membership would drop 90 percent amid continuous raiding.

Harry Bridges, president of the International Longshore and Warehouse Union and a communist fellow traveler, complained at the Cleveland convention that Reuther had not leveled any "charge that says that the UE has not done a good job for its members . . . So now we have reached the point where a trade union is expelled because it disagrees with the CIO on political matters." In the months following the convention, Bridges's own union and eight others that were communist-led or communist-friendly were also kicked out of the CIO.

These Cold War–motivated mass purges would prove to be an epic act of self-sabotage. The CIO not only lost around a million members (23.6 percent of its total membership), but in ousting dedicated union-ists from its ranks, it also lost much of the vitality that enabled it to flourish in the first place.[15] Without a militant, class-conscious orienta-tion, the shrunken CIO's only option for continued survival was to double-down on its reliance on the state by demonstrating its patriotism and hostility toward Washington's foreign foes.

Industrial Pluralism

The CIO's anticommunist turn went hand in hand with its retreat from class struggle. This retreat produced what some would euphemistically call an "accord" between labor and management. Symbolized by 1950's so-called Treaty of Detroit—a five-year collective bargaining agreement between General Motors and Reuther's United Auto Workers that served as a model for other union contracts—the labor-management accord meant unions would formally renounce shop floor militancy and accept employers' "right to manage." In exchange, unionized workers would get cost-of-living raises tied to production increases, ostensibly giving the working class a stake in economic growth under capitalism.

Surrendering the right to strike during the life of the contract, unions instead got bureaucratic grievance procedures to settle workplace disputes. The labor-management accord also created a kind of privat-ized welfare state, with industrial workers receiving benefits like health-care, pensions, and paid time off not as rights of citizenship but rather as employer-provided perks secured through collective bargaining.[16]

Believing the global supremacy of the United States to be in line with the interests of their members, both CIO and AFL officials endorsed the US-dominated international economic system that was emerging thanks in part to the Marshall Plan. In particular, anticommunist US labor leaders supported trade liberalization, or as historian Leon Fink comments, "The principle of 'free' trade unionism also came to imply 'free-trade' unionism."[17] With industry in Western Europe and Japan decimated by the war, the United States was now the chief manufacturer to the entire noncommunist world. An international system of free trade would mean more foreign markets for US exports, which meant more jobs and, under the supposed labor-management accord, higher wages and more benefits for American industrial workers.

As Reuther put it in 1946: "Labor is not fighting for a larger slice of the national pie. Labor is fighting for a larger pie." The way to get "a larger pie" was through economic imperialism. The continued expansion of the US-managed capitalist order around the globe—with American workers getting their share of the spoils through a stable system of collective bargaining—could serve as a substitute for class struggle. In a similar way, labor officials lent their support to the rapidly growing military-industrial complex, believing that substantial federal spending in defense industries would be essential to maintaining high employment and preventing recessions. After all, it was defense-industry spending during World War II that had finally ended the Great Depression and helped unions grow to unprecedented heights.[18]

With union membership at record levels, collective bargaining along the lines of the Treaty of Detroit a generally accepted reality, and the economy booming thanks to American international dominance, a new US industrial relations system developed in the immediate postwar years. Its central assumption was that while unions and management might have different interests, they need not be mortal enemies. Instead, as supposedly equal partners, they could amicably and rationally negotiate pay, benefits, and working conditions to simultaneously increase wages and productivity. In later decades, critical legal scholars and labor historians named this system "industrial pluralism," because it attempted to apply the tenets of liberal pluralism and democratic consensus to industrial relations.[19]

This putatively rational model of industrial relations would be an important tool for waging the Cold War, both at home and abroad. Labor leaders, public officials, and academics aimed to replace what they regarded as the irrational "ideology" of class conflict (which could only lead to national turmoil) with the "science" of labor-management cooperation (which would bring national prosperity).

To counter anti–Marshall Plan propaganda coming from the Soviet Union—which characterized US aid as a Trojan Horse bringing capitalist imperialism—the State Department launched what it called a "Labor

Information Program" in Europe in 1950. The program coordinated the efforts of the Economic Cooperation Administration (the agency carrying out the Marshall Plan), Labor Department, AFL, and CIO to produce propaganda aimed at European workers highlighting the virtues of the US industrial relations system, where mass production was tied to mass consumption.[20] That it was espoused by American unionists made it all the more convincing.

This propaganda included various written and visual materials showcasing the high standard of living enjoyed by American industrial workers, emphasizing the supposed rewards of abandoning outright class warfare in favor of cooperation and consensus. Many of these materials were derived from empirical research conducted by emergent industrial relations schools at prestigious universities in the United States. At the same time, European unionists and business managers were brought to US universities through the auspices of the State Department, taking courses at the new industrial relations schools.[21]

Though labor relations in the United States became more professionalized and routinized in the post–World War II period, worker discontent and union militancy persisted. During the 1950s, for example, over 3,500 large work stoppages were recorded nationwide. But compared to the tumultuous strikes of the late nineteenth and early twentieth centuries—which often ended with the destruction of the union—these industrial conflicts appeared tame, with the continued existence of the union and the eventual achievement of a contract rarely in question.

Further, while the blue-collar prosperity of this period may have been romanticized in later decades, workers and their families (particularly white workers and families) really did see their economic fortunes improve dramatically from where they had been prior to the growth of organized labor in World War II. In addition to having more rights and protections on the job, millions of unionized workers could now afford decent homes, take vacations, send their children to college, and retire with security.

Still, due to the ongoing stratification of the US working class, which manifested itself in both economic and legal structures, millions were systematically excluded from the postwar prosperity—including Blacks, Latinos, agricultural workers, domestic workers, public sector workers, healthcare workers, disabled people, poor people, and women who did not have or did not wish to have a "male breadwinner" to depend on.[22]

As the Cold War began in earnest, those at the center of the American labor movement—white men in the mass production industries and building trades—had reason to believe they were mostly benefiting from patriotic class collaborationism and US international dominance. In the face of a perceived "Red Menace" targeting much of the globe, they were ready to spread their brand of unionism to workers abroad, protect the US-managed international capitalist order, and halt the advance of anything remotely smacking of communism.

The International Confederation of Free Trade Unions

Three weeks after the CIO's 1949 convention where the communist-led UE was formally expelled, top officials from the AFL, CIO, British Trades Union Congress, Force Ouvrière, and nearly sixty other noncommunist trade union centers from fifty-three countries assembled in London for the Free World Labor Conference. At that meeting they founded the International Confederation of Free Trade Unions (ICFTU) as a direct competitor to the World Federation of Trade Unions.

As at the Lima conference, where the Inter-American Confederation of Workers had been formed almost two years earlier, the AFL delegation ensured that the Cold War fight against totalitarianism was at the center of every discussion at the London gathering. Though also anticommunists, many of the socialist and social democratic unionists representing Europe wanted more emphasis on questions of social justice and economic security. On this, they had an ally in Walter Reuther, who headed the CIO delegation. Still regarding himself as a progressive, the UAW president would remain resolute for the rest of his life in paying lip service to social reform even if his conservative calculations as a trade union official only reinforced the capitalist status quo.

"We assert that political and economic democracy are inseparable," Reuther said in an address at the gathering. "We demand full participation by worker organizations in economic decisions affecting planning, production and distribution." Reuther received roaring applause when he used the slogan "Neither Stalin nor Standard Oil," which encapsulated the Western Europeans unionists' vision of combining anticommunism with social democracy. "We do not believe that our choice . . . is between Wall Street and the Kremlin," he argued. "The choice lies down the broad, democratic middle road, where people may fight to have both bread and freedom."²³

The new ICFTU set up headquarters in Brussels. The International's operations would be managed by European unionists, with Dutch labor leader J. H. Oldenbroek selected as general secretary. In the months following the ICFTU's birth, however, officials with the AFL's Free Trade Union Committee grew worried that the International's social democratic leaders were not taking enough initiative in the fight against world communism.

When the Korean War broke out in the summer of 1950—with the United States and United Nations sending troops into South Korea to turn back an invasion by the communist North—Lovestone and Brown wanted Oldenbroek to convene an emergency session of the ICFTU to express public support for the US/UN "police action." To their disappointment, Oldenbroek demurred. He and the ICFTU's other European officials were reticent to get the International overtly involved in Cold War geopolitics, preferring to stick to traditional trade union issues like protecting workers' rights and raising living standards.²⁴

In an ironic twist, then, the left-leaning laborites remained truer to "pure-and-simple" trade unionism than the AFL, which was advocating more politically and ideologically motivated action.

4

Joining the CIA

In trying to get the politically influential unions of Western Europe behind the Marshall Plan and the Cold War more generally, Washington officials knew US labor leaders could open doors that they could not. The State Department's labor attaché program, which began as a wartime experiment in Latin America, was soon expanded to US embassies in Europe, with nearly two dozen labor attachés stationed there by 1946. Increasingly, the men who filled these roles were plucked from the ranks of the AFL and CIO. As the Free Trade Union Committee's executive secretary, Jay Lovestone lobbied the State Department to pick more representatives from the AFL than its rival.

Relying on both his instinctive suspiciousness and deep knowledge of radical politics, Lovestone advised the State Department on which potential candidates were trustworthy and which might be communist sympathizers. He thus came to have near veto power over who got to be a US labor attaché. Owing him their jobs, in many instances the attachés would report to him from their foreign posts just as they would report to their superiors in Washington.

The Marshall Plan only served to duplicate this infrastructure, with the Economic Cooperation Administration—the government agency created to administer the European Recovery Program—appointing labor advisors to its missions in Europe. Like the labor attachés assigned to embassies, the Marshall Plan labor advisors tended to come from US unions and had the job of liaising with and gathering information about foreign labor movements.[1]

The CIA Connection

Concurrent with the launching of the Marshall Plan, the US government established the Central Intelligence Agency (CIA). As the nation's first permanent, civilian-run intelligence arm, the CIA's mandate was to enforce the Truman Doctrine by uncovering and disrupting alleged communist subversion around the world.

The Agency was in many ways the continuation of the wartime Office of Strategic Services. OSS head William Donovan, one of the earliest government officials to call for "containment," had advocated for the CIA's creation and is considered the Agency's founder. During World War II, Donovan and Lovestone frequently corresponded, with the latter eager to gain the OSS's trust by supplying information on foreign labor movements and the international Left.[2]

The CIA's clandestine wing, the Office of Policy Coordination, was run by Frank Wisner, a former Wall Street lawyer and OSS veteran. Wisner believed that containing communism was not good enough, instead favoring a strategy of "rollback"—trying to destabilize and dislocate communist regimes that already held power. He was aware of and impressed by the work of the Free Trade Union Committee (FTUC) thanks to the AFL's extensive links with the US foreign policy apparatus, as well as Lovestone's correspondence with Donovan. As FTUC representative Irving Brown boasted in late 1947, "We have become . . . an army which is about 1,000 miles from its supply bases. Our challenge to the [World Federation of Trade Unions], to the Soviet Union, to world Communism means the AFL has become a world force in conflict with a world organization in every field affecting international . . . labor."[3] Wisner would enlist the aid of the AFL's "army" to carry out the CIA's anticommunist mandate, just as officials with the State Department and Economic Cooperation Administration sought out the assistance of US labor to achieve their objectives abroad.

In December 1948, months after the CIA went into operation, Wisner met with Lovestone and Matthew Woll to arrange a formal partnership.

The Agency would secretly provide the Free Trade Union Committee with funding to continue its work of disrupting communist-led unions overseas, and in return the FTUC would supply the CIA with much-desired intelligence about foreign labor movements.

According to a "Proposed Agreement" between the CIA and FTUC, the two would work together "to attack and break down Communist control of labor groups and unions wherever it exists" and "frustrate Communist design to obtain control over labor and labor movements," as well as "to unmask and discredit the WFTU" and "develop and advance free trade unionism, especially in areas subject to, or potentially subject to, Communist influence." The agreement also specified that both parties would publicly deny the partnership existed at all.[4] The FTUC's Lovestone, Woll, Meany, and Dubinsky were in on the arrangement, as were field representatives like Brown, but other AFL officials and rank-and-file US unionists were kept in the dark.

Though the Free Trade Union Committee would act as a financial conduit for the CIA, Lovestone insisted on operational independence. With the agreement in place, the Agency transferred its first payment to the FTUC in January 1949: $35,000. From then until 1958, the committee would receive a total of $464,167 from the CIA in the form of individual, occasional disbursements officially listed as donations from phony philanthropies. In addition, throughout these years, enormous sums of money (the amount is unknown, but was once said to be $2 million per year) were transferred directly from the CIA to Brown via the US Embassy in Paris. Still more cash made its way to the FTUC through the Marshall Plan's counterpart funds—money retained by the Economic Cooperation Administration from the purchase of American exports.[5]

European Intrigues

Now with generous funding from the CIA, the Free Trade Union Committee's Irving Brown was reputed to travel around Europe carrying "suitcases full of money" to buy the loyalty of European unionists.[6] In France, he endeavored to build the stagnant Force Ouvrière by training organizers to recruit more members so it could compete with the much larger, communist–led CGT.

Brown's top priority was strengthening Force Ouvrière's dockworker unions in France's port cities. In line with the policies of the World Federation of Trade Unions, CGT dockworkers planned to disrupt shipments of NATO-supplied arms bound for Indochina, where France was fighting to maintain colonial control in the face of a national independence movement spearheaded by the communist Viet Minh.

To ensure that the arms shipments moved without disruption, Brown enlisted the aid of Pierre Ferri-Pisani, leader of Force Ouvrière's Mediterranean longshoremen. With a startup fund of $9,150 from the CIA, Brown and Ferri-Pisani created a "Central Vigilance Committee," meant to violently break CGT strikes in Mediterranean ports. The Vigilance Committee hired Corsican gangsters to attack CGT dockworkers in Marseille in the early months of 1950. Details are scarce, but *Time* magazine recounted that a communist who ran afoul of Ferri-Pisani's hired thugs "was chucked into the harbor," while an anticommunist longshoreman later boasted that he "threw 4,400 men into the port of Marseille" during the dispute. The violence worked and the CGT was prevented from blocking the flow of NATO weaponry in French ports.[7]

To guarantee that anticommunist unions remained in control of Mediterranean ports, Ferri-Pisani's CIA-funded outfit was upgraded to become the Regional Vigilance Committee for the Mediterranean, with affiliates from France, Italy, Greece, Algeria, Tunisia, Morocco, and Malta. Besides publishing a monthly propaganda journal, the activities of this Mediterranean committee were shrouded in secrecy, though it was reputedly involved in organized crime, particularly pilfering and drug trafficking. Through a Swiss bank account, Ferri-Pisani received anywhere from $10,000 to $34,000 per month from the CIA in the early 1950s to fund his organization. The Corsican gangsters whom Ferri-Pisani worked with used this arrangement with the CIA to build their international heroin trafficking network from Southeast Asia to the Mediterranean to North America: the notorious "French Connection."[8]

Meanwhile, Brown became more active in Italy after that country's 1948 parliamentary elections, which saw the center-right, CIA-bankrolled Christian Democrats defeat a left-wing coalition of communists and socialists thanks to covert American meddling. Teaming up with US labor attaché Tom Lane, Brown sought to split the CGIL (Italian General Confederation of Labor) much as he had split the French CGT.

Since Serafino Romualdi had departed Italy at the end of his tour with the Office of Strategic Services in 1945, the CGIL continued representing Italian unions tied to different antifascist political movements in the tradition of the Popular Front. After the Italian Socialist Party opted to continue an alliance with the Italian communists in 1946, its anticommunist wing broke off to form the Democratic Socialist Party.

Such division among the socialists meant that within the CGIL, the Communist Party faction held the most power. Brown and Lane hoped to convince the CGIL's Christian Democrats and Democratic Socialists, along with a smaller faction linked to the Italian Republican Party, to break away and form a new trade union center, which would be funded by the United States. They identified Giulio Pastore, leader of the CGIL's Christian Democrats, as their key ally to pull off this strategy. Pastore led the Catholic unionists out of the CGIL in late 1948. He then formed the LCGIL (Free General Confederation of Italian Labor), asking Lane for an astounding $1.5 million over nine months to get the new organization up and running. Lane ran the request up to his superiors and the State Department approved it.

Brown and Lane called on the Democratic Socialist and Republican wings of the CGIL to similarly break away and join with Pastore's new trade union center, but they were initially hesitant out of distrust of the Christian Democrats and Catholic Church. Instead, they broke from the CGIL and formed their own center, called the Italian Federation of Labor. Brown offered financial aid to the group if it would combine with the LCGIL to form a united anticommunist trade union center, but such overtures had little impact because the State Department, via Lane, was already doling out generous donations anyway.

Watching all this from the United States, Lovestone resented the large amounts of money Lane was donating, which were undercutting the AFL's own influence in Italy. "I think our Italian friends have been overfed," Lovestone complained to Brown. "If they keep on with their high caloric diet they will get acute indigestion."[9]

After the establishment of the International Confederation of Free Trade Unions (ICFTU) at the end of 1949, which welcomed in Pastore's LCGIL, the Democratic Socialist and Republican unionists were finally willing to link up with their Christian Democratic counterparts. In May 1950, the LCGIL and Italian Federation of Labor merged to become the Italian Confederation of Labor Unions, consisting of nearly 1 million members. The "free" trade union forces of Italy were now united in opposition against the communist-led CGIL, but only after having been paid off handsomely by the United States.[10]

Besides creating splinter unions, Irving Brown also used his generous CIA subsidy to establish the International Center for Free Trade Unionists in Exile. Founded in 1948 and headquartered in Paris, it was a grouping of anticommunist labor activists who had fled the Soviet-controlled Eastern Bloc. These political refugees often maintained secret lines of communication with workers back in Eastern Europe, giving Brown and Lovestone access to valuable intelligence. But in 1950, the CIA moved the Exile Center out of Lovestone and Brown's hands and placed it under the larger umbrella of its National Committee for a Free Europe, a front organization charged with disseminating anticommunist propaganda to the Eastern Bloc, most famously through Radio Free Europe.[11]

Channeling covert CIA funds, Brown sometimes drifted beyond the world of organized labor, funneling money to Europe's broader Noncommunist Left. For example, he was instrumental in helping the CIA create the Congress for Cultural Freedom—an organization that worked to turn respected intellectuals and artists around the world into ardent anticommunists. From the moment the Congress was founded in Berlin in 1950, Brown served as the CIA's main conduit to secretly bankroll the organization.

"I suppose the attraction of the Congress crowd for Irving—who didn't know his Picassos or his Baudelaires—was that it was glamorous, and the contacts were good," explained Diana Dodge Josselson, whose husband, CIA officer Michael Josselson, ran the Congress. "Brown loved all the strong-arm business, strike-breaking in Marseille and so forth. Michael and I were amused by the whole thing of going to a nightclub and meeting a union tough whom Irving would be giving money to, and I'm sure Irving was equally amused by the intellectuals."[12] Brown continued serving as the CIA's bagman to secretly finance the Congress for Cultural Freedom until 1952, when the Agency set up the phony "Farfield Foundation" to serve that purpose.

Indonesia

CIA cash allowed Lovestone to expand the Free Trade Union Committee's operational scope beyond Europe. Latin America was already under the purview of Romualdi, and Africa was still largely dominated by European colonial powers, making Asia the natural choice. Lovestone soon had agents reporting to him on the national labor scene in Asian countries, including Japan, India, and Indonesia.

After World War II, Indonesian nationalists waged a four-year war for independence against their Dutch colonizers. During this struggle, the country's pro-independence unions united in 1946 with the founding of SOBSI (Central Organization of All Indonesian Trade Unions). Aligned with the Indonesian Communist Party and affiliated with the World Federation of Trade Unions, SOBSI advocated revolutionary class struggle and became the country's largest labor organization. In 1949, Indonesia finally expelled the Dutch and became an independent nation under the leadership of President Sukarno, a noncommunist nationalist who embraced Cold War neutralism and was willing to work with the country's Communist Party.

Lovestone selected Harry Goldberg to be his representative to the vast archipelago nation of 70 million people. A genteel New Yorker and onetime philosophy instructor who had led a Lovestoneite faction in his teachers union, Goldberg had a mission to divide and weaken SOBSI. With $30,000 from the CIA, between 1951 and 1952, Goldberg ran a training program in Bandung to teach pro-Western, "free" trade unionism to Indonesian workers. Among the subjects taught were collective bargaining, grievance procedures, and the "Threat of Communist and other brands of Totalitarianism in the disruption of World Peace and the Destruction of Human Liberty."

But Indonesia's hodgepodge of non-SOBSI unions struggled to coalesce into a united front due to ongoing factionalism. Finding SOBSI all but impossible to counter, and falling into poor health, Goldberg returned to the United States after only a year. Lovestone transferred him to Italy and shuttered the Free Trade Union Committee's Indonesia office.[13]

Goldberg nevertheless remained a close observer of Indonesian politics for many years as he continued working for the AFL and later AFL-CIO as an international advisor. Throughout the 1950s, the US foreign policy establishment grew increasingly concerned about the size and strength of the Indonesian Communist Party—then the third largest communist party in the world—and Sukarno's tolerance of it. In 1959, Sukarno implemented "Guided Democracy": a more centralized governing system meant to unify the country's competing political factions and foster political stability. As part of this new setup, SOBSI was given an official role in the government as the voice of labor.

Goldberg wrote an analysis of Guided Democracy in the AFL-CIO's *American Federationist* that same year and, interestingly, made sure to send a copy to then CIA director Allen Dulles. In his article, Goldberg accused Sukarno of taking Indonesia "an enormous step forward on the road toward authoritarian control" and alleged that Guided Democracy would "only play into the hands of the Communists."[14] Dulles responded that he read the piece "with considerable interest," promising to give Goldberg's "comments and ideas serious consideration" while noting that Indonesia was "an important country with an outstanding potential."[15]

As Goldberg was likely aware, the CIA was already trying to take Sukarno out and replace him with leaders who would crush the Indonesian Communist Party. In the two years leading up to the implementation of Guided Democracy, the Agency had covertly supported anti-Sukarno rebels and bombed some of the smaller islands, killing civilians. Overseen by Frank Wisner, the operation was an attempt to replicate overthrows the CIA had recently orchestrated in Iran and Guatemala.

The US intrigues in Indonesia continued for another six years. Then in late September 1965, after a failed coup attempt that was immediately blamed on the communists, the Indonesian Army and right-wing death squads carried out one of the bloodiest mass murders in world history. SOBSI was declared illegal, its offices raided and destroyed. All across the country, communists and anyone even remotely associated with them—including rank-and-file members of SOBSI-affiliated unions—were imprisoned, tortured, and killed.

Union membership alone was enough to be considered guilty. Magdalena, an apolitical teenager who worked at a Jakarta t-shirt factory, was locked up for being a "communist" because she happened to be a member of the factory's SOBSI-affiliated union. Before her imprisonment, she was forced to endure a seven-day interrogation and was raped by two police officers. Decades later, journalist and author Vincent Bevins met an elderly Magdalena to find her living alone and in poverty, with no family or community support network—still "marked for life" as a subversive.[16]

Aimed at purging Indonesia of communism, the killing spree continued for several months, with an estimated 500,000 to 1 million people murdered. US officials not only looked on approvingly but supplied the Indonesian Army with lists of suspected communists so they would know who to target. By 1967, Sukarno was out of power, and an anticommunist, authoritarian military regime had taken over Indonesia.

While claiming the Indonesian communists had been "drunk with power" in the years leading up to the slaughter, Harry Goldberg nevertheless condemned the "inhuman excesses" and "horrendous methods" of what he called a "holocaust." To approve of the carnage "would mean, morally, to sink down to the same level as that of the communists themselves," he argued. Goldberg baselessly speculated that had Indonesia's communists "succeeded in their bid to capture power," they "would undoubtedly have done the same, probably even more so."[17]

China

The Free Trade Union Committee's most ambitious intervention in Asia, as well as the operation that earned it its single largest contribution from the CIA anywhere in the world, was an effort to brew chaos in the newly minted People's Republic of China. The mission was headed by Willis Etter, a Lovestoneite who, like Brown, had been a staff organizer for Homer Martin's UAW. He had worked for the State Department in the 1940s, assigned to the US consulate in Shanghai between 1946 and 1948.

Shortly after the communist revolution in China, Lovestone recruited Etter to the FTUC and dispatched him to the island of Formosa (Taiwan), where Chiang Kai-shek's Kuomintang forces had retreated in the wake of their defeat at the hands of Mao. On Formosa, Etter reconnected with some of his anticommunist Chinese contacts from his Shanghai days. The CIA's Wisner developed a plan for Etter's mission and funded it first with some seed money in December 1949, then with an enormous disbursement of $145,472 in February 1950. Officially, Etter was on Formosa on behalf of the FTUC to advise pro-Kuomintang unionists. Unofficially, he was there on behalf of the CIA to train and supply anti-communist spies to infiltrate mainland China and carry out espionage and sabotage activities.[18]

At the beginning of 1950, Etter helped found the Free China Labor League, a group of Chinese "free" trade unionists whose ostensible goal was to alert the world to the alleged "slave labor" being practiced by the communist government on the mainland. A secret memo explained the league's true purpose: "To despatch capable comrades, after adequate training, to communist-occupied territories to participate in underground subversive activities." The league would recruit "liberty-loving Chinese workingmen" and put them in training classes where "special attention will be paid to the techniques of group organization, espionage, sabotage, dissemination of information, etc."[19]

Etter formed six teams of Kuomintang spies under the auspices of the Free China Labor League, each consisting of a radio operator, a saboteur, and an intelligence analyst. The teams were supplied with long-range radio transmitters, guns, and explosives. By mid-March 1950, the first teams began secretly arriving on the mainland, sending intelligence back to Etter via radio. He then reported to Lovestone, who in turn reported back to Wisner. General Richard G. Stillwell, who oversaw the Agency's Far East operations, was impressed with Etter and hoped to cut out Lovestone as middleman. Stillwell brought Etter to Washington that spring and attempted to formally hire him as a CIA officer, but ever the loyal Lovestoneite, he refused before returning to Formosa, still as an FTUC representative. Lovestone complained to Wisner that the recruitment attempt was "stupid," as it would risk blowing Etter's cover and "undermine everything worthwhile."[20]

Because China was a critical ally of communist North Korea, Etter moved to expand his radio intelligence network after the Korean War began in the summer of 1950 and ramp up the destabilization operation. A Free China Labor League sabotage team was sent to Shanghai, where it blew up storage tanks of aviation fuel—leading to a massive fire that reputedly killed many civilians. Another team infiltrated a state-run textile mill to stir up unrest among workers by making demands for bonus pay, while still another team attempted to start a movement against the government's conscription of soldiers to fight in Korea.

All of this was overseen by Lovestone on behalf of the AFL, demon-strating how frighteningly far the Federation had strayed from its core mission of "pure-and-simple" trade unionism.

"We have succeeded in creating both among our people on this island of Formosa, and among our fellow-countrymen on the enslaved main-land of China an immeasurable spiritual and moral awareness of the democratic factors involved in the hopes and aspirations of the workers of Asia," Lu Ching-shih, chair of the Free China Labor League's board of directors and Kuomintang loyalist, euphemistically wrote to Lovestone in November 1950. On behalf of the league, he conveyed "our most sincere gratitude for the moral and material assistance given to us during the past year by the American Federation of Labor."[21]

Etter and Lovestone requested more money from the CIA to pay for additional personnel who could relieve their spies on the mainland. Unfortunately, the funds were not forthcoming, since the Agency had already shifted its attention and resources to Korea. Cut off and left to fend for themselves, Etter's teams were gradually captured and executed by Chinese authorities.

"Perhaps this would not have happened if help had come to the boys there in a state of mobility," Etter lamented in a letter to Lovestone. "Many of these men were personal friends of mine. Some of them I bid good luck to from this very place." Highly displeased with the CIA, Lovestone replied to his colleague, "I curse the day I ever introduced you to that pack of bribers and corrupters in Washington. They have gone back on every agreement. They have lied." By January 1952, CIA funding for the FTUC's China operation had ceased entirely, forcing Etter to return home.[22]

The Fizz Kids

Lovestone's frustration with how the CIA treated Etter and his Chinese agents was characteristic of the fraught relationship between the AFL and the Agency. Lovestone chafed at the Agency's slow-moving bureau-cracy and heavy-handed oversight, continuously demanding greater autonomy for the FTUC and a quicker disbursement of monies. For their part, CIA officials demanded more transparent accounting from Lovestone.

Some in the Agency's top ranks—typically Ivy League–educated WASPs—looked disdainfully at their AFL contacts, who were mostly Jews and Irish Catholics with immigrant and working-class upbringings. The feeling was mutual, with Lovestone frequently ridiculing his CIA partners as "Fizz Kids" from "Fizzland" in letters to Brown.

Lovestone had been hatching plots and engaging in secretive activities since his time as a Communist Party leader in the 1920s, and his FTUC had been battling world communism since before the CIA's formal creation. He therefore tended to look at the Agency and its officials as amateurs, which was only exacerbated by their ignorance of the international labor movement. "Scarcely a day passes when I don't get hit by their irresponsibility and slovenliness of work," Lovestone complained in a letter to Brown in late 1950. "I cannot conceive how we can lend our good name and organization to such a group of uninformed and irresponsible sophomores. I absolutely refuse to be put in the position of being run by people who have never been in the labor movement, who have never lived intimately with the problems that we are dealing with and who are merely intellectually on our side for certain moments."[23]

In November 1950, FTUC leaders met with Wisner and General Walter Bedell Smith, then director of the CIA, to try working out a more amicable relationship. In the meeting's secret minutes, each attendee was given a code name. David Dubinsky was "Tailor," George Meany was "Plumber," Matthew Woll was "Photo Engraver," Lovestone was "Intellectual," Wisner was "Lawyer," and Smith was "Soldier." Smith promised to stop circumventing Lovestone, and both sides agreed to develop a "charter of operations" to better clarify the AFL-CIA partnership.[24]

Following this meeting, Lovestone continued bristling at the Agency's watchful oversight, which included incidents of the FTUC's mail being intercepted. Things came to a boiling point at another gathering of the major players in April 1951, which historian Anthony Carew has described as a "shouting match." Tapping into their trade union roots, Dubinsky, Woll, and Meany denounced Smith for attempting to boss them around. "You're not telling us what to do," Dubinsky supposedly told the general. "We are from the labor movement."[25]

In his autobiography, Dubinsky claimed that this meeting marked the definitive end of the AFL's relationship with the CIA. In truth, the

Agency continued bankrolling the Free Trade Union Committee until the latter was disbanded seven years later, and both Lovestone and Brown would each maintain their relationship with the CIA for the rest of their decades-long careers. Nevertheless, the subsidy to the FTUC— not including the money going to Brown through his Paris account— declined year after year. In 1950, for example, the FTUC received $172,882 from the CIA. By 1956, the amount had dropped to $25,239, and then only $10,109 by 1958.[26]

5

Inter-Americanism

_____

ORIT

Anticommunist labor leaders in Latin America welcomed the founding of the International Confederation of Free Trade Unions in late 1949. Advised by the AFL's Serafino Romualdi, they committed to reconfiguring their Inter-American Confederation of Workers (CIT) into the ICFTU's regional body for the Western Hemisphere.

At a conference held in Mexico City in January 1951, delegates representing twenty-nine union centers from twenty-one countries formally dissolved the CIT and in its place established ORIT (Inter-American Regional Organization of Workers), which immediately affiliated with the ICFTU. Romualdi was appointed ORIT's International Affairs Secretary, the same position he had held in the CIT.

Unlike its immediate predecessor, ORIT included union centers that had previously been affiliated with the now-fractured World Federation of Trade Unions like the CIO, Mexico's CTM, and the workers organizations of the British West Indies that were associated with the British Trades Union Congress.

After initially being based in Havana, ORIT moved its headquarters to Mexico City in December 1952 and Luis Alberto Monge was named general secretary. Leader of Costa Rica's ORIT affiliate, Monge was a close ally of Costa Rican president José Figueres, and would himself serve as the nation's president decades later. Monge threw himself into the role of ORIT general secretary, guaranteeing that it became highly active in the political, social, and economic affairs of Latin American countries in the 1950s.[1]

With Monge at the helm, ORIT mirrored the social democratic politics of the larger ICFTU, tending to prioritize questions of economic development over outright anticommunism. While ORIT's Latin American leaders were quite familiar with the history and unpopularity of US imperialism in the region, they also believed that investment and trade from their North American neighbor were prerequisites for their countries' economic growth. Their only demand was that Latin Americans have a say in how foreign capital would be invested.[2]

Argentina

In the early 1950s, the Latin American nation that most concerned the AFL's "free" trade unionists was Juan Perón's Argentina. Peronismo was a noncommunist political movement that articulated a class-conscious anti-imperialism and exuded confidence that Latin American nations could industrialize without having to show deference toward the United States. Worried that Peronismo threatened US influence in the region, and convinced that Perón himself was a crypto-fascist, the AFL, CIO, and Washington were alarmed by the admiration with which he was held among segments of Latin America's working class.

After becoming president in 1946, Perón established a corps of worker attachés within Argentina's foreign service. Like many of the US labor attachés, the Argentine worker attachés came out of organized labor. Unlike their US counterparts, they were not typically high-ranking union officials or staffers, but rather blue-collar workers and rank-and-file activists. They all came from unions affiliated with the CGT. Several hundred worker attachés were dispatched to Argentine embassies around the world in the late 1940s and early 1950s to propagandize the social and economic benefits that Perón's corporatist regime delivered for workers.[3]

With the CGT deliberately kept out of the new ORIT by Romualdi and his allies, Perón and his followers set about creating their own regional labor confederation in 1951. In several Latin American countries, small factions had recently splintered from ORIT-affiliated national labor federations to form their own independent worker organizations that were simultaneously anti-imperialist and anticommunist. The Argentine worker attachés began courting these independent unionists, inviting them to Buenos Aires to meet Perón and his glamorous wife Eva and tour working-class communities to witness Peronismo in action.[4]

This labor diplomacy resulted in the establishment of ATLAS (Association of Latin American Union Workers) in 1952. The Argentine CGT and Mexico's CROM were the largest union centers to affiliate with ATLAS, but independent worker organizations from thirteen other Latin American countries also joined. Funded primarily by the Argentine government, ATLAS sent union leaders on tours across the region to proselytize Peronismo as the Latin American alternative to both US capitalism and Soviet communism.

Though anticommunist, ATLAS propaganda mostly targeted the United States, since the Soviets barely had a presence in the hemisphere.[5] This prompted Romualdi to allege that communists were "infiltrating" Peronista labor movements. "Their main purpose of infiltration," Romualdi explained, "is to steer these nationalist and neo-Fascist movements along the path of anti-Americanism and bitter opposition to the free labor movement."[6]

In 1953, Perón softened his public hostility toward the United States. With a drop in the price of agricultural exports weakening the Argentine economy, and with his nationally beloved wife Eva dying of cancer, Perón's political popularity at home was waning. He reached out to the incoming administration of President Dwight Eisenhower seeking to improve relations between the two countries, blaming past tensions on the Truman administration. Perón's propaganda apparatus let up on its anti-US broadsides and became more vocally critical of communism. Similarly, ATLAS toned down its anti-Yankee rhetoric.

Seeing Perón as a necessary ally in the fight against world communism, Eisenhower agreed to give Argentina a $60 million loan to build a steel mill. But it was too late to save Perón's regime. In 1955, he was overthrown in a military coup. The new government proceeded to expel Peronistas from the CGT, recall the worker attachés, and cut off funds for ATLAS. With its patron out of power and the political movement it championed routed, ATLAS quickly ceased to exist. The sudden disappearance of this potentially powerful rival meant ORIT would indisputably be the largest and most influential labor organization in Latin America.[7]

Volman

In addition to communism and Peronismo, ORIT positioned itself as an enemy of Latin America's multiple military dictatorships in the 1950s. In both Peru and Venezuela, right-wing military officers staged coups d'état in 1948 to oust progressive political parties that had emerged during the war years. Leaders of Peru's American Popular Revolutionary Alliance and Venezuela's Democratic Action Party—who had championed the international "free" trade union cause—were forced into exile.

Meanwhile, the Dominican Republic and Nicaragua had both remained in the grip of dictators since the 1930s. ORIT frequently issued resolutions denouncing all of these autocratic regimes and their abuses of workers' rights, filing formal complaints to the Organization of American States and International Labor Organization. Exiled "free" trade unionists from Venezuela and Peru were given high-ranking positions in ORIT, allowing them a platform to lead and coordinate opposition efforts against their home countries' dictators.[8]

In 1957, ORIT head Monge joined the board of a new, US-funded nonprofit called the Institute of International Labor Research. Its mission was to strengthen Latin America's Noncommunist Left— particularly the exiled political and union leaders from the countries under dictatorial rule. With Monge's assistance, the institute set up an office in Costa Rica, where it ran a political training school and published the anticommunist, anti-dictator newspaper *Combate*.

The driving force behind the Institute of International Labor Research was CIA operative Sacha Volman. After World War II, the anticommunist Volman fled his native Romania as it came under Soviet control. He arrived in Paris in 1948, where he met Irving Brown and became a propagandist for the CIA-funded International Center for Free Trade Unionists in Exile. With help from his CIA paymasters, Volman emigrated to New York in 1952, where he continued working on behalf of Eastern Bloc exiles. There he befriended Socialist Party leader Norman Thomas, a champion of Latin America's Noncommunist Left.[9]

Through his relationship with Thomas, Volman became interested in Latin American politics. He met Monge and, with help from ORIT, arranged for a group of exiled Hungarians to tour Latin America, speaking on the alleged evils of communism. In 1957, Volman formed the Institute of International Labor Research with secret CIA money, which was hidden by being channeled through the J. M. Kaplan Fund, a philanthropic organization founded by the head of the Welch Grape Juice Company. Kaplan was happy to let his foundation serve as a conduit for CIA cash, believing it was his "patriotic duty."[10] As in Western Europe during this period, the Agency believed social democratic political movements offered a strong bulwark against the spread of communism. Thomas—who later claimed to be unaware of the CIA connection—served as the institute's chair and public face, while Volman, in the role of treasurer, ran the institute behind the scenes.

Besides Monge, the institute's other board members included Charles Zimmerman, the Lovestoneite trade unionist who led ILGWU Local 22, and Rutgers sociologist Robert J. Alexander. A one-time leader of the Young People's Socialist League, Alexander specialized in Latin American labor movements, frequently traveling through the region over several decades as both a scholar and an advisor to the AFL.[11]

Like ORIT, Volman's Institute of International Labor Research served as a base for leaders of the Peruvian and Venezuelan democratic opposition parties. It also offered a safe haven for the exiled Dominican Revolutionary Party, the main force opposing Rafael Trujillo's decades-long rule over the Dominican Republic. The party's leader, Juan Bosch, became an instructor at the institute's political training school in Costa Rica, and Volman became one of his most trusted advisors. Bosch's opposition party was allied with the similarly exiled Dominican Democratic Workers Committee, which was welcomed into ORIT as the closest thing the Dominican Republic had to a "free" trade union center. In the 1960s, Bosch would become the Dominican Republic's president, with Volman by his side, but would eventually find himself labeled an enemy of the United States and AFL-CIO.[12]

The Guatemalan Coup

ORIT was generally in lockstep with the AFL and US government in taking positions on political controversies in Latin America, but a notable exception was the infamous CIA-orchestrated coup in Guatemala in 1954. The Central American nation had traditionally been ruled by landed oligarchs, military dictators, and foreign corporations—most notably the US-based United Fruit Company. With its massive banana plantations, United Fruit owned roughly one-fifth of the country's arable land, but cultivated only about 15 percent of it.[13]

In 1944, Guatemala underwent a political revolution that brought to power its first democratically elected president, the progressive schoolteacher Juan José Arévalo. Emulating Franklin D. Roosevelt and Mexican president Lázaro Cárdenas, Arévalo introduced social and economic reforms to benefit the country's poor and working class, including union rights, a forty-eight-hour workweek, a social security system, and taxes on large landholdings. Cutting into their profits, such measures outraged United Fruit's executives and shareholders in the United States.

Arévalo's successor, Jacobo Árbenz Guzmán, was elected president in 1951. He enacted a sweeping agrarian reform law the following year that aimed to put an end to Guatemala's semi-feudal agricultural system and begin modernizing the national economy. The measure would allow the government to expropriate large uncultivated landholdings—including those owned by United Fruit—and redistribute them to impoverished campesinos. United Fruit would be compensated at the same minimal amount at which it had officially valued the landholdings for tax purposes.[14]

Determined to continue exploiting Guatemala's campesinos and fertile lands, United Fruit launched a sophisticated propaganda campaign in the United States to discredit the Árbenz government. With the help of public relations expert Edward Bernays, the company fed stories to the *New York Times* and other major publications painting the Guatemalan president as a puppet of the Soviets. In reality, although Árbenz was supported and advised by Guatemala's vibrant Communist Party, his government did not have relations with the USSR beyond the barest diplomatic formalities.

Several important figures in the US foreign policy establishment owned stock in the United Fruit Company, including CIA director Allen Dulles. His brother, Secretary of State John Foster Dulles, had previously worked as a top lawyer for the company. The Dulles brothers and other officials in the Eisenhower administration with ties to United Fruit eagerly embraced the notion that Árbenz was a Moscow agent and therefore needed to go. Although he enjoyed widespread popularity among the Guatemalan people and was only the second democratically elected president in the country's history, Árbenz was depicted as little more than an illegitimate "totalitarian" by the US political, corporate, and media establishments.[15]

For AFL officials, Árbenz's biggest crime was tolerating the country's largest trade union center—the General Confederation of Guatemalan Workers—which was an affiliate of the WFTU. The confederation's leader, Víctor Manuel Gutiérrez, was both a communist and an Árbenz ally. Romualdi considered the Guatemalan president's acceptance of a WFTU-tied labor federation as proof that he was "a willing tool of the Communists." In 1953, a small group of anticommunists in Guatemala City founded the so-called Union of Free Workers, trying to organize transport workers and the unemployed. The group's leaders flatly refused an invitation to join the General Confederation of Guatemalan Workers in January 1954, positioning their tiny organization as a rival to the communist-led national trade union center.

The AFL agreed to fund the Union of Free Workers to oppose the Árbenz government. On a visit to Guatemala, sociologist Robert Alexander met with the group's leader, Rubén Villatoro, who asked him to pass along a request to the AFL for money to purchase two jeeps "for getting to the countryside for organizing purposes." Alexander noted that the trade union backgrounds of Villatoro and the other Union of Free Workers leaders were "rather skimpy."

Suspicious of the Union of Free Workers' budding relationship with the AFL and well aware of the US animus against him, Árbenz had the group's headquarters raided and its leaders arrested in early 1954. Villatoro alleged he was beaten into confessing that he was in league with the AFL to overthrow the Guatemalan government. He was deported to Mexico, while the other leaders of the Union of Free Workers fled to Honduras.[16]

Although they were also troubled by Árbenz's leftist politics and the General Confederation of Guatemalan Workers' association with the WFTU, ORIT's Latin American officials avoided publicly supporting US efforts to undermine the Guatemalan government. They knew that Yankee imperialism was unpopular among the region's working class and did not want to be seen as collaborating with it.[17] "We reject all attempts of any government or public or private institutions to intervene violently or pacifically, in internal affairs, even less so to invoke the name of the so-called crusade against Communism, violation of sovereignty of any country," Monge declared in a 1953 public statement. He added that any suggestion ORIT favored destabilizing or deposing the Árbenz government was "calumnious."[18]

Nevertheless, by spring 1954 ORIT was partnering with the AFL to support Villatoro from his exile in Mexico City. With financial help from ORIT, the Union of Free Workers—which now went by the name "Union of Guatemalan Workers in Exile"—was publishing a monthly anti-Árbenz newspaper that was clandestinely circulated in Guatemala. This support was arranged by Romualdi, who also convinced the AFL's Free Trade Union Committee to provide Villatoro with a $200 monthly subsidy to pay for his living expenses. "He is . . . very friendly to our country," Romualdi told AFL leaders, "we can safely cooperate with him."[19]

In December 1953, Eisenhower signed off on CIA director Dulles's secret $4.5 million plan to oust the Guatemalan president. Only a few months earlier, the Agency had successfully engineered a coup against Iran's democratically elected prime minister, Mohammad Mosaddegh, after he sought to nationalize that country's British-controlled oil industry. While Árbenz did not know when or how a coup would be attempted against him, he wanted to be ready and sought to beef up Guatemala's national defenses. Unfortunately for him, Washington convinced its allies in NATO and the Organization of American States not to sell weapons to the Guatemalan government. With no other options, Árbenz turned to the Soviet Bloc, purchasing a shipment of outdated weaponry from Czechoslovakia, which arrived in May 1954. In the United States, the shipment was treated as definitive evidence that Árbenz was a communist with nefarious intentions.[20]

The coup was executed the following month. Romualdi appears to have been briefed on the plot by US government officials. Weeks before the coup, he informed AFL leaders that there was "reason to believe the last word on Guatemala has not yet been spoken." He continued, "Extra ordinary events are likely to occur in the very near future with the possible result that the communist influence in the government will be wiped out for good. In such event, it would be extremely important to have a group of trusted trade unionists [like Villatoro] who could go back to Guatemala and take over on behalf of the free trade union movement."[21]

To overthrow Árbenz, the CIA recruited Carlos Castillo Armas, a right-wing Guatemalan military officer living in Honduras. After months of preparation, Castillo Armas marched a small army from Honduras into Guatemala in June 1954. Using equipment and weapons secretly supplied by the United States, the force of about 500 men consisted of mercenaries and exiled Guatemalans who opposed Árbenz, including leaders of the AFL-supported Union of Free Workers.[22]

At the same time this incursion took place, unidentified CIA planes attacked military and civilian targets inside Guatemala City, while a radio broadcast called the "Voice of Liberation" started beaming into the city. Purporting to be the mouthpiece of a spontaneous movement of freedom-loving Guatemalans, the broadcast told listeners that Árbenz was a closet communist on the verge of asserting totalitarian rule and that an epic struggle for democracy was now under way. The "Voice of Liberation" was actually manufactured by the CIA from a base near Miami to spread fake news and sow mass confusion in the Guatemalan capital.

The combined effect of the air attacks, radio broadcasts, and Castillo Armas's invasion indeed served to create chaos. The communist-led General Confederation of Guatemalan Workers assembled 350,000 unionists into defense committees and asked the government for arms, but fearing such a move might alienate the military, Árbenz hesitated. He instead pleaded with the United Nations Security Council to conduct an investigation to expose the CIA's authorship of these events, but under US diplomatic pressure the Security Council refused. Guatemalan military commanders were then told by US ambassador John Peurifoy, who had been in on the plot from the beginning, that the only way to restore order would be for Árbenz to step down.

The commanders promptly called on the president to resign. Outmaneuvered on every front, Árbenz complied, bringing an untimely end to Guatemala's ten-year experiment in social democracy.[23]

Árbenz escaped to Mexico, where he would live out the remainder of his life in obscurity. Castillo Armas was installed as Guatemala's new head of state, with full US backing. The new regime quickly moved to destroy all leftist and pro-Árbenz elements. Within weeks of Castillo Armas taking over, 9,000 Guatemalans were killed, 7,000 were jailed, and 18,000 union workers were fired from their jobs.

"They killed whomever they pleased," factory worker Carlos Escobar, who was living in Guatemala City at the time of the coup, later told historian Deborah Levenson-Estrada. "According to the archbishop everything was OK and would be normal, but son of a bitch!—you saw dead people everywhere, even in rivers. They said they had been killed by the Árbenz regime, but a dead person starts to decompose after a few days and these were appearing fresh every day."[24]

"The American Federation of Labor rejoices over the downfall of the Communist-controlled regime in Guatemala," wrote Meany, who by now had assumed the AFL's presidency, in a public statement a few days after the coup. Árbenz's ouster, Meany said, had been "brought about by the refusal of the Army to serve any longer a Government that had betrayed the democratic aspirations of the people and had transformed the country into a beachhead of Soviet Russia in the Western Hemisphere."[25]

Sensitive to the anti-imperialist views of Latin American workers, ORIT concurrently put out a very different message, condemning the "subversive" movement against Árbenz and repudiating the "infamous" and "imperialistic" policy of "the United Fruit Co. to meddle in the destiny of the people of Guatemala." Acknowledging the "regrettable circumstances" of the Guatemalan labor movement being "under control of Communist elements," ORIT nonetheless praised the social and economic reforms enacted by Arévalo and Árbenz. "ORIT is opposed to every interventionist policy, whether from the United States or Russia or any other country," the statement read. "Instead of placing its trust in the noisy but ineffective anti-Communism of the dictators, the Government of the United States should realize that world democracy can be saved only by those movements that are based on genuine democratic ideals and social progress."

Despite voicing strong disapproval of the coup, Monge and ORIT soon equivocated, expressing a hope that "democratic forces" might take control of Guatemala's labor movement now that affiliation with the WFTU would be proscribed under the new anticommunist regime.[26]

Shortly after the coup, in July–August 1954, Romualdi traveled to Guatemala to advise the new dictatorship on labor policy. He was joined by Daniel Benedict, a CIO international affairs official; Rafael Otero Borlaff, an ORIT organizer; and Raul Valdiva, a leader of the Cuban Workers Confederation, to help form a National Committee for Trade

Union Reorganization. Chaired by anti-Árbenz unionist Rubén Villatoro, now returned from his brief exile, the committee dismantled the General Confederation of Guatemalan Workers, commandeering its old headquarters and painting over the leftist slogans on the walls. All of the country's unions were ordered to bar communists from leadership positions.

Romualdi contended that the newly established right-wing military dictatorship of Castillo Armas—which was allied with Guatemalan oligarchs and the United Fruit Company—would somehow allow a "free" trade union movement to blossom. Instead, labor rights were severely curtailed and the National Committee for Trade Union Reorganization collapsed by 1955. There was at least some success in creating a new ORIT affiliate called the Guatemalan Trade Union Council, but this was mostly a paper organization that disappeared after a few years.[27]

Guatemala became a drastically less democratic, equitable, and peaceful country after the CIA-engineered overthrow of Árbenz. From 1960 to 1996, the country was wracked by a bloody civil war between leftist guerillas and a repressive, US-supported military regime, which killed an estimated 200,000 people. Trade unionists who refused to support the dictatorship were frequently targeted for torture, imprisonment, and assassination.[28]

The Cuban Revolution

Another country sparking controversy within ORIT during the 1950s was Cuba. The Cuban Workers Confederation, led by Romualdi's friend Eusebio Mujal, was one of the founding national union centers of both the CIT and ORIT. The confederation was initially led by Cuban communists, but with Romualdi's backing, the anticommunist Mujal took it over and expelled the reds from leadership in 1947.

Despite its own corrupt and antidemocratic leanings, Cuba's ruling Authentic Party in the late 1940s aligned itself with the Noncommunist Left and played host to some of the political exiles from the region's military dictatorships. Further, the Authentic Party government helped bankroll ORIT through the Cuban Workers Confederation, making Cuba the second largest financial contributor to the hemispheric "free" trade union movement after the United States.[29] Havana was therefore chosen to be ORIT's original headquarters in 1951, and Cuban unionist Francisco Aguirre was selected to serve as the organization's first general secretary.

At the time of ORIT's founding, Mujal, Aguirre, and the Cuban Workers Confederation's other leaders were allied with the Authentic Party. But in March 1952, former president Fulgencio Batista overthrew the government and imposed a dictatorship. Mujal soon reached an unsavory accord with Batista: the dictator would allow the Cuban Workers Confederation to continue operating, and in exchange, the union center would support his regime. Mujal justified this arrangement by arguing that Batista's dictatorship was not the same as a totalitarian one, since his labor confederation was allowed to remain independent. Of course, it was only "independent" on the condition that Mujal remained loyal to Batista. Many ORIT leaders were disgusted by Mujal's sellout, and it was under these circumstances that ORIT's headquarters were relocated to Mexico City and Monge replaced Aguirre as general secretary.[30]

US capitalists had significant investments in Cuba, owning sugar plantations, mines, public utilities, and railroads. Because the anticommunist Batista got along well with US businessmen and promised to protect their Cuban investments, the Eisenhower administration supplied him with arms and military equipment to bolster his repressive rule. Knowing that both Washington and the Cuban Workers Confederation were on friendly terms with Batista, the AFL and CIO muted any criticisms they may have had about his undemocratic regime.

On July 26, 1953, a group of anti-Batista rebels attacked the Moncada military barracks in Santiago de Cuba, hoping to spark an armed revolution. They were led by a young lawyer named Fidel Castro. As a student at the University of Havana, Castro had gotten involved in anti-imperialist, anti-racist activism and was an outspoken opponent of the Trujillo regime in the nearby Dominican Republic. He was running for the Cuban House of Representatives in 1952 when Batista seized power and canceled the planned elections.

For the next year, Castro's attempts to challenge the dictatorship through legal means were unsuccessful, prompting him to organize and lead the assault on the Moncada barracks. Unfortunately for Castro, his group's attack was repelled and he was imprisoned, though the ambitious gambit won him heroic status on the island. Under public pressure, Batista freed Castro in 1955, believing he posed no threat. The young revolutionary headed to Mexico, where he and the members of his 26th of July Movement—so named because of the date of the Moncada attack—made plans to return to Cuba and launch a guerilla war to overthrow the dictatorship.

While in Mexico, Castro met and became friends with Monge. The ORIT general secretary was disappointed in the Cuban Workers Confederation's accord with Batista. Rather than cheer Castro's failed attack on the Moncada barracks, Mujal had condemned it. In return, Batista changed national labor laws to give Mujal more autocratic control over the Cuban Workers Confederation and its finances, which he then used to enrich himself. After befriending Monge in Mexico, Castro reputedly asked ORIT to support his planned revolution. Though Monge was sympathetic as an individual, the Cuban Workers Confederation, AFL, CIO, and US government would never approve of assisting an anti-Batista rebellion, so ORIT's leadership turned down Castro's request.

In November 1956, Castro and eighty-one fellow revolutionaries famously sailed from Mexico back to Cuba aboard the yacht *Granma*. The few who survived the initial landing soon established a guerilla base in the Sierra Maestra mountains. As the 26th of July Movement swept the nation over the next two years—with attacks on military targets, mass urban protests, and strong support for guerilla fighters in the countryside—Mujal and the Cuban Workers Confederation repeatedly quashed attempts to organize a general strike in solidarity with the rebellion.

Even before Castro's guerilla war began, anti-Batista urban protesters had led a series of one-day strikes and boycotts, briefly shutting down Havana and rendering it a "dead city." After Batista's police murdered 26th of July activist Frank País in Santiago in 1957, outraged workers in that city led a spontaneous general strike without the Cuban Workers Confederation's endorsement. In April 1958, Castro's rebels hastily called for a general strike that they hoped would be the final nail in the regime's coffin. Presenting itself as neutral, the Cuban Workers Confederation warned that any workers who participated in the strike would lose their jobs. Though the general strike was partially observed— especially outside Havana—without the trade union center's support, it failed to bring down Batista.[31]

Mujal's corruption and ongoing partnership with the dictatorship caused internal disagreements in ORIT over whether the Cuban Workers Confederation still belonged in the "free" trade union camp at all. ORIT leader Monge could no longer keep silent and in 1957 began openly denouncing Batista, alienating Mujal in the process. The following year, Monge stepped down from his position as ORIT general secretary, returning home to Costa Rica, but remaining involved in the hemispheric labor organization.[32]

On December 31, 1958, the rebellion in Cuba finally succeeded in deposing Batista, with Castro's forces taking control of the government. Within months, hundreds of members of Batista's brutal security forces were put on trial and executed. Though several of his fellow revolutionaries were openly Marxists—including his younger brother Raúl and the legendary Ernesto "Che" Guevara—Castro initially hid his own ideological position to avoid alienating potential allies, even momentarily convincing the CIA that he was an anticommunist.[33]

Still, in the first year of the Cuban Revolution, Castro enacted bold measures to redistribute wealth to the country's poor and working class, including a sweeping agrarian reform program that instantly earned him the scorn of US capitalists who owned land in Cuba. The new Cuban government made overtures to the United States, with Castro meeting Vice President Richard Nixon, but these ultimately went nowhere due to Washington's distaste for Castro's left-wing nationalist policies.

The AFL-friendly sociologist Robert Alexander made three visits to Cuba in 1959 to ascertain the situation. While back in the United States that June, he reported to Jay Lovestone that there was "still a good deal of confusion in Cuba," explaining that the "revolutionary euphoria and exuberance" were ongoing but that "they have stopped shooting people."

Like their counterparts in the US foreign policy establishment, labor officials like Lovestone and academics like Alexander were unsure what the Cuban Revolution would mean in the framework of the Cold War. The 26th of July Movement was allied with the country's Communist Party, but Castro had never been a party member. During Batista's first presidential term back in the 1940s, the communists had supported him in exchange for control over the nation's unions.[34]

"The best chance for the Communists to get influence is through Fidel himself. He is certainly not a Communist," Alexander told Lovestone. "It seems to me which way he goes depends a lot on what happens, particularly in this country [the United States]. He is a guy who tends to be impetuous, to say things off the cuff, to make decisions quickly then stick with them." Alexander warned that Castro might be pushed into the arms of the Soviets if the United States failed to win him over.[35]

Mujal fled the country shortly after Batista's ouster, eventually winding up in the United States. The Cuban Workers Confederation was now under new, provisional leadership made up of communists and noncommunists who all shared a hatred of Mujal and his followers because of how they had collaborated with the dictatorship for their own personal benefit. The noncommunists wanted to keep the Cuban Workers Confederation in ORIT, but only on the condition that members of the ORIT executive board who had been allied with Mujal—including Romualdi—be stripped of their leadership positions.

For his part, Castro was cold toward ORIT given the organization's prior refusal to support his rebellion. Monge visited Havana on behalf of ORIT in January 1959 hoping to patch things up, but Castro refused to meet with him despite their former friendship. Romualdi was similarly snubbed by the Cuban Workers Confederation's new leaders when he visited the island the following month. In October 1959, noncommunist Cuban unionists met with Meany, Romualdi, and other US labor officials in New York to discuss a path for the Cuban trade union center to remain in ORIT. The Cubans continued insisting that Romualdi step down from ORIT leadership, which Romualdi himself interpreted as a move to placate the communists.[36]

That November, the Cuban Workers Confederation held its first national convention since Batista's overthrow. At the gathering, the communists won complete control of the union center and, following Castro's wishes, voted to disaffiliate from ORIT. As they were still angling to retake control over the national labor movement, several anticommunist union leaders were soon imprisoned.[37] Meanwhile, Castro established diplomatic ties and trade relations with the Soviet Union. In early 1960, Eisenhower signed off on a covert CIA plot to overthrow the new revolutionary Cuban government, partly modeled on the operation that took out Árbenz.

The Executive Council of the now-merged AFL-CIO issued a statement in May declaring that the left-wing, Russia-friendly actions of the Cuban government could "no longer be lightly dismissed as outbursts of inexperienced, youthful leaders," but instead had "all the earmarks of a well-planned strategy designed to make Cuba an advanced outpost of the Soviet Union's drive to infiltrate the New World."[38]

Meanwhile, the CIA assembled and financed a secret invasion force of anti-Castro Cuban exiles in Miami. This network of exiled Cubans included a trade union group called the Cuban Democratic Revolutionary Labor Front, which included former Cuban Workers Confederation members who opposed both Mujal and Castro. Aware of the plot, in late 1960 Romualdi advised the Labor Front to welcome Mujal supporters into its ranks to give the group a wider base of support. This advice was rejected and, according to Romualdi, he was then excluded from participating in the invasion planning.

Sailing from Nicaragua and Guatemala, the 1,400-man invasion force arrived at Cuba's Bay of Pigs in April 1961, three months into the administration of new US president John F. Kennedy. Castro's defensive forces quickly pinned down the invaders and forced them to surrender after three days—a major defeat for US imperialism.

Naturally, the botched CIA-backed invasion of Cuba irrevocably turned Castro away from Washington. As the Bay of Pigs attack unfolded, he announced that Cuba would be a socialist state, and by the end of 1961 he openly declared himself a Marxist-Leninist. To ensure his northern neighbor would not try mounting another invasion, Castro made a secret agreement with the Soviets to begin placing nuclear missiles on the island in the summer of 1962.

When US reconnaissance planes discovered the missiles in October, Kennedy ordered a naval blockade of Cuba to prevent any more weapons from reaching the country and strongly considered a full-scale invasion or bombing campaign. The ensuing two-week Cuban Missile Crisis brought the United States and Soviet Union to the brink of nuclear war, but ultimately ended with a negotiated settlement.

In exchange for the Soviets removing their missiles from Cuba, Kennedy ordered US nuclear missiles be removed from NATO bases in Turkey and Italy, though this was not made public at the time. While Castro felt betrayed by the Soviets for not being included in the negotiations, a long-term consequence of the crisis would be that the United States would not attempt another outright invasion of Cuba, though it would incessantly try overthrowing Castro's government through economic, diplomatic, and clandestine means. But for all practical purposes, Washington—along with the "free" trade union movement—would have to learn to live with the reality of a communist nation in the Western Hemisphere.

6

Merger

In November 1952, the presidents of the AFL and CIO—William Green and Phillip Murray—both died within twelve days of each other. George Meany was chosen to succeed Green as leader of the 8.1-million-member AFL, while Walter Reuther was narrowly elected president of the 4.2-million-member CIO. Labor reporter A. H. Raskin wrote at the time that it was "hard to imagine two men more different in physical appearance, personal habits, and ideological background." Raskin described Meany as "a cross between a bulldog and a bull" who "says what he means," avoiding "windy platitudes" and "diplomatic double-talk." Reuther, on the other hand, looked "more like a stand-in for Van Johnson or some other movie prototype of clean-cut American young manhood than . . . a labor leader."[1]

Reuther and Meany's respective ascensions to the top of the CIO and AFL came only weeks after a national election in which Republicans won control of the White House and House of Representatives. Further, the economy was experiencing a recession in the aftermath of the Korean War. Under such circumstances, and since the AFL and CIO now had fewer ideological differences, the two new leaders agreed that the time had come to reunite the US labor movement by merging their organizations.[2]

The merger negotiations lasted two years. There were tense discussions over union jurisdiction, racial discrimination, organizing policy, political priorities, and corruption, but the largest source of disagreement between Meany and Reuther was international affairs. Reuther strongly believed the US labor movement should conduct its foreign policy solely through the multilateral auspices of the International Confederation of Free Trade Unions. This would mean the AFL would have to shutter its CIA-funded Free Trade Union Committee run by Jay Lovestone. The CIO president's position was informed by principle as much as it was by personal animosity toward Lovestone, who had been Reuther's enemy during the UAW factional fight in the late 1930s.

By the time a unity agreement was signed in February 1955, the question of what to do with the FTUC remained unresolved.

The Reuthers and the CIA

During the merger negotiations, Lovestone experienced ongoing disagreements with the "Fizz Kids" at the CIA, especially over their interest in funding the CIO's overseas activities. Lovestone came into conflict with Thomas Braden, head of the Agency's International Organizations Division. Braden disliked Lovestone, complaining to CIA director Allen Dulles about his refusal to fill out reports detailing how the Free Trade Union Committee was spending the Agency's money.

Despite being an aggressive cold warrior, Lovestone was distrusted by many key figures in the Eisenhower administration due to his communist past. Eisenhower's Assistant Secretary for International Labor Affairs, Spencer Miller, told the FBI that Lovestone was a "Rasputin-like character who desires to dominate the labor picture throughout the world." FBI director J. Edgar Hoover, always paranoid about "subversives" infiltrating US institutions, kept a watchful eye over the FTUC leader.

As a professed liberal, Braden preferred the CIO over the traditionally more conservative AFL, believing its officials would be easier to work with than the likes of Lovestone. He sought to establish a covert relationship between the CIA and CIO similar to that between the Agency and AFL. Protective of their special arrangement with the Agency, Lovestone and the FTUC's other leaders objected to this proposal. Nevertheless, Braden attempted to recruit the CIO in the early 1950s by approaching Victor Reuther, Walter's younger brother.[3]

In February 1951, Victor arrived in Paris to serve as the CIO's European representative. His mission was to promote the Marshall Plan among workers, serve as a liaison between the CIO and the ICFTU, and offset the AFL's outsized presence in Europe personified by the Free Trade Union Committee's Irving Brown. Couching his appeals to workers in the language of economic security rather than fierce anticommunism, the younger Reuther quietly disapproved of the AFL's heavy-handed attempts to "dictate" policy to Europe's unions. Victor was more of an idealist and intellectual than his older brother. To Brown and Lovestone, he was a "boy scout" with "hare brained schemes."[4] But through Braden, the CIO representative got encouragement from the CIA.

According to Braden, in 1952, he gave Walter Reuther "$50,000 in $50 bills" at his request, which Victor then spent from his post in Europe to support unions in West Germany. Victor would later admit that the UAW had indeed transferred $50,000 in CIA money to European unions, but swore it was a one-time-only transaction.

In his memoirs, Victor disputed some of Braden's claims, stating that he and Walter had never requested the money, but had been actively courted by Braden, and that the money had been given to unions in France and Italy, not West Germany. Victor said that when Braden first approached him, he had assumed Braden worked for the State Department or Marshall Plan, accepting the $50,000 "with what was probably unjustified innocence about the source of the money."

It was only after the funds were transferred that Braden revealed he worked for the CIA and tried recruiting Victor to be an operative in the same vein as Irving Brown. Claiming to have been shocked, Victor "rejected the idea on the spot." "I had known that Communist and fascist unions operated with government funds, both overtly and covertly," he would later write. "Now I knew that our own government resorted to the same methods, but entirely covertly. Indeed, I had been naïve!"[5]

Despite Victor's apparent objection to partnering with the CIA, his activities in Europe were funded by the Agency on more than one occasion. He may not have been aware of this, because the funds were transmitted through CIO international affairs director Michael Ross. Lovestone caught wind of this arrangement, writing to Irving Brown that he was "convinced that Victor and his friends are operating . . . with the aid of substantial injections from Dr. Fizzer." Victor's European operations were also partly funded through a grant from the philanthropic Michigan Fund—but the Michigan Fund was itself a CIA conduit.

In October 1953, Walter Reuther had the CIO's European office closed as part of his commitment to conducting foreign policy more strictly through the ICFTU. Victor returned to the United States and became the CIO's director of international affairs. Having "personal misgivings" about the merger due to his distrust of Meany, Victor voluntarily stepped down from his CIO post in 1955 and instead became head of the UAW's own International Affairs Department, correctly believing he would have a "freer hand" there. He would remain in that position for the next eighteen years.[6]

Following the unity agreement signed earlier that year, in December 1955 the AFL-CIO held its founding convention in New York City. Meany would serve as the newly merged Federation's president, with Walter Reuther taking a subordinate role as one of several vice presidents. Still, as the dynamic leader of the UAW, Reuther enjoyed more fame and popularity than Meany, both in the United States and around the world.

It was clear to most observers that Reuther saw himself as Meany's heir apparent, ready to take the reins of the Federation as soon as the Bronx plumber retired. With Meany as the gruff labor "boss" and Reuther as the suave politician, the two men's opposite styles served as a constant reminder that the AFL-CIO marriage was a rocky one. This was especially obvious in their different approaches to Cold War anticommunism, which was on full display immediately after the merger was formalized.

Contending with the Third World

In the spring of 1955, political and intellectual leaders from across Asia, Africa, and the Middle East gathered for the Afro-Asian Conference in Bandung, Indonesia, to assert their political, economic, and cultural independence as a rising Cold War order replaced a collapsing European colonialism.

The leaders of postcolonial nations like India's Jawaharlal Nehru, Indonesia's Sukarno, and Egypt's Gamal Abdel Nasser were eager to quickly develop their country's economies. Rejecting the superpower conflict at the heart of the Cold War, they pursued friendly relations with both the United States and Soviet Union, uniting under the neutralist banner of the "Third World." As historian Vijay Prashad explains, the Third World was more of a project than a place—a political and intellectual movement for equity, dignity, and peace: "The colonized world had now emerged to claim its space in world affairs, not just as an adjunct to the First or Second Worlds, but as a player in its own right."[7]

To hawkish anticommunists like Meany and Lovestone, Third World neutralism was equally as unacceptable as Popular Front unity had been. World communism had to be totally repudiated in the zero-sum game of the Cold War. The embrace of nonalignment and neutrality, they believed, was merely a ruse to conceal Third World leaders' true affinity for the Soviets.

Days after the AFL-CIO's formal launch that December, Meany unloaded on foreign neutralists in a speech written by Lovestone. "No country, no people, no movement can stand aloof and be neutral in this struggle," Meany declared to a crowd of 1,200 unionists and clergy at a luncheon in New York hosted by the National Religion and Labor Foundation.

He called out Indian prime minister Nehru by name, charging that leaders like him were "not neutral" but rather "aides and allies of communism in fact and in effect, if not in diplomatic verbiage." Meany was particularly cross with Nehru because earlier in the year India had accepted economic and technical assistance from the USSR to build a steel plant in the city of Bhilai. Soviet leaders Nikita Khrushchev and Nikolai Bulganin, who took over after Stalin's death in 1953, saw neutralism as an opportunity to establish cordial relations with the Third World and demonstrate why communism was a better framework for economic development than capitalism.[8]

The AFL-CIO president's remarks at the luncheon came as a shock to many in the audience. Eleanor Roosevelt was in attendance and said that Meany had made a "sad mistake" in suggesting Nehru was a communist. Also in the audience was K. T. Tripathi, general secretary of the Indian National Trade Union Congress, which was allied with

Nehru's Congress Party and affiliated with the ICFTU. Tripathi said that Meany sounded to him like a "spokesman for the American War Department," explaining that the unwarranted attack on the Indian prime minister might very well lead to his organization's disaffiliation from the ICFTU.

Walter Reuther, who spoke right after Meany at the luncheon, went into immediate damage-control mode. "We have no right to preach morality to the world or point an accusing finger at other nations unless we are fighting equally hard against injustices at home," he said.[9]

Impressed by Reuther's more sympathetic remarks, Tripathi urged him to visit India. John Sherman Cooper, the US ambassador to the country, made a similar appeal to Reuther, fearing Meany's vitriol might only push India further into the arms of the Soviets. In April 1956, Reuther flew to New Delhi. In a twelve-day whirlwind tour, the UAW president visited more than twenty cities and gave over 100 speeches. He was accompanied by US labor attaché David Burgess, a former CIO organizer who had been nominated to the State Department by Reuther himself.

In addition to having an audience with Nehru, Reuther met Indian unionists, factory workers, politicians, intellectuals, and journalists. In his speeches, he said that "free" trade unions should not put forward "a negative program of anti-Communism, but rather . . . a positive program for social justice." He drew connections between the Gandhian legacy of nonviolent resistance and the Montgomery bus boycott then under way in the United States.

All in all, Reuther was a hit. The *Hindustan Times* called him a "whiff of fresh air" who had "revived Indian faith in American democracy." An Indian security official who guarded Reuther during his visit told Burgess he "had received the warmest reception of any American traveling in India since India's independence in 1947." Tripathi and the Indian National Trade Union Congress decided not to withdraw from the ICFTU after all.[10]

Meany was irate, especially after the Voice of America aired one of Reuther's India speeches in which he criticized the AFL-CIO's opposition to Third World neutralism. He publicly insisted that Reuther had gone on the trip "strictly as a tourist" and not as an official representative of the Federation. Believing that a nuanced approach to waging the Cold War was needed in postcolonial societies like India,

Reuther complained to the UAW Executive Board that "George Meany's position really is based upon the assumption that Europe is Asia and Asia is Europe. You cannot mechanically apply a foreign policy point of view that may make sense in Europe to Asia . . . where conditions are so different."

Six months after Reuther's visit, Lovestone's international agent Irving Brown traveled to India. Addressing the Indian National Trade Union Congress's annual conference, Brown preached about the dangers of Soviet influence on developing nations.

While Brown spoke, the nation's labor minister reportedly whispered to Burgess that "Reuther's approach is the correct one. He told us what the American labor movement does and what the American people have achieved in economic growth since the Second World War . . . But Brown spends little time telling us about the American labor movement. Instead he gives us a lecture as if we were completely ignorant."

Burgess remained critical of the Meany/Lovestone approach to labor internationalism. He would later allege that a CIA officer based at the US Embassy in New Delhi asked him to pass along some "walking-around money" to Indian unionists during the 1957 elections in Kerala state to help the Congress Party edge out the communists at the polls. Burgess refused, "not wanting to become a briber." The Kerala communists wound up winning that election.[11]

Reuther vs. Khrushchev

Another noteworthy foreign policy disagreement between Meany and Reuther was whether/how the US labor movement should interact with representatives of the Soviet Bloc. This disagreement garnered widespread attention, both because organized labor was a major force in national politics in the 1950s, and because the Cold War contest between capitalism and communism was ostensibly about which system best served the working class.

Throughout his career, Meany would never waiver from his belief that there was no point in trying to meet or have discussions with communists, instead assuming a position of complete hostility. Reuther, on the other hand, was more in line with European social democrats and most US political leaders in that he saw value in diplomatically engaging with the Soviets for the sake of world peace, especially as the nuclear arms race continued apace.

The controversy over whether to engage with the Soviets came up twice in 1959. In January of that year, Anastas Mikoyan, the deputy premier of the USSR, came to Washington. His diplomatic visit occurred in the context of a growing crisis in Berlin, with the Soviets demanding Western forces pull out of the divided city. But it was also part of the new post-Stalin leadership's stated desire to have a less combative relationship with the United States.

Mikoyan requested a meeting with AFL-CIO leaders. Unsurprisingly, Meany refused, but Reuther agreed, along with AFL-CIO vice presidents James Carey of the International Union of Electrical Workers, Joseph Beirne of the Communications Workers of America, and William Doherty Sr. of the National Association of Letter Carriers.

These men were all ardent anticommunists. Carey had once even gone as far as to say, "In the last war we joined the Communists to fight the fascists; in another war we will join the fascists to fight the Communists."[12] Nevertheless, Meany belittled their willingness to talk with Mikoyan, arguing that any such conversation with the Soviets was a form of appeasement. "Those who feel that we can meet the Soviet challenge at the conference table," the AFL-CIO president said, were shirking their "responsibility as trade unionists to preserve" democracy.[13]

Reuther and the other union presidents grilled Mikoyan over lunch. Carey accused the Soviets of trying to "dominate" the World Federation of Trade Unions in the late 1940s, alleging that this is what had led the CIO to pull out of the organization. Mikoyan did not argue with Carey, instead admitting that the "Russian trade union movement made a mistake and we made other mistakes during that period. But two neighbors who have made mistakes in the past should not let their past mistakes dominate their future."

Reuther then criticized the Soviets for depicting US workers as miserable, and Beirne denounced Moscow for having sent the Red Army into Hungary in 1956 to crush a popular uprising. Mikoyan accused them of being prejudiced and misinformed about the USSR, and invited them to come tour the country. When Beirne questioned whether they would be able to travel freely, Mikoyan responded, "All doors will be open to you and other American labor leaders." Not convinced that it was a genuine offer, and probably knowing Meany would never stand for it, the US labor representatives did not take him up on the invitation.

Upon returning home, the Soviet deputy premier said that he had received a warm and friendly reception in the United States from everyone except the combative Reuther and his associates.[14]

A few months later, in September 1959, Soviet leader Nikita Khrushchev came to the United States on Eisenhower's invitation for a two-week visit—the first time a Soviet head of state had ever come to the country. As he stopped in California, Khrushchev asked to address the biennial AFL-CIO convention then under way in San Francisco. Meany of course refused, describing Khrushchev's attempts to rebrand the USSR and ease Cold War tensions as a campaign of "deceit" and "treachery."

Meanwhile, Reuther arranged a dinner meeting with the Soviet premier on one of the nights of the AFL-CIO convention. "We do not intend to pull any punches in the discussion any more than we did with Mikoyan," the UAW president promised. "We think it is important for Khrushchev to hear first hand from the representatives of free American labor of our total opposition to communism and our dedication to the American system of freedom."[15] Carey, Beirne, and Doherty planned to attend as well, along with five other union presidents and Victor Reuther. After being pressured by Meany, Beirne and Doherty decided not to participate after all.

The three-hour, late-night meeting took place on September 21 at San Francisco's Mark Hopkins Hotel. Victor Reuther noted that both sides consumed copious amounts of alcohol. When Khrushchev arrived with his entourage, Walter Reuther explained that the Soviet leader's chair had been moved slightly to the right because it had been directly in front of a table leg. "Even though I have shifted you to the right, Mr. Chairman, I assure you there is no political significance in it," Reuther said. Laughing, Khrushchev responded, "No matter how much you move me, I will still hold to a basic communist position. Everything is fluid and everything progresses toward communism."

The US unionists proceeded to press the Soviet leader on a host of issues, including disarmament, repression in Hungary, and trade union rights in the USSR. As the night wore on, an increasingly fatigued Khrushchev began losing his patience. When asked whether Soviet workers had the right to strike, Khrushchev replied that they did, but chose not to exercise it because "workers and unions and the Government have one thought, because in what other country would the Government announce that wages would be raised and the working day reduced without pressure? In capitalist countries they would need to fight for this."

Reuther argued that unions in the USSR were extensions of the government. "Does a union ever disagree with the Government? Can you give us one single example in which one of your unions ever disagreed with Government policy?" he asked.

Khrushchev responded with a question of his own: "Why poke your nose into our business?"

"Freedom is everybody's business," Reuther answered. He referenced his sojourn at the Gorky Auto Works near Moscow in the early 1930s. At the time, he and Victor had praised work in the factory as a wonderful experiment in "proletarian industrial democracy." But he now told Khrushchev, "I was a member of a union, and it was what we would call a company union."

Annoyed, the Soviet premier called Reuther and the others "capitalist lackeys," adding that the "capitalists have certainly trained some very good cadres."

By the end of the contentious meeting, Khrushchev summarized the "irreconcilable" difference between communists like him and the AFL-CIO's "free" trade unionists: "We are progressing toward communism. You want to strengthen capitalism." He also noted that he read Meany's speeches and that they "sound like Dulles," a reference to either (or both) Secretary of State John Foster Dulles or CIA director Allen Dulles. Reuther did not dispute this characterization and admitted to having some "disagreements" with Meany. "However, when we have disagreements, no one is exiled," the UAW president said.[16]

This was not completely accurate, since communists and several communist-led unions had been "exiled" from the mainstream US labor movement over political disagreements—often at the hands of Reuther himself.

The Demise of the FTUC

Though Reuther was making international headlines by wooing the Third World and confronting the Soviets face to face, the AFL-CIO's foreign policy was still dominated by Lovestone, something the UAW president aimed to change with help from his social democratic allies in Europe.

With Reuther's endorsement, in 1955 the Brussels-based International Confederation of Free Trade Unions made plans to establish its own department of organizing to support anticommunist unions around the world. This new department was meant to replace the AFL's Free Trade Union Committee, which Reuther and the ICFTU's European leaders— who disdained Lovestone and Brown's arrogant, go-it-alone approach— wanted shut down.

Matthew Woll, the Free Trade Union Committee's chair, died in June 1956. Meanwhile, David Dubinsky, who had cofounded the FTUC, was growing tired of its troubled relationship with the CIA and was open to Reuther's calls for conducting foreign affairs through the ICFTU. The Free Trade Union Committee at this time was nearly moribund. After Woll's death, no one was selected to replace him as chair, meaning there was nobody to cosign checks for new projects. "I have no authority," Lovestone complained to Brown. "I can't initiate anything big . . ." Further, the FTUC's annual subsidy from the CIA had been continuously dropping, reaching $25,239 by 1956—about half what it had been only four years earlier.

CIA officials like Thomas Braden increasingly sidestepped the abrasive Lovestone and conducted their foreign labor intrigues through some of the international trade secretariats. Today known as "global union federations," the trade secretariats were worldwide bodies of noncommunist unions organized along particular sectors like transportation, metalwork, hospitality, and agriculture. Primarily headquartered in Europe, they had been in existence since the late nineteenth and early twentieth centuries, and they had affiliated with the ICFTU upon its founding. Starting in the late 1950s, the Agency established covert ties with some of the trade secretariats, including Public Services International, which comprised the Western world's public sector unions, and the Postal, Telegraph and Telephone International, which included communications workers' and letter carriers' unions.[17]

With Woll dead, Dubinsky siding with Reuther, and the CIA seeking out new labor partners, by 1957 Meany was ready to let go of the Free Trade Union Committee. During the AFL-CIO's convention in Atlantic City that December, an informal gathering was held between Federation leaders and the heads of the ICFTU's largest European affiliates. The meeting ended with an agreement that the FTUC would be closed down and that the AFL-CIO would give $1 million to the ICFTU's new International Solidarity Fund, which had been established earlier that year to raise money from affiliates to support union organizing and humanitarian aid in the Third World.

As part of the agreement, Irving Brown would remain in Europe as an AFL-CIO liaison to the ICFTU. "As far as we are concerned, we can yell, complain, etc., but the Brussels bureaucracy has things in hand," Brown complained to Lovestone. "I have never felt so helpless and frustrated."

Victor Reuther greeted news of the FTUC's demise much differently, commenting, "At long last, I think we have reached a turning point, and for the better."[18] It appeared that US labor's days of running its own shadowy, Washington-backed foreign policy were over.

Both Brown's defeatism and Victor Reuther's triumphalism were premature. The Free Trade Union Committee was disbanded in the first half of 1958, but its executive secretary and the hardline interventionism for which he was known were there to stay. "I have been buried many times and I've had my carcass picked at," an undaunted Lovestone wrote to one of his associates soon after the Atlantic City meeting. "There will be many a vulture forced down before getting at me. I take a special delight in strangling vultures before they get to me."[19]

Though the FTUC was shut down, Lovestone not only remained editor of the *Free Trade Union News* but also attained the powerful position of director of the AFL-CIO's International Affairs Department in 1963.[20] What's more, though the formal partnership between the CIA and FTUC ended with the latter's closing, Lovestone and Irving Brown remained on the Agency's payroll as freelancers for many years to come.

Already in the mid-1950s, as the FTUC's subsidy from the CIA was shrinking, Lovestone was redefining his relationship with the Agency through his newfound friendship with James Jesus Angleton. As the longtime head of the CIA's counterintelligence division, Angleton was one of the most influential figures in the history of espionage. While Lovestone had detested many of his early "Fizz Kid" contacts in the CIA, he found a kindred spirit in Angleton, with whom he started working around 1955. Bonding over their shared sense that they were among the chosen few who truly understood the Soviet threat, the two men became lifelong friends.

Over the next few decades, the ex-communist would use his vast international networks to supply the CIA's counterintelligence chief with information and advice about global labor affairs. For his part, Brown would also continue doing "extra-curricular" work for the CIA, secretly transferring money on the Agency's behalf to key organizations and individuals in Europe and elsewhere.[21]

PART II

Free Labor Development (1960–1973)

7

Comradely Brainwashing

Modernization Theory

By the mid-1950s, with the reconstruction of Western Europe a success and with decolonization under way, liberal cold warriors increasingly turned their energies toward the Third World. They feared that Latin America, Africa, and Asia, like Europe after the war, were susceptible to communist revolution due to their low standards of living and economic "backwardness."

Washington favored a controlled transition to independence for Europe's colonial possessions in the Third World, with the idea that the new states of Africa and Asia would be integrated into the US-managed international capitalist system. The latter would be accomplished through "development," in the form of economic and technical aid administered by the US foreign policy apparatus and multilateral institutions like the World Bank.

To find ways of advancing rapid, dramatic, but noncommunist transformation in these regions, liberal social scientists searched for an all-encompassing theory of social change to rival Marxism. Many of them, particularly economic historian Walt W. Rostow through his Center for International Studies at the Massachusetts Institute of Technology, had helped develop early Cold War propaganda touting the superiority of US capitalism over Soviet communism.

In the mid-1950s, they molded modernization theory to serve as a blueprint for US international development policy. Modernization theory posited that all societies follow a similar, linear trajectory of development, with "traditional" at one end and "modern" at the other. Traditional societies were said to be characterized by economic stagnation, rigid social hierarchies, rural livelihoods, a belief in superstition, and a cultural acceptance of fate. Modern societies, on the other hand, were defined by constant economic growth and technical innovation, pluralist-democratic institutions, urban and industrial wage work, a reliance on scientific rationalism, social mobility, and mass consumption. Rostow's *Stages of Economic Growth*, published in 1960 as "a non-communist manifesto," served as the principal guidebook to modernization.

Industrial relations scholars and international labor specialists were prominent among experts writing about modernization and development in the late 1950s and early 1960s. Many grappled with the apparent paradox of workers in an unabashedly capitalist society like the United States attaining the highest standard of living in the world—which seemed to fly in the face of Marx—and wondered whether the US experience could be replicated in the newly industrializing nations of the Third World.

The ideas propounded and knowledge produced by this band of social scientists, industrial relations professionals, and labor diplomats would need to be disseminated to Third World workers as a counter-argument to leftist propaganda and class resentments. Accordingly, throughout the 1950s and into the 1960s, labor education targeting the so-called underdeveloped nations became an important tool not only of Cold War liberal intellectuals, but also of "free" trade unionists in the AFL-CIO. Labor education programs, especially those aimed at Third World workers, could help spread anticommunist, pro-Western attitudes in foreign labor movements without appearing to be geopolitical propaganda.

Understanding the value of labor education, the European leaders of the International Confederation of Free Trade Unions launched educational initiatives for their Third World affiliates during the 1950s, for example, in India and Uganda. These labor schools were premised on the idea that would-be rabble-rousers in developing countries should be shaped into rational technocrats, since noncommunist modernization required cadres of unionists who could be expected to deal "responsibly" with employers and government officials. This, it was hoped, would effectively combat the potential appeal of communism among workers in weak economies, as it had in Western Europe after World War II.[1]

It was in this context of robust and highly professionalized efforts to develop and transmit knowledge about industrial relations and trade unionism in the Third World that the AFL-CIO would create the American Institute for Free Labor Development (AIFLD)—the single largest, most generously funded, and consequential overseas initiative the Federation would undertake during the entire Cold War period.[2]

Founding AIFLD

AIFLD was the brainchild of Joseph Beirne, president of the Communications Workers of America (CWA) and a member of the AFL-CIO's Executive Council. After a 1957 visit to South America, Beirne was inspired to start a union training program specifically for Latin American workers.

With funds from the US International Cooperation Administration, a descendent of the Marshall Plan's Economic Cooperation Administration, Beirne organized a three-month course on "free" trade unionism in 1959. He had the support of Latin America specialists from the Postal, Telegraph and Telephone International, the Switzerland-based international trade secretariat of unions in the communications sector.

The course was held at a former hunting lodge owned by the CWA in Front Royal, Virginia, and attended by at least fifteen Latin American unionists.[3] It included a subject explicitly warning students about the apparent dangers of communist infiltration in their unions. Entitled "Democratic Safeguards," the class was taught by the eminent industrial relations professional David Saposs, who had previously served as the chief economist of the National Labor Relations Board and special advisor to the Marshall Plan.[4] Graduates each received a nine-month stipend when they returned home to help them carry out self-designed organizing and educational projects promoting "free" trade unionism.

As the Cuban Revolution set off fears that communism was on the march in the Western Hemisphere, Beirne was eager to institutionalize and scale up his new labor training initiative. In July 1960, he reached an agreement with sociologist John McCollum, director of the University of Chicago's labor education program, to realize his vision for a permanent union training program for Latin Americans. The following month, Beirne and McCollum convinced George Meany and the AFL-CIO Executive Council to appropriate $20,000 to get the project off the ground.

McCollum, who, by all accounts, was not a Latin America expert and had never visited the region, dove into the project with enthusiasm. After months of research and conversations, he assembled a committee of prominent union leaders and businessmen to design the initiative. Attendees at the committee's first meeting in May 1961 included Meany, Romualdi, Nelson Rockefeller associate Berent Friele, and J. Peter Grace of W. R. Grace and Company—a US conglomerate active in Latin America since the mid-nineteenth century. At the meeting, it was suggested that a nonprofit organization be created to administer the education project, which would seek to raise $4 million over five years to annually bring 100 to 150 Latin American unionists to the United States for training and to fund them for nine months of anticommunist organizing once they returned home.[5]

It was further proposed that a handful of regional training centers in Latin America be established, partly to identify which students would be best to bring to the United States for advanced training. In the months following this meeting, McCollum contacted over a dozen foundations asking to finance the new nonprofit, which by September was being called the American Institute for Free Labor Development.[6]

Though McCollum envisioned AIFLD as akin to the International Confederation of Free Trade Unions' contemporaneous labor colleges for Third World workers, by late 1961, Meany, Beirne, and other anticommunist hawks in the AFL-CIO had plans to make it into a formidable Cold War weapon. Having shut down the Free Trade Union Committee a few years earlier to appease Walter Reuther, Meany and his allies remained distrustful of the ICFTU's European social democrats, concerned by past disagreements within ORIT over Guatemala and Cuba, and especially anxious after the rise of Castro. They hoped AIFLD would allow them to bring the fight to world communism on their own terms once again.

Particularly encouraging to them in 1961 was the new occupant of the White House. Influenced by modernization theory and wanting to wage a smarter Cold War than his predecessors, President John F.

Kennedy enunciated an ambitious foreign aid policy upon taking office. Meany and Beirne saw an opportunity, but McCollum was not on the same page.

In the latter part of 1961, McCollum struggled to attract funds for AIFLD as he waited for the federal government to grant the new nonprofit its tax-exempt status. He suggested to Beirne that the institute start off with only twenty-five students until it was on better financial footing. "I am dismayed at the loss of 15 months and winding up where I was in 1958," Beirne told the young sociologist in November. McCollum took offense and histrionically declared that he was prepared to submit his resignation.

Beirne called his bluff, saying that McCollum's suggested resignation was "the only sound alternative," as he believed there was "a very sharp difference between you and me" and feared "greater discord as time goes on." McCollum initially resisted and offered "to try and clear up this mess," but it was too late.[7] Just after AIFLD attained tax-exempt status in December, Meany—at Beirne's urging—asked McCollum to step aside, accusing him of "thinking too small in regard to the envisioned program."[8] In the first week of January 1962, McCollum made his resignation official.

With the young academic out of the picture, Meany and Beirne moved forward with their bolder vision for AIFLD, tapping the AFL's long-time Inter-American Representative Serafino Romualdi to be the Institute's new executive director.

USAID

According to diplomat Ben Stephansky, Romualdi initially disliked Beirne's AIFLD idea because he worried it would "undercut his work," but ultimately, since "he couldn't defeat it, he joined it."[9] Hoping to get AIFLD up and running as soon as possible, Romualdi and Meany turned to the White House for support. Upon taking office in 1961, President Kennedy set about making international development a top priority. Under Presidents Truman and Eisenhower, the United States had carried out modest, short-term technical assistance projects in Third World countries. Originally called Point Four—so named because it was the fourth foreign policy objective Truman laid out in his January 1949 inaugural address—the program later evolved into the International Cooperation Administration under Eisenhower.

Inspired by modernization theory, Kennedy entered the White House promising national assistance "for whatever period is required" to "those people in the huts and villages of half the globe struggling to break the bonds of mass misery."[10] He created the Peace Corps to send idealistic young Americans to assist in small-scale community development efforts in the Third World, signed the 1961 Foreign Assistance Act— which transformed the International Cooperation Administration into the US Agency for International Development (USAID) to administer grants, long-term loans, and technical assistance to poor countries— and declared to the United Nations that the 1960s would be the "Decade of Development." Advised by Walt Rostow and other liberal intellectuals, Kennedy hoped that through long-term modernization programs and goodwill efforts, Washington could integrate the Third World into the informal US empire while blocking the potential appeal of communism and leftism.

One of Kennedy's most wide-reaching new initiatives was the Alliance for Progress, which would provide $20 billion in economic and technical aid to anticommunist governments in Latin America over ten years. A reaction to the Cuban Revolution, the Alliance for Progress combined the Marshall Plan with modernization theory. It was an ambitious attempt to spark economic growth and mass consumption in Latin America while undercutting left-wing influence in the region. Secretary of Labor Arthur Goldberg, the labor lawyer who had previously headed the OSS Labor Desk during World War II and helped engineer the AFL-CIO merger, encouraged the administration to seek the Federation's help in promoting the Alliance's goal of noncommunist development.

At Goldberg's urging, in January 1962, a committee was formed to bring together high-ranking officials from the Department of Labor, AFL-CIO, and USAID to consider providing federal funds to the newly established and under-resourced AIFLD. Top officials from the CIA were also involved, though not as formal members of the committee.[11]

The Kennedy administration promised an initial $350,000 to kick-start AIFLD's education program. Going through ORIT-affiliated unions, the Institute assembled its first group of forty-three Latin American and Caribbean students to take the three-month course in Washington that summer. The Institute received $1.5 million from

USAID in 1963, then $2.3 million the following year, and $4.7 million the year after.[12]

Just like the AFL's Free Trade Union Committee, then, AIFLD started out as an autonomous labor initiative only to willfully become an instrument of US foreign policy.

J. Peter Grace

Meany and Romualdi recruited businessmen from US corporations active in Latin America to serve on AIFLD's new Board of Trustees. Charles Brinckerhoff of the Anaconda Company and Juan Trippe of Pan American World Airways were recruited, among others. J. Peter Grace, who had attended the AIFLD's initial planning meeting in May 1961, agreed to become board chairman. These men and the companies they represented were no strangers to union busting, which made the AFL-CIO's eagerness to partner with them particularly questionable. That they agreed to be part of AIFLD demonstrates that US capitalists saw no threat—only opportunity—in the kind of unionism the Institute was encouraging.

Though these men contributed relatively modest corporate donations to the Institute, their real function was to demonstrate industrial pluralism's commitment to class consensus. The "fundamental credo" of AIFLD, Romualdi said, was "the concept of the various economic power elements in a free society working together, instead of in opposition."[13] For years, he had aimed to convince employers in Latin America that "free enterprise" and "free labor" were natural allies in the fight against communism, noting that dictatorships often arose by exploiting the "economic disorder" caused by conflicts between workers and capitalists.[14]

In a speech about AIFLD to Chicago business leaders in September 1963, Meany lauded US corporate titans like Grace, Trippe, and Brinckerhoff, who were "well aware that the choice today [in Latin America] is between democracy and Castroism; and that if democracy is to win, it must meet the needs and the desires of the people, starting with a higher standard of living." Meany contended that although US "unions and management may quarrel over the terms of a contract" and "may be deeply divided on a wide range of domestic issues," it was necessary for the two to "stand together in the great struggle of our times, the struggle that will determine the future and perhaps survival of mankind"—the Cold War.[15]

Grace fully agreed. He approved of AIFLD because it urged "cooperation between labor and management and an end to class struggle" while teaching workers that they could "have better living conditions within the framework of a free, democratic and capitalistic society," precepts that ran "completely counter to Communist propaganda."[16]

Grace had been particularly alarmed by the Cuban Revolution and feared that anticapitalist, anti-Yankee sentiment would spread throughout the region and threaten his family's century-old conglomerate, which had interests across Latin America in a variety of industries, including shipping, agriculture, chemicals, finance, and textiles. He was an early supporter of Kennedy's Alliance for Progress, urging fellow businessmen to get behind the initiative and calling for a kind of corporate social responsibility for US firms operating abroad.[17]

Watching the creation of AIFLD from a distance, Victor Reuther, serving as the United Auto Workers' director of international affairs, warned early on that "this program is not well-conceived."[18] He predicted that AIFLD would "be a source of great tension" between the AFL-CIO and the ICFTU, with he and Walter still believing that the ICFTU was the ideal vehicle for US labor to carry out its foreign policy. He was especially skeptical about the inclusion of corporate businessmen in the project, privately complaining in June 1962 that the "presence of J. Peter Grace on the board of the Institute needlessly compromises our effort in the eyes of tens of thousands of trade unionists . . . throughout the hemisphere." Despite Grace's potential "personal merits," he continued, "the name, Grace, arouses painful memories of 'Yankee imperialism' in its worst forms" in Latin America, including "generations of ruthless exploitation."

Indeed, as recently as 1960 W. R. Grace and Company had teamed up with state security forces in Peru to violently put down a three-week strike at a Grace-owned sugar plantation. Victor Reuther was especially troubled by the fact that AIFLD graduates would be on the Institute's payroll for nine months on their return home. "Each of them will not only be open to the charge by our opposition that they are agents of the US but they clearly will be in the pay of a US institution which includes employers and government in what is presumably a 'labor training' program," he warned.[19]

Education

Between 1962 and 1974 alone, AIFLD received $52.52 million in funding from USAID, compared to $2.46 million from the AFL-CIO and $1.6 million from corporations.[20] With its robust federal funding, the Institute set up extensive field operations to supplement its main education center in Washington.

By late 1964, AIFLD had opened thirteen national resident training centers across Latin America and the Caribbean running eight- to twelve-week courses, including Brazil's Cultural Institute of Labor and the Peruvian Labor Studies Center.[21] According to Romualdi, by 1967 AIFLD was directing schools or running seminars in every country in the region, with the exceptions of Haiti, Paraguay, and Cuba.[22] By the end of the decade, the Institute would boast of having trained some 128,515 Latin American and Caribbean workers.[23]

Most students participated in AIFLD-sponsored programs in their home countries, with only a select number traveling to Washington for the more advanced, three-month residential course. Students were recruited to local training programs by ORIT-affiliated unions within their respective countries, while the Institute's field representatives and country directors played a larger role in selecting participants for the course in Washington, often described as a kind of "graduate school." The preferred characteristics of prospective students included "militancy [for anticommunism], the desire for education . . . trade union dedication . . . and the age range of 21–35."[24]

Courses explored US democracy, collective bargaining, labor economics, and "threats to unionism and democracy" (by which was meant "Communism and other forms of totalitarianism").[25] In the summer of 1963, the Dominican Republic's José Dolores Bautista, secretary of the Santo Domingo Masons' Union, participated in AIFLD's residential school in Washington. "Before I left my country, I was warned by some of my co-workers that I would be 'brainwashed' in the United States," Bautista told interviewers during his US sojourn. "I can now answer that I am very happy to be brainwashed in the free, friendly, and comradely manner in which we are being brainwashed at the Institute."[26]

A writer for the *Reader's Digest* sat in on one of AIFLD's Washington training courses in 1966, providing this account of how trainees used roleplays to practice countering left-wing arguments:

> Another session rehearsed a meeting of auto workers wherein "Red infiltrators" were trying to divert matters to political ends. "You are a puppet of Yankee imperialists trained in Washington!" shouted planted hecklers at Juan, the Argentine chairman. "American workers are the highest paid in the world under the free enterprise system of class cooperation," Juan shot back. "And what did you communists learn in Cuba? How to reduce living standards by 15 percent in five years? How to destroy free unions and destroy them with government bosses and forced labor? Is that how you plan to 'emancipate the working class'? If that's the best you have to offer us, take your doctrines back to Moscow—or is it Peking [Beijing] you're taking orders from this week?"[27]

Such roleplays constituted the education program's most important function: preparing graduates to combat radicalism in their native labor movements. AIFLD described the nine-month internships awarded to graduates as "a concrete attempt to counter the vigorous efforts of communists" who were "constantly trying to subvert and undermine democratic unions and to organize workers into vehicles of agitation and destruction."[28]

Latin American unionists participated in AIFLD's education programs for varying reasons. Some saw it as an opportunity to make useful connections. A Brazilian worker who took an AIFLD course in the 1970s, for example, told historian Larissa Rosa Corrêa decades later that the training had offered "a good political network" with "all the support of the US embassy," and had been considered "very modern, since it came from the United States."[29] Others, like Uruguayan Mabel Bermúdez Pose, were true believers. In a December 1968 letter to AFL-CIO headquarters, Bermúdez wrote (in English) that she had just completed her second course at the local AIFLD-sponsored training center in Montevideo, noting that she "was the only woman in it." She explained she was "so grateful to the Institute" that she "decided to start to do something"—namely to "make a plan" to "throw away" the general secretary of her unnamed union "because he is the communist."[30]

As her remarks suggest, women unionists were underrepresented in AIFLD-sponsored trainings. The Institute attempted to address this in early 1965, recruiting seven women to attend its ninth Washington course out of a total of twenty-five students, but it would not be until the mid-1970s that AIFLD focused serious attention on gender inclusivity through scholarships and specialized courses for women.[31]

AIFLD staff struggled to keep track of the graduates of its residential program but noted in 1966 that three-quarters of those "of whom we have knowledge" had advanced or maintained their union position and remained active apostles of "free" trade unionism.[32] Graduates like Jorge Vicente Tur, who attended the sixth residential course in 1964, said that they felt a "moral obligation towards the United States and especially to the AFL-CIO" for allowing them "to share in the experiences and every-day life of the North American worker," and accordingly dedicated themselves to putting their AIFLD training to use.[33] Roberto Guillermo Payano of the Dominican Republic, a graduate of the Institute's first residential course, went on to be elected general secretary of his country's railroad workers' union, where he expended "a great deal of energy and talent in his efforts to ward off communist infiltration."[34]

Bill Doherty

Washington saw AIFLD as a crucial partner in the Alliance for Progress's mission to challenge leftist currents in Latin America through development aid. Labor diplomats and modernization theorists argued that Third World unions could act as social welfare agencies to temper workers' demands for higher wages and thereby further capital formation and industrialization.[35] Consequently, AIFLD established a Social Projects Department in 1962 to complement its educational activities. Its mission was to enable anticommunist Latin American unions to provide housing, healthcare, and credit to their members.

The department was initially led by William "Bill" Doherty Jr., who, as the inter-American representative for the Postal, Telegraph and Telephone International, had assisted Beirne with his Front Royal school in 1959. Labor internationalism was in Doherty's blood. His father served as president of the National Association of Letter Carriers for over twenty years, participated in the founding congress of the ICFTU in London, and was named the first US ambassador to independent Jamaica by Kennedy in 1962.[36]

The younger Doherty credited getting his position with the Postal, Telegraph and Telephone International to "a good kind of nepotism," since his father's union was a powerful affiliate in the trade secretariat. "I mean a lot of people condemn nepotism," he explained, "but I figured that when God himself saw the world in deep trouble he turned to his own son to save it and I figured if nepotism was good enough for God, it was good enough for me."[37] Like Meany, Beirne, and his own father, Doherty was a devout Catholic whose zealous anticommunism partly sprang from his religious identity.

Thanks to the relationship he had forged with Beirne in organizing the Front Royal training program, Doherty was hired to head AIFLD's Social Projects Department in 1962. Though the department would carry out many ambitious projects, the Institute's educational program remained the top priority, with a budget $1.3 million higher than that of the Social Projects Department in 1966.[38]

Subsidized by USAID, AIFLD's Social Projects Department implemented scores of development initiatives across Latin America. A representative example was a workers' housing bank in Peru. A partnership with the Peruvian Confederation of Workers, the bank received a $6 million line of credit from USAID, and by 1969 had reportedly given out over 800 loans.[39]

The department also launched an Agrarian Union Development Service in 1965, which worked to train and organize landless campesinos, particularly in Central America and northern Brazil, who US officials feared were ripe for radicalization due to their exploitation at the hands of elite landowners. Following the same counterinsurgency logic put forward by the State Department, Doherty believed that "where a Latin American country escapes a violent revolution from which only communism will benefit it will be because the campesino has been given reason to believe that at long last his voice is being heard, his identity is recognized, his dignity honored." AIFLD's agrarian program was envisioned as "a multifaceted undertaking including education, establishment of cooperatives, community development and training in improved agricultural techniques, etc."[40]

Additionally, in late 1964 the AFL-CIO began putting up its own money to fund small-scale "impact projects" through AIFLD, with grants for individual schemes totaling no more than $5,000 each. Some of these grants went, for example, to a construction workers' union in the Dominican Republic to repair a school, a Peruvian textile workers' union to develop a sewing cooperative, a maritime union in Chile to establish a library, and a Brazilian hospitality workers' union to set up a consumer cooperative.[41]

AIFLD Housing Projects

With many Latin American cities facing overcrowding and the growth of slums due to rural-to-urban migration, itself brought on by industrialization and privatization of farmlands, the construction of affordable worker homes became a top priority of AIFLD's Social Projects Department.

Importantly, the intended beneficiaries of such housing developments would be members of Latin America's ORIT-affiliated unions to showcase the rewards of siding with "free" trade unionism. This would help stratify the region's working class, with members of pro-US unions able to get comfortable, modern housing while nonunion workers or members of leftist unions might be stuck in slums. Ironically, AIFLD's efforts to house workers loyal to the United States mirrored state-led efforts in communist countries to provide the growing urban working class with public housing.

In its first five years of existence, AIFLD coordinated $35 million in loans to build housing cooperatives in Brazil, Uruguay, Honduras, British Guiana, the Dominican Republic, and elsewhere, with the money coming from the pension funds of AFL-CIO affiliates.[42] The first and most prominent of these AIFLD-sponsored worker housing developments was in Mexico City. Opened in 1964 and christened the "John F. Kennedy Housing Project," the development was championed by the Confederation of Mexican Workers (CTM), the country's ORIT-affiliated trade union center, which had become an appendage of the ruling Institutional Revolutionary Party (PRI). By 1971, it was estimated that 22,000 people were living at the Kennedy Housing Project. As of 2018, the development was still home to thousands and still bore Kennedy's name.[43]

Other AIFLD housing projects, such as in Costa Rica and Uruguay, faced criticism for the Institute's attempts to control who the residents would be.[44] As part of the application process, AIFLD would usually require potential residents to fill out extensive questionnaires seeking detailed information about their respective unions—including the number of members, the political orientation of union officers, and any internal conflicts brewing—which were irrelevant to the applicants' housing needs. Such questionnaires were an obvious attempt by the Institute to compile intelligence about different unions, as well as to screen out applicants belonging to unions deemed "radical."[45]

Often, the Institute's housing projects were delayed because of various technical and logistical issues. This occasionally led to clashes between AIFLD and USAID, as in Colombia in 1964 when a Bogotá housing development was put on hold over an inability to find a suitable contractor and unresolved budgeting questions. AIFLD blamed USAID for dragging its feet on approving the project and goaded Colombian unionists to complain to national authorities, who in turn complained to Washington. Under diplomatic pressure, USAID approved the project despite believing it was premature to do so. Indeed, it would take AIFLD another three years of planning before construction could even begin.

Despite such controversies, the Social Projects Department's housing program remained a source of pride for the Institute until it was finally discontinued in 1978 due to rising worldwide interest rates. AIFLD claimed that it had helped construct a total of 18,048 units in fourteen countries, housing 125,000 people.[46]

8

Intervenors

By the early to mid-1960s, dramatic social change was under way in the United States as those who were excluded from post–World War II economic prosperity—African Americans, women, poor people, farmworkers, Latinos—mobilized to demand civil and economic rights. Knowing that the rest of the world was watching, President Lyndon Johnson signed sweeping civil rights legislation and launched a "war on poverty" to help bring long-neglected segments of US society into the era of high mass consumption, much as the Marshall Plan had done in postwar Europe and the Alliance for Progress was currently trying to do in Latin America.

Although some of the more liberal labor leaders like Walter Reuther tried to get the AFL-CIO to tap into the social movements' energy to expand unions into unorganized sectors, the Federation's Executive Council, dominated by George Meany, opted to keep organized labor mostly on the sidelines. Even as industrial corporations increasingly moved production outside of the heavily unionized Northeast and Upper Midwest to the non-union South and Southwest, the top officials of the AFL-CIO and most of its affiliates were uninterested in organizing new workers.

Meany and his anticommunist clique instead devoted much of their time and attention to waging the Cold War overseas. Between 20 and 25 percent of the AFL-CIO's annual budget was devoted to foreign activities throughout the 1960s (not including the millions in USAID funds it was spending), while organizing the unorganized at home was barely on the radar.[1]

The overseas modernization efforts championed by the AFL-CIO took a violent turn as leftists and nationalists in the Third World resisted Washington's attempts to pull their countries into the US-managed international capitalist system. Despite its lofty rhetoric around democracy and pluralism, the Alliance for Progress—which prioritized national security as a prerequisite for development—frequently facilitated the installation of authoritarian governments in Latin America for the sake of establishing "order."[2] A similar dynamic would soon play out in Southeast Asia, where US-sponsored modernization went hand in hand with counterinsurgency and a brutal war killing millions of civilians. These developments would parallel the US domestic scene, as movements of the oppressed and their allies became more radical and militant by the late 1960s, only to be met with some of the same repressive tactics first developed and tested overseas.

Like their allies in the US government, whenever faced with the problem of how to promote political stability and economic development while simultaneously living up to their professed democratic pluralist ideals, the AFL-CIO's cold warriors did not hesitate to sacrifice the latter as long as the defeat of leftists was assured. In the Third World, particularly in the Western Hemisphere, this sometimes took the form of the AFL-CIO's American Institute for Free Labor Development (AIFLD) actively undermining a democratic government if Washington deemed it untrustworthy.

Guyana

AIFLD's first attempt at dramatically altering a country's political dynamic occurred between 1962 and 1964 in the small South American nation of Guyana, which was then a colony of the United Kingdom called British Guiana. The semi-autonomous colony of only 600,000 people was led by democratically elected Chief Minister Cheddi Jagan, who expected to see his country through a planned transition to full independence from Britain.

A devoted socialist who did not hide his admiration of the Soviet Union and Cuba, Jagan frightened the Kennedy administration and its allies in the AFL-CIO, including Meany and AIFLD director Serafino Romualdi, who saw him as another Fidel Castro. US officials were especially wary of the influence of Jagan's activist wife, Janet, a Jewish American he had met while studying dentistry at Northwestern University. Janet Jagan had been a member of the Young Communist League as a college student and was perhaps an even more ardent leftist than her husband.

The Kennedy administration pressed the British to stall the transition to independence until Cheddi Jagan could be forced out of power and replaced by his main political rival, Forbes Burnham. Kennedy's secretary of state, Dean Rusk, wrote to the British foreign secretary in early 1962 explaining that "it is not possible for us to put up with an independent British Guiana under Jagan." Soon after, Kennedy issued a memo to the British government demanding to know whether "Great Britain can be persuaded to delay independence for a year" and whether "a new election before independence" would be possible. Prime Minister Harold Macmillan gave in to Kennedy's pressure and pushed back the timetable on British Guiana's independence.[3]

British Guiana's political divide between the Indo-Guyanese Jagan and the Afro-Guyanese Burnham fueled racial tensions, with the colony's East Indians (49 percent of the population) generally backing Jagan, and Blacks (40 percent of the population) generally supporting Burnham. When AIFLD held its first residential course in Washington in the summer of 1962, eight of the trainees were Guyanese labor officials from unions affiliated with the pro-Burnham British Guiana Trade Union Council (BGTUC), who returned home that fall with nine months of funding as part of AIFLD's internship program—each getting paid a $250 monthly stipend. Meanwhile, several AFL-CIO officials made visits to British Guiana in 1962, including AIFLD social projects director Bill Doherty, to meet with BGTUC leaders to discuss strategies for opposing Jagan.[4]

In March 1963, Jagan's government introduced a bill to rehaul the colony's labor relations system. Jagan argued that the legislation was modeled after the US National Labor Relations Act, allowing workers the opportunity to vote for which union they wanted to have as their collective bargaining agent. He hoped the new law would enable Indo-Guyanese sugar workers to break away from their Burnham-aligned union and instead join an alternative one allied with his own People's Progressive Party.

Fearing that this labor bill would undercut their influence over Guyanese workers, BGTUC leaders called a general strike that April in protest. The colony was brought to a standstill as the strikers—practically all of them Afro-Guyanese—included workers in essential sectors like transportation, communications, and the civil service. Loyal to Jagan, Indo-Guyanese workers refused to strike but were attacked by mobs of strikers, leading to reprisals and an ugly cycle of race riots.

AFL-CIO leaders championed the work stoppage as a putative fight to preserve "free" trade unionism in the face of legislation they alleged aimed to turn unions into an instrument of the government. Six of the Guyanese AIFLD graduates—still funded by the Institute as interns—were instructed by Romualdi to devote all their time and energy to serving on the BGTUC strike committee. Their internship funding, scheduled to end in June, was extended to August by AIFLD. In other words, the strike leaders were on the AFL-CIO's payroll.[5]

Meanwhile, William Howard McCabe, an international representative with the AFL-CIO-affiliated American Federation of State, County, and Municipal Employees (AFSCME), was dispatched to British Guiana to help sustain the strike. McCabe was ostensibly working on behalf of Public Services International, the international trade secretariat for civil service employees. He was assisted in British Guiana by Gerard O'Keefe, a former Marine and foreign affairs director of the Retail Clerks International Union, another AFL-CIO affiliate.

With McCabe's coordination, US labor dished out between $800,000 and $1 million to the BGTUC strike fund, which provided food relief for some 50,000 strikers—an unprecedented level of support for a foreign work stoppage. But as would later be revealed, most of the money donated by McCabe and O'Keefe originated not with rank-and-file US union members, but rather the CIA. The Agency had established covert relationships with Public Services International and some other international trade secretariats in the late 1950s, and was working through McCabe and O'Keefe to destabilize Jagan's government.[6]

As the general strike continued into June 1963, Jagan published a letter to the editor in the *New York Times* defending his labor bill, explaining that his government had "bent over backward attempting to reach a compromise" with the BGTUC. He charged that the strike was "not industrial but rather politically inspired," directly calling out AIFLD for training Guyanese unionists "to overthrow my Government."[7] For many US readers, including union members, Jagan's accusatory letter was possibly the first time they had ever heard of AIFLD, which had only begun operations a year earlier.

As the strike neared the three-month mark, the colony's economy was in tatters and racial violence was spiraling out of control. Nine people had been killed and many others injured. Finally, with his government on the brink of collapse, Jagan shelved his proposed labor bill in early July. Victorious, Burnham and his loyalists in the BGTUC then suspended the strike. By the time it ended, the eleven-week US-backed work stoppage had cost the tiny colony an estimated $40 million.[8]

Elections were held in December of the following year. Adhering to US pressure, the British colonial office changed the colony's electoral system to proportional representation, meaning that a single party would need to secure a *majority* of the vote in order to form a government, instead of a plurality as had previously been the case. Both the CIA and AFL-CIO worked hard in the run-up to the 1964 election to ensure that Jagan's People's Progressive Party would be denied more than 50 percent of the vote.

Gene Meakins of the AFL-CIO-affiliated American Newspaper Guild was sent to British Guiana to disseminate anti-Jagan propaganda in print and over the radio. The CIA also funded the creation of new Indo-Guyanese political parties to split the PPP vote. In the end, the PPP secured 45.8 percent of the vote, while Burnham's party won 40.5 percent and another anti-Jagan party won 12.4 percent. With no party securing a majority, the colonial governor invited the anti-Jagan parties to form a coalition government, with Burnham as chief minister. Under Burnham, the AIFLD graduates who had helped lead the 1963 strike attained high-ranking positions in Guyanese unions, with one of them becoming president of the BGTUC.[9]

Now that Jagan was out of power, the decolonization process was allowed to move forward, with British Guiana becoming the independent nation of Guyana in 1966. That same year, AIFLD began work on a new housing development in the suburbs of Georgetown, Guyana's capital. With a $2 million USAID-guaranteed loan from the AFL-CIO, the Institute went about building 568 two- to four-bedroom houses. Problems with the contractor and disagreements between the Institute and USAID not only led to delays, but also served to make the houses more expensive than originally expected.

When the housing development—named TUCville—was finally completed, the homes were financially out of reach for poorer workers, and only members of BGTUC-affiliated unions were allowed to live there. Illustrating how AIFLD's interventions served to stratify foreign workers, the Guyanese families who could not buy a TUCville house instead set up a shantytown on the project's outskirts, leading to a drainage backup and mosquito infestation linked to a malaria outbreak.[10]

The unanticipated problems with AIFLD's housing development were emblematic of the detrimental consequences of the Institute's role in elevating Burnham at Jagan's expense. To prevent the majority Indo-Guyanese population from voting him out of office, Burnham would turn to election fraud and voter intimidation, becoming an authoritarian ruler who remained in office until his death in 1985.

Brazil

Like their allies in the US foreign policy establishment, AFL-CIO leaders in the early 1960s distrusted Brazil's left-leaning president, João "Jango" Goulart, whom they considered "an erratic opportunist" making the country vulnerable to a communist takeover.[11]

Leader of the Brazilian Labor Party and the nation's former minister of labor, Goulart was twice elected vice president, in 1956 and 1960. He maintained good relations with the country's Communist Party, making him suspect in the eyes of the AFL-CIO. Carlos Lacerda, a conservative Brazilian politician and one of Romualdi's closest allies in the country, constantly warned that Jango's Labor Party was being infiltrated by communists.

Upon President Jânio Quadros's resignation in 1961, Goulart ascended to the presidency in accordance with Brazil's constitution. Leftists in Brazil's ORIT-affiliated trade union center felt emboldened by Jango's rise to power, proposing the creation of a new national labor organization that would unite communists and noncommunists. A year later, 600 unions led by communists and noncommunist progressives formed the General Workers Command, with Goulart ally Clodsmidt Riani at the helm.

Though the creation of this new trade union center technically violated Brazil's restrictive industrial relations system, wherein the state traditionally maintained tight control over collective bargaining, the Goulart government tolerated it. While this could have been regarded as a sign that the country's labor movement was becoming more autonomous—the kind of development that "free" trade unionists would be expected to celebrate—Romualdi, Meany, and Jay Lovestone interpreted it merely as an attempt by Goulart to exercise personal, dictatorial control over organized labor.

About this same time, Goulart and Riani visited the United States, holding a testy meeting with AFL-CIO leaders. Goulart expressed interest in replacing the anticommunist ORIT with a new regional labor confederation that was tied to neither the International Confederation of Free Trade Unions nor the World Federation of Trade Unions, an obvious nonstarter for the North Americans. When Meany pointedly asked the Brazilian president whether he was pro-ICFTU or pro-WFTU, Jango deflected and offered only ambiguous answers.

United Auto Workers president Walter Reuther offered an olive branch by suggesting to Riani that the US labor movement find ways to collaborate with Brazilian unions through the international trade secretariats, namely the International Metalworkers Federation, with which his UAW was affiliated. Romualdi believed Reuther was "overly optimistic" and that the discussion was "an exercise in futility," having already written off Riani as a tool of the communists.[12]

For three months in early 1963, a year before the US-backed military coup that would oust Goulart, AIFLD hosted a special all-Brazilian class of thirty-three unionists at its school in Washington. Each of the course participants had earlier attended AIFLD's Cultural Labor Institute in São Paulo and were deemed trustworthy. The Washington course included fifty hours' worth of instruction on thwarting communist infiltration, with lectures on this topic by Romualdi and Lovestone, as well as field trips to Philadelphia and New England to visit factories and union halls.[13] As with AIFLD's other courses, graduates were sent home with nine-month stipends to instruct their fellow workers in the ways of "free" trade unionism. Before returning to Brazil, ten of the course participants first traveled to Western Europe and Israel with Romualdi to learn more "techniques and practices of democratic labor."

Meanwhile, reactionary forces in Brazil—unhappy with Goulart's plans for pro-worker social and economic reforms—made preparations to overthrow him, with support from US ambassador Lincoln Gordon, the CIA, and the Kennedy and Johnson administrations. On a visit to Brazil in the fall of 1963, Romualdi was informed by Adhemar de Barros, governor of São Paulo state, that "plans were already underway to mobilize military and police contingents to counter any attempt by Goulart to establish dictatorial control by force." Further, conservative politician Carlos Lacerda told Romualdi that sooner or later Jango would "make a fateful faux pas that would give the Brazilian armed forces the right and duty to intervene."[14]

When right-wing military officers launched their coup d'état against Goulart on April 1, 1964, which they characterized as a "revolution" to "save" the country from following in Cuba's footsteps, AIFLD graduates helped ensure that the overthrow went smoothly. One of them, Rômulo Teixeira Marinho of the Radio, Telegraph and Telephone Workers' Union, said that when the Communist Party called for a general strike to defend the Brazilian constitution during the coup, the party exhorted communications workers to walk off the job. But thanks in part to Marinho's efforts, the left-wing agitators were ignored so that "the wires kept humming, and the army was able to coordinate troop movements that ended the showdown bloodlessly."[15] Goulart and his family fled to Uruguay.

In the days after the coup, an estimated 10,000 to 50,000 suspected leftists were arrested, including union members and student activists. Hundreds faced brutal torture, much of it centered in Guanabara state, where Romualdi ally Carlos Lacerda served as governor.[16]

The new coup regime especially targeted organized labor, Jango's main base of popular support. Riani, the pro-Goulart head of the General Workers Command, was thrown in prison. Allegedly communist-led unions were put into government trusteeships, with outside "intervenors" sent to take control of these unions and systematically purge them of all leftists and Goulart sympathizers. The coup leaders appointed three graduates of the 1963 AIFLD course in Washington and one former student of AIFLD's Cultural Labor Institute to be intervenors. Many other graduates of the Washington course were "recalled" by AIFLD and "employed . . . on a full-time basis to organize teams that would not only undertake educational activities but would also assist in rescuing unions that were for so many years under communist control."[17]

Three months after the coup, AIFLD social projects director Bill Doherty openly bragged in a radio interview that Brazilian graduates of the Institute "became intimately involved in some of the clandestine operations of the revolution before it took place on April 1." He continued:

> What happened in Brazil . . . did not just happen—it was planned— and planned months in advance. Many of the trade union leaders— some of whom were actually trained in our institute—were involved in the revolution, and in the overthrow of the Goulart regime.

Whether this was mere bravado on Doherty's part, or if AIFLD graduates really had participated in "clandestine operations" in Brazil, remains a mystery. Upon hearing these comments, a distraught Victor Reuther—the UAW's international affairs director—privately remarked that there was "no statement that more clearly admits and confirms the major charge of Latin American Communists . . . that the military takeover was US-engineered. If this be the case . . . at least the AIFLD should know enough to keep their mouths shut."

Years later, Doherty explained to documentary filmmaker Allan Francovich that the Brazilian students had not been "in any kind of course for revolutionary activities or clandestine activities," but rather "they were in a regular collective bargaining course. It so happens that when many of those students went back home from that course, their unions were involved in the struggle against the attempt of the Communists to take over some of the unions, and that's precisely what I meant by the statement."[18]

The coup regime set about implementing its plan for rapid modernization in Brazil, which centered on a wage-control policy meant to curb inflation and attract foreign investment. Under Goulart, despite the country's traditional corporatist industrial relations system, unions had been allowed to negotiate salary increases with their employers. The military government soon nullified these agreements and passed what it called the Law of Salary Compression, tying all wage raises to the regime's own determination of the cost of living.[19]

In the same 1964 radio interview, Doherty defended the wage controls. Advocating his belief in "responsible" unionism, he confidently stated that Brazil's unions were "perfectly willing to accept any type of wage freeze necessary" and that even the destitute would have to sacrifice for the sake of development. "You can't have the poor suffer more than the rich, or *the poor less than the rich*," he stated.[20]

Victor Reuther said he was "horrified that all of this is being done in the name of establishing a 'strong, virile trade union movement in Latin America,' " adding that "not even the most servile, company-union-minded workers' organization in the US would dare to advocate this kind of sell-out."[21]

The AFL-CIO and AIFLD's enthusiasm for the coup was partly driven by the expressed "hope that the new government would provide an atmosphere in which free labor unions could prosper."[22] At a September 1964 AIFLD graduation ceremony in Washington, Brazil's new ambassador declared that "the Brazilian Revolution which saved the country from Communism and corruption wants to establish trade union freedom" and promised that unions would no longer be "subjected to [government] intervention," even as intervenors were being dispatched to purge leftists from union office.[23]

AFL-CIO Inter-American Representative Andrew McLellan—a Scottish-born former ORIT organizer who replaced Romualdi after the latter became executive director of AIFLD—assisted the regime in drafting a new labor law that would replace state-managed corporatism with free collective bargaining. But fearful that a more independent form of trade unionism would undermine the government's economic development policies, Brazil's minister of finance killed the legislation. At the same time, the government implemented new restrictions on the right to strike.

In October 1965, the coup's right-wing leaders formalized their dictatorship. Throughout 1966, the regime decreed numerous anti-union measures in the name of anticommunism and modernization. That June, McLellan confided to the US labor attaché in Rio de Janeiro that "perhaps our efforts have been nothing more than an exercise in futility," explaining that he "had hoped that by now, after all the effort that has gone into the Brazilian labor movement through AIFLD . . . we would begin to see something positive emerge."[24] Despite this bleak assessment and recognition that there was little hope of US-style industrial pluralism taking root under such draconian conditions, AIFLD continued its educational and development activities in Brazil for many years to come.

Now operating in an outright dictatorship, the Institute's stated purpose in the country changed from fighting a no-holds-barred battle against totalitarianism to the more watered-down goal of preparing workers "for the day when the military regime would relax its control of organized labor and permit both free trade unionism and collective bargaining"[25]—but doing nothing in particular to hasten when that day might come.

For his part, Jay Lovestone said that there was a distinction between "totalitarian" dictatorships and military dictatorships like that in Brazil, because the latter supposedly allowed unions a greater degree of autonomy than the former.[26] Such flexibility in the face of an anticommunist military regime stood in stark contrast to the brash determination with which AIFLD had confronted the democratic Goulart government. The AFL-CIO's tolerance of Brazil's repressive regime similarly contrasted with its uncompromising hostility toward world communism.

Through the entirety of Brazil's nineteen-year dictatorship, AIFLD quietly continued its training programs in the country through its Cultural Labor Institute and, according to US ambassador John Crimmins in 1975, rarely challenged the dictatorship even as local unionists were disappeared and tortured. Instead, AIFLD remained fixated on anticommunism in Brazil, seeking "to train people who could, when the time came, confront the Communists."[27]

The Dominican Republic

In 1961, Dominican dictator Rafael Trujillo's three-decade reign was brought to a sudden end when he was gunned down by a group of assassins. The CIA had been in on the conspiracy to kill Trujillo, fearing that his continued rule might spark another Castro-like revolution. But in the wake of the Bay of Pigs debacle, the Kennedy administration unsuccessfully tried to pull the plug on the assassination plot at the last minute, worried that a fresh power vacuum in the Dominican Republic might just as easily allow the rise of a new Castro.[28]

In the months following Trujillo's demise, a new national trade union center was formed called FOUPSA (United Front for Autonomous Unions). AFL-CIO Inter-American Representative Andrew McLellan was sent to the country to partner with US labor attaché Fred Sommerford to gauge whether FOUPSA's leaders could be trusted. In late 1961, FOUPSA threatened a general strike as part of a popular movement demanding the resignation of Trujillo's puppet president, Joaquín Balaguer, who remained in power.[29] With the US Embassy believing that pro-Castro elements were agitating for the strike, McLellan allegedly offered FOUPSA general secretary Miguel Soto $30,000 to call it off. As researcher Susanne Bodenheimer revealed, when Soto refused the money and went ahead with the work stoppage, the AFL-CIO and US Embassy labeled him and FOUPSA's other top officials as communists.[30]

Mimicking the same tactics employed by the Free Trade Union Committee's Irving Brown in Europe after World War II, McLellan and Sommerford engineered a split in FOUPSA in February 1962. They helped create a new, rival trade union center named CONATRAL (National Confederation of Free Workers). CONATRAL quickly affiliated with ORIT. Its leaders participated in some of AIFLD's earliest union training courses in Washington, utilizing their post-graduation stipends to preach "free" trade unionism to Dominican workers while branding rival unionists as crypto-communists. What remained of FOUPSA merged with another labor federation—the CESITRADO (Central Union of Dominican Workers)—to become the FOUPSA-CESITRADO, or FC.[31]

Meanwhile, longtime opposition leader Juan Bosch returned from exile, along with other members of his social democratic Dominican Revolutionary Party. Bosch came back only after his friend and advisor Sacha Volman first visited the Dominican Republic to survey the post-Trujillo political situation. An anticommunist Romanian exile, Volman ran the CIA-financed Institute of International Labor Research (which, unlike AIFLD, was not part of the AFL-CIO) alongside his friend, US Socialist Party leader Norman Thomas.

After Balaguer stepped down as a result of mass pressure, a US-backed interim government took over at the beginning of 1962. National elections were planned for later that year, with Bosch running for president. Volman helped build a popular base of support by sending Dominican campesinos first to the Institute of International Labor Research's political training school in Costa Rica, then to a new training center he established in Santo Domingo.

Once trained, the campesinos formed political organizations that did electoral campaigning for Bosch in the countryside. The urban unions affiliated with FC also backed Bosch. He won the election that December in a landslide, taking office in February 1963.

Informally advised by Volman and Norman Thomas, Bosch's government wrote and enacted a new national constitution in the first two months of his presidency. The document gave Dominican workers and campesinos basic rights and legal protections for the first time.[32]

Bosch traveled to Washington shortly before taking office to meet with Kennedy, as well as the AFL-CIO's Meany, Lovestone, and McLellan. The US president was eager to make the Dominican Republic the centerpiece of his Alliance for Progress. The country would become the largest per capita recipient of US foreign aid between 1962 and 1966. This was not so much out of enthusiasm for Bosch, but out of concern that the Dominican Republic might otherwise go the way of its Caribbean neighbor, Cuba.

As Kennedy told his advisors shortly after Trujillo's assassination, there were "three possibilities in descending order" of a preferred successor government: "A decent democratic regime, a continuation of the Trujillo regime or a Castro regime. We ought to aim at the first, but we really can't renounce the second until we are sure that we can avoid the third."[33] Kennedy's assessment perfectly summed up the Cold War calculus of both the US government and the AFL-CIO: brutal, corrupt, right-wing dictators were preferred to leftists, and Washington would endeavor to ensure that the former held power at the expense of the latter.

In his meeting with Meany, Lovestone, and McLellan, Bosch expressed his desire to reunite the Dominican labor movement. The rivalry between FC and CONATRAL was creating civil unrest, with workers from the competing trade union centers reportedly fighting in the streets of Santo Domingo over strike disagreements. McLellan and Sommerford were so unpopular for having split FOUPSA that Dominican workers burned them in effigy. There was also a third major union center, affiliated with the Catholic labor movement, that was rapidly growing.

The AFL-CIO officials had no interest in Bosch's proposal to build a united national trade union center. If CONATRAL—whose AIFLD-trained and funded leaders were loyal to the North Americans—were to be subsumed into a larger organization, it would likely mean the loss of AFL-CIO influence over the Dominican labor movement. While cordial with Bosch in person, after the meeting, Meany and the others accused him of having the ulterior motive of wanting to build a state-dominated union federation to give himself more power, hinting that perhaps he was a totalitarian in the making.[34]

Bosch continuously faced these kinds of accusations. Conservative Dominican elites, who had long benefited from the Trujillo dictatorship, were outraged by the new president's constitution and social democratic impulses, including his plans for land reform. Accordingly, they called him a communist.

Particularly troubling to both the Dominican military and US Embassy was Bosch's lifting of anti-subversive laws and leniency toward the country's Communist Party—more a reflection of his commitment to civil liberties than an affinity for reds. Officials in Washington labeled Bosch "soft" on communism and right-wingers in the Dominican Republic began openly discussing ousting him.

CONATRAL's anticommunist, AIFLD-trained leaders were also among the growing opposition to Bosch. In a July 1963 radio broadcast, CONATRAL general secretary Robinson Ruiz López heaped praise on Ecuador's armed forces for having recently overthrown that country's president, calling on the Dominican military to do the same in order to save the nation from communism. Following this controversial plea, leaders of both the FC and the Catholic union center issued a newspaper declaration defending Bosch's government and the Dominican constitution. CONATRAL officials then responded with a newspaper notice of their own, expressing full faith in the armed forces to defend against communist subversion.

Shortly afterward, in September, Bosch met the same fate as Árbenz and Goulart before him—he was ousted by a military coup. He once again went into exile. Coming only seven months into Bosch's presidency, the coup was approved by the US Embassy and applauded by the AFL-CIO, AIFLD, and CONATRAL.

In violation of the Dominican constitution, the coup regime installed conservative politician Donald Reid Cabral as the country's new president. While the pro-Bosch FC and Catholic trade union center faced repression under the new government—with their offices raided and leaders arrested—CONATRAL thrived, growing to 100,000 members by 1965. Cabral got along well not only with Washington, but with the AFL-CIO. AIFLD social projects director Bill Doherty praised the new president as "a warm friend of the workingman and the labor movement."[35]

On April 12, 1965, in an official state ceremony at the National Palace in Santo Domingo, Cabral inducted AIFLD's Serafino Romualdi into the prestigious Order of Duarte, Sanchez y Mella at the rank of "Knight Commander." It was a special honor from the Dominican government to reward him for "lifetime services on behalf of the free trade union movement" and to recognize "what the labor movement of the United States ... has done in defense of freedom in the Dominican Republic." With the US ambassador in attendance, the ceremony and high honor bestowed on Romualdi represented the cementing of a special relationship between the United States, AFL-CIO, and the coup regime.[36]

Two weeks later, a rebellion began.

Seeking a return to constitutional rule, on April 26, a group of junior military officers arrested Cabral's chief of staff and took over the National Palace. The country was immediately plunged into civil war between two factions: pro-Bosch Constitutionalists and so-called Loyalists who supported the coup regime.

Armed with the help of the junior officers who sparked the rebellion, the Constitutionalists consisted of civilian Bosch supporters, progressives, and nationalists who resented Cabral's subservience to Washington. The Loyalists were composed of the same military leaders who had overthrown Bosch two years earlier and backed by right-wing elites. The FC and Catholic trade union center immediately mobilized to support the Constitutionalists, but CONATRAL leaders stayed out of the conflict.

Only two days into the civil war, US ambassador William Tapley Bennett Jr. recognized that the pro-Bosch forces were on the verge of victory. He begged the State Department to assist the Loyalists, cabling on the afternoon of April 28: "The issue here is now a fight between Castro-type elements and those who oppose it [sic]. I do not wish to be over-dramatic but we should be clear as to the situation." A few hours later, he cabled again recommending that US Marines stationed off Santo Domingo immediately be sent ashore to assist the Loyalists. Knowing that this might look bad, Bennett suggested a pretext: "If Washington wishes, [the Marines] can be landed for the purpose of protecting evacuation of American citizens."

President Lyndon Johnson ordered 536 Marines ashore that same evening, explaining in a public statement that their mission was simply to help escort Americans out of the country. Bennett and the Dominican Loyalists had hoped the mere presence of US troops would be enough to dissuade the pro-Bosch forces from continuing their rebellion, but it did not. "Santo Domingo will never be taken nor our people vanquished in their democratic struggle," the Constitutionalist command declared via radio broadcast on April 29. "We will accept no solution but the complete re-establishment of constitutional government with Professor Juan Bosch as President of the Republic."

Fearing that a victory for the Constitutionalists and return to power for Bosch would make Washington appear "weak" in Castro's neighborhood, Johnson decided a full-scale invasion was necessary. On April 30, he ordered 2,500 soldiers into the Dominican Republic, the first wave of a US invasion that grew to a total of 23,000 troops over the next ten days. "Communist leaders, many of them trained in Cuba, seeing a chance to increase disorder, to gain a foothold, joined the revolution," Johnson told the American public, without evidence. "And what began as a popular democratic revolution, committed to democracy and social justice, very shortly moved and was taken over and really seized and placed into the hands of a band of Communist conspirators."[37]

The US soldiers were soon followed by a peacekeeping force of troops from multiple member nations of the Organization of American States, with Brazil's military dictatorship sending the largest contingent. CONATRAL leaders, who until now had been quiet, echoed Johnson's talking points and endorsed the US-led invasion, as did the AFL-CIO Executive Council.[38]

Thanks to the US-led military intervention, by June the Constitutionalist revolution had been defeated. All fighting stopped and the international forces pulled out of the country. Still, Bosch was allowed to return to again run for president in new elections set for 1966. His opponent was Joaquín Balaguer, the former figurehead president under Trujillo.

With Johnson determined to keep Bosch from winning, Balaguer's campaign received substantial financial support from the CIA and State Department. The AIFLD-backed CONATRAL also championed Balaguer's candidacy. Meanwhile, the State Department refused to grant Sacha Volman a visa to travel to the Dominican Republic to assist Bosch's campaign.

Two years earlier, Texas Congressman Wright Patman had publicly exposed how the J. M. Kaplan Fund—the main benefactor to Volman's institute—was a conduit for CIA funds. After this embarrassing revelation, the Agency's covert subsidy to Volman was cut off. In the 1966 Dominican election, the anticommunist Volman ironically found himself on the opposite side of his former CIA patrons, wanting to aid a presidential candidate whom they were actively trying to defeat.

This turning of the tables signified the Agency's abandonment of its former strategy of supporting the Noncommunist Left. Now, especially in the wake of the Cuban Revolution, the CIA felt safer supporting right-wing reactionaries.[39] US Socialist Party leader and Bosch ally Norman Thomas, who had unsuccessfully lobbied for Volman to be allowed into the Dominican Republic, traveled to the country himself to be an election observer.

Facing overt hostility from the Dominican military and the US Embassy, and knowing that if he won he would only be overthrown again, Bosch ran a lackluster campaign. Further, the labor movement—which might have provided a strong base of support for Bosch—remained divided. On election day, Balaguer won a decisive victory. Despite some reports of fraud, Thomas declared the election to have been free and fair, thus granting legitimacy to the result.[40] Balaguer would remain the nation's paternalistic, often repressive president off and on over the next thirty years.

In the aftermath of the civil war, US intervention, and 1966 election, it was clear to many Dominican workers that CONATRAL was an instrument of the AFL-CIO and US Embassy. Its leaders had not only opposed Bosch and welcomed foreign troops into the country, but they also had supported various wage freezes and austerity measures enacted first by Cabral, then by Balaguer, in the name of development. Multiple affiliate unions soon broke from CONATRAL, with the labor federation's overall membership plummeting from 100,000 in early 1965 to only 25,000 by 1966.[41]

Even José Dolores Bautista—the onetime AIFLD trainee who had approvingly commented on being "brainwashed" by the Institute in a "free, friendly, and comradely manner"—quit CONATRAL and joined the FC instead. His brainwashing had apparently failed to stick.[42]

AIFLD attempted to bolster CONATRAL through a housing development built for sugar workers in the town of San Pedro de Macorís between 1965 and 1966. Like the AIFLD housing project in Mexico City, the development would be named after Kennedy. The project initially promised between 700 and 900 units. Sixty-seven percent of the cost would be financed by a loan from the Inter-American Development Bank, with the remaining 33 percent coming from USAID-guaranteed loans by AFL-CIO affiliates.

But the Inter-American Development Bank pulled out of the project, citing AIFLD's insistence that bidding on the construction contract be kept closed in order to favor US firms, which violated Dominican laws, as well as the Institute's demand that only CONATRAL members be allowed to live in the development. Without the bank's support, the project had to be significantly downsized, with ultimately only 110 units being built. The project was criticized by a US technician for being "obviously designed to impress the USA with the tremendous impact of the AIFLD rather than serve the practical necessities of the Dominican Republic and Dominican labor."[43]

By December 1967, AIFLD country director Joe Bermudez complained to the head of USAID's Dominican mission that CONATRAL's loss of membership meant there was no money to pay its officers and staff or maintain an office. "For all intents and purposes, the CONATRAL has ceased to exist except in name," he wrote.

But with an injection of funds, the Institute and USAID managed to keep the trade union center alive, with a 1969 AIFLD report noting that "it can be said with certainty that any gains made by CONATRAL during 1967 and 1968 have been as a result of the AIFLD technical advice, social projects, and education programs."[44]

9

Mama Maida

At a meeting with AFL-CIO officials in January 1964, USAID administrator Daniel Bell noted the American Institute for Free Labor Development's "fine progress" and expressed his wish that "a somewhat similar mechanism could be established for the African labor scene." By March, the AFL-CIO was drawing up plans for a new institute that would aim to bring AIFLD-style education programs and social projects to African workers, with the possibility of later expanding into Asia. USAID offered full support for the project. A few months later, the initiative was named the African American Labor Center.[1]

But this would hardly be the AFL-CIO's first foray into Africa. The Federation already had firm allies on the continent thanks to the diplomacy of one of US labor's most celebrated internationalists: Maida Springer.

Springer

Born Maida Stewart in 1910 to Barbadian and Panamanian parents, Springer spent the first seven years of her life in the Panama Canal Zone before moving to New York City with her family. Settling in Harlem, she was influenced at an early age by Marcus Garvey's Pan-Africanism, which sought to unite all people of African descent and cultivate a spirit of Black pride.

In 1932, a few years after marrying Barbadian immigrant Owen Springer, she went to work as a dressmaker and soon joined Local 22 of the International Ladies' Garment Workers' Union (ILGWU). This was the same local headed by Lovestoneite Charles "Sasha" Zimmerman. An ally of A. Philip Randolph and his Brotherhood of Sleeping Car Porters— the only Black-led union in the AFL—Zimmerman took Springer under his wing and introduced her to Randolph. With these men as her mentors, Springer developed a firm commitment to trade unionism as well as an aversion to communism.

She became a member of ILGWU Local 22's executive board in the late 1930s, later serving in the role of business agent for the union. In 1945, Springer was selected to represent the AFL on a goodwill exchange of women unionists between the United States and Britain, sponsored by the Office of War Information. As she headed out to England that January, the *New York Times* noted Springer was making history as the "first American Negro woman to represent American labor abroad."[2]

The trip ignited a lifelong passion in Springer for labor internationalism. With funding from private foundations, she returned to Europe in 1951, studying workers' education in Scandinavia, touring France and Italy to observe labor conditions, then spending a year studying at Oxford's Ruskin labor college on a fellowship from the Urban League, a US civil rights organization.[3]

As a prominent Black union official with impressive international credentials, by the mid-1950s, Springer was a natural choice to represent the AFL-CIO in Africa, where nationalist movements—often led by unionists—were demanding independence from European colonizers. What's more, through Zimmerman, she had gained the confidence of Jay Lovestone. Both Springer and Lovestone supported anticolonialism in Africa, though for different reasons. For Springer, African liberation was an end in itself: the manifestation of self-determination and self-worth after centuries of exploitation, plunder, and racism; as well as an inspiration to the Black Freedom Movement then under way in the United States.

Lovestone, on the other hand, viewed African liberation as a geostrategic problem to be solved. He surmised that African independence was inevitable after World War II had critically weakened the old European empires, and that this presented a potential opening for the communists to gain influence in another region of the world. The most effective way to stave off such influence would be for Washington and the AFL-CIO to befriend and aid African nationalist movements early on, winning them over to the West.[4]

In late 1955, Springer embarked on her first trip to Africa to observe an International Confederation of Free Trade Unions (ICFTU) seminar in the Gold Coast—a British colony that would soon become the independent state of Ghana. She then spent much of 1957 and 1958 touring East, West, and Central Africa on behalf of the AFL-CIO.

Unlike other Western diplomats, who were almost always white men, Springer connected with Africa's youthful nationalist leaders on a deeply personal level. Her brownstone in Brooklyn became something of a home away from home for these leaders whenever they were in New York on diplomatic business, like during the annual meetings of the UN General Assembly. Mostly young men in their twenties and thirties, they nicknamed the middle-aged, matronly Springer "Mama Maida" as a sign of respect.

At Lovestone's urging, in 1960, she was hired full-time with the AFL-CIO's International Affairs Department to be the Federation's main ambassador to Africa. Years later, Springer would face accusations from some on the Left of being a CIA-funded operative like Lovestone and Irving Brown. Not only was she an associate of those two men, but she was also on the board of directors of Norman Thomas's CIA-financed Institute of International Labor Research. But her biographer, historian Yevette Richards Jordan, found no evidence of any direct connection to the Agency. If anything, rather than being flush with cash from mysterious sources, Springer's African activities tended to be underfunded and overlooked, forcing her to constantly plead with the Federation for more support.[5]

Decolonization

The stage for Springer's efforts in Africa had been set as far back as the 1930s. Anticipating modernization theory by nearly two decades, British and French colonial officials sought to maintain control over their African subjects through development and "stabilization" programs. Though most Africans were subsistence farmers, sizable numbers toiled as wage workers in vital areas of the colonial economies like mines, railroads, ports, plantations, and the civil service.

The colonial administrations' dependence on the labor of these work-ers made them a potential threat that would need to be contained and controlled. Having slowly begun coming to terms with a rebellious working class in Europe through collective bargaining and social legis-lation in the early twentieth century, the British and French govern-ments hoped to re-create this relatively orderly arrangement by intro-ducing "stable" industrial relations mechanisms to Africa. According to historian Frederick Cooper, colonial authorities believed an identifiable and manageable African working class would be a "positive alternative to the unbounded mass" and could be "socialized and tamed by tech-niques that were familiar in Europe."

The British established labor departments in their African colonies to set wage standards and create trade unions—always keeping the unions small and fragmented to prevent them from becoming too powerful. The British Trades Union Congress aided colonial officials in training African unionists in the hopes they would be "responsible" bureaucrats instead of radical agitators. France, meanwhile, intro-duced a Code du Travail (Labor Code) in its colonies and allowed African workers to set up their own branches of French unions affili-ated with the CGT (General Confederation of Labor) and, later, the anticommunist Force Ouvrière.[6]

The more Africans were treated by white colonizers as rights-bearing citizens entitled to the fruits of their labor, the more they demanded an end to foreign domination so they could lead their own citizenries and develop their own economies. By the 1940s, such demands frequently took the form of work stoppages in key economic sectors, as well as general strikes.

African calls for decolonization only grew more forceful after World War II demonstrated the vulnerability of colonial regimes. With educa-tional opportunities and access to the halls of power, African trade union leaders became some of the most influential figures in the emerg-ing nationalist movements. One of the most notable examples was Sékou Touré, head of the CGT branch in the French West African colony of Guinea. After leading general strikes in the early 1950s to demand more rights for Guinean workers, Touré used his popular union base to enter politics. He led Guinea to independence at the end of the decade, then served as the nation's first president. Other nationalist leaders, including the US-educated Kwame Nkrumah of Ghana, were allied with labor movements and advocated using strikes to dislodge the power of colonial rulers.[7]

By the time Maida Springer first visited Africa in 1955, relations were strained between the ICFTU's European trade union centers and their African affiliates. Without always explicitly saying so, the International's white leaders—particularly those from Britain, France, and Belgium—expected African unions to remain subservient to the labor movements of the colonial powers. While these European unionists were frequently involved in the politics of their own countries through social democratic parties, they chauvinistically expected their colonized African counterparts to steer clear of political issues, especially the question of independence. Because of her association with Lovestone, who had a record of hostility toward them, the European laborites were naturally suspicious of Springer. Her steadfast support for decolonization and the respect she gained from African nationalists only solidified this distrust.

Springer was an especially controversial figure to the British in East Africa. The colonies of Kenya and Tanganyika (Tanzania) each had large settler populations of whites, which fostered heightened racism and sharper repression against Black nationalist leaders, including unionists. When Springer made her first two trips to East Africa at the beginning and end of 1957, she was surveilled by colonial authorities and denounced in the pro-colonial press. That same year, at an ICFTU conference in the newly independent Ghana, the Europeans relegated her and fellow AFL-CIO representative Irving Brown to the lowly status of nonparticipating "guests."[8]

Brown had been engaged in African affairs since the early 1950s, particularly in French North Africa. Following Lovestone's advice, the AFL championed anticolonial struggles in Tunisia and Morocco partly to hedge against any potential Soviet support for such movements. To the ire of the French government, Brown arranged for Tunisian nationalist leader Habib Bourguiba to visit the United States in September 1951. Bourguiba attended that year's AFL convention and delivered an address over the State Department's Voice of America radio broadcast, during which he called for an end to European control over Arab nations.

Lovestone's Free Trade Union Committee gave money to anticolonial unions in Tunisia and Morocco in the early 1950s, helping fund the Tunisian General Labor Union and the Moroccan Labor Union. In 1956,

Brown was welcomed to the now-independent Tunisia and was a guest of honor at the Tunisian General Labor Union's annual congress. With his interest in Africa growing, at the beginning of 1957 Brown accompanied Springer to the ICFTU conference in Ghana, where plans were made to begin forming a new regional organization of African trade unions similar to ORIT in Latin America.[9]

Springer's closest friend among African nationalists was Kenya's Tom Mboya, who would become the AFL-CIO's most reliable ally on the continent. Initially a public employee for the city of Nairobi, Mboya became active in the labor movement and served as general secretary of the Kenya Federation of Labor (KFL) in the years leading up to that country's independence in 1963. Still only in his twenties, he toured the United States multiple times in the late 1950s to promote Africa's anticolonial cause and propose an "international new deal" to raise living standards around the world.

It was during his first visit in 1956 that Mboya befriended Springer. Welcoming him into her home and inspired by his political idealism, Springer came to regard Mboya almost as a son. She convinced the AFL-CIO to donate $35,000 to Mboya in early 1957 so his KFL could build a new headquarters in Nairobi. During Mboya's 1959 visit to the United States, he addressed one thousand delegates from Springer's ILGWU at the union's national conference in Miami Beach, where he received the "warmest" reception "accorded any guest in four days of meetings." He also established a scholarship program to send young Kenyans to study at US universities—one of whom was Barack Obama Sr., who would father the forty-fourth president of the United States.[10]

Systematically denied educational opportunities by the British, East African workers were eager for scholarships to study in the United States. During her stop in Tanganyika in early 1957, Springer was asked by Tanganyika Federation of Labor general secretary Rashidi Kawawa if there were any possibilities of sending African trade union members to American universities. On her return to the United States, Springer took up the issue with the AFL-CIO Executive Council, with A. Philip Randolph's backing. In August 1957, the Executive Council approved a plan to fund scholarships for approximately twelve African union leaders to take a course at Harvard's industrial relations center and then be provided one-year stipends to organize in their home countries. Two months later, Springer was back in East Africa to begin recruiting participants.

The AFL-CIO's African scholarship program proved to be another source of tension with ICFTU officials, who had been considering the possibility of opening an African labor college and felt that the Federation was now trying to undermine that effort. Accordingly, they protested to Meany. Wary of Springer's connection to Lovestone and keen to approach international affairs more multilaterally, Walter Reuther also objected. The issue came up that December in Atlantic City at the same high-level meeting between AFL-CIO and ICFTU officials that saw Meany agree to do away with the Free Trade Union Committee. Meany promised to scrap Springer's African scholarship program and instead support the establishment of an ICFTU labor college in Kampala, Uganda. African labor leaders had no say in this deal, and neither did Springer and Randolph.[11]

The ICFTU's African Labor College opened in Kampala in November 1958. The college held four-month courses for unionists from anglophone Africa. Its small international staff consisted of four Europeans and one African American: George McCray. A dedicated Pan-Africanist and civil rights activist, McCray had entered the labor movement by leading a union of public sector workers in Chicago. He was friends with the noted sociologist St. Clair Drake, who was a professor at Chicago's Roosevelt University but was teaching at the University of Ghana around the time of that country's independence. Through his connection with Drake, McCray toured Ghana in 1957 and early 1958, reporting back his observations to the AFL-CIO. This experience prompted Federation leaders, particularly Randolph, to tap McCray to be an instructor at the Kampala labor college.

In its first few years, the college was housed within a British-owned hotel. The management initially barred the African trainees from eating in the main dining hall with the white hotel guests, instead telling them to eat with employees in an uncomfortable spot close to the kitchen. While the ICFTU's European staff were willing to tolerate this arrangement, McCray and the trainees protested, forcing the hotel to change course. McCray would continue clashing with his white colleagues at the college over their racist and paternalistic attitudes until he eventually left Uganda in 1965.[12]

The ICFTU in Africa

In 1957, Ghana became the first European colony in sub-Saharan Africa to win independence, followed by Guinea the next year. With political autonomy secured, nationalists like Nkrumah and Touré called for more economic and cultural freedom from former colonizers, which they believed could be facilitated through stronger African unity. To achieve this vision, African workers would need to cut their ties with European unions. Already in 1956–57, Touré had broken with the French CGT and formed the General Union of Black African Workers to bring together the unions of French West Africa into a single, autonomous body.

Meanwhile, as prime minister of Ghana, Nkrumah oversaw passage of an industrial relations law in 1958 that created a "New Structure" for the Ghanaian labor movement. The sixty-four national unions that comprised the Ghana Trades Union Congress were consolidated into ten unions. Further, the Ghana Trades Union Congress became an official wing of Nkrumah's Convention People's Party, strikes were outlawed in favor of compulsory arbitration, and the government maintained the right to control union finances. The purpose of the corporatist New Structure was to transform the Ghanaian labor movement into a partner in state-led economic development, instead of an independent force that Nkrumah worried might get in the way of his modernization plans. The ICFTU and International Labor Organization criticized the legislation for violating standards on freedom of association, which only strengthened Nkrumah's desire for increased independence from European-dominated institutions.[13]

Positioning himself as the leader of a nascent continent-wide movement against colonialism and neocolonialism, Nkrumah hosted the All-African People's Conference in December 1958. Held in the Ghanaian capital of Accra, the meeting was organized by the continent's only independent countries at the time—Ghana, Guinea, Ethiopia, Liberia, Libya, Morocco, Tunisia, and Egypt—and welcomed some 300 delegates from twenty-eight African nations, most of them still colonies.

Springer, Brown, and McCray all attended as observers on behalf of the AFL-CIO, which was more popular among Africans than the European-led ICFTU. Adopting the slogan "Hands Off Africa," the delegates discussed strategies to hasten decolonization and ideas for a postcolonial future. During the proceedings, Touré advocated the creation of a new, Africa-wide labor confederation, expanding on the General Union of Black African Workers he had founded in French West Africa. Nkrumah championed this idea, calling on African unions affiliated with the ICFTU to disaffiliate.

Mboya, representing the Kenyan delegation, argued that African trade union unity and affiliation with the ICFTU need not be mutually exclusive. Mboya understood that breaking with the ICFTU would irritate US cold warriors, which he was in no rush to do. He argued that the International, if pressured by the AFL-CIO, would do more to support African nationalism. While Ghana Trades Union Congress leader John Tettegah initially sided with Mboya, soon after the conference, he was pressured by Nkrumah into also supporting disaffiliation.

By early 1959, there were two rival camps in the African labor movement: one in favor of sticking with the ICFTU, led by Mboya, and one that wanted to pull out of the International, led by Nkrumah and Tettegah.[14]

Springer, Brown, and McCray warned Meany that unless the ICFTU did more, the international "free" trade union movement was at risk of being shunned from Africa. Meany had the AFL-CIO Executive Council issue a statement pledging full support for African decolonization.

Meanwhile, the Ghana Trades Union Congress officially withdrew from the ICFTU in 1959 and led the charge in forming a new, Pan-African trade union organization. As part of this campaign, anti-Western unionists in Nigeria published a pamphlet entitled the "Great Conspiracy Against Africa." Widely circulated around the continent with Nkrumah's help, and also picked up by the Soviet press, the publication centered on what was alleged to be a leaked document from inside the upper echelons of the British government. The document appeared to lay out plans for the Western powers to continue dominating Africa after independence through control of unions, with the help of the AFL-CIO and CIA. Several errors in the document led researchers to conclude it was a fake, yet the neocolonial machinations the pamphlet warned about certainly rang true—especially after events in Congo.[15]

After a century of brutal colonial rule at the hands of the Belgians, the Congolese won independence in June 1960 under the leadership of the young nationalist Patrice Lumumba. Irving Brown had met Lumumba at the All-African People's Conference in 1958 and believed him to be a trustworthy liberal leader, encouraging his contacts in the US foreign policy establishment to support Lumumba.[16]

But Brown's advice was ultimately ignored. Soon after Congo became independent, two of its mineral-rich provinces seceded with backing from Belgium. Lumumba pleaded with Washington and the UN to help resolve the crisis. After being rebuffed, he reached out to the Soviets. This latter move outraged officials at the CIA, who became convinced that the Congolese prime minister was a communist puppet and began plotting his assassination.

In the end, with the collusion of the US and Belgian governments, Lumumba was forced out of office, captured, and murdered by his domestic political enemies. Within a few years of Lumumba's January 1961 assassination, the anticommunist General Joseph-Désiré Mobutu emerged as the country's undisputed head of state, renaming the country Zaire and instituting a corrupt, repressive, and US-backed dictatorship that would last until his ouster in 1997. The CIA role in this affair prompted many African nationalists to abandon their once-held belief that the United States was any better than European colonizers.[17]

It was in this atmosphere that African labor leaders gathered in Casablanca for a May 1961 conference to discuss the idea of forming a continental trade union organization. Both the pro- and anti-ICFTU groups were present. The Ghana Trades Union Congress and Touré's General Union of Black African Workers led the faction arguing that membership in a Pan-African union federation would require disaffiliating from all outside organizations, namely the ICFTU, while the Kenya Federation of Labor and Tunisian General Labor Union took the position that dual affiliations should be permissible. After a few days of debating the issue, the delegates finally voted on it. Dual affiliation would not be allowed, or as the New York Times put it, "unionists resentful of the West triumphed over their more moderate comrades."[18]

The conference formally established the All-African Trade Union Federation (AATUF), which adopted African unity, Cold War neutralism, and opposition to all forms of colonialism and neocolonialism as its core principles. The new organization would be headquartered in Accra. Already believing that neutralism was merely a cover for procommunist sympathies, Meany and Lovestone viewed the creation of the AATUF as a victory for the Soviet-led World Federation of Trade Unions.

With help from Mboya, the ICFTU responded in 1962 by founding the African Trade Union Confederation to be its regional wing. While remaining firmly connected to Europe and North America, this organization also adopted the language of Pan-African unity. Further, under the new leadership of Belgian unionist Omer Becu, the ICFTU gave the AFL-CIO approval to resume its own independent activities on the continent, which had previously been restricted by the 1957 Atlantic City agreement.[19]

Vocational Training

Now working directly for the AFL-CIO's International Affairs Department, in the early 1960s Maida Springer endeavored to maintain friendly relations with African labor leaders in the face of the growing divide between Nkrumah's pan-African AATUF and the pro-Western "free" trade union movement. She was especially eager not to let the Cold War blind the Federation to African realities. "Soviet domination, though real, is less evident than the terror, violence, discrimination endured by Africans in parts of North, South, East, and Central Africa," she wrote Lovestone after a six-week tour of the continent in late 1960, referring to the abuses of the colonial regimes.[20]

Springer was sympathetic to the new governments' desire for rapid economic growth and, unlike some of her fellow internationalists in the AFL-CIO, cautioned against trying to mold African labor relations in the image of US industrial pluralism.[21] After attending a conference of international labor education experts held at Michigan State University in 1962, an unimpressed Springer wrote Lovestone to express her frustration that "many of these good folk think they can create labor leaders, can find assurances that overseas unionists will react in a certain way and even love us if we tell him what is good for him."[22] Instead of preaching "free" trade unionism, Springer favored providing practical assistance to African unionists. She was instrumental in the establishment of two union-sponsored vocational training centers.

The first was the Kenyan Institute of Tailoring and Cutting, based in Nairobi and run by the local Tailors and Textiles Workers' Union, part of Mboya's Kenya Federation of Labor. In 1961, the Nairobi tailors' union reached out to the AFL-CIO "begging" for financial help in opening a training school because "the countrymen of Kenya want good clothes and therefore there must be experienced tailors."[23] Going through her contacts in the International Ladies' Garment Workers' Union, Springer managed to secure funds to help open the tailoring school in March 1963. Starting with an initial fifty-one students, the school offered four- to six-month tailoring courses, including beginner classes for women trying to start a career in the garment industry.

The second vocational program Springer helped start was the Nigerian Motor Drivers School, located near Lagos. The brainchild of the ICFTU-affiliated Nigerian United Labor Congress, the school was intended particularly for taxi drivers and other transport workers to promote safety by learning to read road signs, follow traffic rules, and safely operate vehicles. Springer persuaded the AFL-CIO Executive Council to partner with the Nigerian unionists on the project and provide an initial $2,500 in 1963, though the school would not formally open until early 1965.[24]

Despite Springer's efforts, more and more African countries and trade union centers were following the Ghana model of breaking with the ICFTU. Upon Kenya's independence in 1963, Mboya—with reputed CIA backing—served first as the minister of labor, then minister of justice, then minister of economic planning and development. With its leading figure now more focused on his political career, the Kenya Federation of Labor gave in to mounting pressure from Pan-Africanists and disaffiliated from the ICFTU in 1964.[25]

Nkrumah's All-African Trade Union Federation grew closer to the communist-led World Federation of Trade Unions, which gladly encouraged Africans to resist neocolonialism. Following Khrushchev's lead, the WFTU welcomed neutralism as an opportunity to forge friendly relations in the Third World. Now a pariah in the West—especially after establishing one-party rule and attempting to break all connections with Western capital—Nkrumah increasingly looked to the Soviets and especially the People's Republic of China as examples to follow for both economic development and cultural autonomy. Under Nkrumah's influence, the pan-African AATUF modified its definition of foreign domination to specifically mean exploitation by foreign capitalists, thereby opening it up to partnering with foreign communists and accepting funds from the WFTU.

The All-African Trade Union Federation continuously attacked the ICFTU and AFL-CIO for their presence in Africa, particularly criticizing the African Labor College in Uganda. The Ugandan government forced the AFL-CIO's George McCray out of the college in 1965 after effectively banning him from the country by not renewing his visa. Three years later, after Ugandan authorities made it clear that the ICFTU was no longer welcome, the International handed control of the school over to the government.[26]

The African American Labor Center

Amid this rise of left-wing Pan-Africanism and anti-Western sentiment, the AFL-CIO and US Agency for International Development agreed to create the African American Labor Center (AALC) as a new mechanism to influence African labor movements, similar to how AIFLD was influencing Latin American labor.

Headquartered next door to the United Nations in New York City, AALC was formally established between December 1964 and January 1965. Irving Brown was named executive director. Though he was officially working as a representative of the International Confederation of Free Trade Unions at this time, Brown's first loyalty was still to Meany and Lovestone. He accepted the job at the new African institute without even consulting his ICFTU supervisors.[27]

Perhaps influenced by Springer, Brown had a more nuanced take on Africa than he did on much of the rest of the world, as noted by historian John Stoner. "I think the whole subject of neutralism, especially for Africa, has to be treated in much more serious fashion than merely labeling people in terms of two categories," Brown had told Lovestone in 1960. "I certainly would have strong reservations if certain statements gave an impression of the AFL-CIO sitting in judgement on what Africans are doing or should do."[28]

Upon opening in early 1965, the AFL-CIO's new African institute established a presence in Kenya, Nigeria, Tanzania (the new name for a united Tanganyika and Zanzibar), Ethiopia, Zambia, Sierra Leone, Liberia, South Africa, the Gambia, and Uganda. By the end of 1967, it was operational in over twenty countries.[29] Around this same time, in 1966, Springer retired from the AFL-CIO after battling sporadic health problems and getting remarried.

In running the new African American Labor Center, Brown shared Springer's assessment that unions in newly independent African states needed practical assistance more than lectures on pluralism. This meant that he, Meany, and Lovestone would abandon their stated belief in "free" trade unionism, to the extent that the term indicated union freedom from state control. It was the ICFTU's insistence that African governments keep their hands off organized labor that had helped fuel the rise of Nkrumah's anti-Western labor federation, and Brown did not want to make the same mistake. His AALC was therefore willing to partner with tightly controlled labor movements in one-party states that failed to live up to the "free" trade union ideal. AFL-CIO officials tried to excuse this without appearing hypocritical, arguing that African nations had only just thrown off the shackles of colonialism and still needed time to "mature."

As Meany pointed out, "in the first years after the American Revolution, there was much to be desired from the functioning of a multiparty system." He added that "we must have some patience and hope through such efforts as those of AALC that Africans will eventually develop a free and democratic society in which trade unions can grow."[30]

From the start, the African American Labor Center prioritized the kind of development work being done by AIFLD's Social Projects Department, correctly surmising that African leaders would be amenable to activities aimed at promoting nation-building. Borrowing from the language of modernization theory, the AFL-CIO therefore declared that the African American Labor Center's purpose was to assist the African trade union movement "fulfill its primary reason for existence," namely "to ensure a smooth transition from the subsistence economy to the market economy, to the industrial economy of tomorrow" and "to be the intermediary between the tribal hierarchy and the political democracy of tomorrow."[31]

Unlike AIFLD, the new AALC did not include any corporate executives on its board, though part of its stated mission was to "encourage labor-management cooperation to expand American capital investment in the African nations" in the name of spurring economic growth.[32] Receiving over $1 million in USAID funding between 1966 and 1970 alone, the African institute worked with noncommunist unions across the continent to establish credit unions, cooperatives, clinics, and educational programs, and also assisted several unions in obtaining office equipment for their headquarters.[33]

The African American Labor Center in addition financed the Kenya tailoring school and Nigerian motor drivers' school that Springer had helped get off the ground, reasoning that vocational training programs were vital for the transition from a "traditional" to a "modern" economy. In its first six years of existence, AALC coordinated more than 100 small-scale development projects in thirty-three countries and helped establish a Trade Union Institute for Social and Economic Development at the University of Ibadan in Nigeria.[34]

In 1967, AALC convened a meeting of academics, journalists, and development professionals in New York to discuss the problems of South Africa.[35] Since 1948, the country's dominant white minority had imposed apartheid—an authoritarian system of racial segregation and subjugation. The AFL-CIO publicly opposed apartheid, but the Federation struggled to find a foothold in South Africa because the country's only legally recognized unions were exclusively white.

Under apartheid, Black workers did not have the legal right to unionize or strike, and were restricted from better-paying jobs, but they organized nevertheless. The country's primary Black-led labor federation at this time—the South African Congress of Trade Unions—was allied with the African National Congress, the main political center of anti-apartheid resistance. Because the latter worked in cooperation with the Communist Party and, after 1961, was willing to fight the apartheid regime through armed struggle and sabotage, the AFL-CIO kept its distance. Instead, between 1959 and 1965, the Federation and the ICFTU supported a short-lived trade union center meant to rival the South African Congress of Trade Unions, which, despite being inclusive to Black workers, was funded by the white labor movement and failed to confront apartheid.[36]

Like AIFLD, the African American Labor Center's self-styled humanitarianism was politically calculated. Among other things, it was meant to challenge the popularity of the Ghana-based All-African Trade Union

Federation. Using "hot dollars and the usual communist scare propaganda," the AATUF warned in early 1965, the AFL-CIO's new African institute would attempt to succeed where the "decadent imperialists" of the "neo-colonialist ICFTU" had failed in subverting and destroying African labor unity.[37]

A turning point in this rivalry came in February 1966, when Nkrumah was overthrown in a military coup while he was on a state visit to China. After the Ghanaian economy was hit hard by a drop in world cocoa prices, causing Nkrumah's popularity to fall, the CIA station in Accra conspired with dissidents in the armed forces and police to execute the coup d'état. Originally, the CIA station chief had hoped to use the confusion of the coup as cover to attack the Chinese Embassy, kill everyone inside, and steal its records—but the Agency higher-ups back in Langley rejected that idea.[38]

With Nkrumah replaced by a pro-Washington "National Liberation Council," which set about privatizing state-run industries, the AFL-CIO saw an opportunity to make inroads in the Ghanaian labor movement by using development aid as a Trojan Horse. In discussing a proposed African American Labor Center low-cost housing project, for example, Lovestone did not attempt to gauge the actual housing needs of Ghanaian workers, but rather explained that it was "most imperative that we *do something* in Ghana to prevent a recurrence of bad sentiment."[39] Along with other "impact projects," AALC set up a new mobile medical clinic near Accra in 1967, stocked with $7,000 in medicines.[40]

Also in Accra that year, AALC helped establish a labor college in partnership with the Ghana Trades Union Congress—which was now under new, pro-Western leadership—by providing instructors, furnishings, and other materials. The college offered courses on industrial relations, labor law, and economic development for up to fifty students at a time.[41] As if to gloat, Ghana's coup leaders and their US allies housed the college in the same building as the former headquarters of the anti-Western All-African Trade Union Federation, which had relocated to Tanzania following Nkrumah's ouster.[42]

From then on, with its major patron out of power, the AATUF became more of a paper organization. The ICFTU's regional organization for Africa was not particularly active either. In 1973, political and labor leaders across the continent agreed to dissolve both the AATUF and the ICFTU's African arm and in their place form the Organization of

African Trade Union Unity. While championing Pan-African ideals and not allowing dual affiliation with either the anticommunist ICFTU or communist WFTU, the new entity was more friendly toward the West than the AATUF had been.

By the early 1970s, the AFL-CIO managed to establish a robust presence among labor movements on the continent by successfully tapping into Africans' desire for development and education through the USAID-funded African American Labor Center. The only thing marring this apparent triumph for Western trade unionists was the sudden loss of their greatest African ally. In 1969, Tom Mboya was shot and killed on a Nairobi street as he left a pharmacy. He was only thirty-eight. It was speculated—but never proven—that the assassination was orchestrated by Mboya's Kenyan political rivals, who had always viewed him as an upstart threat due to his popularity overseas.

Whatever the motivation, for Maida Springer, Mboya's untimely death in many ways symbolized the end of the youthful idealism associated with Africa's anti-colonial movement.[43]

10
Vietnam

Throughout the first two decades of the Cold War, repeated US intrusions into other countries' affairs were generally accepted by the majority of the American people—including most union members—because they believed these interventions were being done to protect democracy. Intense anticommunism served to silence most would-be dissenters.

The Vietnam War, waged by the United States from the mid-1960s to early 1970s, drastically changed all that. Because of the war's simultaneous brutality and futility, as well as the lies told by Washington to justify its continuation, large numbers of Americans began openly questioning their government's foreign policy and argued that it was more imperialistic than altruistic. This was especially true of younger people.

Vietnam was thus a turning point in the Cold War, the point at which the anticommunist consensus that had taken root in the late 1940s shattered. This had reverberations across US society, particularly within the labor movement. For the first time, union leaders and members began paying serious attention to the AFL-CIO's foreign policy, and many did not like what they saw.

Tran Quoc Buu

As historian Edmund Wehrle has thoroughly documented, the AFL-CIO's principal ally in Vietnam from the 1950s to 1970s was Tran

Quoc Buu, an anticommunist nationalist and labor leader. Partnering with France's Catholic trade union center, Buu founded the CVTC (Vietnamese Confederation of Christian Workers), which by 1953 claimed upwards of 39,000 members across the country. Despite its association with Catholicism, the CVTC was open to workers of all religions. Buu himself was a Buddhist.

The AFL paid close attention in the early 1950s as France fought a war to maintain colonial rule over Indochina, battling an armed independence struggle led by the communist Viet Minh. AFL international agent Irving Brown used CIA money to successfully counter attempts by communist French dockworkers to disrupt arms shipments bound for Indochina. At the same time, Brown was also urging the International Confederation of Free Trade Unions (ICFTU) to support the growth of anticommunist unions in Vietnam.

Like their friends in the US foreign policy establishment, AFL officials wished to see not only the defeat of the Viet Minh, but also an end to French rule in Indochina, with a pro-Western government taking over. "Resistance to communist aggression in Indo-China should be made more effective by stripping it of every appearance of a nineteenth century colonial campaign," read a 1952 AFL statement criticizing the French. The Federation was impressed with Buu's anticommunist CVTC, regarding it as the perfect "free" trade union alternative to both communism and colonialism.[1]

After the Viet Minh decisively defeated the French at Dien Bien Phu in 1954, a conference was held in Geneva to work out a peace plan for Indochina. Jay Lovestone sent Harry Goldberg to represent the AFL at the Geneva gathering. Goldberg—who previously served as the Free Trade Union Committee's operative in Indonesia—urged independence alongside increased military support to Vietnamese anticommunists. Issued that July, the Geneva Accords split Vietnam along the seventeenth parallel, with the communist Viet Minh getting control of the north, setting up their capital in Hanoi, and the south going to the pro-Western government of Ngo Dinh Diem, with its capital in Saigon. The division was meant to be temporary, with reunification elections planned for 1956 to determine who would lead a united Vietnam.

Outraged at this so-called appeasement, which he felt surrendered too much to the Viet Minh, AFL president George Meany said the accords "would make Munich pale into insignificance."[2] He and the Federation's other hawkish internationalists would not be satisfied until the Vietnamese communists were completely destroyed. Washington and the Diem regime agreed, both conspiring to make sure the reunification elections never happened.

Buu also opposed the partition. Immediately after the accords, leaders and members of his anticommunist CVTC, which had over 200 affiliated unions in the north, fled to South Vietnam and took refuge at the CVTC headquarters in Saigon. Determined to protect his labor federation in this new political environment, Buu formed an alliance with the corrupt and repressive Diem government. He also befriended CIA officer Edward Lansdale, the Agency's expert in Asian counterinsurgency campaigns. With Diem's patronage, along with protection from the CIA and US Embassy, Buu's CVTC grew to approximately 350,000 members in the mid-1950s.

In 1961, Irving Brown visited the country on behalf of the AFL-CIO, reporting back that he was "so impressed with Buu" that "he should be considered in terms of any possible reshuffling of the political control of the government." Brown even went so far as to suggest that the CVTC, with its tight organization and anticommunist politics, should receive the weapons and training necessary to become a paramilitary force. In such a role, he contended, the labor federation and its members could repress the growing communist insurgency in South Vietnam led by the National Liberation Front (commonly known in the West as the Viet Cong).[3]

In November 1963, Diem was overthrown and assassinated in a CIA-backed military coup. The coup had been greenlit by the Kennedy administration, believing the corrupt and unpopular South Vietnamese president had become too much of a liability in the ongoing standoff with the communists. Only three weeks later, Kennedy himself was assassinated. His successor, President Lyndon Johnson, falsely claimed the following August that North Vietnamese forces attacked a US Navy ship in the Gulf of Tonkin, resulting in Congress giving him authorization to use military force in Vietnam.

Meanwhile, with US support Buu and his CVTC grew more powerful. Buu visited the United States in early 1964 and, in a meeting arranged by the AFL-CIO, was welcomed into the Oval Office by Johnson himself. Around the same time, to broaden its international appeal, Buu had the

CVTC drop the "Christian" from its name, so that it became simply the Vietnamese Confederation of Labor, or CVT.[4]

In March 1965, the US war in Vietnam began in earnest. To wipe out the National Liberation Front's insurgency, which was spreading through the countryside and supported by Hanoi, Johnson deployed combat troops to South Vietnam while also bombing targets in the North. Around this time, Air Marshall Nguyen Cao Ky became the south's new head of government. Ky was initially hostile to Buu's CVT, but he changed his mind after being personally pressured by Lovestone associate Harry Goldberg, who visited the country on the AFL-CIO's behalf.

Ky came around to see Buu as an important ally in the war against the communists, particularly as the CVT-affiliated tenant farmers' union directly challenged the Viet Cong in the battle for the "hearts and minds" of rural peasants. When the communist guerillas briefly took over a Michelin-owned rubber plantation, they struggled to pay or feed the workers—prompting the CVT to step in and negotiate a new favorable labor contact with Michelin.[5]

Back in Washington, Meany was pleased with Johnson's aggressive intervention in Vietnam and advocated increased US financial support to the CVT. But not everyone in the US labor movement was as enthusiastic about the new military conflict. The Vietnam War and the mass movement that arose to oppose it created a political and cultural environment in which, for the first time since the Cold War began, American unionists were willing and able to voice dissent against the Federation's foreign policy.

Unions against the War

The first US union to come out against the war was Local 1199 of the Retail, Wholesale, and Department Store Union.[6] Though traditionally representing Jewish pharmacy workers in New York City, by the 1960s Local 1199 was busily unionizing the predominantly Black and Puerto Rican workforce in the city's private hospitals. As early as July 1964, Local 1199's longtime president, Leon Davis, warned against US military escalation in Vietnam. In February of the following year, just weeks before the first US combat troops were deployed, Local 1199 issued a public letter to New York senators Robert F. Kennedy and Jacob Javits.

Calling the conflict "a war no one can win," the union made clear it was "unalterably opposed to extension of the war" and urged the senators to back "an all-out effort to negotiate a peaceful settlement."[7]

This antiwar position was not totally surprising, given that many of Local 1199's leaders were leftists, including Davis, who was a former member of the Communist Party USA. Despite the political leanings of its officers, the local had managed to survive the anticommunist purges of the early Cold War years in part because, at the time, it was still "too small and insignificant to attract sustained public attention," according to historians Leon Fink and Brian Greenberg.[8]

As 1965 continued, more opposition to the war was voiced within the ranks of organized labor. In May, the Negro American Labor Council, an organization of Black unionists led by A. Philip Randolph, passed a resolution critical of President Johnson's military adventures in both Vietnam and the Dominican Republic. Meanwhile, some of the independent, leftist-led unions that had been expelled from the CIO in 1949 and 1950—including the United Electrical Workers (UE), International Longshore and Warehouse Union (ILWU), and International Union of Mine, Mill, and Smelter Workers—also issued formal criticisms of the war.

Particularly significant was the open hostility to the war expressed by Emil Mazey, secretary-treasurer of the United Auto Workers, then the AFL-CIO's largest affiliate. Mazey spoke at some of the earliest antiwar rallies in Detroit and at teach-ins at the University of Michigan.[9] In one speech, he bluntly argued there was neither freedom nor democracy in South Vietnam and that the United States was waging the war "to bolster and maintain an oppressive military dictatorship." Walter Reuther, who supported Johnson's aggressive foreign policy, rushed to dissociate himself and the UAW from what he described as Mazey's personal opinions.[10]

At Mazey's urging, the UAW leadership issued a tepid statement in 1965 calling on the Johnson administration to seek a peaceful resolution to the conflict. But in October of that year, members of the AFL-CIO Executive Council, including Reuther, reaffirmed steadfast support for Johnson's military escalation while simultaneously denouncing the budding antiwar movement.

Things came to a head that December at the Federation's national convention in San Francisco. After delegates were addressed by high-ranking members of the Johnson administration—including Secretary of State Dean Rusk, Vice President Hubert Humphrey, and Johnson himself (by telephone)—Meany presented a resolution pledging the AFL-CIO's "unstinting support" of "all measures the Administration might deem necessary" to drive communism out of South Vietnam, noting that the war would only end when the communists "were willing to sit down at the conference table." The last part about sitting at the table had reportedly been added at Reuther's request in an attempt to satisfy those in the UAW calling for peace.[11]

As the delegates prepared to approve the resolution without any discussion or debate, a group of students from the University of California, Berkeley, and San Francisco State College, sitting in the balcony as observers, arose to chant "Get out of Vietnam!" and "Debate! Debate!" Banging his gavel, Meany had the protesters removed, shouting, "Will the sergeant of arms clear these kookies out of the gallery?" The prowar resolution was then adopted unanimously.

Later in the convention proceedings, the UAW's Mazey addressed the delegates to rebuke what he called "the vulgar display of intolerance" shown toward the college students. He said the situation in Vietnam was complicated and called for nuanced discussions, noting that many Vietnamese viewed the United States as the successor to French colonialists, and again calling the South Vietnamese government a "corrupt military dictatorship." Mazey insisted that the AFL-CIO should be more tolerant toward antiwar protesters and not try to shut down democratic debate over Vietnam. His speech on the convention floor received only minimal applause.[12]

Victor Reuther

Sympathizing with the students who were derided by Meany as "kookies," Victor Reuther, the UAW's international affairs director, agreed with Mazey that there needed to be a deeper discussion within the US labor movement over foreign policy. After being disgusted by AIFLD's support for the 1964 Brazilian coup, between 1965 and 1966, the younger Reuther brother had spearheaded the founding of the UAW's own nonprofit to assist Third World workers, naming it STEP (for Social, Technical, and Education Programs).

Unlike AIFLD, STEP aimed to work in close partnership with the ICFTU, as well as with the International Metalworkers' Federation—the international trade secretariat with which the UAW was affiliated. Through STEP, UAW members repaired discarded materials such as hospital equipment, furniture, or vehicles and then donated them to worker organizations in Latin America, Africa, and Asia. The nonprofit had a modest annual budget of around $60,000, funded through grants, private donations, and interest from the UAW's strike fund. STEP was not financed by USAID or other government agencies, though it occasionally partnered with Peace Corps volunteers in the Third World.[13] In mid-1966, AIFLD leaders privately complained about STEP, grumbling among themselves that "five years later Victor is discovering what AIFLD is all about and seems to be trying to duplicate our efforts."[14]

Displeased overall with the Federation's foreign policy, especially the Executive Council's steady support for the increasingly unpopular Vietnam War, Victor went against the wishes of his older brother by making his concerns public. During the UAW's own national convention in Long Beach, California, in May 1966, he suggested to a *Los Angeles Times* reporter that the AFL-CIO was "involved" with the CIA abroad. Leftist and liberal publications had previously made similar accusations, but this was the first time a high-profile union official had gone on record alleging linkages between the AFL-CIO and the Agency. The "tragedy" of the AFL-CIO's foreign activities, Victor told the *Los Angeles Times*, was that they were "in the vest pocket" of CIA-connected Jay Lovestone.[15]

Victor Reuther hoped to spark a debate within organized labor's ranks over Meany and Lovestone's tight control of the Federation's international affairs, but his statement about the AFL-CIO being "involved" with the CIA naturally got the most attention. Meany vehemently denied the claim. In a public statement approved that summer by all but two its members—one of them Walter Reuther—the AFL-CIO Executive Council charged Victor with "conduct unbecoming a trade unionist," because, in making "false and unfounded accusations," he had "maliciously attempted to sabotage the successful efforts of the American labor movement in its overseas program of helping to strengthen the free and democratic trade union movement."[16]

At the same time as Victor Reuther was making waves, Leon Davis and over 170 other local union officers and staffers in New York and

New Jersey came together to form a new organization of antiwar labor activists. Linking up with the National Committee for a Sane Nuclear Policy (SANE)—a peace group founded in 1957 to protest the nuclear arms race between the superpowers—they created the Trade Union Division of SANE to demand debate within organized labor over the Vietnam War. More chapters of the Trade Union Division of SANE were soon founded by local union leaders in Chicago, San Francisco, and other cities. Meanwhile, at the national conventions of multiple unions—including the UAW, United Packinghouse Workers, Amalgamated Clothing Workers, and Davis's Retail, Wholesale, and Department Store Union—delegates made clear their dissatisfaction with Johnson's military escalation.

"A quiet uprising is developing inside the ranks of organized labor over the AFL-CIO high command's unswerving, uncritical allegiance to the Administration's course in Vietnam," progressive *New York Post* editor James A. Wechsler wrote in May 1966. "In the small beginning of an insurgency now at hand there may be the glimpse of an overdue debate. The sons of union men are perishing in Viet Nam, along with other Americans."[17]

Walter Reuther

As this "quiet uprising" took root, tensions over foreign policy mounted between Meany and Walter Reuther. A major disagreement came in June 1966 over the annual International Labor Organization conference in Geneva. At the start of the conference, the ILO's governing body elected Leon Chajn—Poland's former deputy minister of labor—to the largely ceremonial post of chair of the ten-day meeting. To protest the election of a communist to the chairmanship, US worker delegate Rudolph Faupl stormed out of the conference, refusing to participate. In contrast, the US business delegate, Edwin P. Neilan of the Bank of Delaware, chose to stay, as did the US government representatives. Faupl, an official from the AFL-CIO-affiliated International Association of Machinists, answered to Meany.

Walter Reuther worried that Faupl's histrionic boycott of the ILO meeting would damage US labor's international credibility, and believed the move had been planned without his knowledge. Meany claimed that

Faupl had spontaneously walked out on his own initiative. In any case, Meany and his loyalists on the AFL-CIO Executive Council backed the boycott decision over Reuther's protestations, even as the Johnson administration reportedly urged them to reconsider. After this incident, Reuther was convinced that the UAW would need to chart a more independent course.[18]

In the months following the ILO conference, Reuther became increasingly vocal over his uneasiness with the AFL-CIO Executive Council's aggressive anticommunism overseas, including its hawkish stance on Vietnam. He was especially outraged after the council, without his approval, issued a statement in August doubling down on its support for the war and declaring that antiwar protesters were effectively "aiding the Communist enemy of our country."[19] After denouncing the statement as "intemperate, hysterical, and jingoistic," he requested that the Executive Council hold a special meeting to review its foreign policy, to be held in November 1966.

But in the months leading up to this meeting, Reuther reflected on his many years of disagreement with Meany, who had no plans to retire any time soon and allow Reuther to ascend to the AFL-CIO presidency, and concluded that a break between the UAW and the Federation was probably inevitable. Reuther ultimately opted not to attend the November foreign policy meeting that he himself had called, blaming it on a last-minute scheduling conflict. The meeting went forward anyway, but absent Reuther there was no serious debate.[20]

The next month, the UAW Executive Board sent a letter to the auto union's general membership laying out their differences with the AFL-CIO leadership on international affairs. "We believe that anticommunism in and of itself is not enough," the letter read. "We must take positive steps to abolish poverty and hunger and to eliminate social and economic injustice, which are the ingredients that communism exploits and attempts to forge into political power." The letter made it clear that the disagreements were as much about domestic issues as foreign ones, citing the AFL-CIO's failure to put its resources toward fighting for an expanded welfare state and organizing the unorganized, especially farm workers and public sector workers. Above all, the UAW Executive Board exhorted the AFL-CIO to allow more democratic debate and decision-making over the important issues of the day, especially in foreign affairs.[21]

In February 1967, the UAW Executive Board took the bold step of issuing a statement declaring that the promise of the 1955 merger between the AFL and CIO had gone unfulfilled, and that the Federation under Meany had become a "comfortable, complacent custodian of the status quo." Accordingly, UAW officials formally resigned from their positions on the AFL-CIO Executive Council, general board, and standing committees, with Reuther resigning from his symbolic position on the boards of AIFLD and the African American Labor Center.[22] Meany showed no indication he was interested in changing the AFL-CIO's direction, but rather denounced the UAW president for trying to divide the labor movement. As both sides dug in their heels, the prospects of a reconciliation became dimmer.

Though Walter Reuther was locking horns with Meany over labor's foreign policy, in the spring of 1967, he still supported the Vietnam War. Reuther clung to the same strategic wager he had made during World War II of relying on access to Washington's power centers to allow organized labor to thrive. He was careful not to anger allies in the Democratic Party or damage his close relationship with Lyndon Johnson, which meant supporting the president's foreign policy—or, at the very least, not openly challenging it. Like many other prominent liberals, he hoped to sidestep the war question altogether to avoid causing a rift within the decades-old New Deal coalition and allowing anti-union Republicans a political opening.

But at a Passover seder hosted by his friend and fellow UAW officer Irving Bluestone, Reuther was confronted on this position. Attending the dinner were Bluestone's son, Barry, and Leslie Woodcock, the daughter of UAW official Leonard Woodcock. Both college students, Leslie and Barry were dedicated antiwar activists at the University of Michigan, and hoped to use the private gathering to convince Reuther to take a stand against the war. The young couple did a short presentation for the seder guests, reading excerpts from Martin Luther King Jr.'s famous speech condemning the war, delivered at New York's Riverside Church only weeks earlier, as well as some antiwar poetry.

Knowing that this was all directed at him, Reuther lectured the two student activists about how the UAW could not afford to alienate President Johnson, adding that it was "no time to split the union on this kind of ideological issue."

Instead of paying deference to the powerful, fifty-nine-year-old labor leader, Leslie Woodcock surprised everyone by unloading on Reuther. "You really said that, didn't you?" she asked rhetorically. "What are you trying to do, maybe get eighty cents an hour in the pay envelope, five cents here, five cents there? You're telling me that you are unwilling to make a statement that may save fifty thousand lives or one hundred thousand lives or maybe a million lives because you want to get fifty more cents in your God-damn fucking contract . . . That's the most inhumane thing I have ever heard in my life."[23]

Reuther, who prided himself on being a progressive liberal and was once an idealistic young activist himself, was hurt. At home, he faced similar criticisms from his own daughters. Scenes like this were playing out at dinner tables across the country as young people confronted their elders about the violence and immorality of the Vietnam War.

In September 1967, Reuther finally began expressing some tepid public opposition to the war, calling for an end to the US bombing of North Vietnam and arguing that there were no military solutions to the political problems in Asia.[24]

The Labor Leadership Assembly for Peace

As the UAW president was cautiously criticizing the war, the Trade Union Division of SANE convened a National Labor Leadership Assembly for Peace. The gathering of antiwar unionists occurred over Veterans Day weekend 1967 at the University of Chicago. While the event's organizers had anticipated about 250 people showing up, 523 wound up attending, representing fifty unions from thirty-eight states.

Most of the participants were union officials at the local or state level, but some heavy hitters attended, including Victor Reuther, Emil Mazey, and veteran unionist Frank Rosenblum of the Amalgamated Clothing Workers. Guest speakers included Martin Luther King Jr., famed liberal economist John Kenneth Galbraith, dovish Senator Eugene McCarthy, and a now eighty-two-year-old Norman Thomas. Though a frequent ally of the AFL-CIO's international "free" trade union crusade, Thomas was a pacifist first and foremost.

The gathering represented an important break in Cold War orthodoxy within the labor movement, with officers from AFL-CIO-affiliated unions and leftist-led, independent unions like the UE and ILWU meeting together on a national stage for the first time in nearly twenty years. But notably missing were any student antiwar activists, whom figures like Mazey intentionally excluded, believing they were too radical and that the labor movement should avoid associating with them.[25]

In his address to the Labor Leadership Assembly for Peace, Rosenblum lamented the fact that Meany not only backed the Johnson administration's aggressive foreign policy, but was "if anything to the right of the Administration."

"On the crucial questions of peace," Rosenblum insisted, "labor must be in the vanguard."

Victor Reuther gave perhaps the fieriest address at the event, lambasting the AFL-CIO International Affairs Department for propping up "fascist corporate unions" abroad and excoriating AIFLD for its role in Brazil's military takeover. Victor argued that the only way to change the Federation's overseas activities for the better would be opening them up to rank-and-file scrutiny and debate. "The determination of foreign policy within the labor movement must not be permitted to remain the vest pocket operation of any individual or small leadership group," he said. "As with union collective bargaining objectives and domestic legislative goals, foreign policy decisions should flow upward from the membership following the widest possible discussion in depth by the rank and file."[26]

A few weeks later, Meany struck back during the AFL-CIO's annual convention, held near Miami in Bal Harbour, Florida. At Meany's invitation, President Johnson addressed the convention in person. Immediately after his speech, a pro-war resolution was put to the delegates. At the direction of his union's membership, American Federation of Teachers president Charles Cogen presented a counter-resolution calling on the AFL-CIO to take no position on the war. Cogen's resolution was seconded by Leon Davis of Local 1199 and Americo Toffoli, secretary-treasurer of the Colorado Labor Council. In his comments to the delegates, Toffoli cited the recent Labor Leadership Assembly for Peace to illustrate that the union movement was not unanimous on whether to support the war.

Meany responded by denying there was any division within organized labor over the war. He explained that the 500 or so unionists who had attended the recent antiwar gathering in Chicago were hardly

representative of the hundreds of thousands of local union officials affiliated with the AFL-CIO. Meany then baselessly alleged that the peace
assembly was "planned in Hanoi by a special committee that went there"
and that "every line" of the peace assembly's official statement had been
published in a Communist Party newspaper "two weeks before the
meeting was held in Chicago."

The convention delegates then voted overwhelmingly in favor of the
pro-war resolution. Afterward, an irate Mazey called Meany's red-
baiting accusations against the Assembly for Peace "libelous and slan-
derous, the kind you'd expect from a senile old man."[27] A Gallup poll a
few weeks after the AFL-CIO convention found that, contrary to Meany's
characterizations, rank-and-file union members were evenly divided on
whether Washington should continue escalating the war.[28]

By early 1968, the Reuther brothers and Mazey had had enough. They
were ready for a full break with the Federation. In May, the UAW
Executive Board began withholding the union's per capita dues payments
to the AFL-CIO, ostensibly to pressure Meany into adopting reforms.
Predictably, Meany's response was to "suspend" the union, a mainly
symbolic move. On July 1, 1968, the Executive Board of the 1.3-million
member UAW voted to formally disaffiliate the union from the
Federation, representing the ultimate failure of Meany and Reuther to
work together almost thirteen years after the merger.[29]

Soon after, the UAW joined with the International Brotherhood of
Teamsters—which had been expelled from the AFL-CIO a decade
earlier over corruption charges—to form the Alliance for Labor Action,
a short-lived and relatively ineffective attempt to carry out Reuther's
progressive agenda.

Tet

In late January 1968, coinciding with the Tet holiday observing the
beginning of the new year, the North Vietnamese and National
Liberation Front launched a coordinated series of surprise attacks
targeting South Vietnamese and US forces, including an attack on the
US Embassy in Saigon. In addition to causing thousands of fresh casual-
ties, the Tet Offensive completely undermined the Johnson administration's claims that the war was nearly won. Johnson was in the early stages

of his re-election campaign, but in March, he came within a hair's breadth of losing the New Hampshire primary to antiwar candidate Eugene McCarthy—an embarrassment for a sitting president.

Realizing how unpopular he had become because of the war, Johnson soon after announced that he would not seek a second term after all and would begin peace negotiations with Hanoi. This move stunned Meany and Lovestone, who remained convinced that the United States should continue aggressively waging war on the Vietnamese communists until they were totally defeated, despite every indication that such a victory would be impossible to achieve. Meany successfully urged Hubert Humphrey, Johnson's prowar vice president, to enter the presidential race. For their part, UAW leaders backed antiwar candidate Robert F. Kennedy until his assassination that June.[30]

In the wake of the Tet Offensive, Meany and the AFL-CIO were eager to increase support for Buu and the CVT. The CVT and its officers were not only targeted by the communists during the offensive, but also by the South Vietnamese government under the recently elected president, Nguyen Thieu. Despite Buu's anticommunism, the notorious head of Thieu's national police—Nguyen Ngoc Loan—was wary of the CVT's power and considered its activists to be potential subversives. Loan, who is best remembered in the United States for being filmed summarily executing a suspected Viet Cong cadre by casually shooting him in the head, arrested two CVT leaders during the Tet attacks. The AFL-CIO dispatched Irving Brown to Saigon in March, where he successfully pressured Thieu and Loan to release the CVT officials and forge a better relationship with Buu.

Brown was also there to help inaugurate the AFL-CIO's newest foreign nonprofit, the Asian American Free Labor Institute (AAFLI), which opened an office inside the CVT's Saigon headquarters.

Like AIFLD and the African American Labor Center, the new Asian institute was funded by USAID. The AFL-CIO and US foreign policy establishment originally envisioned AAFLI as supporting labor-friendly modernization projects in a postwar, communist-free Vietnam. Instead, the Asian institute's first initiative upon getting up and running was providing emergency relief packages to CVT members displaced by the Tet Offensive.[31] AAFLI also set up training programs for South Vietnamese workers and donated tractors to farmers affiliated with the CVT.

For Buu, who was accustomed to dealing directly with the USAID mission in Saigon, AAFLI seemed only to serve as an extra layer of bureaucracy.[32] Under the acting directorship of Gerard O'Keefe—the foreign affairs chief for the Retail Clerks International Union, who had previously worked to undermine Cheddi Jagan's government in British Guiana—AAFLI set up training seminars on union leadership and collective bargaining in other Asian nations, including India, South Korea, the Philippines, Singapore, and Indonesia.[33] USAID gave the new institute $3.74 million between 1968 and 1972, compared to the $330,000 given by the AFL-CIO during the same period. [34]

Near the end of a raucous political year in the United States that witnessed Johnson's decision not to seek re-election, followed by the assassinations of Martin Luther King Jr. and Robert Kennedy, and a chaotic Democratic National Convention in Chicago, Republican Richard Nixon was elected president in November 1968 on a promise to end the Vietnam War and restore "law and order" to the United States.

For Meany and the AFL-CIO, who had endorsed Humphrey, Nixon's victory signaled a new and uncertain relationship with the White House, particularly when it came to foreign policy. In a positive sign for the "free" trade unionists, shortly after taking office, Nixon assured AIFLD chair J. Peter Grace that he was "greatly interested in the work of the American Institute for Free Labor Development" and admired its success in "strengthening democratic labor unions" abroad.[35]

At the same time, Buu was gaining more political influence in South Vietnam. To realize Brown's vision of the CVT serving as a paramilitary force, Buu convinced the Thieu government to train his union members in defensive military techniques in order to fend off any possible future attacks in the style of the Tet Offensive. Further, Buu and the US Embassy convinced Thieu to sign a land reform law in early 1970, transferring ownership of rented farmlands to tenants to try sapping support for the National Liberation Front in the countryside. The CVT formed new producer cooperatives as part of this land reform initiative.[36]

The Cambodia Invasion

In a televised address to the nation on April 30, 1970, President Nixon announced that he was sending US troops into Cambodia, South

Vietnam's neighbor to the west. Unbeknown to Congress and the US public, the Nixon administration had already been bombing that neutral country for over a year to try to take out North Vietnamese supply lines and bases believed to be there. The architect of this illegal and secretive policy, National Security Advisor Henry Kissinger, contended that the bombing would put psychological pressure on the North Vietnamese government, leading to concessions at the negotiating table. It did not.

The covert bombing campaign did, however, manage to destabilize Cambodia by sparking a March 1970 military coup against the country's leader, Prince Sihanouk. The new military government dispensed with neutrality and joined the United States in its war on communism. Now that Cambodia was officially an active participant in the war as a direct result of their secret bombing campaign, Nixon and Kissinger decided to invade the country to prevent any possible communist takeover from happening there.[37]

Despite promises to wind down and end the Vietnam War, Nixon was only expanding it. Millions of Vietnamese and 40,000 Americans had already been killed in the war, 400,000 US troops were still in Southeast Asia, and 56 percent of the US public now wanted the war to end.

Nixon's April 30 announcement of the invasion of Cambodia immediately reawakened the antiwar movement, which had been relatively quiet since the tumult of 1968. In the first week of May, students went on strike at 400 university campuses to protest the war.[38] "You see these bums, you know, blowing up the campuses," Nixon grumbled. "Listen, the boys that are on the college campuses today are the luckiest people in the world, going to the greatest universities, and here they are burning up the books, storming around about this issue."[39]

On Monday, May 4, National Guard troops opened fire on a crowd of protesters at Kent State University in northern Ohio, killing four students and wounding nine others. Eleven days later, police fired on protesters at Jackson State College, a historically Black institution in Mississippi, killing two students. The tragedies shocked the nation, and the wave of student strikes at universities and high schools only grew. For the US labor movement, it would be a critical moment to choose a side in the unfolding domestic unrest.

Meany issued a public statement celebrating the invasion of Cambodia. "As other Presidents before him have done, [Nixon] acted with courage and conviction," the AFL-CIO chief wrote. "In this crucial hour, he should have the full support of the American people. He certainly has ours."[40]

In the days following the deadly incident at Kent State, union locals and labor councils from Philadelphia to Cleveland to the Bay Area formally called for an end to the war. Holding its national convention that same week, the American Federation of State, County, and Municipal Employees (AFSCME), led by its progressive president Jerry Wurf, demanded the "total and immediate withdrawal" of all US troops from Southeast Asia.[41]

With a Republican now in the White House, it was easier for liberal labor leaders to publicly take an antiwar stance. Most significant was an open letter to Nixon from Walter Reuther. Sent on May 7, the letter was unanimously approved by the UAW Executive Board. "Your decision to invade the territory of Cambodia can only increase the enormity of the tragedy in which our nation is already deeply and unfortunately involved in that region," Reuther wrote to Nixon. He continued:

> Widening the war at this point in time once again merely reinforces the bankruptcy of our policy of force and violence in Vietnam . . . However this dangerous adventure turns out militarily, America has already suffered a moral defeat beyond measure among the people of the world . . .
>
> We must mobilize for peace rather than for wider theaters of war in order to turn our resources and the hearts, hands and minds of our people to the fulfillment of America's unfinished agenda at home.[42]

This would be Walter Reuther's final public statement. Two days later, he, his wife May, and four others were killed when their chartered Learjet crashed outside Pellston, Michigan.[43] One of the most consequential and controversial labor leaders of the twentieth century, Reuther died unequivocally opposed to the Vietnam War, though he had arrived at that position several years late.

The Hard Hat Riot

Reuther was hardly the only trade unionist expressing antiwar views in early 1970. In February, 110 labor officials from twenty-two unions signed a statement published in the *Washington Post* calling for an immediate end to the war, arguing that the war was driving inflation and diverting resources from housing, education, and healthcare.

This effort was spearheaded by Tony Mazzocchi, a progressive officer in the Oil, Chemical, and Atomic Workers union who cochaired a committee of antiwar unionists in Washington, DC, called Labor for Peace. The committee later expanded the statement into a booklet entitled *A Rich Man's War, A Poor Man's Fight: A Handbook for Trade Unionists on the Vietnam War.*[44]

Despite such antiwar activity, it was the labor movement's pro-Nixon elements in 1970 who would receive the most attention and be most remembered.

On Friday, May 8, New York City's liberal Republican mayor, John Lindsay, declared a citywide "day of reflection" in honor of the Kent State tragedy earlier that week. Around lunchtime that day, about a thousand young antiwar activists—mainly students from area colleges and high schools—gathered for a peaceful rally in Lower Manhattan at Wall Street's Federal Hall National Memorial, the spot where George Washington had been inaugurated president in 1789.

Midway through the relatively quiet demonstration, 200 construction workers marched into the crowd from all directions, coming from their nearby job sites, including the construction site of the World Trade Center towers. Using their tools as weapons, the workers began beating the young antiwar demonstrators without provocation while chanting "USA, all the way!" and "Love it or leave it!" Police officers on the scene turned aside and allowed the attack to unfold. The students ran away, but were chased by the construction workers through the streets of Lower Manhattan.

Eventually, many of the antiwar activists found refuge in Trinity Church. The construction workers then marched up Broadway to City Hall, where Mayor Lindsay had ordered the US flag be lowered to half-staff in memory of the students killed at Kent State. One of the "hard hats"—as the belligerent counterprotestors commonly came to be called—made his way inside City Hall, went up to the roof, and raised the flag back to full mast. The crowd of construction workers outside then cheered and sang the National Anthem. A little while later, a contingent of hard hats broke off from the main group and stormed nearby Pace College, where they smashed windows, attacked students, and tore down and burned an antiwar banner. All told, the "Hard Hat Riot" left more than seventy people injured, including several bystanders who had nothing to do with the antiwar protest.

The attack was not spontaneous but carefully planned and coordinated by Peter Brennan, president of the AFL-CIO-affiliated Building and Construction Trades Council of Greater New York, and approved by local construction contractors, who made sure the workers still got paid for the time they spent rioting. One of the most powerful union leaders in the city, Brennan spoke for the traditionally more privileged, skilled, white strata of the US working class.

Like other conservatives, Brennan and many of the building trades workers he represented were repulsed by the progressive social movements of the time. They opposed affirmative action policies meant to open up construction jobs to racial minorities, denounced the antiwar movement, and reflexively rejected efforts to remake the social status quo. They were particularly incensed by antiwar protesters, arguing that they were unpatriotic and disrespectful to the working-class kids fighting in Vietnam. Their premeditated assault on the student protesters on May 8, only days after the Kent State tragedy, was a violently delivered right-wing political statement.[45]

Nixon saw an opportunity. Through his notorious advisor Charles Colson—who would eventually go to prison for obstruction of justice in the Watergate scandal—the president had been attempting to woo the white working class as part of his re-election strategy for 1972. Colson and the president initially struggled to gain the support of blue-collar voters, who had remained loyal to the Democratic Party since the New Deal.

For their part, Meany and Lovestone initially thought that Nixon was too soft on world communism, disapproving of his stated plans to wind down the war before total victory. But after Nixon announced the Cambodia invasion, their opinion of the president changed. Impressed by the administration's expansion of the war, on May 5 Lovestone privately met with Colson to promise the AFL-CIO's full support of Nixon's Southeast Asia policy. Three days later, the Hard Hat Riot occurred. Immediately, Lovestone put Colson in touch with Brennan so the two could widen the blue-collar backlash against the rejuvenated antiwar movement.[46]

With the help of Colson and the administration, Brennan organized a mass march of jingoistic hard hats in New York City on May 20. Holding signs reading "We Love Our Police, Flag and Country," between 100,000 and 150,000 participated in the demonstration. "The word was passed around to all the men on the jobs the day before. It was not voluntary," one building trades union member later reported. "You had to go. You understand these are all jobs where the union controls your employment absolutely."[47] The overall message was less pro-war than it was pro-USA, with even Brennan admitting that the war needed to be brought to an "honorable" end.[48] Similar, smaller rallies were held the same day in San Diego, Pittsburgh, Buffalo, and other cities.

Soon after, in a highly publicized spectacle, Nixon invited Brennan to the White House. In front of a throng of reporters, the union leader placed a flag pin on the president's lapel and ceremoniously gave him a white hard hat with the words "Commander in Chief" emblazoned on the front. The helmet, Brennan said, was "a symbol, along with our great flag, of freedom and patriotism to our beloved country."[49] In return for this photo op and the general support for his foreign policy, Nixon rewarded Brennan by moving to weaken affirmative action and, after his re-election, appointing Brennan to be his new secretary of labor.

Nixon and Colson's "blue-collar strategy"—aided by Lovestone in the spring of 1970—would pay off, though not immediately. In that year's midterm elections, working-class voters stuck with the Democrats. Immediately following the events in May, a survey found that 53 percent of US union members disapproved of the hard hat violence, compared to only 33 percent approving.[50] Over the following two years, Nixon was incessantly attacked by Meany over his economic policies as well as his historic moves to open diplomatic relations with the People's Republic of China. Nevertheless, Meany and the administration remained close allies when it came to the Vietnam War.[51]

When George McGovern—a liberal senator who promised immediate US withdrawal from Southeast Asia—was nominated by the Democrats to run for president in 1972, Meany and the AFL-CIO opted to remain neutral, which served as a tacit endorsement of Nixon. It was at this moment that Nixon's blue-collar strategy finally bore fruit. The president was re-elected in a landslide, losing only Massachusetts and the District of Columbia, and securing the white working-class vote he and Colson had long been chasing.

Perhaps more important than his 1972 re-election, a triumph that would soon be spectacularly undermined by the Watergate scandal, the long-term result of Nixon's alliance with Meany, Lovestone, and Brennan on the Vietnam War would be the public perception that the US labor movement was a reactionary force. The image of hard hats beating young antiwar protesters would be burned into the nation's collective memory, while the impassioned moral appeals of countless unionists to end the war would be largely forgotten.

For many in the antiwar movement and other social movements associated with the New Left, organized labor came to be seen as just another part of the corrupt, soulless establishment that needed disman-tling. In the popular imagination, the term "working class" would become almost synonymous with white conservatives violently and stubbornly standing in the way of peace and progress, even though in reality much of the working class, particularly the less privileged strata of service workers, Black and Latino workers, and women workers had consistently opposed the Vietnam War.[52]

The End of the War

The Nixon administration's escalation of the war failed to bring the United States any closer to victory; it only resulted in more bloodshed. Finally, in January 1973, with Nixon's re-election secured, the peace talks originally begun by President Johnson five years earlier concluded with an agreement by Washington, Hanoi, Saigon, and the National Liberation Front to end direct US military involvement in the war.

Though presented by Nixon as "peace with honor," the agreement heralded the defeat of US forces by the North Vietnamese and Viet Cong. American combat operations ended, and US troops were pulled out of the country by the end of March. A ceasefire between North and South Vietnam was officially in place, but the communists were already poised to take full control over the bifurcated nation.

The South Vietnamese economy had become dependent on the money spent by the tens of thousands of US military personnel in the country. Now, with the withdrawal of US forces, the economy nose-dived, leading to new financial hardships for the Vietnamese Confederation of Labor and its members. What's more, Tran Quoc Buu faced domestic and international criticisms for corruption and nepotism, having used the CVT's political connections to land cushy government jobs for his family while also personally enriching himself. On top of all this, the Thieu regime became even more repressive, outlawing strikes and restricting union activity.[53]

When the North Vietnamese invaded in early 1975, Buu beseeched Meany and the AFL-CIO to lobby President Gerald Ford—who had stumbled into the White House upon Nixon's scandal-induced resignation—to increase US aid to South Vietnam in the hope of propping up the Thieu government a little while longer. The AFL-CIO leadership was eager to help, bringing Buu to Washington that March to plead his case to Congress. Kissinger, then serving as Ford's secretary of state, referred to Buu as "the George Meany of Vietnam."

But it was too late. Soon after Buu returned home from his US visit, North Vietnamese forces entered Saigon. He and about 200 other CVT officers and their families took refuge in the labor federation's Saigon headquarters in late April, uncertain of their fate. Meany successfully pressured the State Department to evacuate the union leaders, and Buu was whisked away to the Philippines in a helicopter, while others were ferried out of the country by boat. After the so-called Fall of Saigon on April 30, Vietnam was reunited as an independent, communist nation. The CVT was unsurprisingly disbanded under the new government, and Buu moved to Paris with his family, where he died the following year.[54]

A few months before the final collapse of the South Vietnamese government, Meany did something that, for him, was practically unheard of: he publicly admitted to making a mistake. Appearing on *The Dick Cavett Show* on November 13, 1974, Meany was asked by Cavett if he still thought he was right to have supported Johnson and Nixon's prosecution of the Vietnam War. "Well," Meany replied, "if I'd known then what I know now, I don't think we would have backed them." He continued:

> But we backed them on the information that was given by the President of the United States. The President of the United States has

access to more information than anyone else . . . He's the Commander-in-Chief of our Army. And we felt that this was the man we had to back and we did back LBJ and we did back Nixon. And you say, "do I think I was right?" I thought I was right at the time. But I would say to you, if I knew then what I know now, I would not have backed them. No.

In response, Local 1199 president Leon Davis, who had been against the war from the beginning, wrote in his union's newsletter, "So George, in admitting your mistake about Vietnam, how about examining the relationship of the American labor movement all over the world? For it's essential that we come to some understanding on how to live together on this planet—or surely we will perish together." Meany offered no reply.[55]

11

Exposed

The Vietnam War shattered the early Cold War consensus in the United States that economic and military interventions abroad were necessary to defend supposedly liberal pluralist values against the perceived threat of communism. The simultaneous fracturing of the Democratic Party, the shortcomings of Lyndon Johnson's "war on poverty," and the outbreak of urban uprisings around the country served to radicalize many of the young activists who had been participating in the social movements of the 1960s.

The AFL-CIO leadership positioned itself in opposition to the radical political currents of the era by supporting the Vietnam War and tacitly endorsing Richard Nixon's re-election. Still, some unions channeled the frustrations of workers who had traditionally been left out of organized labor—Blacks, Latinos, women, and rural workers—into successful organizing campaigns. These included Leon Davis's Local 1199, Cesar Chavez's United Farm Workers, and the American Federation of State, County, and Municipal Employees (AFSCME) under the progressive leadership of civil rights ally Jerry Wurf. The public sector in particular saw a significant rise in union density during the 1960s and 1970s, punctuated by high-profile strikes by municipal sanitation workers, public healthcare workers, and postal employees.

Although United Auto Workers president Walter Reuther publicly challenged the AFL-CIO to lead the way in pushing for civil rights and social reforms before his untimely death in 1970, he was himself accused of racism and indifference by Black members of his own union. Inspired by the Black Power movement and tired of being relegated to the lowest-paid jobs in the auto factories, in the late 1960s African American UAW members in Detroit formed the short-lived League of Revolutionary Black Workers. Articulating a Marxist-Leninist ideology, the League and its associated caucuses in the auto plants staged a series of wildcat strikes and ran in union elections to challenge Reuther's authoritarian control over the UAW, arguing that he and his fellow white union officers did nothing for rank-and-file Black auto workers.[1]

In the radical political environment of the Vietnam War era, it became increasingly common for Americans to question what their government was doing in other parts of the world. This also meant the AFL-CIO's international program—essentially an appendage of official US foreign policy—came under heightened scrutiny and criticism, particularly from journalists, congressmembers, and union members.

After years of meddling in the labor movements of other countries with little public oversight, the overseas empire the Federation had slowly built up through entities like the Free Trade Union Committee, American Institute for Free Labor Development (AIFLD), African American Labor Center, and Asian American Free Labor Institute became more visible to the general public in the late 1960s and early 1970s. As some startling revelations came to light during this period, the Federation was unflatteringly referred to as the "AFL-CIA" by many leftists.

CIA Connections Revealed

On February 15, 1967, the New Left magazine *Ramparts* released its March issue, with a feature story detailing how the CIA had for years been secretly channeling funds to organizations of US university students—such as the National Student Association—and turning their overseas activities into "an arm of United States foreign policy." Funneling money through tax-exempt foundations, the spy agency had given the National Student Association some $4 million from 1950 to

1965 to ensure that the "American point of view" would always be represented at international student gatherings attended by youth groups
from communist countries. The story was confirmed by the student
organization as well as by the State Department, and its appearance
created a national controversy.[2]

It had been public knowledge since the fall of 1964 that the CIA used
foundations—some real, others "dummy" foundations that only existed
on paper—as conduits to fund a variety of civil society organizations.
That discovery had been brought to light by Texas Congressman Wright
Patman during a probe into the finances of tax-exempt foundations.[3]
But the *Ramparts* article on the CIA financing of student organizations
was the first time the US public had gotten a real glimpse of how this
process worked.

Victor Reuther wasted no time in using the revelations to redirect
attention to organized labor's foreign affairs, telling the *New York Post*
on February 16 that there was "a lot bigger story in the CIA's financial
and other connections with the AFL-CIO than with the students,"
adding that he had already done his best to "lift the lid on it" and was
confident that "some day it will all come out." Jay Lovestone responded
by "blast[ing] Victor Reuther in unprintable language," ominously
warning he would "take care of Mr. Reuther."[4]

In the next week, investigative reporters from the *Washington
Post*, *New York Times*, and other papers broke multiple stories proving Victor Reuther right. After looking carefully at the donations
given by the nearly two dozen foundations already identified as CIA
conduits, journalists discovered several connections to AFL-CIO-
affiliated unions.

The first batch of articles revealed fresh details about the role of US
unions in the 1962–1964 destabilization campaign targeting Cheddi
Jagan's leftist government in British Guiana. Journalists found that
the American Newspaper Guild had accepted nearly $1 million in
funds over three years from four CIA-connected foundations. Not
coincidentally, the Guild had sent a representative, Gene Meakins, to
British Guiana to help undermine Jagan through a propaganda
campaign. It was then reported that between 1958 and 1964, AFSCME
had received up to $60,000 in donations per year from the "Gotham
Foundation"—a confirmed CIA dummy—to fund the union's international activities.

The arrangement with AFSCME was in place when the union's president was Arnold Zander, who used funds under the cover of Public Services International, the international trade secretariat for public sector workers. AFSCME had dispatched William Howard McCabe to British Guiana to help sustain the 1963 general strike against the Jagan government with CIA money. Further reports indicated that the AFL-CIO-affiliated Retail Clerks International Union—which sent its representative Gerard O'Keefe to assist McCabe in British Guiana— had similarly received CIA funds via foundations. Jerry Wurf, who narrowly defeated Zander in a 1964 election for the AFSCME presidency, had already severed his union's CIA ties by the time of the exposés.[5]

Another discovery was that CIA money had helped expand the global reach of the International Federation of Petroleum and Chemical Workers (IFPCW), the international trade secretariat for the world's energy sector unions, which was based in Denver. The IFPCW was founded in 1954 by the CIO-affiliated Oil Workers International Union (later the Oil, Chemical, and Atomic Workers) under the presidency of O. A. "Jack" Knight. While many IFPCW affiliates paid little to no dues to the trade secretariat, its budget nevertheless rose dramatically from $65,692 in 1960 to $193,838 in 1961 and $230,363 in 1962. This was thanks to financial contributions from Knight's union, money that came directly from CIA-linked foundations. The growth of the IFPCW allowed US labor to build and maintain relationships with unions in the strategic petroleum sector in the Middle East and Venezuela.[6]

Meanwhile, the defunct Institute of International Labor Research— Sacha Volman and Norman Thomas's project to strengthen Latin America's Noncommunist Left—was also implicated in the growing scandal. Reporters revealed that the institute received $1 million from a confirmed CIA conduit, the J. M. Kaplan Fund, between 1961 and 1963. The money, which accounted for all but $25,000 of the institute's total budget during that period, had been used to create the political education school in Costa Rica. The eighty-two-year-old Thomas pleaded ignorance over the source of the Kaplan Fund money, while trying to mitigate the damage to his reputation by reminding reporters that his Institute of International Labor Research had supported the Dominican Republic's Juan Bosch even as Washington had undermined him.[7]

Following these reports in February 1967, Victor Reuther appeared vindicated. But a few months later, former CIA officer Thomas Braden publicly accused Reuther of being a hypocrite. Braden had served as the CIA liaison to the AFL's Free Trade Union Committee in the early 1950s, and had attempted to establish a similar relationship with the CIO. By now retired from the Agency, in May 1967, Braden responded to the public outrage at the recent CIA exposés by penning an essay in the *Saturday Evening Post* entitled "I'm Glad the CIA is 'Immoral,' " in which he defended the CIA's early Cold War tactics as necessary to prevent the spread of communism. In the piece, he claimed that he had once given Walter Reuther "$50,000 in $50 bills" at the latter's request, which Victor then spent from his post in Europe to bolster "free" trade unions in West Germany.

For disingenuously criticizing CIA sponsorship of foreign labor activities, Braden said that "Victor Reuther ought to be ashamed of himself."[8] Victor admitted to the press that the UAW had indeed transferred $50,000 in CIA money to European unions, but swore it was a one-time-only transaction.[9] Soon after his public defense of the CIA in the *Saturday Evening Post*, Braden became a popular Washington-based political commentator, with his family life later serving as the inspiration for the TV comedy-drama *Eight Is Enough*.

For his part, Meany did damage control by telling inquisitive reporters that regardless of what its affiliates may have been up to, the AFL-CIO itself had "absolutely not" received any financial or other support from the CIA, and that he was opposed to union acceptance of Agency funding. Behind the scenes, Meany ordered Lovestone to cease doing freelance work for the CIA's counterintelligence chief James Jesus Angleton.[10] Lovestone's failure to comply would later prove to be a fateful choice.

Journalists naturally began questioning whether AIFLD was financed by the Agency. Meany denied that it was and, pointing to the millions of dollars the Institute annually accepted from USAID, rhetorically asked, "When you get that kind of money, why do you have to run to the CIA?"[11] While AIFLD officials undoubtedly coordinated their overseas missions with the CIA—just as they very openly did with USAID and the State Department—hard evidence proving that the Institute was funded or directed by the CIA has yet to be uncovered.

In early 1967, however, former AIFLD staffer Joseph Palisi wrote a curious letter to the *Washington Post* describing the damage "CIA front groups" were doing to the "innocents" who were being "carefully recruited for the timely exploitation of their professional skills to help mask other activities hardly in keeping with the publicly defined aims and objectives of their apparent employers." Palisi had briefly worked for AIFLD's Social Projects Department in Washington in the mid-1960s. Though not explicitly saying in his letter that the Institute itself was a CIA front, he bemoaned "the damage done to the imagery of legitimate organizations in the labor, religious, charitable and other fields of overseas activities by CIA connections which may range from levels of complete control to that of continuing infiltration."[12]

President Johnson responded to the uproar over the Agency's clandestine funding operations by prohibiting hidden government subsidies to private organizations, including unions. Former beneficiaries of the secret monies, which became known as "CIA orphans," would now have to receive government funds through new mechanisms. In May 1968, the AFL-CIO's International Affairs Department and USAID signed a contract allowing AIFLD, the African American Labor Center, and the Asian American Free Labor Institute to transmit a total of $1.3 million in USAID funds to certain "CIA orphans" in the realm of organized labor, including the Retail Clerks union and the International Federation of Petroleum and Chemical Workers.[13] "Same operation—new cover," Victor Reuther wrote of the arrangement. "Thus the AFL-CIO became, quite literally, a disbursement agent for the State Department."[14]

Overall, this series of bombshells and accusations created a sense that organized labor had compromised its independence and integrity to secretly serve US imperial interests, earning it the derisive moniker "AFL-CIA." This led to book-length excoriations by leftist writers of "the subversion of the AFL-CIO's foreign policy" in the last years of the 1960s.[15] In 1969, New Left historian Ronald Radosh wrote *American Labor and United States Foreign Policy*, which would become the seminal study of US labor imperialism. Radosh described the AFL and later AFL-CIO's role in world affairs as evolving from an attempt to gain recognition by government and business in exchange for industrial peace during World War I to an anticommunist-fueled integration into the "machinery of the corporate-capitalist state" in the post–World War II era.[16]

In 1971, New York playwright Eric Bentley also openly attacked labor's foreign affairs in his satirical musical *The Red, White, and Black: A Patriotic Demonstration*. The musical included a song set to the tune of the classic union ballad "Which Side Are You On?" entitled "AFL/CIA":

> They say in Detroit nowadays
> There ain't no neutrals here
> You're either for the cold war
> Or you just plain disappear:
>> Which side are you on, George?
>> Which side are you on?
>
> George Meany was a worker
> But he ain't a worker no more
> Instead he helps the government
> To stir up hot 'n cold war
>> Which side are you on, George?
>> Which side are you on?
>
> When Meany heard the workers
> In foreign lands were red
> He said: Let us explain to them
> It's better to be dead.
>> Which side are you on, George?
>> Which side are you on?
>
> When AFL joined with CIO
> 'Twas a great Union day
> Still greater was when AFL
> Joined with CIA.
>> Which side are you on, George?
>> Which side are you on?
>
> So, how about it, fella?
> Defend George if you can!

Are you CIO or CIA?
A Meany? Or a man?
Which side will you be on, fellas?
Which side are you gonna be on?

Don't listen to Mean George's gab
Just put an end to it
Stand up to him and tell him straight:
George, you are full of shit.
That's which side you're on fella,
That's which side you're on.
Right, right?[17]

As Radosh's book and Bentley's song indicate, Victor Reuther's goal of "lifting the lid" on the AFL-CIO's controversial alliance with the US foreign policy establishment had been accomplished by the start of 1970s.

Fulbright vs. Meany

In 1969, after press reports revealed USAID's $1.3 million disbursement to the AFL-CIO to fund labor's "CIA orphans," Senator J. William Fulbright called on the General Accounting Office (GAO) to conduct an audit of USAID's contracts with AIFLD. A previous such audit the year before had been unable to reach any clear conclusions about the effectiveness of AIFLD's government-subsidized programs due to poor monitoring and evaluation on the Institute's part.[18]

Chairman of the Senate Foreign Relations Committee, Fulbright was an outspoken opponent of the Vietnam War, believing he had been duped by President Johnson into voting for the 1964 Gulf of Tonkin Resolution. In July 1969, as Secretary of State William Rogers and USAID administrator John Hannah testified about foreign aid before the committee, Fulbright pointed to the millions of dollars the AFL-CIO's three foreign institutes had received from USAID since 1962 and remarked, "I have wondered if this is the price we paid for Mr. Meany's support in Vietnam." Two weeks later, as the GAO's new audit was under way, Fulbright called a hearing to explore the "unusual amount of flexibility accorded AIFLD in the expenditure of public funds," bringing Meany in to offer testimony.

In his opening statement, the AFL-CIO president attacked Fulbright's earlier words suggesting that his backing of the Vietnam War had been bought. "It is a gratuitous insult to the American labor movement to accuse us of receiving a payoff for supporting the foreign policy of an administration," Meany stated. In a heated exchange with Fulbright, Meany rhetorically asked, "Did you get a payoff for supporting the Tonkin Gulf Resolution? I don't think you did. But neither do I think you should suggest any payoff to us for promoting the free trade union movement in Latin America, Africa or Asia." Fulbright conceded that "perhaps the term payoff was too strong," but added that "I think it amounts to the same thing."[19]

Throughout his testimony, Meany forcefully defended the AFL-CIO's development activities in the Third World. "The AFL-CIO has always had an interest in workers in every part of the world. That is fraternal solidarity, humanitarianism in the best sense of the word," he told the Foreign Relations Committee. "Now I'm not going to tell you that we have never made mistakes or performed miracles . . . But we are trying to make a contribution to help the working people of these lands play a constructive role in building democratic societies through free trade unions."

When Fulbright pointed out the involvement of AIFLD graduates in the overthrow of Goulart in Brazil, Meany did not deny it, but instead replied, "We're interested only in building effective free trade unions in free societies. If our graduates later find themselves living under repressive and dictatorial regimes and decide to do something about it, that's their business."[20] Meany's response omitted the fact that Goulart's constitutional, democratic government had not been a dictatorial regime, but that his AIFLD-assisted overthrow had facilitated the installation of a repressive military dictatorship.

The GAO completed its audit in the spring of 1970. Once again, it could not come to any specific conclusions regarding AIFLD's effectiveness due to the Institute's lax standards on monitoring and evaluation. Fulbright expressed dismay at what he considered both AIFLD and USAID's lack of transparency. "The more I learn about the American Institute for Free Labor Development," the senator told the press after the audit came out, "the more convinced I am that it is both a drain on the taxpayers' dollars and counterproductive in bettering our labor relations within the hemisphere." He added that "AID should be phasing out this program" instead of "classifying the details" around the Institute's "questionable activities."[21]

Leaving the ICFTU

A major change for the AFL-CIO's foreign policy going into the 1970s involved a dramatic break with the International Confederation of Free Trade Unions (ICFTU), the anticommunist global labor body the Federation had been instrumental in creating. In 1968, with the UAW's disaffiliation from the AFL-CIO on the horizon, the Reuther brothers met with several Western European trade union officials— including the newly installed ICFTU general secretary, Harm Buiter of the Netherlands—to discuss the auto union's future role on the world stage.

The Reuthers wanted the UAW to remain part of the ICFTU and for Walter to retain his post on the International's board. Buiter was sympathetic, preferring Reuther's cooperative style to Meany's unilateralism and general disdain for Europe's social democratic trade unionists. A few years earlier, Meany had gone so far as to publicly disparage the ICFTU and its European officials using a homophobic slur, saying that they were an "ineffective bureaucracy right down to the fairies."[22]

Buiter's eagerness to allow the breakaway UAW to remain in the ICFTU infuriated Meany, who viewed it as a betrayal of the AFL-CIO. In November 1968, Meany demanded that the ICFTU board formally denounce the UAW's alleged divisiveness and declare its full support for the AFL-CIO, but the board only voted to delay the UAW's application for admission. The following month, the AFL-CIO Executive Council announced a boycott of all ICFTU activities until the matter of UAW admission was satisfactorily resolved.

Further fueling Meany's anger were the ICFTU's attempts at rapprochement with trade unions in the Soviet Bloc, following the lead of West German chancellor Willy Brandt and his "Ostpolitik" policy of normalizing relations with the communist countries of Central and Eastern Europe. After twenty years of clashing with the ICFTU's social democratic leaders, Meany had finally had enough. In February 1969, the AFL-CIO Executive Council took the extreme step of voting to disaffiliate from the International altogether.

The move served to effectively kill the UAW's application for admission. Desperate to bring the AFL-CIO back into the fold because of the resources and political clout it brought to bear, ICFTU leaders knew that admitting the UAW would only further antagonize Meany and close off any possibility of the AFL-CIO's return. The UAW's application was therefore dropped from consideration.[23] It would be over a decade before the Federation finally rejoined the ICFTU.

PART III

Free Market Revolution (1973–1995)

12

Crisis

Capitalism is inherently prone to crises, such as the multiple depressions of the nineteenth century, the Great Depression of the 1930s, and the numerous recessions since. After experiencing what some have called a "golden age" during the post–World War II years, capitalism once again went into crisis beginning in the late 1960s. More precisely, the postwar international capitalist order the US government had carefully crafted broke down, in many ways a victim of its own success.

With ever greater industrial production in the United States, Western Europe, and Japan naturally came declining corporate profit rates, leading to slower economic growth, which in turn led to higher unemployment. At the same time, more state spending on social welfare, higher wages, and (for the United States) spending on the Vietnam War all contributed to prices going up. The US inflation rate had averaged 1.3 percent a year in the early 1960s, only to grow to 6 percent in 1970 and then 11 percent by 1974. The combined problem of slower growth, rising unemployment, and high inflation was dubbed "stagflation," and economists and policymakers were initially unsure of what to do about it.[1]

For their part, industrial corporations squeezed out as much profit as possible by forcing their workers to labor faster and longer through speed-ups and mandatory overtime. Companies increasingly moved manufacturing out of the unionized, industrial core of the Northeast and Upper Midwest to the South and Southwest, where anti-union "right-to-work" laws prevailed. They also downsized their workforces and production facilities though automation. Top union officials, who viewed corporate executives as their partners in maintaining economic growth, generally tolerated these strategies. Meanwhile, US union membership was shrinking, not only because of corporate machinations, but also because labor leaders failed to prioritize organizing the unorganized. Between 1960 and 1980, for example, the AFL-CIO's affiliated unions organized only 2 million of the 35 million new workers added to the national labor force.[2]

Dissatisfaction with ever more strenuous industrial labor, combined with union bureaucrats' complacency and opposition to the progressive movements of the period (especially the antiwar movement), served to alienate a younger, more diverse, and more class-conscious generation of workers. In this context, a wave of internal dissent emerged within the US labor movement demanding more workplace rights and greater union democracy. For many younger union members, labor officials like the octogenarian George Meany were out of touch, too close to the political establishment, and hardly distinguishable from their corporate employers.

In the late 1960s and 1970s, a series of rank-and-file rebellions and reform movements challenged the entrenched bureaucracies within a number of US unions like the United Mine Workers, United Steelworkers, UAW, and Teamsters.[3] Women and people of color—who were entering the ranks of organized labor thanks to the unionization of the public sector and the antidiscrimination measures in the 1964 Civil Rights Act—formed their own rank-and-file organizations like the League of Revolutionary Black Workers, Coalition of Labor Union Women, and Coalition of Black Trade Unionists.[4] Union democracy and shopfloor militancy became the rallying cry of these various rank-and-file movements, with an uptick in the number of work stoppages.

Like many rank-and-file US unionists, leaders in the Third World also grew more assertive in the 1970s amid the growing crisis of capitalism, partly inspired by the stunning US defeat in Vietnam. The "Decade of Development" had not lived up to the promises of American liberals, and modernization theory—with its simplistic assumptions of linear development that failed to account for power relations between countries and classes—came under heavy criticism from left-wing social scientists like Andre Gunder Frank and Immanuel Wallerstein. The brutality of the US war in Vietnam, waged in the name of modernizing

Southeast Asia, had also damaged modernization theory's reputation. Walt Rostow, whose name was synonymous with modernization theory, was one of the war's most prominent boosters in his role as President Johnson's national security advisor. Modernization theory had thus lost its political and intellectual currency as a development model by the start of the 1970s.[5]

Wanting to escape from the economic dependency and neocolonial status that the informal US empire had only exacerbated, Third World leaders with the nonaligned movement demanded a "New International Economic Order" in 1973, and a set of principles was adopted by the UN General Assembly the following year. It called for foreign-owned assets in the Third World to be nationalized, for postcolonial countries to have the right to implement whichever economic system they deemed most appropriate, for more equitable terms of trade, and for the creation of public cartels of raw commodity exporters in the style of OPEC (Organization of Petroleum Exporting Countries) to stabilize prices. Officials in Washington aimed to put down this geopolitical insurgency even as they worked to improve relations with Moscow and Beijing, with the result that the Cold War increasingly shifted in the 1970s from an East versus West struggle to a North versus South one.[6]

AIFLD and the Chilean Coup

Serafino Romualdi, the AFL-CIO's longtime representative in Latin America, retired in 1965 and died of a heart attack two years later at the age of sixty-six. Replacing him as head of AIFLD was Bill Doherty, who had previously served as the Institute's social projects director.

Under Doherty, AIFLD in 1966 moved its residential training center from a building in Washington to a seventy-five-acre property in Front Royal, Virginia. It was the same former hunting lodge near the Shenandoah River where Joseph Beirne had held his pilot training program for Latin American unionists back in 1959, which AIFLD acquired from Beirne's Communications Workers of America. The facility included dormitories, a cafeteria, and classrooms able to accommodate up to forty students at a time.

Front Royal would remain home to the Institute's residential training program throughout the 1970s, becoming the "free" trade union version of the US Army's notorious School of the Americas in the Panama Canal Zone. At the School of the Americas, anticommunist Latin American military personnel studied the violent techniques of counterinsurgency. At AIFLD's Front Royal school, anticommunist Latin American unionists studied the class collaborationist techniques of business unionism and ways to counter working-class radicalism.[7]

Despite moving away from ambitious foreign aid programs like the Alliance for Progress, President Nixon saw the geopolitical value provided by AIFLD and the AFL-CIO's other foreign institutes. During Nixon's six years in office, the amount of USAID's grants to AIFLD increased, averaging $6 million per year—almost double the average $3.2 million per year the Institute received during the Kennedy and Johnson administrations. USAID's funding for the AFL-CIO's African and Asian institutes similarly rose, annually topping $1 million for each.[8]

By 1978, AIFLD claimed that over 338,000 participants had graduated from its educational initiatives: 2,550 from the Front Royal program, 205 from a specialized economics program in partnership with Georgetown University, and the rest from one of the Institute's many in-country training centers across Latin America and the Caribbean.[9]

As it had in the previous decade, AIFLD continued inviting controversy in the 1970s, especially in the aftermath of a bloody military coup in Chile.

In 1970, Chilean socialist Salvador Allende became the first Marxist to be democratically elected president of a Latin American nation. In his first year in office, Chilean workers saw a 30 percent average increase in real wages. Meanwhile, the country's Left-led labor movement was consulted in setting government policy and union membership grew to roughly a third of the nation's workforce.[10]

Allende's 1970 electoral victory horrified US capitalists with interests in the South American nation and their anticommunist allies in Washington, who had secretly funneled campaign contributions to his right-wing opponent, Jorge Alessandri. The Nixon administration and multinational corporations active in Chile, including International Telephone & Telegraph and Anaconda Copper, feared that Allende's democratic road to socialism, which included nationalization and wealth redistribution, might set an example for the rest of Latin America.

President Nixon infamously ordered the CIA to "make the [Chilean] economy scream" in order to destabilize Allende's government. Nixon's foreign policy team—including the secretive "40 Committee" oversee-ing covert activities—spent the next three years undermining Allende's government by cutting off all aid, loans, and credit to the country (but continuing to fund and arm the military) and helping Allende's domes-tic political opposition wreak havoc on the Chilean economy.

The resultant instability gave the country's military a pretext to execute a coup d'état on September 11, 1973, in the name of "restoring normality." With Washington's blessing, coup leader General Augusto Pinochet became Chile's military dictator and went about murdering thousands of Allende sympathizers and imprisoning tens of thousands more, all while protecting US investments in the country.

Central to the subversion campaign against Allende was a series of crippling and costly strikes beginning in late 1972 and continuing throughout much of 1973. These work stoppages occurred despite Allende's immense popularity with the Chilean working class, particu-larly among the communist leaders of the nation's largest labor federa-tion, the CUT (Unitary Central of Workers).

During the 1960s, AIFLD—whose board members included busi-nessmen with investments in Chile—had attempted to split the coun-try's left-oriented labor movement by courting unionists aligned with the center-right Christian Democrats and trying, unsuccessfully, to create a more conservative national trade union center to rival the CUT. After Allende's election in 1970, the Institute, supported as always by the State Department and USAID, ramped up its efforts to sow discord within the CUT by bringing noncommunist union officials to the United States to participate in AIFLD's Front Royal training program.

As explained by Robert O'Neill, AIFLD's Santiago-based country director for Chile, the Institute's goal was to ensure that conservative union forces could "grow and eventually control the trade union move-ment here." O'Neill hoped AIFLD's Chilean allies "could initially form a block within CUT to defend their positions and eventually be the basis for a break-up of CUT," though he admitted that "undeniably and unfor-tunately, the majority of organized Chilean workers still back Marxist leadership, at least in trade union elections."[11]

The number of Chileans attending AIFLD training programs skyrock-eted during Allende's presidency. In the decade between 1962 and 1972, a total of seventy-nine Chileans had participated in AIFLD's residential course in the United States, an average of about eight per year. But in the single year between February 1972 and February 1973, there were twenty-nine trainees. Altogether, the Institute trained 2,877 Chilean unionists in the three years from 1970 to 1972—nearly all in-country— compared to 5,963 who had been trained in the eight years from 1962 to 1969.[12]

Ultimately unable to gain a real foothold inside the CUT, the Institute's only major trade union ally was the Maritime Confederation of Chile, an independent union of conservative maritime workers based in Valparaiso. In addition to building a library for the union, AIFLD also contracted CIA money launderer Nicholas Deak to ensure that the Maritime Confederation got an advantageous exchange rate on the dollar.[13]

Around the time of Allende's electoral victory, AIFLD leaders adjusted their Chilean strategy, shifting attention away from traditional unions and instead focusing on professional associations known as *gremios*. Gremios consisted of property-owning, middle-class opponents of Allende, who feared wealth-redistribution policies would disadvantage them.

In Chile's complex and stratified class structure, much as in that of the United States and many other countries, the comfortable middle class was particularly hostile toward socialism, determined not to lose any of the economic or social privileges that kept them above the working class and the poor. The word "gremio" can mean both employer and worker, and thus the term perfectly captured "the AIFLD concept of labor-management solidarity moreso [*sic*] than any word in English."[14] The Institute's partnership with the gremios was part of Washington's larger strategy of bankrolling the Chilean middle class's opposition to Allende.

AIFLD first made inroads with professional associations inside Chile's recently nationalized copper mines. There, middle-class engineers and supervisors were unhappy that Allende's government was prioritizing raising wages for the lowest-paid mine workers instead of their own salaries. To curry favor among these disaffected professionals, in 1970, AIFLD spent $5,000 constructing a beachside country club for the Professional Employees Union at the Andes Mining Company. The Institute next helped form a national gremio association in May 1971. Called the CUPROCH (Confederation of Chilean Professionals), it was centered in the mines. Other AIFLD-aligned gremios consisted of truckers, shopkeepers, physicians, and members of other professions opposed to Allende's socialism.

With Washington having cut off all aid, loans, and credit, the Chilean economy predictably experienced a sharp downturn. In October 1972, 12,000 truckers staged a strike that brought the country's internal commerce to a halt. A protest against a shortage of spare auto parts and plans for a nationalized road haulage system, the trucking strike was also part of the broader, US-backed strategy to breed chaos and weaken Allende's government. The socialist president reached an accommodation with the trucking gremios after the strike lasted a month and cost the country $170 million. Only months later, in the spring of 1973, CUPROCH-affiliated gremios in the El Teniente copper mine staged a work stoppage of their own, demanding pay increases. While the mining strike stretched on for over seventy days, costing the government $75 million, gremios representing doctors and shopkeepers ratcheted up the pressure by holding their own short-term strikes to protest all the economic woes since Allende had come into office.

Then, only three weeks after the government negotiated a settlement to end the unrest in the mines, the trucking gremios staged yet another anti-Allende strike—halting the transportation of fuel, food, seeds, and fertilizers and costing the country $6 million per day. The economic hardship wrought by the trucking strike inspired still more work stoppages by merchants and physicians, as well as by bus and taxi drivers, all protesting high inflation and stagnating incomes.

These protests were organized by the National Command for Gremio Defense, a coalition of CUPROCH and several employer groups whose leaders had been trained by AIFLD. While much of the country's population was forced to rely on food rations, *Time* correspondent Rudolph Rauch encountered striking truckers near Santiago "enjoying a lavish communal meal of steak, vegetables, wine and empanadas." When Rauch asked where the money for the meal came from, they laughingly answered, "From the CIA."[15]

The mass disruptions caused by these strikes provided the excuse needed for General Augusto Pinochet and the Chilean armed forces to orchestrate a violent coup on September 11, 1973. The first major city to fall to the coup plotters that morning was the Maritime Confederation of Chile's home base of Valparaiso, which was captured by the navy.[16]

As tanks rolled through the streets of Santiago and the presidential palace was bombed by the Chilean air force, Allende refused to resign. Instead, he gave one last defiant speech over the radio, lambasting "the sedition that was supported by professional associations"—the gremios—accusing them of defending "the advantages of capitalist society." By mid-afternoon, infantrymen had overtaken the bombed-out presidential residence, finding Allende dead from an apparent self-inflicted gunshot wound to the head, though a theory has persisted for many years that he was murdered.[17]

As with the Brazilian coup in 1964, AIFLD leaders argued that the new military regime in Chile would somehow open the door to "free" trade unionism. Once again, the exact opposite happened.

The new dictatorship led by Pinochet suspended the constitution and all political rights and civil liberties. The military took over universities and purged them of faculty, students, and books deemed too left-wing. In the first few weeks after the coup, an estimated 100,000 people were arrested, many of them detained in sports stadiums where they faced interrogation and torture. At least 1,500 were murdered in these early days of the dictatorship.[18]

Pinochet unsurprisingly moved to destroy the labor movement, outlawing the CUT and arresting or killing thousands of union leaders. The more right-wing Maritime Confederation of Chile, which AIFLD had long supported, was allowed to exist, but had little legal room to operate. As in Brazil after its military takeover, AIFLD continued its training programs in Chile despite the apparent impossibility of a free labor movement.

According to researcher Robert Alexander, the Institute was "making the best of a very bad situation" in Chile, using its relationship with the US Embassy to provide cover for a handful of independent unionists who were critical of the regime. Alexander claimed that under the dictatorship, AIFLD allowed unionists of all political stripes—including even communists—to have a safe space to meet and discuss worker issues.[19]

Rank and File Against AIFLD

A year following the Chilean coup, and shortly after Nixon resigned under the cloud of the Watergate scandal, a series of congressional hearings and investigative news reports confirmed what many already knew: that the US government had played a critical role in toppling Allende. In particular, it came out that the CIA had been authorized to spend up to $8 million to fund opposition activities, with most of the money going toward sustaining the antigovernment trucking strikes that paralyzed the Chilean economy in the lead-up to the coup—just as the Agency had financed the general strike in British Guiana a decade earlier to disrupt and discredit the government of socialist Cheddi Jagan.[20]

Around the same time these revelations came to light, Fred Hirsch—a plumber and local union activist in San Jose, California—wrote a report on the AFL-CIO's role in the coup entitled *Under the Covers with the CIA: An Analysis of Our AFL-CIO Role in Latin America*. A lifelong leftist, Hirsch used his connections in both the labor and peace movements to get hold of various AIFLD and State Department documents. His report, which pieced together AIFLD's role in supporting the gremios and destabilizing Allende's government, was completed in early 1974 on behalf of the Emergency Committee to Defend Democracy in Chile, a small labor study group of San Jose activists. In March 1974, the Santa Clara County Labor Council, of which Hirsch was a member, adopted a resolution demanding that the AFL-CIO explain its activities in Chile. The council then published Hirsch's report as a pamphlet and helped mass-mail it to labor activists all over the United States.

Thanks to the whistleblowing of United Auto Workers international affairs director Victor Reuther and the journalistic exposés of the late 1960s, the groundwork had already been laid for Hirsch's pamphlet to be well received by thousands of rank-and-file unionists troubled by the AFL-CIO's suspect relationship with the government, particularly with the CIA. The longstanding lack of member input and involvement in the Federation's foreign activities was a prime example of the secretive, top-down decision-making culture the union democracy movements of the 1970s were combating. Several union locals requested bulk reprints of Hirsch's booklet and permission to translate it into other languages.[21]

AFL-CIO leadership was compelled to respond, sending Doherty to meet with the Santa Clara County Labor Council in July 1974. Unsurprisingly, he denied any AIFLD involvement in the coup, going so far as to tell the bald-faced lie that the Institute "didn't even have a program in Chile."[22]

Still, in light of this growing criticism, George Meany and the AFL-CIO Executive Council finally issued a public statement criticizing Pinochet in August 1974, nearly a year after the coup. Federation leaders could not, however, resist also taking a gratuitous swipe at the deceased Allende. "Free trade unionists did not mourn the departure of a Marxist regime in Chile which brought that nation to political, social and economic ruin," the statement read, "but free trade unionists cannot condone the autocratic actions of this militaristic and oppressive ruler."[23]

Disturbed by the accusations laid out by Hirsch, in early 1975 several dozen local labor leaders in the Bay Area, speaking under the name Union Committee for an All-Labor AIFLD, disowned the Institute on behalf of rank-and-file unionists. "Whether or not [Hirsch's] charges are true," the committee wrote, "AIFLD . . . is wide open to such accusations because of its connections" to multinational corporations and the US government. "This situation puts the labor movement out front to take all the knocks for the multinationals and the State Department. We don't need that." They called for the development of "a completely new approach" to labor's foreign policy, for AIFLD to break ties with all corporations and government agencies, and for direct union-to-union foreign relations. "The genuine help we can offer to Latin American unions will not match the government and corporate monies, but neither will it carry the stigma of company unionism and the CIA," the committee explained.

Some union locals around the country, including the Teaching Assistants Association at the University of Wisconsin-Madison and Maryland's Montgomery County Federation of Teachers, also responded to Hirsch's booklet by passing resolutions in 1975 demanding that AIFLD be dissolved and that all AFL-CIO links to government and corporate money be immediately cut.[24]

At the 1974 national convention of the AFL-CIO-affiliated American Federation of Teachers (AFT), delegates overwhelmingly passed a resolution condemning the Chilean coup. A similar resolution calling for an investigation into AIFLD's role in the coup was, however, beaten back by the union's newly elected president, Albert "Al" Shanker. An arch anti-communist and onetime member of Norman Thomas's Socialist Party, Shanker was allied with officials in the AFL-CIO's International Affairs

Department and aimed to develop a closer relationship between the teachers' union and AIFLD.

At the AFT's 1978 convention, Shanker angered many rank-and-filers by inviting the AFL-CIO's veteran international agent Irving Brown to speak about labor's foreign affairs at a lunch event. Brown's CIA connection was by then well known. When asked by a reporter a year earlier about his relationship with the Agency, Brown answered cryptically, "If I was a CIA agent, I would deny it. And if I denied it, you wouldn't believe me."[25]

Members of the teachers' union's Black Caucus urged fellow delegates to skip Brown's lunchtime speech at the convention—handing out leaflets reading "Boycott CIA Goods"—and instead go to their own luncheon, occurring at the same time, honoring the life of singer, actor, civil rights activist, and communist fellow traveler Paul Robeson, who had died two years earlier. The expected turnout for Brown's event wound up being so low that Shanker was forced to move it to a smaller room to avoid the embarrassment of a visibly sparse audience.[26]

In this same period, the progressive North American Congress on Latin America published new exposés of AIFLD's activities across the region, while a small California-based nonprofit called Research Associates International, which was spearheaded by journalist and former union official Rodney Larson and included "several former intelligence officers," produced and distributed reports tracing the AFL-CIO's alleged connections with the CIA around the Third World.[27]

Meanwhile, in 1975, former CIA officer Philip Agee published *Inside the Company*, an explosive, tell-all memoir of his life as a spy. In the book, Agee alleged that AFL-CIO officials like Doherty and Andrew McLellan were CIA agents and that several international trade secretariats were essentially CIA fronts. Besides his own diary entries, Agee did not provide documentary evidence backing up his claims, and his publisher was successfully sued for libel by the Geneva-based International Federation of Plantation, Agricultural, and Allied Workers. Still, his book only further fueled concerns about the "AFL-CIA."[28]

The same year that Agee's book came out, a Senate committee chaired by Idaho Senator Frank Church was busily investigating and bringing to light some of the abuses of the CIA and other US intelligence agencies over the years. After reading up on their own union's close ties to AIFLD, fifteen rank-and-file members of the Communications Workers of

America in San Diego wrote to Senator Church. Only a year earlier, the CWA's longtime president and AIFLD cofounder, Joseph Beirne, had retired and died of cancer at age sixty-three.

Citing Agee's book and noting how AIFLD was run out of an office inside their union's national headquarters in Washington, the CWA members told Church they hoped that "short-sighted political concerns" like campaign donations from the AFL-CIO would not stop him "from getting to the bottom of this situation." If the CWA had "been used by the CIA," they wrote, "we want to know the truth—the whole truth. Your committee can find it out."[29] However, no new major revelations about the CIA's ties to organized labor came out of his committee's investigation.

Neoliberalism

The 1973 Chilean coup and its aftermath were harbingers of the dramatic transformations that would reshape the world's political economy in response to the crisis of capitalism. Under the Pinochet dictatorship, Chile served as a laboratory for a new Third World development model—one that ostensibly put the private sector in the driver's seat. Following the advice of economists trained at the University of Chicago, Pinochet privatized public utilities, lifted regulations on businesses, opened up international trade, and substantially curtailed workers' rights. The South American nation became what many scholars consider ground zero for neoliberalism.

Neoliberalism became the preferred solution to economic crisis for US policymakers and capitalist elites. Couched in the anticommunist rhetoric of individual freedom and the rights of private property, neoliberalism entailed privatization, liberalization, and deregulation in lieu of the social democratic and New Deal–style economic policies that had dominated much of the noncommunist world since the late 1940s.

Manufacturing companies in the United States merged into ever-larger conglomerates and increasingly invested overseas—especially in the Third World—where they could get higher profit rates. New telecommunications technologies, innovations in logistics, and the growing power of the financial sector all helped facilitate the rise of multinational corporations. The Nixon administration also helped by moving away from government-funded development aid in favor of supporting private foreign investment.

The Third World vision of a New International Economic Order would not come to pass. Instead, throughout the 1970s, governments in poor nations took out loans from the financial institutions of the wealthy industrial countries to cover the cost of imports and fund ongoing state-led development schemes, only to become mired in debt. By the latter half of the decade, they were turning to the International Monetary Fund (IMF) for debt relief. Founded at the end of World War II as one of the pillars of the US-managed international capitalist system, the IMF's original purpose was to coordinate monetary policy across borders and guarantee liquidity in financially struggling economies by serving as a "lender of last resort." But under the de facto control of the US Treasury, the IMF in the late 1970s became a vehicle to impose neoliberal priorities on the Third World as a precondition for debt relief.

If they wanted the IMF's help (and they often desperately needed it), indebted countries would have to implement "structural adjustment" programs—which typically meant devaluing their currency, privatizing publicly owned industries and utilities, slashing social welfare spending, reducing or eliminating tariffs, and rolling back labor rights. Such measures were intended to make the Third World more attractive to foreign direct investment, so that multinational corporations from the US and other wealthy nations would come in, set up manufacturing operations using low-paid, non-union workers, and then export cheaply made products back home for consumption.

Just as Pinochet's military dictatorship forcibly imposed neoliberalism onto Chile, the IMF forced structural adjustment onto the indebted countries of the Third World. Despite its rhetoric of "freedom," neoliberalism was adopted by coercion, not democratic or popular choice.

The same kinds of neoliberal policies enacted under Pinochet and dictated by the IMF would gradually be embraced in the United States itself as an antidote to the stagflation of the 1970s. With looser regulations, US companies moved manufacturing into cheaper, less regulated labor markets abroad, or simply sold off their factories altogether in the race for short-term profits.

Employers now forcefully abandoned the supposed labor-management accord. The model of collective bargaining symbolized by 1950's

"Treaty of Detroit"—where increased productivity was tied to cost-of-living raises in an ever-growing economic pie—was anathema to the emerging multinational conglomerates, whose executives were increasingly distant (both physically and financially) from their employees.

The divisions within the labor movement and the collapse of the government-led approach to foreign aid were combined with increasing flows of private capital into the Third World. The resulting processes of deindustrialization and globalization over the next few decades devastated American workers and their communities while precipitating a staggering decline in union membership. Class cooperation and factory-level collective bargaining—the hallmarks of industrial pluralism—did nothing to prevent US capitalists from shutting down plants and laying off union workers by the tens of thousands between the 1970s and 2000s.

The clothing industry was one of the first in the United States to take advantage of the emerging neoliberal world order. In the early 1960s, imports accounted for only 2.5 percent of domestic apparel sales in the United States. By 1976, that number had dramatically risen to 31 percent and would only continue climbing in the years to come. Early on, apparel imports came from Japan, Hong Kong, and Taiwan—part of trade agreements brokered by Washington to provide an economic incentive for them to stave off communist influence from mainland China. But with the growth of foreign direct investment and IMF-imposed structural adjustment, by the late 1970s, Central America and the Caribbean became important apparel exporters to the United States, with US clothing brands facilitating the opening of sweatshops there.

Unsurprisingly, US unions like the International Ladies' Garment Workers' Union (ILGWU) were hit hard. As more imports came in and garment-manufacturing jobs moved overseas, the ILGWU's membership dropped from 457,517 in 1969 to 308,056 in 1980. Now that free trade was no longer a one-sided boon to American workers as it had been in the 1950s and 1960s, the AFL-CIO abandoned its long-held support for trade liberalization.

As labor historian Dana Frank has noted, though US labor could have responded by fostering greater solidarity with exploited garment workers abroad to take on the power of multinational corporations together, the AFL-CIO instead embraced protectionism and economic nationalism under the slogan "Buy American." The ILGWU ran a series of memorable TV commercials featuring its members singing a catchy tune encouraging consumers to "look for the union label" because "it says we're able to make it in the USA."[30]

The AFL-CIO vs. Détente

For AFL-CIO president George Meany, the most troubling issue of the 1970s was not the economic restructuring that was beginning to decimate the US labor movement, but rather détente—the policy of easing tensions between the Cold War superpowers. Always far more concerned about the struggle of democracy against "totalitarianism" than the conflict between workers and capital, and smarting from US defeat in Vietnam, Meany and the Federation's other "free" trade unionists only doubled down on their hawkish anticommunism amid the crisis of capitalism.

To Meany's dismay, the Nixon administration not only negotiated limits on nuclear weapons with the Soviet Union but also opened diplomatic relations with the People's Republic of China, with Nixon visiting Beijing in 1972 and meeting communist leader Mao Zedong face-to-face. In a familiar refrain, the AFL-CIO president compared the opening of US-Chinese relations to the appeasement approach of the 1930s that had emboldened the Nazis. Leonard Woodcock, president of the now-independent United Auto Workers and successor to Walter Reuther, disagreed. After retiring from the UAW in 1977, Woodcock was sent to Beijing by President Jimmy Carter to negotiate fully normalized relations between China and the United States, a task he saw through. Once full diplomatic relations were established in 1979, Woodcock became the first US ambassador to communist China.[31]

But Meany was an ardent opponent of what he derided as "this thing called detente," blaming it for the country's growing economic problems in the 1970s, particularly the liberalization of trade with the USSR and Eastern Bloc—something US corporations, eager for new markets, were successfully lobbying for. As Presidents Gerald Ford and Carter continued détente in the years following Nixon's 1974 resignation, a distrustful AFL-CIO clung to its hardline anticommunism, demonstrating how the Federation had internalized its traditional role as a bulwark against radicalism.

"There is a basic problem . . . with these Soviet promoted ideas like peaceful co-existence and detente," Meany said in 1975. "The Communists just don't mean it. They don't really believe in these propaganda slogans."[32] The same year, the Federation invited famed Russian novelist and exiled dissident Aleksandr Solzhenitsyn to tour the United States and honored him with a banquet in Washington, where he assailed détente as nothing but a Soviet trick to gain the upper hand in the Cold War.[33]

In contrast, the social democratic unionists of Western Europe welcomed the diplomatic thaw, forging relationships with communist unions in the Eastern Bloc. No longer part of the Brussels-based International Confederation of Free Trade Unions (ICFTU), there was little the AFL-CIO could do to disrupt this growing labor unity in Europe, despite Irving Brown's continued presence in Paris.

So, in late 1977, the Federation established a fourth government-funded foreign nonprofit—the Free Trade Union Institute (FTUI)—to bring the AIFLD model to Europe. With its name clearly inspired by the AFL's Free Trade Union Committee from the early Cold War period, the new FTUI's initial focus in the late 1970s was stymieing the growth of the Left in Spain and Portugal as both countries emerged from decades-long fascist dictatorships.[34]

By the 1970s, it was obvious to virtually everyone that the purpose of the AFL-CIO's foreign institutes had less to do with development or labor rights and more to do with neutralizing leftist movements around the world. In a 1976 report by the General Accounting Office, for example, officials from the US Department of Labor were quoted saying that the institutes' "real objectives are more political and ideological than economic or technical."[35]

That is precisely why Washington continued funding the AFL-CIO's overseas operations long after the enthusiasm behind the "Decade of Development" had dried up. The Federation had repeatedly proven its geopolitical usefulness in keeping militant, class-conscious labor movements abroad in check—something especially helpful for Washington planners looking to spread neoliberalism.

13

New Blood

In the years following the exposés of organized labor's shadowy relationship with the US foreign policy establishment, Jay Lovestone—by now in his mid-seventies—became a lightning rod for public controversy.

With Lovestone often characterized as a Rasputin-like figure manipulating the AFL-CIO president behind the scenes, George Meany was eager to prove he was not under the ex-communist's spell. In 1973, a check from the CIA's James Angleton for services rendered was misplaced by Lovestone's new secretary and unintentionally forwarded to the Federation's headquarters in Washington. This alerted Meany to the fact that, contrary to his express wishes, his international affairs director was still doing freelance intelligence work for the Agency. The following spring, Meany formally replaced Lovestone with his own son-in-law, Ernest Lee, a Korean War vet who had served as the AFL-CIO's assistant director for international affairs for over a decade.[1] After nearly thirty years at the center of US labor's global empire, Lovestone was out.

In November 1979, Meany himself retired at the age of eighty-five. Two months later, he died of cardiac arrest. "George Meany was an American institution," President Carter said in a White House statement. "He was an enemy of totalitarianism in all its forms, a fighter for social justice at home and abroad, and a friend of freedom everywhere."[2] Carter ordered all flags on federal buildings to be lowered to half-mast in tribute to the Bronx plumber who had, more than any other single individual, defined the US labor movement in the Cold War era.[3]

Lane Kirkland

Meany's handpicked successor was fifty-seven-year-old Lane Kirkland. A South Carolina native and the descendant of a Confederate senator, Kirkland served as an officer in the US Merchant Marine during World War II and was a member of the International Organization of Masters, Mates and Pilots, the union of licensed US mariners.

After the war, he studied at Georgetown University's School of Foreign Service. In 1948, AFL president William Green spoke at Georgetown and was approached by Kirkland, who told Green of his membership in the mariners' union. The two hit it off, and Kirkland soon accepted a job offer at the AFL's Research Department. Aside from stints as a speechwriter for Adlai Stevenson's presidential campaigns in the 1950s, he would remain at the Federation's headquarters for the rest of his career.[4]

In 1960, Kirkland became Meany's chief assistant, then was elected secretary-treasurer of the AFL-CIO in 1969. In 1973, he married Irena Neumann, a Czech-born Auschwitz survivor who had fled Eastern Europe after the Soviets took over. On visits to Washington, anti-Soviet dissidents like Solzhenitsyn would regularly be welcomed into the Kirklands' home as dinner guests.[5] As Meany's right-hand man at the Federation, Kirkland became a skilled political operator, developing close relationships with Washington's top power brokers.

During Richard Nixon's presidency, he often served as an AFL-CIO liaison to the White House, particularly on matters of foreign policy. In this function, Kirkland became lifelong friends with Henry Kissinger. The two men and their wives made it a tradition to spend their annual Thanksgiving holiday together.[6] Meany was impressed by Kirkland's unwavering commitment to aggressive anticommunism, praising him as "a strong and vigilant defender of liberty." By the early 1970s, Kirkland was already rumored to be the AFL-CIO president's heir apparent.

When Meany retired in November 1979, he personally nominated Kirkland to be his successor. This met no opposition from the rest of the

Federation's leadership, who proceeded to install the South Carolinian as the new president.[7] As historian Timothy Minchin notes, Kirkland had a softer, more tactful style as AFL-CIO chief than his blunt, acerbic predecessor. "Mr. Kirkland looks more like a Cabinet member or corporate lawyer than a grass-roots organizer," the *New York Times* opined. "He is a man who seems more comfortable in Washington's salons than on a picket line."[8]

One of his top priorities on taking charge of the Federation was healing some of the rifts inside the labor movement that Meany had helped create. In 1981, he welcomed the United Auto Workers back into the AFL-CIO. Now under the leadership of Douglas Fraser—a Scottish-born auto worker and associate of the late Walter Reuther—the UAW hoped that reaffiliation and increased labor unity could be an answer to the ongoing decline in US union density.[9]

Trained as a diplomat at Georgetown, Kirkland's primary interest was always international affairs. Some in the AFL-CIO joked that if he were ever offered a White House Cabinet position, he would sooner choose secretary of state than secretary of labor. Foreign policy, Kirkland said, was "far too important to be left in the hands of a tight, incestuous breed of economists and diplomats."[10] Upon taking over the Federation, he responded to years of criticism from within labor's ranks by amicably dismissing J. Peter Grace and all other corporate representatives from AIFLD's Board of Trustees in 1981 and bringing the AFL-CIO back into the International Confederation of Free Trade Unions the following year.[11]

But Kirkland certainly had no intention of dismantling the AFL-CIO's overseas empire or ending its Cold War activities abroad. He retained Bill Doherty as the director of AIFLD, moved the Institute's residential training program from Front Royal to the George Meany Center for Labor Studies in Silver Spring, Maryland, and named Irving Brown the new head of the AFL-CIO's International Affairs Department. Although he accepted the job, Brown, who was now in his early seventies, remained at his station in Paris. Running the department on Brown's behalf in Washington was Tom Kahn, the leading figure among a new generation of labor anticommunists and Kirkland's most trusted international advisor.[12]

Kahn, Rustin, and Shanker

A Brooklyn native, Kahn cut his political teeth as a teenager in the 1950s by joining the Independent Socialist League, a small group of socialist intellectuals who identified themselves as champions of democracy and completely opposed to the USSR for its "communist totalitarianism."

The League's founder, Max Shachtman, had once been a member of the Communist Party USA. But because of his heretical anti-Stalinism and support for Leon Trotsky, Shachtman was expelled from the party in 1928 by none other than Jay Lovestone, who was then the CPUSA's executive secretary. In the decades that followed, Shachtman broke with Trotsky and formed the Independent Socialist League.

The young Kahn embraced Shachtman's politics and became an enthusiastic anticommunist. In 1958 Shachtman ended his group's relative isolation by bringing its members, including Kahn, into Norman Thomas's Socialist Party.[13]

Kahn became a leader in the Young People's Socialist League, the youth wing of the Socialist Party, advocating increased unity between labor liberals and the civil rights movement. His fundraising for the Montgomery bus boycott brought him into contact with renowned civil rights activist and ex-communist Bayard Rustin. Kahn's senior by twenty-five years, Rustin had spent two years in a federal prison during World War II for adhering to his pacifist beliefs and refusing to fight in the war. More than anyone else, Rustin brought the Gandhian principles of nonviolence into the African American civil rights movement.

The young Kahn was enamored with Rustin, who became his mentor, close friend, and, for a while, his lover.[14] Kahn, who was white, partnered with Rustin and A. Philip Randolph to organize the 1963 March on Washington for Jobs and Freedom, where Martin Luther King Jr. famously delivered his "I Have a Dream" speech.

Soon afterward, Kahn and fellow socialist Michael Harrington both took jobs at the League for Industrial Democracy (LID), a decades-old group devoted to promoting social democracy. As the respective chairman and executive director of LID, Harrington and Kahn set about trying to implement Rustin's "from protest to politics" strategy of achieving tangible social democratic reforms by cozying up to institutions like the Democratic Party and AFL-CIO. Much to Kahn's dismay, LID's youth branch—the Students for a Democratic Society—broke away in

1965 and became one of the central organizations of the emerging New Left, which rejected Cold War anticommunism.[15]

Through LID, Kahn established relationships with a handful of union officials, including Al Shanker, who would be an important ally on international matters in the years to come. Shanker was then president of the 50,000-member United Federation of Teachers (UFT), the New York City local of the AFT. He was a close friend of Max Shachtman, whose wife, Yetta Barsh, served as his assistant at the UFT.

Shanker came to national prominence when he led the UFT on three citywide teacher strikes in the fall of 1968 demanding the reinstatement of several white educators who had been fired by Black members of a community-controlled school board in the Ocean Hill-Brownsville area of Brooklyn. The board members in the majority African American neighborhood were aiming to replace the white, Jewish teachers with Black teachers, leading Shanker to accuse them of anti-Semitism. During the Ocean Hill-Brownsville dispute, which appeared to pit the white-led teachers union against Black parents, Rustin and Kahn came to the UFT's defense.[16]

Shanker publicly opposed US withdrawal from Vietnam. This was not only a product of his hawkish anticommunism, but also a strategic move to gain favor with the conservative AFL-CIO leadership and climb the ladder of labor bureaucracy. "Once a boat-rocker as a young Socialist rebel," labor reporter A. H. Raskin wrote in 1973, "Shanker has moved steadily rightward inside organized labor until he now ranks among the most orthodox of union establishmentarians, a highly articulate defender of almost everything George Meany does."[17]

His critics accused him of being recklessly power crazed. This was famously articulated in the 1973 comedy film *Sleepers*, in which Woody Allen's character awakens in a distant future to learn that the world as he knew it was destroyed because "a man named Albert Shanker got ahold of a nuclear warhead."[18]

Shanker became national president of the AFT in 1974 and joined the AFL-CIO Executive Council.

From Social Democrats to Neoconservatives

In 1965, Bayard Rustin helped found the A. Philip Randolph Institute, a new, AFL-CIO-funded nonprofit aiming to bridge the civil rights and labor movements. Under Rustin's direction, in early 1967, the Randolph Institute published A *"Freedom Budget" for All Americans*, a pamphlet that advocated massive federal spending on social programs to elimi- nate US poverty, which was endorsed by dozens of prominent civil rights activists, academics, and labor leaders.

But noticeably absent from the Freedom Budget was any mention of the Vietnam War, which the Johnson administration was increasingly prioritizing over its "war on poverty" at home.[19]

Rustin, the lifelong pacifist, ironically wanted to sidestep the ques- tion of Vietnam, surmising that it would only divide the kind of mass political coalition he hoped to build. Or, as Harvard Students for a Democratic Society activist and future historian Michael Kazin put it, Rustin and the other architects of the Freedom Budget were "willing to keep all the defense money intact just so they can get George Meany on their side."[20]

Rustin advised Martin Luther King Jr. not to condemn the war, predicting that doing so would lead to a swift public backlash. But believing it was a matter of moral principle, King denounced the war anyway, beginning in April 1967. As a result, he was castigated and abandoned by many of his liberal allies in what would be the final year of his life.[21]

Kahn and other Shachtmanites wanted nothing to do with the New Left or the antiwar movement—not only because they feared alienating the Democratic Party and AFL-CIO, but also because they believed the antiwar movement was only giving comfort to world communism. Kahn scolded the New Left for its "anti-anti-communism," describing it as a "reverse McCarthyism which refuses to differentiate between civil libertarian and rightist opposition to Communism."[22] He accused New Left activists of being an out-of-touch intelligentsia that ignored the issues concerning real-life workers in favor of abstract political theories.

Regarding the AFL-CIO as the genuine face of class struggle in the United States, Kahn and fellow Shachtmanites advocated greater unity between the Socialist Party and the labor federation. They particularly admired Meany for his fierce devotion to anticommunism and unapologetic opposition to the antiwar movement.[23]

For his part, Michael Harrington went from similarly criticizing the New Left and antiwar movement to eventually calling for US military withdrawal from Southeast Asia. During the 1972 presidential election, Harrington supported the Democrats' antiwar nominee, George McGovern, while Kahn and Rustin refused to endorse the dovish candidate. Shachtman died that year, and Thomas had already died in 1968, leaving the Socialist Party at a crossroads. Rustin became the party's new cochair, alongside union official and former Lovestoneite Charles Zimmerman, while Harrington also remained an influential figure in the party.

At the Socialist Party's 1972 convention in New York, differences over the war came to a head, with Rustin and Kahn's side winning majority control of the party and renaming it Social Democrats, USA (SDUSA).

They deliberately dropped the word "socialist" because, they argued, it had "become hopelessly identified in the public mind with the communist world, which constantly uses the term." Harrington was "very saddened" by this move, arguing that it was "not simply the abandonment of a name but of a tradition, and in an attempt to become more acceptable to the American people and the American trade unions, it would result in our giving up our socialist content. I think the Socialist party should forthrightly stand for socialism."[24]

Harrington and his followers did not stick around, instead forming their own separate organization called the Democratic Socialist Organizing Committee (DSOC). Among the most prominent trade unionists to join DSOC were AFSCME president Jerry Wurf and Victor Reuther, who became one of its national vice presidents around the same time he retired from the UAW in 1973.[25] A decade later, DSOC would merge with the New American Movement, a New Left organization, to become the Democratic Socialists of America.

The newly christened Social Democrats, USA positioned itself as anti–New Left, focusing most of its attention on foreign policy and unions, regularly echoing Meany's denunciations of détente and mimicking his die-hard commitment to anticommunism. Shanker became one of SDUSA's most high-profile spokespersons despite never formally joining the group. Like Meany and Shanker, SDUSA members were particularly fond of Democratic Senator Henry "Scoop" Jackson because of his simultaneous commitment to anticommunism and New Deal liberalism. Kahn, Rustin, and Shanker backed Jackson's failed 1976 bid for the Democratic presidential nomination.[26]

SDUSA members and AFL-CIO officials in the 1970s were both part of an emerging network of hawkish liberals often referred to as "Scoop Jackson Democrats" or "right-wing socialists," but would later be known as neoconservatives (while some of them rejected that label, others embraced it). Despising the New Left and fearful of antiwar radicalism seeping into the Democratic Party, the neoconservatives would gradually move further rightward while increasingly prioritizing foreign policy concerns over domestic issues.

To counter what they viewed as the Democratic Party's leftward drift, they formed the Coalition for a Democratic Majority, which received much of its funding from the AFL-CIO and its affiliated unions. Neoconservatives also helped found the Committee on the Present Danger to encourage greater US military spending, especially for nuclear weapons. In addition to Kirkland, Rustin, and Shanker, the committee's members included a potpourri of anticommunists like J. Peter Grace, former Secretary of State Dean Rusk, modernization theorist Seymour Martin Lipset, and future members of the Ronald Reagan administration William Casey and Jeane Kirkpatrick.

For hawkish social democrats, there was no reason social programs should be prioritized over the defense budget. "Our country need not choose between [guns or butter]," Shanker once argued: "we can do both." Another time, the teachers' union president scoffed at the idea that investments in public education should come from Pentagon cuts, saying, "You won't have very much education if you don't have a free country."[27]

Kahn left his position at the League for Industrial Democracy in 1972 and got a job at the AFL-CIO's headquarters as an assistant and speechwriter to Meany. Together with Shanker, Kahn brought multiple SDUSA members into staff positions within the Federation and its affiliated unions over the next several years. Prominent examples included David Jessup, who became a top staffer at AIFLD; Joel Freedman, who worked for the international affairs department of the Bricklayers and Allied Craftsmen Union; and Kahn's longtime friend Rachelle Horowitz, who served under Shanker as the AFT's political director.

Though a relatively tiny outfit, with a membership never exceeding 1,000, SDUSA gradually attained significant influence in the labor movement's bureaucracy.[28] The marriage between SDUSA and labor officialdom was especially palpable in the literal marriage of Horowitz and AFL-CIO secretary-treasurer Tom Donahue in 1979.

Once Lovestone was put out to pasture in 1973, Kahn became the new editor of the *Free Trade Union News*, the AFL-CIO's anticommunist publication printed in multiple languages and distributed around the world. He also developed a good relationship with the Paris-based Irving Brown, becoming his primary liaison in Washington. By the early 1980s, after Kirkland took over the Federation and made Brown the nominal director of the International Affairs Department, Kahn effectively ran the AFL-CIO's foreign affairs day-to-day.[29]

14

Endowing Democracy

Poland

On August 14, 1980, approximately 17,000 workers at the Lenin Shipyard in Gdańsk, Poland, went on strike. The work stoppage followed years of turmoil in the Polish economy—which had become dependent on loans from Western banks—as well as a recent increase in national food prices. Initially a protest against the firing of a popular worker activist, the strike quickly became a rebuke to Poland's communist government, with the workers demanding an autonomous trade union and more civil liberties.

Upon hearing the news, the Carter administration treaded carefully, fearing that any overt effort by the United States to support the Gdańsk workers might provoke the Soviet Union. The AFL-CIO Executive Council, on the other hand, saw a golden opportunity.

For years, the Federation had been building an ever-growing empire of foreign institutes in the Third World to "contain" communism. With the worker uprising in Poland, AFL-CIO officials were encouraged to become even more audacious, believing they could now take their fight into the communist world itself. Wasting no time in taking advantage of the situation, the Executive Council issued a statement on August 20 declaring the strike "a profoundly important development for human rights, free trade unionism, and democracy in the communist world."[1]

The strike ended on August 31, when the Polish government agreed to the workers' demands, including the right to form a union independent of the ruling United Workers' (Communist) Party. A week later, Lane Kirkland announced the creation of the AFL-CIO's Polish Workers' Aid Fund, which immediately raised an initial $25,000 from the Federation's affiliates. Run by Tom Kahn, the fund would allow US labor to help grow and fortify Poland's newborn trade union—named Solidarność (Solidarity)—which grew to a reputed 10 million members by the end of September 1980, or about half of the country's workforce.[2]

Thanks in part to the International Confederation of Free Trade Unions (ICFTU)'s engagement with the Eastern Bloc over the previous decade, that September, a Swedish labor representative was able to visit Poland on behalf of the International and meet with Lech Wałęsa, the mustachioed electrician who had led the Gdańsk strike and cofounded Solidarność. Wałęsa explained to his ICFTU visitor that his nascent union needed in-kind donations of materials like office equipment, printing paper, cameras, and mimeograph machines.

Kirkland and Kahn responded by using their workers' aid fund to provide at least $100,000 in material donations to Solidarność over the next year. Kahn made no secret of the AFL-CIO's intentions, openly advocating for "the dismantling, by non-nuclear means, of the Communist system."[3]

The cautious Carter administration, and even the normally hawkish neoconservative intellectuals advising Republican presidential candidate Ronald Reagan, warned that the AFL-CIO's interventionist approach might inadvertently trigger a hostile response in the Eastern Bloc. But Kahn and Kirkland dismissed such concerns, confident that their fervent support for Solidarność would not provoke a crackdown.[4] In September 1981, the Polish union held its first national congress, where delegates articulated a desire to create an economy centered on worker cooperatives instead of state-run industries.[5]

Two months later, the AFL-CIO awarded Wałęsa with its first-ever George Meany Human Rights Award (a newly established annual honor curiously named after the man who had enthusiastically endorsed a brutal war on Vietnam that was rife with human rights abuses). The Polish government did not allow Wałęsa to travel to the United States to receive the award in person.[6]

On December 13, 1981, recognizing the potential threat posed by Solidarność and its stridently anticommunist foreign patrons, the recently installed government of General Wojciech Jaruzelski declared martial law in Poland, banning the union and arresting Wałęsa.

Five days later, Kirkland met with President Reagan, who was then nearing the end of his first year in office. Reagan had already declared war on the American working class, cutting taxes on the wealthy while gutting social welfare programs. Having won a significant proportion of blue-collar voters in the 1980 election, Reagan suggested that generally pro-Democratic labor leaders like Kirkland were "out of step with their own rank and file."[7] In August, he had infamously fired and replaced 11,345 striking air traffic controllers from the Professional Air Traffic Controllers Organization (PATCO)—an action the likes of which not even the purportedly "totalitarian" Polish government had taken during the Gdańsk strike.

Reagan's harsh treatment of the air traffic controllers gave encouragement to corporate employers across the country who were busily busting unions, shutting down factories, and moving production to cheaper labor markets overseas. To protest the increasingly anti-labor political climate, Kirkland and the AFL-CIO led a massive march of over 250,000 union members and civil rights activists in Washington, DC, on September 19, an event dubbed "Solidarity Day" in tribute to Solidarność.[8]

Upon greeting Kirkland that December to discuss the imposition of martial law in Poland, Reagan joked, "Well, at least we have something we can agree on," referencing their shared hatred of communism.[9]

Kirkland urged Reagan to impose tough sanctions on Poland and the Soviet Union as punishment for declaring martial law. He demanded slapping a trade embargo on the Eastern Bloc, suspending all aid and credit to the Soviets, and calling in all $25 billion of Polish debt to Western banks. Reagan had been elected as an opponent of détente, and to Kirkland that meant the new president should oppose Western business dealings with communist countries. But Reagan's secretary of state, Alexander Haig, favored a softer approach, believing Poland's Jaruzelski could be persuaded to lift martial law through economic incentives.

A week after meeting with the AFL-CIO president, Reagan announced milder sanctions that included the suspension of $100 million in agricultural aid to Poland, ending incoming flights to the United States from LOT Polish Airlines, canceling scientific exchanges, and halting negotiations on restructuring Poland's foreign debt.[10]

Kirkland was irate. He described the administration's response as "unacceptably weak," complaining that "bankers and businessmen" were running US foreign policy instead of genuinely committed cold warriors.[11] A month later, despite Kirkland and Kahn's ongoing demand that Poland's debts be called in, the US government paid off $71 million that Poland owed to American banks, concerned that allowing default would have negative ramifications on world financial markets. "In effect, President Reagan told the Soviets to disregard his tough talk," Kirkland complained.[12]

On January 30, Kirkland went to the Polish Embassy in Washington to personally deliver a petition demanding the release of Wałęsa and all detained Solidarność activists, which had hundreds of thousands of signatures gathered by the AFL-CIO and its affiliates.[13] Jaruzelski eventually released Wałęsa in November 1982 and ended martial law in July 1983, though Solidarność remained officially banned.

As the administration began lifting US sanctions—a move Wałęsa approved of—Kirkland and Kahn continued calling for hardline measures, speculating that Jaruzelski's liberalizing policies were nothing but a "sham."[14]

One area where the AFL-CIO and Reagan administration were in full agreement was their desire to financially bolster Solidarność. Once martial law was declared and the union was forced underground, anti-communist Polish émigrés opened an office in Brussels for Solidarność to coordinate with foreign allies. Kahn had the AFL-CIO link up with Eric Chenoweth, an associate of his from the League for Industrial Democracy who was running the New York–based Committee in Support of Solidarity. Together, the Federation and Chenoweth's committee sent around $200,000 to Solidarność in 1982 via the Brussels office and other avenues.[15]

Meanwhile, the CIA also got in on the action. Apparently caught off guard by Jaruzelski's crackdown in December 1981, the Agency was less prepared than the AFL-CIO to offer aid to Solidarność. Director of Central Intelligence William Casey thought Kirkland and the Federation "were doing a 'first-rate' job in Poland helping Solidarity—better . . . than CIA could do."[16]

Nevertheless, Reagan tasked Casey and the CIA with covertly providing money and communications equipment to Solidarność leaders operating underground in Poland. Working with Israeli intelligence from an office in Frankfurt, the Agency smuggled radio transmitters into Poland and spun together a complex web of financial channels to secretly send money to the trade union. The operation was so covert that, at least according to CIA sources, Solidarność leaders were largely unaware they were being supported by the Agency at all. Over the course of five years, Solidarność received an estimated total of $10 million in funds that originated with the CIA.[17]

While neither the AFL-CIO nor the Reagan administration had much difficulty getting aid to their Polish allies, both sought to establish a new and permanent mechanism to bankroll anticommunist movements all over the world in the name of "democracy promotion." Working together, they would succeed in late 1983 with the creation of the National Endowment for Democracy (NED).

Covert to Overt

The founding of the NED represented the reaffirmation of an anticommunist consensus among the US institutional establishment, urged on by the neoconservative movement that had grown in the 1970s in reaction to détente.

It began with a series of proposals put forth in the 1970s by US academics, politicos, and foreign policy experts seeking new ways to influence the Third World as modernization theory fell out of style. These eventually sparked high-level discussions between the AFL-CIO, US Chamber of Commerce, and both major political parties, prompting Reagan to announce the launch of what he called "Project Democracy" in June 1982.[18] The project was an attempt to finally solve the problem of the "CIA orphans"—the anticommunist civil society organizations, including unions, that had once been covertly funded by the Agency until the exposés of the late 1960s. In particular, the project studied the feasibility of creating a new, quasi-private agency that would use government money to support anticommunist organizations in other countries, including unions, political parties, news outlets, small businesses, and universities—but doing so openly rather than secretly.

Project Democracy brought to life the shared foreign policy vision of neoconservative Reaganites and members of Social Democrats, USA

(SDUSA). Both wished to revive the ideological Cold War, which had suffered a setback thanks to the rise of the New Left over a decade earlier. While the catastrophe in Vietnam had not stopped Washington's relentless efforts to "contain" left-wing, anticapitalist political movements abroad—as evidenced by the continuation of bloody interventions in the Third World like the 1973 Chilean coup—it had severely weakened the once-popular notion that anticommunism was a moral crusade. Through the policies of détente in the 1970s, the belief that the United States could peacefully coexist with the communist world had started becoming more accepted. The Reagan administration, AFL-CIO, and SDUSA all hoped to dramatically reverse this trend through Project Democracy.

Throughout much of 1982 and 1983, Kirkland served as organized labor's advisor to the Reagan-funded project, as did SDUSA member Eugenia Kemble, an assistant to American Federation of Teachers president Al Shanker. (Kemble's brother, Penn, was also a major figure in SDUSA and in Democratic politics.)

Some congressional Democrats were skeptical of the idea of a new instrument to fund private organizations abroad, with Representative Peter Kostmayer of Pennsylvania calling it a "multimillion-dollar propaganda" program and Representative Stephen Solarz of New York questioning whether the administration was prepared to also promote democracy in authoritarian countries that happened to have pro-US regimes. Many critics accurately saw the proposal as an effort to simply revive and rebrand the CIA's old money-funneling operations that had been exposed in the 1960s.[19]

As AFL-CIO officials lobbied Congress to pass the "democracy promotion" plan, they ironically received the most support from anti-union Republicans. Senator Orrin Hatch of Utah, who only a few years earlier had helped defeat a bill that would have made it easier for US workers to unionize, was an outspoken champion of providing more federal funding to labor's international operations. "The AFL-CIO in general has foreign policy positions to the right of Ronald Reagan," an aide to Hatch told the Washington Post. Though the senator had to do "considerable soul-searching before he decided to deal with the devil," he was ultimately impressed by the Federation's "tremendous leverage for political activity compared to, say, CIA covert operations, which often fail," the aide said.[20]

Thanks to the alliance between the AFL-CIO and Reagan—which developed even as the Federation was gearing up to try defeating the president in the next election—Congress passed legislation creating the National Endowment for Democracy in November 1983. As envisioned, the NED would be a privately run, government-funded foundation transmitting millions of dollars to "pro-democracy" civil society groups in over 100 countries.

Four key nonprofits were designated to receive the lion's share of the NED's grant money, each said to represent a different pillar of pluralist democracy: the Chamber of Commerce's Center for International Private Enterprise, the Democratic Party's National Democratic Institute for International Affairs, the Republican Party's National Republican Institute for International Affairs (later renamed the International Republican Institute), and the AFL-CIO's Free Trade Union Institute.[21]

Originally focused solely on influencing unions in Europe, the FTUI would now function as an umbrella organization for the AFL-CIO's other three foreign institutes, channeling funds from the NED to AIFLD and its offshoots in Africa and Asia—which would as well all continue being partly funded by the US Agency for International Development, as they had been since the 1960s.

The NED

The NED went into operation in April 1984. Kirkland, Shanker, Hatch, and an odd assortment of cold warriors and neoconservatives were appointed to serve on its Board of Directors. Eugenia Kemble—the SDUSA member and Shanker aide who had advocated for the NED's creation—became the Free Trade Union Institute's new director.

The *New York Times* noted how the NED "resembles the aid given by the Central Intelligence Agency in the 1950's, 60's and 70's to bolster pro-American political groups," with the main difference being that the NED operated out in the open. "It would be terrible for democratic groups around the world to be seen as subsidized by the CIA," NED president Carl Gershman, also an SDUSA member, explained. Gershman argued that overt funding to anticommunists abroad was smarter poli-tics. "We saw that [covert funding] in the 60's, and that's why it has been discontinued. We have not had the capability of doing this, and that's why the endowment was created."[22]

For its first fiscal year, Congress allocated a total of $31.3 million to the NED, with $11 million going specifically to the AFL-CIO's Free Trade Union Institute. While the FTUI dispersed most of these funds to AIFLD and the African and Asian institutes, about half a million dollars was devoted to European unions.

Each year between 1984 and 1988, the FTUI gave an average of $300,000 in NED grants to Solidarność's Brussels office, accounting for two-thirds of the office's budget. In total, the NED provided slightly less than $10 million to Polish opposition groups in the mid- to late 1980s. According to historian Gregory Domber, the money was consistently funneled through various sub-grantees and intermediaries like the FTUI before finally getting in the hands of Poles, but it was ultimately Poles who determined how the money was spent.[23]

Only a month after it was launched, the NED and its connection to organized labor sparked outrage. In the run-up to Panama's 1984 presidential election, AIFLD gave $20,000 in NED money to the campaign of Nicolás Ardito Barletta—the candidate backed by Panama's anticommunist strongman, General Manuel Noriega. Upon discovering AIFLD's financial contribution, the US ambassador, James Briggs, lodged a complaint. "It would be embarrassing to the United States if the labor institute's use of endowment funds to support one side in Panama's elections became public knowledge," Briggs wrote in a cable to Washington. "The Ambassador requests that this project be discontinued before the US Government is further compromised in Panama." Ardito Barletta would go on to "win" the election only thanks to extensive vote-stealing orchestrated by his patron Noriega.

After getting ahold of Ambassador Briggs's cable, congressional critics of the NED pounced, arguing that the new government-funded foundation was doing exactly the kind of underhanded meddling they had warned it would do. They managed to rally enough votes in the House of Representatives to discontinue all funding for the Endowment. But after the Reagan administration intervened, the House backed down from its initial vote and narrowly approved an $18 million budget for the NED for the next fiscal year.[24]

In late 1985, the NED was again the target of criticism because of its ties to the AFL-CIO's foreign institutes. That December, a Paris-based investigative reporter uncovered that the Free Trade Union Institute had given $1.4 million in NED money to groups opposing French president François Mitterrand. Leader of the country's Socialist Party, Mitterrand had controversially invited the Communist Party into his coalition government. The bulk of the money had gone to Force Ouvrière, the anticommunist "free" trade union center Irving Brown helped create in the 1940s, while $575,000 went to the National Inter-University Union, a right-wing student organization with reputed ties to the illegal paramilitary group Civic Action Service.

The revelation also included details of an informal agreement between the NED and the AFL-CIO stating that the use of these funds was to remain secret. Indeed, the NED's annual report had not included anything about the Free Trade Union Institute's subsidies to the anti-Mitterrand groups. As the *New York Times* noted, the arrangement was startingly reminiscent of Brown's intrigues in France after World War II.[25]

The Philippines

Meanwhile on the other side of the globe, NED money allowed the AFL-CIO's Asian institute to strengthen its regional presence. Since its founding at the height of the Vietnam War, the Asian American Free Labor Institute had been promoting "free" trade unionism in South Korea, India, Thailand, Indonesia, Turkey, and elsewhere.

By the time the NED was established, the Asian institute's most important program was in the Philippines, a nation gripped by political unrest in the 1980s. The country was ruled by Ferdinand Marcos, who was elected president in 1965 but instituted a dictatorship eight years later in the name of crushing a communist guerilla insurgency. Marcos was a reliable Washington ally, which especially mattered because the Philippines was a former colony of the United States and continued to be home to several US military installations, particularly the large Subic Bay Naval Base.

In 1983, longtime opposition leader Benigno Aquino Jr.—a former senator who had been exiled by Marcos—returned to the Philippines only to be assassinated upon arriving at Manila's airport. This brazen murder, combined with a nationwide economic slump, triggered sustained popular protests against Marcos in the mid-1980s.

The only legally recognized union center in the country was the Trade Union Congress of the Philippines (TUCP). Formed in 1975 with the assistance of the AFL-CIO's Asian institute and the blessing of the Marcos regime, the TUCP embraced pro-US, anticommunist "free" trade unionism. In response, left-wing Filipino unionists founded the KMU (May First Movement) on May 1, 1980. An independent trade union center with reputed ties to the country's Communist Party, the KMU was committed to militant class struggle and openly opposed both the Marcos dictatorship and US imperialism. Accordingly, the new union center led a series of powerful strikes, securing gains for workers and putting the TUCP's more tepid brand of business unionism to shame. By 1985, the KMU's membership had grown to 500,000, while the TUCP's had dropped from 2 million to 1.2 million.[26]

Fearing the growth of this rival organization, especially amid the mass social unrest following Aquino's assassination, the AFL-CIO's Asian institute provided $5.7 million in NED money to the TUCP between 1983 and 1988.[27] The funds were used for housing projects, training programs, and public relations campaigns, but the ultimate purpose was to drive Filipino workers away from the militant KMU. As Don Phillips, the Asian institute's country director for the Philippines, said in 1985: "Imagine if you have $100,000 to give out to families in $500 chunks. Your stock goes way up, faster than the stock of any of the militant labor groups."[28]

To their US patrons, TUCP officials presented themselves as the alternative to an unpopular dictatorship on the one hand and to the specter of communism on the other. In 1985, the AFL-CIO bestowed TUCP general secretary Ernesto Herrera with the annual George Meany Human Rights Award. "The dictatorial Marcos regime cannot possibly like us. Nor can the communists in the guise of unionists," Herrera said upon accepting the award at the Federation's convention in Anaheim.[29]

At the urging of the Reagan administration, which hoped to restore legitimacy to the Marcos regime, the Philippines held a snap presidential election in February 1986 pitting the dictator against Corazon Aquino, widow of the assassinated opposition leader. After extensive fraud and violence at the polls, Marcos declared victory. But Aquino, who had mass public support behind her, refused to concede and quickly won the backing of reform-minded military officers and the archbishop of Manila.

After a tense, three-day standoff that saw millions of Filipino protesters take to the streets in defiance of the regime, the military defected to Aquino's side and Marcos fled the country. The People Power Revolution, as it came to be called, was hailed as a nonviolent transition from dictatorship to democracy. A bipartisan committee of US senators, including Orrin Hatch, took partial credit, claiming that the NED money that had made its way into the country was "an important element in the successful democratic elections and transition in the Philippines."[30]

In the more liberal political atmosphere under President Aquino, the KMU grew in prominence as its leader, Rolando Olalia, formed a new leftist political party. This alarmed anticommunist forces in the Philippines, who murdered Olalia and his driver in November 1986.[31] On the island of Cebu, copper miners who were members of a KMU-affiliated union also faced violent attacks at the hands of what scholar Kim Scipes calls an "unholy alliance" between the Atlas Mining company, police, right-wing vigilantes, and a TUCP-affiliated union. The TUCP affiliate had previously represented the mine workers in the 1970s. Unhappy with business unionism, the miners eventually switched to the KMU in 1985 and proceeded to strike, winning raises and better job security. Wanting to reclaim their position at the copper mine, and flush with AFL-CIO-provided cash, the TUCP pushed for a new union representation election.

As Scipes explains, the TUCP used its own local radio station to churn out anticommunist propaganda targeting KMU activists—stoking violence, paying vigilantes (some of them the former officers of the TUCP union that had previously represented the mine workers), and effectively helping the mining company in its union-busting efforts. Despite repeated violent attacks by right-wing mobs targeting KMU activists, including the firing of machine guns at their homes and union offices, the local police did nothing. The company even allowed vigilante leaders to hold seminars at the mine, where they told employees that the KMU-affiliated union was a communist front.

Between 1987 and 1989, at least ten members of the KMU affiliate at the copper mine were murdered, partly thanks to the anticommunist hysteria whipped up by AFL-CIO-backed TUCP. Nevertheless, when the union representation election finally took place in 1989, the workers voted overwhelmingly to stay with the KMU.[32]

South Africa

While AFL-CIO leaders waged an unapologetically interventionist campaign of "democracy promotion" in communist Poland during the 1980s, they took a decidedly more ambivalent approach to opposing apartheid in South Africa.

The countries of southern Africa had avoided the decolonization trend of the 1950s and 1960s. South Africa and Zimbabwe (then called Rhodesia) each had white settler populations maintaining repressive, racist governments, while Namibia (then called South West Africa) was ruled by South Africa in violation of international law. For their part, Angola and Mozambique remained formal Portuguese colonies until 1975, becoming independent only after a revolution in Portugal the previous year.

When Angola and Mozambique won independence, white rule in the region was jeopardized. South African forces invaded Angola, with US support, to prevent the communist-aligned MPLA (People's Movement for the Liberation of Angola) from taking power. Despite being thousands of miles away and not holding superpower status, Cuba remarkably sent tens of thousands of troops into Angola to help the MPLA successfully fight off the white South African invaders.[33] A civil war ensued between the MPLA and its anticommunist rivals, which functioned as a proxy war between the Cubans and Soviets on one side and the United States, South Africa, and the US-backed dictatorship in Zaire on the other. For Washington, concerns about the potential spread of communism in southern Africa trumped any opposition to white supremacy and apartheid.

Amid this newfound regional instability, South Africa's apartheid regime was continuously challenged by the county's majority Black population. Beginning in 1973 with mass strikes in the port city of Durban, a wave of work stoppages and demonstrations broke out across the country. These were met with violent repression—most notably when the police and army opened fire on thousands of protesting schoolchildren in Soweto in 1976—prompting widespread international condemnation. In early 1978, for example, the AFL-CIO Executive Council called on Washington to scale back its social, economic, and athletic ties with South Africa and demanded that Black-led unions in the country be legalized.[34]

At the same time, an intensifying anticolonial war in Rhodesia waged by African nationalists finally forced that country's white government to accept Black control in the last years of the 1970s, leading to the establishment of the Republic of Zimbabwe in April 1980. Feeling the pressure on all sides, but still hoping to maintain apartheid rule, the South African government made very limited concessions, including moving toward gradually granting independence to Namibia and, in 1979, allowing Black-led unions to register for legal status.

In response to these fast-moving developments, the AFL-CIO decided the time was right to ramp up its presence in South Africa. For decades, the Federation had struggled to gain a foothold in the country, as the only legally recognized unions were whites-only. As in many other places during the Cold War, the AFL-CIO's "free" trade unionists wanted to help mold a pro-US, nonradical labor movement among Black South Africans to deny power to the Left.

This would be a tall order, since most of the anti-apartheid movement was unapologetically leftist, including the African National Congress (ANC), the country's major anti-apartheid political center, which had long been allied with communists and was supported by the Soviet Union. The ANC and other anticapitalist groups sought nothing less than the complete and immediate dismantling of the apartheid system.

But top AFL-CIO officials like Kirkland preferred a more moderate strategy of gradually weakening apartheid in hopes that it would wither away. In particular, they hoped that with the ability to form legally recognized, "responsible" business unions, Black workers in South Africa would improve their economic lot and attain middle-class status, which would theoretically allow them entry into the country's existing political system to change it from within.[35] Despite the violent racism and brutal repression of the apartheid regime, the AFL-CIO's internationalists preferred tepid reformism to the possibility of allowing leftists to win power in South Africa.

The AFL-CIO's foreign institute for Africa—the African American Labor Center—saw its annual subsidy from USAID increase from $3 million in 1979 to $8.5 million by 1982, with much of the money going toward educational programs for South African unionists. Multiple South African union activists were brought to New York City for a training program with the help of Maida Springer, who had been US labor's key diplomat to Africa in the 1950s and 1960s before retiring, but who now returned to work as a consultant to the AFL-CIO's African institute between 1977 and 1982. At Springer's urging, the African American Labor Center recruited participants from more left-wing unions to try convincing South African workers that US labor was not playing favorites. This backfired, with several of the leftist participants openly criticizing the AFL-CIO's international policies during the training, and at least one of them accusing Springer of keeping close tabs on him during his time in the United States.[36]

In February 1981, Kirkland and the Executive Council announced the "Program of Action in Support of Black Trade Unions in South Africa." Run by the African American Labor Center, the program was meant to foster better coordination between US and South African labor to promote racial equality through peaceful means. Tapped to lead this initiative was Nelson "Nana" Mahomo. A South African living in the United States, he had cofounded of the Pan Africanist Congress, a rival to the ANC formed in 1959. As the Pan Africanist Congress's foreign representative in the early 1960s, Mahomo met Irving Brown, toured the United States, and became a friend of the AFL-CIO.

After his rivals back home accused him of being a CIA agent—an allegation never definitively substantiated—Mahomo was expelled from the Pan Africanist Congress and moved to London. By the 1970s, he was living in the United States, where he made a documentary film about apartheid with AFL-CIO funding. Though he had no trade union experience and had been living outside South Africa for nearly two decades, in the 1980s he was selected to run the AFL-CIO's new South Africa program from an office in Washington, where he spent much of his time pressing USAID for more funding.[37]

The AFL-CIO's Program of Action encouraged more training and education for Black unionists, but sidestepped the question of boycotting, sanctioning, or divesting from South Africa—the primary tactics embraced by the ANC-led international anti-apartheid movement. Despite issuing resolutions opposing apartheid, Kirkland and other Federation officials were in line with the Reagan administration's policy of "constructive engagement," which rejected putting hard pressure on the South African government through boycotts and divestment in favor of a softer approach.

"Constructive engagement" was a Cold War calculation, since Washington feared the spread of communism in southern Africa and

knew that the apartheid regime—which routinely redbaited the ANC—
could be counted on to remain firmly anticommunist. The soft approach
was also unsurprisingly favored by US corporations with extensive
investments in South Africa, like General Motors and Mobil.

To promote its Program of Action, the AFL-CIO Executive Council
dispatched a small delegation to South Africa for two weeks in September
1982 consisting of Irving Brown, African American Labor Center director Patrick O'Farrell, International Ladies' Garment Workers' Union
president Sol Chick Chaikin, and A. Philip Randolph Institute vice president Frederick O'Neal.[38]

The four men were greeted with suspicion on the part of many Black
unionists and journalists. Some of the English-language South African
press "chose to misrepresent the purpose of the visit and cultivate a
climate of hostility," the delegation later reported, especially through
"misleading articles which raised a CIA scare, attempting to character-
ize the AFL-CIO as an arm of the CIA."[39] Two unions—the Motor
Assembly and Component Workers' Union and the South African
Allied Workers' Union—refused to meet with the AFL-CIO visitors, but
the delegation reported having cordial meetings with twenty-eight other
unions.[40]

Two months after the delegation, the AFL-CIO gave its second annual
George Meany Human Rights Award to South Africa's Mangosuthu
Gatsha Buthelezi. A Zulu chief and head of the Inkatha Freedom Party,
Buthelezi was anticommunist and ostensibly anti-apartheid. He was
also one of the few Black South African leaders to oppose boycotts,
divestments, and sanctions. While much of the anti-apartheid movement considered him a collaborationist, in the eyes of the AFL-CIO's
top officials, Buthelezi and his Inkatha party appeared to be the perfect
alternative to the leftist ANC.[41]

After the left-wing, pro-ANC Congress of South African Trade
Unions (COSATU) was formed—a significant development in the
growing anti-apartheid movement—Buthelezi founded his own "avowedly capitalist trade union" in early 1986. At an inaugural rally for his
United Workers Union of South Africa, Buthelezi's supporters held a
mock funeral for COSATU and trampled on the symbolic coffin. The
new union openly opposed divestment and strikes, arguing that such
tactics would only harm the South African economy and hurt Black
workers. Buthelezi's union attacked anyone who supported divestment,

including Nobel Peace Prize–winning Bishop Desmond Tutu—with its members carrying signs that read "Bishop Tutu deserves execution."

The AFL-CIO had likely encouraged Buthelezi to form the union, though Federation officials denied providing any financial support.[42] It would later be revealed that Buthelezi, recipient of the Meany Human Rights Award, was secretly funded by the apartheid regime, specifically the South African Police and its ruthless Security Branch. What's more, members of Buthelezi's union violently attacked COSATU-affiliated workers at a coal mine near the town of Vryheid in June 1986, killing 11 and injuring over 100 others.[43]

In proclaiming their opposition to divestment and sanctions, the AFL-CIO and the Reagan administration all regularly cited Leon Sullivan, an African American Baptist minister and board member of General Motors (which had several operations in South Africa). In his role at GM, Sullivan devised the "Sullivan Principles" in the late 1970s, a set of fair labor practices for US corporations in South Africa to follow. The argument behind the Sullivan Principles was that as long as companies treated their Black South African workers well, they need not be pressured to divest from the country. Like Reagan's "constructive engagement" policy and the AFL-CIO's Program for Action, the Sullivan Principles promoted a go-it-slow and procapitalist approach to ending apartheid.

Backers of the Sullivan Principles, including AFL-CIO officials, went so far as to implicitly argue that boycotts, divestments, and sanctions were racist because they would negatively impact Black workers in South Africa. "No Black trade unionist I have met, no Black worker . . . supports that idea," veteran AFL-CIO internationalist Irving Brown preposterously said of divestment, a tactic championed by the ANC.[44]

But after facing mounting criticism from many African American anti-apartheid activists, in early 1985, the AFL-CIO invited about a dozen South African unionists to a conference in Washington to discuss selective divestment. Leon Sullivan was brought in to speak, but leftist anti-apartheid activists who supported full divestment were not welcome, a point that reportedly angered some of the South African unionists who attended.[45]

The Sullivan Principles had little real impact in South Africa. Only 66,000 out of 6 million workers were employed by US companies that had signed on to the principles, and even within those firms, 97 percent of managerial positions belonged to whites while Black workers were at the very bottom of the wage scale.[46]

A key turning point for the international anti-apartheid movement came in late 1984. In November, nearly 1 million Black workers staged a two-day general strike in South Africa to protest apartheid. The mass work stoppage was met with a bloody crackdown by the government, with nearly 200 strikers killed and thousands jailed or fired from their jobs. Among those imprisoned were a dozen leaders of the nation's Black unions.

In the United States that same month, Reagan was re-elected president. Earlier in the 1984 election season, African American civil rights leader Jesse Jackson had waged an energetic campaign to be the Democratic Party's presidential nominee, ultimately losing to former vice president Walter Mondale. Jackson's progressive campaign—the most successful of any Black presidential candidate up to that point—had emphasized the moral imperative of using US influence to bring apartheid in South Africa to a swift end.

Learning of the unfolding repression in South Africa that November, US civil rights and anti-apartheid activists decided that there was no time to be dispirited by Jackson's defeat and Reagan's re-election. On November 21, three African American leaders who had supported the Jackson campaign—Randall Robinson of the advocacy organization TransAfrica, US Civil Rights Commissioner Mary Frances Berry, and District of Columbia congressional delegate Walter Fauntroy—staged a civil disobedience protest at the South African Embassy in Washington, refusing to leave the building until they were arrested.[47]

In the days after Robinson, Berry, and Fauntroy's protest, more civil rights activists held similar nonviolent actions in front of the South African Embassy and were also arrested, including Rosa Parks, Yolanda King (daughter of Martin Luther King Jr.), and several Black members of Congress. White liberals also began participating, and the protests soon spread to college campuses and South African consulates across the United States in what came to be known as the Free South Africa Movement.[48]

In San Francisco, left-wing, African American dockworkers with the International Longshore and Warehouse Union (ILWU) Local 10 provided what scholar Manning Marable called "the most militant contribution" to the nascent movement. Starting on November 24, ILWU Local 10 members refused to unload a Dutch cargo ship carrying goods from South Africa, including steel and auto glass. "It's a matter of conscience," explained Local 10 member Leo Robinson, noting that he and his fellow workers were "thinking about our brothers and sisters in apartheid-run South Africa."[49]

As labor historian Peter Cole has shown, the actions of Robinson and his fellow dockworkers were nothing new for the ILWU, which—as a traditionally leftist union that was independent of the AFL-CIO—had a long track record of using its position at a strategic chokepoint in the global economy to support social justice causes around the world. In 1976, rank-and-file members of Local 10, led by Leo Robinson, had formed the Southern African Liberation Support Committee. Working with religious and community activists in the Bay Area, the committee had similarly boycotted a ship containing South African cargo on Easter Sunday 1977, and had also donated funds and supplies to liberation movements in southern Africa.

Local 10's boycott of the cargo ship in late 1984, which was in violation of their union contract, lasted eleven days. It was finally ended by a court injunction that threatened to impose hefty fines on Local 10 and possible prison sentences for the local's leaders. The dockworkers' protest inspired students at the nearby University of California, Berkeley, to ramp up their own anti-apartheid organizing, holding large campus rallies with Local 10 members as guest speakers. Student activists successfully got the university to divest $3 billion in South Africa–related stock in 1986.[50]

Incensed by the imprisonment of the South African union leaders following the November general strike, Kirkland called on the AFL-CIO to also join the Free South Africa Movement. On December 4, three top US labor officials were among a group of protesters arrested at a demonstration outside the South African Embassy in Washington: AFL-CIO secretary-treasurer Tom Donahue, Newspaper Guild president Charles Perlik, and United Steelworkers vice president Leon Lynch. The imprisoned South African union leaders were released a few days later.[51]

Sit-ins and demonstrations at the South African Embassy, consulates across the United States, and other institutions with ties to South Africa continued throughout the winter, with over 2,000 people arrested by mid-1985, including UAW president Owen Bieber, United Mine

Workers president Richard Trumka, and AFSCME secretary-treasurer William Lucy. One of the highest-ranking African American unionists, Lucy was one of the most prominent anti-apartheid activists in the US labor movement.

The UAW, UMW, and AFSCME—which all had large Black memberships—were the most vocally anti-apartheid unions within the AFL-CIO. The UAW advocated for the release of imprisoned Black South African unionists, the UMW called on the US Customs Service to halt the importation of South African coal, and AFSCME pressured state employee pension funds to divest $20 billion from South Africa.

Meanwhile, state and local lawmakers across the country introduced bills calling for divestment. Even some congressional Republicans began openly criticizing Reagan's "constructive engagement" policy. The AFL-CIO came out in opposition to any new US investments in South Africa, but still refused to support divestment and sanctions.[52]

The Federation changed its position only in 1986 amid pressure from African American union members with the Coalition of Black Trade Unionists, civil rights activists, members of Congress, and South African unions.[53] That summer, Kirkland paid a visit to South Africa and met with Black workers and union officials. On returning to the United States in August, the AFL-CIO president finally came out in favor of sanctions and divestment. He explained that Black South Africans understood how economic sanctions may inadvertently hurt them, but that they felt it was worth it. "One of the black union leaders told me, 'We know more freedom isn't cheap. Freedom is worth any price,'" Kirkland said.[54]

Though Kirkland and the AFL-CIO's leadership had not hesitated to demand harsh sanctions against communist Poland in 1981, it took years for them to finally reach the same position on apartheid South Africa. That same month, August 1986, Congress passed the Comprehensive Anti-Apartheid Act over Reagan's veto. The law slapped South Africa with US sanctions until such time as the country ended apartheid. It was the beginning of the end of white rule in South Africa.

15

Civil War

After a decade of détente, President Ronald Reagan and his neoconservative advisors in the 1980s were eager to revive the Cold War and resurrect the spirit of US militarism after it had been dealt a severe blow in Vietnam. Nowhere was the president's belligerence more apparent than in Central America and the Caribbean, where he made it a top priority to destroy left-wing nationalist movements that he alleged were part of a communist conspiracy to bring the Americas into a Soviet orbit.

In Guatemala and El Salvador, the Reagan administration supported authoritarian regimes in their efforts to eliminate guerilla insurgencies by any means, including genocidal massacres targeting rural and Indigenous civilians. In Nicaragua, where the leftist Sandinista revolutionaries had already ousted the US-backed Somoza dictatorship in 1979, Reagan and the CIA worked to destabilize the new government by financing and training right-wing Contras (counterrevolutionaries) and mining the nation's harbors—actions the International Court of Justice later ruled were violations of international law.

Most egregiously, in 1983, Reagan launched a full-scale US military invasion of the tiny Caribbean island nation of Grenada to overthrow its Marxist government. All told, Washington sent billions of dollars in military aid to the region during the 1980s, fueling terrifying levels of violence. According to historian Greg Grandin, "US allies in Central America during Reagan's two terms killed over 300,000 people, tortured hundreds of thousands, and drove millions into exile."[1]

Nicaragua and Grenada

Despite Reagan's anti-labor policies at home, the AFL-CIO's leadership readily went along with his anticommunist aggression in the Western Hemisphere. In Nicaragua, AIFLD bankrolled the Confederation of Trade Union Unity, an anti-Sandinista labor organization. Formed in the 1960s with the Institute's help, the confederation had been the only national trade union center tolerated by the Somoza dictatorship due to its cozy relationship with the regime.

The Sandinistas understandably did not trust the confederation— which was allegedly in league with the Contras to coordinate acts of industrial sabotage—and placed legal restrictions on it. AIFLD decried this as an assault on "free" trade unionism and, claiming it could not function under such "totalitarian" conditions, the Institute pulled out of Nicaragua in 1982, something it had not done during the Somoza era and did not do in Brazil or Chile after those countries were taken over by right-wing dictatorships. Still, AIFLD continued generously funding the Confederation of Trade Union Unity from afar with money from the National Endowment for Democracy.[2]

In October 1983, Reagan unilaterally and unexpectedly deployed 6,000 US troops to Grenada, where the leftist New Jewel Movement had been in power since a 1979 revolution. At the time, Reagan claimed the revolutionary government posed a threat to 800 US medical students in Grenada and that the island was on its way to becoming a base for the Soviets and Cubans to "export terror and undermine democracy," but he later admitted that he believed a quick and decisive military victory could help shake off the American public's reluctance to use armed intervention abroad after the Vietnam War.[3] As the invasion got under way, AIFLD immediately sprang into action. The Institute's executive director, Bill Doherty, "wangled his way into Grenada before the shooting stopped," according to the *Reader's Digest*.[4]

With the Grenadian labor movement in disarray amid the invasion, Doherty strengthened the more conservative union leaders who had opposed the revolutionary government. With AIFLD's direction, anticommunist unionists quickly went about replacing pro–New Jewel graffiti with messages welcoming the invasion forces, which the US military pointed to as proof that the invasion had popular support. A US interagency government report two months later stated that the Institute was already "developing an extensive plan to reorient and train the labor leadership."[5]

El Salvador

Working in close coordination, the State Department and AIFLD stepped up their presence in El Salvador after a group of reformist military officers seized control of the government in October 1979. Supported by the United States, the new junta aimed to keep El Salvador from going the way of revolutionary Nicaragua. Both the State Department and AIFLD endorsed a counterinsurgency strategy that hinged upon propping up political centrists in El Salvador, a venture doomed to fail as the country's Left and Right became ever more polarized.

Resenting even token attempts at social and economic reform, the Salvadoran Right mobilized death squads that murdered with impunity, while the Left—faced with escalating repression—became convinced that armed struggle was the only way to topple the country's elites. By late 1980, El Salvador was in the grips of a bloody civil war. Determined to deny victory to the leftist guerillas, the incoming Reagan administration resolved to increase military assistance to the Salvadoran government, ensuring that the conflict would drag on throughout the 1980s and ultimately leave some 80,000 people dead.

In the late 1960s, AIFLD's Agrarian Union Development Department used training programs and small-scale community development projects in El Salvador's countryside to begin organizing campesino associations called "communal unions." Under the direction of AIFLD staffer Michael Hammer—a former Air Force mechanic who graduated from Georgetown's School of Foreign Service—these associations were in 1969 combined into a politically moderate national campesino organization called UCS (Salvadoran Communal Union).[6]

From the start, UCS was meant to steer rural workers away from radicalism by helping them form cooperatives and advocating for modest reforms to improve their standard of living. But any type of campesino organizing was a highly sensitive issue in El Salvador, which was still scarred by a failed 1932 rural uprising that resulted in the systematic state murder of between 10,000 and 30,000 campesinos, a traumatic event known as *La Matanza* (the massacre).[7]

In 1973, large landholders complained UCS was becoming "overly enthusiastic" in trying to empower campesinos. In response, Salvadoran president Arturo Molina kicked AIFLD out of the country.[8] Despite the Institute's departure, UCS continued to exist with protection from the US Embassy and AIFLD continued influencing the campesino organization from outside the country over the next several years. UCS membership increased to as much as 100,000, and the organization remained on friendly terms with the Salvadoran government, which established an "agrarian transformation" agency meant to eventually implement some kind of land reform. In the late 1970s, José Rodolfo Viera, himself a campesino, became the head of UCS. Though his formal education only went up to the fourth grade, Viera was a shrewd and competent leader trusted by the UCS rank and file.[9]

In mid-1979, facing growing left-wing protests and watching in horror as the Sandinistas took over neighboring Nicaragua, the Salvadoran regime welcomed AIFLD back into the country, with Hammer serving as the Institute's lead representative. Only months later, reformist military officers seized control of the government and, after a power struggle among them, a new ruling junta embraced a counterinsurgency strategy that adopted a combination of repression and reform. UCS leader Viera was tapped to serve as head of the government's agrarian transformation agency.

In March 1980, with technical support from AIFLD's Hammer and UCS's Viera, the junta implemented the first phase of agrarian reform, which involved expropriating large estates comprising about 15 to 17 percent of El Salvador's arable land and handing them over to newly formed cooperatives. But this was accompanied with declaration of a state of siege, which imposed severe restrictions on travel, press freedom, and freedom of association, while also granting state security forces virtually unlimited power to arrest and detain "subversives."

Soldiers were deployed to the countryside as part of the siege, primarily in areas affected by the agrarian reform. Ostensibly there to enforce the reform by ensuring that landlords peacefully gave up their estates, the military actually hunted down suspected guerillas and their sympathizers. In the first year of the agrarian reform, state security forces murdered an estimated 500 campesino leaders and hundreds more cooperative members. Though initially scheduled to last thirty days, the state of siege would be continuously extended over the next seven years.[10]

Implementation of the agrarian reform's second phase, which would have transferred ownership of 70 percent of the country's most fertile and productive land from a tiny elite to poor campesinos, was perpetually blocked by right-wingers in the oligarchy and military, meaning that the reform could never live up to its promise of genuine social and economic change. In the meantime, in the face of escalating repression, the country's mass left-wing organizations, guerilla armies, and Communist Party united in late 1980 to form the Farabundo Martí National Liberation Front (FMLN). Named in honor of one of the organizers of the 1932 campesino uprising, the FMLN dedicated itself to overthrowing the oligarchy and military regime through armed struggle.

Though they had effectively defeated agrarian reform and used its accompanying state of siege to terrorize campesinos, the Salvadoran Right was nevertheless outraged that such a reform had ever been conceived of in the first place, and swore revenge. On the night of January 3, 1981, Hammer, Viera, and Mark David Pearlman—a young agrarian reform expert who had recently begun working for AIFLD— were fatally shot in the coffee shop of San Salvador's Sheraton Hotel. It was the first time in AIFLD's nineteen-year history that any of its staff had been murdered.

The audacious attack, carried out by two plainclothes national guardsmen, was later determined to have been ordered by right-wing military officers with ties to notorious death squad leader Roberto D'Aubuisson, who had engineered the assassination of Archbishop Óscar Romero the year before. Nevertheless, AIFLD director Doherty openly speculated that maybe leftists were responsible. "We don't know who did the killing," he said in his first public remarks after the incident. "It could have been people either from the extreme right or extreme left."[11]

Coming one month after a death squad raped and killed four US churchwomen near El Salvador's international airport, the Sheraton murders shocked Washington. The incoming Reagan administration— eager to increase military assistance to El Salvador to defeat the

FMLN—pleaded with the junta to bring the killers to justice to avoid jeopardizing the flow of US aid. Doherty and the AFL-CIO helped convince Congress to require President Reagan to "certify" that the Salvadoran government was making progress toward the prosecution of all those involved in the murders of the churchwomen and AIFLD staffers as a condition of future military assistance.

Between 1982 and 1985, a succession of Salvadoran courts, stacked with judges from the country's elite, threw out all charges against the officers who had masterminded the AIFLD murders on the basis of "insufficient evidence." These decisions were upheld by El Salvador's Supreme Court. Only the two gunmen were ever tried. They were convicted in February 1986, but released in December 1987 as part of a peace plan granting amnesty to those imprisoned for political crimes.

All the while, Reagan continued certifying to Congress that progress was being made in bringing the death squads to heel so military aid would continue. For their part, AFL-CIO officials went back and forth on their support for ongoing US military assistance depending on the latest developments in the Sheraton case. AIFLD's program in El Salvador became its most expensive of any country in the 1980s, receiving between $2 million and $4 million per year from USAID.[12]

Besides backing the failed agrarian reform, AIFLD devoted most of its resources in El Salvador to supporting the nation's center-right Christian Democratic Party and its leader, José Napoleón Duarte. In late 1980, the Institute helped form a coalition of six nonradical unions and campesino organizations called the UPD (Democratic Popular Unity), which claimed to represent 300,000 workers and peasants.

In addition to being moderate, all the organizations within the UPD relied on funding from USAID via AIFLD. During El Salvador's high-stakes 1984 presidential election, the Institute gave up to $800,000 to Duarte's campaign through the UPD, while the CIA also gave an estimated $200,000. In exchange for the UPD's support, Duarte and the Christian Democrats promised to enact genuine social and economic reforms, rein in the death squads, cease the repression, and sue for peace with the FMLN guerillas—promises that would quickly be broken.

Much to the delight of AIFLD and the State Department, the Christian Democrats were victorious in the 1984 election and Duarte became El

Salvador's new president. But soon afterward, some in the UPD began publicly criticizing Duarte for brushing off their pleas to work on finding a negotiated settlement with the guerillas. Such criticisms dismayed AIFLD leaders because, along with the Reagan administration and Duarte himself, they still believed the guerillas would be defeated outright and were therefore unserious about resolving the civil war through peace talks.

Fearing the UPD might be becoming too sympathetic with the FMLN, in December 1984, the Institute created a new Salvadoran labor confederation over which it could maintain more direct control. Disillusioned with both Duarte and AIFLD, in early 1986 the remaining UPD affiliates joined forces with El Salvador's more radical, leftist unions to form the National Union of Salvadoran Workers. By the late 1980s, then, the Salvadoran labor movement was divided into two major factions, one tied to the FMLN revolutionaries and the other almost totally a creation of AIFLD and the US Embassy.[13]

The National Labor Committee

AIFLD's many intrigues in El Salvador did not escape the notice of US labor leaders and union members. Like much of the public, US unionists feared that Reagan's aggressive interventionism in Central America might escalate into another Vietnam-style quagmire.

Many US labor activists questioned why the AFL-CIO was working so closely with the blatantly anti-union Reagan on foreign policy issues, especially in El Salvador. Moreover, left-leaning US unionists were still wounded from the AFL-CIO's staunch support for the Vietnam War—which damaged organized labor's progressive credibility—and did not want to see that mistake repeated.

After the AIFLD murders in January 1981, several cross-union committees were formed in cities like New York, Boston, San Jose, and Seattle with the goal of getting the wider labor movement to oppose Reagan's Central America policy. By July, over 100 union locals had passed resolutions opposing further US military aid to El Salvador.[14]

The cross-union committee on Central America that was organized in New York City held its first meetings at the headquarters of the Amalgamated Clothing and Textile Workers Union (ACTWU), with union staffer David Dyson playing an unofficial leadership role. An ordained Presbyterian minister turned organizer, Dyson worked for ACTWU's Union Label Department where he helped mobilize public support for high-profile campaigns at companies like J. P. Stevens. ACTWU's then secretary-treasurer (and future president), Jacob "Jack" Sheinkman, took special interest in building national labor opposition to Reagan's foreign policy to prevent another Vietnam.

Representing clothing workers, ACTWU was already being hit hard by the offshoring of textile manufacturing, and progressive figures like Sheinkman and Dyson were determined to challenge the power of multinational corporations by supporting militant trade unions in Central America.

In September 1981, Sheinkman reached out to the presidents of the United Auto Workers and International Association of Machinists— Douglas Fraser and William Winpisinger, respectively—and together the three union officials founded the National Labor Committee in Support of Democracy and Human Rights in El Salvador (NLC). By November, six other national union presidents had signed on to the NLC, and the group went public calling on Washington to cease military aid to El Salvador and advocating for a peaceful resolution to the country's civil war. Dyson would serve as the new group's sole full-time staff person.

The launching of the National Labor Committee would prove to be one of the most significant developments for US labor internationalism since the start of the Cold War. While openly opposing Reagan, the group was also tacitly lodging a "vote of no confidence in the way the AFL-CIO was handling the Central America policy questions and the question of unions in Central America," Dyson later said.[15]

NLC membership was restricted to national union presidents (with the exception of Sheinkman, who only became ACTWU's president in 1987), while local labor leaders and rank-and-file unionists participated in the local cross-union committees, which sometimes coordinated with the NLC. By 1983, twelve national unions belonged to the National Labor Committee through their top officials, including ACTWU; the UAW; the Machinists; the American Federation of State, County, and Municipal Employees; the Newspaper Guild; the Oil, Chemical and Atomic Workers; the United Farm Workers; and the National Education Association, among others. In June 1983, the National Labor Committee sent a delegation of seven union leaders to El Salvador on a fact-finding mission, including Sheinkman and Dyson of ACTWU.[16]

After meeting with US Embassy officials who mistakenly assumed they were there on behalf of AIFLD, visiting imprisoned Salvadoran trade unionists whom the AFL-CIO had abandoned due their left-wing politics, and getting a grim picture of the overall violence and repression facing union activists in the country, the NLC delegation published their findings in a report widely circulated within US labor circles. The report charged that there was "no trade union freedom in El Salvador" and that Salvadoran unionists were "workers who have organized to fight for dignity and decency," which made them supposed "subversives" according to "the twisted logic of politics in El Salvador."

The report further asserted that the AIFLD-supported agrarian reform was "not working" and was even "structured not to work" because rightists in the Salvadoran government were blocking its full implementation. Overall, the NLC delegation argued that by supplying the Salvadoran government with military aid, Washington was complicit in severe labor and human rights abuses—a message that directly went against the AFL-CIO's official line that thanks to US assistance, progress was being made toward turning El Salvador into a beacon of democracy.[17]

As a result of the fact-finding mission, the National Labor Committee developed friendly relationships with several leftist Salvadoran unions whose leaders and members routinely faced violent repression at the hands of death squads and state security forces. For the next several years, the National Labor Committee and its network of US labor activists would rapidly jump into action whenever reports emerged of Salvadoran unionists getting arrested or being "disappeared." Pressuring both the US and Salvadoran governments, the NLC helped as many as forty unionists get out of jail or avoid torture or murder during the civil war. Dyson made multiple visits to El Salvador to try helping union activists targeted by the Right, sometimes even doing the morbid work of searching for their bodies in the landfill where death squads callously disposed of their victims.[18]

In addition to defending them from persecution, the NLC and the network of local union committees invited leftist unionists from El Salvador to go on speaking tours for labor audiences across the United States. Some of the invited speakers belonged to organizations that were affiliated with the communist-led World Federation of Trade Unions.

This especially irked AFL-CIO president Lane Kirkland, who wanted to ensure that US union members stayed far away from any WFTU affiliates or their representatives. He and the AFL-CIO Executive Council issued a so-called shunning decree in 1985 advising state labor federations and local labor councils to slam the door on any foreign unionists who belonged to "Marxist-Leninist" unions. But for the most part, these warnings went unheeded and the touring speakers were well received.[19]

Confrontation

As Kirkland's "shunning decree" demonstrates, by the mid-1980s, the AFL-CIO's anticommunist leaders were beginning to fear the National Labor Committee's growing influence within the US union movement. What especially bothered Kirkland was that the NLC's reports, press releases, and speaking tours were breaking the information monopoly long held by the Federation's International Affairs Department and foreign institutes like AIFLD.

But since NLC members were mostly the national presidents of AFL-CIO affiliates, Kirkland was wary of openly attacking them. Instead, the International Affairs Department and AIFLD organized speaking tours and delegations of their own while disseminating bulletins and reports to US union members—all aimed at winning rank-and-file support for the AFL-CIO's aggressively anti-Left activities in Central America. This was a hard sell, however, as the Federation's Central America policy was in lockstep with Reagan's, and most US union members had no love for the union-busting president.

The simmering tensions between the National Labor Committee and AFL-CIO leadership eventually exploded into outright conflict. Just as the Federation, AIFLD, and Reagan administration waged an all-out public relations effort to paint the Christian Democrats as El Salvador's great centrist hope—attempting to convince Congress and the American public that a turning point had been achieved with Duarte's election—the National Labor Committee undermined these claims through a second fact-finding delegation in early 1985.

By then, several more unions had joined the NLC through their presidents, such as the American Federation of Government Employees

(AFGE), International Union of Operating Engineers, National Association of Letter Carriers, and National Union of Hospital and Health Care Employees. John Sweeney, president of the Service Employees International Union (SEIU) and future AFL-CIO president, also joined after being pressured to do so by his own union's membership, as did Morton Bahr of the Communications Workers of America.[20] The United Electrical Workers and the International Longshore and Warehouse Union—two traditionally leftist, independent unions that had been cast out of the CIO during the anticommunist purges decades earlier—also joined the NLC.

The February 1985 NLC fact-finding mission again comprised Sheinkman and Dyson of ACTWU, as well as eight others, including AFGE president Ken Blaylock and UAW Local 909 shop chairman Frank Hammer, the brother of slain AIFLD staffer Michael Hammer. They met with persecuted trade unionists and with government officials, including Duarte himself. The delegation reported that the anti-labor repression was only continuing under Duarte, and that no progress was being made in bringing the murderers of Hammer, Viera, and Pearlman to justice.

The delegates also paid a visit to neighboring Nicaragua, where the US-backed Contras were wreaking havoc. Only two months before the National Labor Committee's visit, Congress had defied Reagan by suspending military aid to the Nicaraguan counterrevolutionaries amid public outcry over reports of Contra war crimes. The AFL-CIO had taken no official position on the question of whether Washington should be aiding and arming the Contras, but the Federation repeatedly echoed Reagan's characterization of the Sandinistas as nefarious "totalitarians."

After their visit to Nicaragua, the NLC delegates criticized the Sandinista government for its restrictions on press and trade union freedoms, but argued that it was "not the oppressive, totalitarian regime of President Reagan's pronouncements." They also condemned the Contras for their "systematic atrocities" and called US policy in the country "an unwise, self-fulfilling prophecy of cold war fears," arguing that Contra aid had only spurred violence and forced the Sandinistas to take a more "hardline" stance against any opposition.[21]

Eight months after the NLC's second fact-finding mission, the AFL-CIO held its biennial convention in Anaheim. There, a resolution on Central

America ignited the first truly open debate on foreign policy in the Federation's history. Drafted by the International Affairs Department, the resolution offered a simple condemnation of the Sandinistas—without mentioning the atrocities of the Contras—and praised Duarte while ignoring the ongoing repression in El Salvador.

Recounting his recent visit to Central America, AFGE president Blaylock took to the convention floor to demand the resolution be revised to include criticism of Washington's role in fueling right-wing violence in the region. "Now, I don't know about the rest of you people here," Blaylock said, "but when I look at Iran, I look at Nicaragua, I look at El Salvador, Guatemala, I would like for one time for my government to be on the side of the people, not on the side of the rich dictators living behind high walls." He continued that because Congress had "finally got the balls to stand up and cut off military aid to Nicaragua" in accordance with public opinion, "the American labor movement ought to hear that message, too."[22]

Jerry Brown, secretary-treasurer of the NLC-affiliated National Union of Hospital and Health Care Employees, also rose to the convention floor to insist that the resolution include a denunciation of the Contras. "For this labor movement to sidestep, to fudge, to waffle on this issue seems to me that we haven't learned a thing from the history of the past 20 years, and the shame of the labor movement in not speaking out against American involvement in Vietnam," Brown said. "We ought to look at how somehow or other we are always, always the shock troops of the cold war."[23]

Several union officials pushed back against Blaylock and Brown's comments, chief among them American Federation of Teachers president and arch-anticommunist Al Shanker. Shanker blasted the Sandinistas, warning that Nicaragua was "on its way to full dictatorship, well on its way." He further claimed the AFL-CIO could be "very proud" of its work in supporting the Salvadoran government, saying that "the worst thing that we can do is to say that it's a tough job and not everything is perfect and there continue to be some violations, therefore, we are going to walk away from it all."[24]

As the back-and-forth on the convention floor unfolded, transforming from a discussion on a single resolution on Central America into a debate on labor's support for US imperialism, it was television star Ed Asner who delivered the most poignant remarks. President of the Screen

Actors Guild (the same union Ronald Reagan had once led), Asner was best known for playing the curmudgeonly news producer Lou Grant on *The Mary Tyler Moore Show*. His spinoff series, *Lou Grant*, was canceled by CBS in 1982 after Asner publicly protested US policy in Central America and used his celebrity platform to raise funds for a leftist medical relief committee in El Salvador.[25]

On the convention floor, Asner noted the hypocrisy of the AFL-CIO condemning alleged rights violations of the Sandinistas while remaining silent about the United States illegally mining Nicaragua's harbors and the murder of left-wing unionists and journalists in El Salvador under Duarte, saying that "support of the Nicaraguan Contras is unforgiveable" and "labor support of brutally repressive regimes is unforgiveable."

He then turned the discussion to AIFLD and its recent splitting of the UPD in El Salvador: "Where are our voices when the American Institute for Free Labor Development suddenly decides that even the pro-Duarte unions they supported only months before are suddenly too liberal, too uncontrollable? How far to the right are we willing to travel in the name of free democratic trade unions?"

Asner pointed out that under Duarte, AIFLD and the AFL-CIO were "no closer to justice in the murder of our two representatives, Hammer and Pearlman." He concluded by expressing his pride at being part of the labor movement, but added:

> It does not make me proud to see us bolstering the foreign policies of those whose stated goals include the destruction of our own labor movement like Orrin Hatch and Ronald Reagan. I do know which side I'm on, and it's not theirs.
>
> I don't want the labor movement to do the dirty work of President Reagan or our large multinational corporations. And I don't want any of Orrin Hatch's National Endowment for Democracy money to do it either.
>
> When Senator Hatch is ready to endow true democracy and trade unionism here at home, then maybe I'll talk to him about Central America . . . I love the labor movement and the things it stands for. It makes me more of a human being. That's why I'm here. It is because I love the labor movement that I don't want to see it sullied by any foreign policy that belies our highest ideals.[26]

An angry Kirkland responded that any suggestion the Federation was "in league" with conservatives like Reagan or Hatch was "beneath contempt." He also promised that the murderers of Hammer and Pearlman would be brought to justice, weirdly saying, "I'm Scottish and I'm southern and I like revenge."

Kirkland further suggested that any criticism of AIFLD or the Federation's other foreign institutes amounted to a betrayal of the people who worked for them. "When we send our people out around the world, expose them to conditions of great danger, I think they deserve your support and not a knife in the back," he grumbled.[27]

Following the ninety-minute floor debate, the convention delegates voted in favor of a compromise resolution that took no position on further military aid to the Contras or the Salvadoran government, but instead explicitly stated that "a negotiated settlement, rather than a military victory, holds the best hope" for establishing the "justice that the people of Nicaragua and El Salvador deserve."[28] The National Labor Committee chalked this up as a victory, using the resolution as a tool to support its lobbying to stop the flow of US military assistance to Central America. But organized labor's cold warriors were by no means deterred.

The Mobilization for Peace and Justice

As the Iran-Contra affair made headlines in 1987—revealing the Reagan administration's shadowy attempts to continue arming the Nicaraguan counterrevolutionaries despite Congress making it illegal—the National Labor Committee lobbied Capitol Hill to permanently cease all military aid to Central America. By this time, the leaders of twenty-five unions were part of the NLC, representing a combined 7.2 million US union members.[29] Dyson believed the moment was right to increase the pressure on lawmakers by holding a mass protest in Washington.

On April 25 of that year, in partnership with religious organizations and progressive advocacy groups, the National Labor Committee organized the Mobilization for Peace and Justice in Central America and Southern Africa. Held on the National Mall, the demonstration urged Congress to cease all further aid to the Salvadoran government and the Nicaraguan Contras, as well as to do more to push for an end to apartheid in South Africa.

In the days leading up to the protest, Kirkland and other anticommunist union officials like Shanker publicly called on unionists not to attend, telling them they were being duped into supporting "Marxist-Leninist guerillas" and warning them to avoid fraternizing with "the wrong crowd."[30] But the red-baiting did not work. NLC unions brought their members from different parts of the country to the rally by the busload. Out of a crowd of 100,000 marchers, an estimated 30,000 to 45,000 were members of at least twenty national unions.

"There is no real division in the ranks. The only split I see is with Lane Kirkland," Blaylock told the *New York Times*. Some of the unionists in the crowd chanted, "Lane Kirkland, you said No. We came anyway, Ho, ho, ho!"[31]

Prominent individuals at the rally included veterans of the anti–Vietnam War movement like Pentagon whistleblower Daniel Ellsberg and Yippie prankster Abbie Hoffmann. Jesse Jackson, then gearing up for his second presidential run, was also there. Ed Asner of the Screen Actors Guild, who had spoken eloquently on labor's foreign policy at the 1985 AFL-CIO convention, was one of the event's main speakers. Addressing the tens of thousands of union members in the crowd, Asner said:

> It is hard to believe the AFL-CIO's rhetoric about free speech abroad, in the face of their abysmal disregard for free speech and expression at home; they have redbaited this march and hounded its supporters within the house of labor, and the resistors deserve our gratitude— and have my utmost respect.
>
> Likewise, it is painfully hard to swallow the AFL-CIO's rhetoric on democratic trade unionism, when faced with the shady, truly subversive activities of their American Institute for Free Labor Development, its meddling in politics in Central America, mirroring the role of the administration and, quite possibly, the CIA.
>
> And to them I say, as I say to the US government, our labor movement also belongs to me. You cannot deny my voice. You cannot commit injustice in my name.[32]

The huge union turnout at the April 1987 mobilization and the continuous growth of the National Labor Committee signaled an unprecedented defeat for labor's hardline cold warriors who for so long had dominated the AFL-CIO's foreign policy. At the Federation's convention later that year, delegates passed a resolution calling on Washington to permanently end Contra aid—though to appease the anticommunist faction, the resolution also called for an end to Soviet and Cuban aid to the Sandinistas (a purely symbolic gesture since the AFL-CIO obviously had no influence with the Soviet and Cuban governments).

As Reagan begged Congress to renew military assistance to the Nicaraguan counterrevolutionaries, Kirkland said nothing, but the NLC utilized the convention resolution to make clear to lawmakers that organized labor officially opposed more aid. The ongoing popular pressure, combined with the political fallout from the Iran-Contra affair, led Congress to vote down Reagan's request in February 1988. It served as the final defeat of military assistance to the Contras.

16

Hollow Victory

Eastern Europe

In the years following the lifting of martial law in Poland in 1983, Solidarność continued leading the country's opposition movement, though from underground since the union was still banned by the communist government. With funds primarily from the National Endowment for Democracy, the AFL-CIO channeled an estimated $4 million to Solidarność during the 1980s. At the same time, Lane Kirkland continuously pressured the Reagan administration to maintain sanctions on Poland by restricting trade and credit.[1]

By 1988, the Polish economy was in severe crisis, owing some $40 billion in international debt and suffering steep inflation. The economic woes, felt most acutely by Poland's working class, gave additional energy to Solidarność, leading to a wave of work stoppages that rocked the country all summer. The strikes were sustained with financial support from the AFL-CIO's Free Trade Union Institute.[2] With the nation in turmoil, in late 1988, the communist government of Wojciech Jaruzelski had no choice but to open negotiations with Solidarność.

After months of talks, the government and Solidarność signed the Round Table Agreement in April 1989. Under this groundbreaking accord, the union would be legalized, Poland would get a new bicameral legislature, and national elections would be held that June. Solidarność established a political wing to run candidates for 261 seats in the new legislature. In the run-up to the election, the union turned to Washington for help, receiving $30,000 from the NED to publish and distribute its own newspaper.

Solidarność advisor Bronisław Geremek flew to Washington and met with Kirkland, returning home with a suitcase filled with $100,000 in cash from the AFL-CIO and the Polish American Congress.[3] When the election was held on June 4, Solidarność shocked the world by winning all but one of the seats its candidates were competing for, thus taking control of the Polish government. It would be Eastern Europe's first noncommunist government since the end of World War II.

This unexpected turn of events in Poland was possible not only thanks to generous US financial aid, but also in part because the Soviet Union—which for decades had maintained tight control over Eastern Europe—allowed it. Since 1985, the USSR had been led by Mikhail Gorbachev, a committed reformer and the country's youngest leader since Stalin. Gorbachev came to power wanting to shake up Soviet society by making the government more open and transparent (a policy known as "glasnost") and by introducing limited market reforms ("perestroika").

He adopted a softer foreign policy than his predecessors: ending the USSR's decade-long war in Afghanistan, pulling hundreds of thousands of Soviet troops out of Eastern Europe, and promoting nuclear disarmament. Though Gorbachev hoped that Poland and the rest of the Eastern Bloc would remain communist, he was, crucially, not inclined to use military force to achieve that aim.

Within months of Solidarność's electoral victory, the Berlin Wall would come down, the communist governments in Czechoslovakia and Romania would be toppled, and Bulgaria and Hungary each announced elections for the following year that would see the Communist parties defeated. Suddenly, the countries of Central and Eastern Europe were no longer satellites of the USSR. It was widely recognized that all of this began in Poland with the steadfast opposition of Solidarność.

Because they had strongly supported the underground Polish union throughout the 1980s, AFL-CIO leaders received some of the credit for bringing down communism in the Eastern Bloc. Taking a victory lap in December 1989, Kirkland called the situation "a vindication of our central belief in free and democratic trade unionism and our shunning of any contacts with unions created by state power."[4] But this celebration would later prove to be premature.

Almost poetically, the upheavals of 1989 were bookended by the deaths of two of US labor's original "free" trade unionists. In February of that year, Irving Brown died at the age of seventy-seven. The veteran labor diplomat and CIA agent had served as director of the AFL-CIO's International Affairs Department from his office in Paris from 1982 until 1986, when he suffered a stroke from which he never fully recovered. Four months before Brown's death, the outgoing President Reagan awarded him the Presidential Medal of Freedom, calling him "one of the architects of Western democracy" for his postwar anticommunist intrigues.

Just over a year later, in March 1990, Brown's old boss and mentor died too. Jay Lovestone was ninety-two years old and had lived to see the Berlin Wall come down. In the years following his forced retirement from the AFL-CIO in 1974, the communist-turned-anticommunist had served as a consultant to the Federation while remaining close friends with his longtime CIA contact, James Angleton. A memorial service for Lovestone was held at the AFL-CIO's headquarters shortly after his death. "There were more CIA men there than labor men," one attendee remarked.[5]

Dissolution of the Soviet Union

While Central and Eastern Europe's communist governments were being ousted in 1989, change was also brewing within the Soviet Union itself. That July, 400,000 coal miners in Siberia and Ukraine went on strike, demanding that Gorbachev's market reforms start benefitting workers—what some observers called "perestroika from below." The Soviet government responded with certain concessions like pay increases and the provision of new consumer goods.

Then in October, another strike of 26,000 coal miners in and around the far-northern town of Vorkuta began. Alleging the government had not fulfilled its promises from the summer, the Vorkuta miners made political demands aimed at reducing the authority of the Communist Party. About two weeks into their strike, they telegrammed the AFL-CIO asking for help, noting the Federation's "world fame in the struggle for the rights of workers." Kirkland sprang into action, assembling a would-be delegation comprising himself, AFT president Al Shanker, and UMW president Rich Trumka to go visit the Soviet strikers. Not surprisingly, the Soviet Embassy in Washington denied their visa applications, and the visit never materialized.

But in the spirit of glasnost, Gorbachev allowed a delegation of nine Soviet miners who were involved in the strikes and had formed their own independent union to travel to the United States for a month-long visit in early 1990. Hosted by the AFL-CIO, the delegates toured multiple states and met with various US unionists and officials, making sure to state that they were not seeking to overthrow the Soviet government, only to reform it.[6]

Whatever the intentions of the coal miners, their strikes were part of a larger rebellion inside the USSR. Gorbachev's market reforms only encouraged nascent capitalists in the Soviet Union to subvert state socialism, while his deliberate weakening of centralized authority inspired nationalist movements in several Soviet republics to demand independence. By late 1991, with multiple republics seceding, and after a bungled coup attempt by hardline communists trying to preserve the USSR, Gorbachev threw in the towel.

On Christmas Day, he announced his resignation and the dissolution of the Soviet Union. The republics that had once comprised the communist superpower were now fifteen independent states. "An end has been put to the 'Cold War,' the arms race, and the insane militarization of our country, which crippled our economy, distorted our thinking and undermined our morals," Gorbachev declared.[7]

The Cold War was officially over. The United States and the forces of capitalism had triumphed.

As with the end of communism in the Eastern Bloc, the breakup of the Soviet Union was punctuated by the death of a key AFL-CIO official. In March 1992, only three months after Gorbachev's resignation, Tom Kahn passed away due to complications from AIDS. He was fifty-three. Though Kahn had effectively been running the Federation's International Affairs Department in Washington since 1982, he was formally made director of the department only on Brown's retirement in 1986. In that role, he continued coordinating AFL-CIO support to Solidarność, while also opening contacts with rebellious Soviet workers, including the coal miners who went on strike in 1989.

Kahn and his compatriots in the world of "democracy promotion" had actively encouraged the rapid demise of Soviet communism. The

National Endowment for Democracy, for example, had championed the nationalist opposition movements in the various Soviet republics, channeling funds to separatist groups in the Baltics, Armenia, Ukraine, and Russia in the years prior to the dissolution of the USSR.[8] In 1991, *Washington Post* columnist David Ignatius attributed "the great democratic revolution that has swept the globe" to "a network of overt operatives who during the last 10 years have quietly been changing the rules of international politics. They have been doing in public what the CIA used to do in private—providing money and moral support to pro-democracy groups, training resistance fighters, working to subvert communist rule."

Ignatius singled out the role of the NED, the "sugar daddy of overt operations," for its central role in doing "openly what had once been unspeakably covert—dispensing money to anti-communist forces behind the Iron Curtain." The AFL-CIO, he wrote, was especially deserving of high praise for expertly channeling Endowment funds to Solidarność throughout the 1980s. "The CIA old boys spent a generation fantasizing about this sort of global anti-communist putsch. But when it finally happened, it was in the open," Ignatius explained. NED cofounder and dedicated "democracy-promoter" Allen Weinstein agreed, telling Ignatius that "a lot of what we do today was done covertly 25 years ago by the CIA."[9]

Mandela

The Soviet Bloc was not the only place experiencing dramatic political change at the dawn of the 1990s. Faced with mounting racial tension at home and growing sanctions and divestment from abroad, South Africa's new president, Frederik Willem de Klerk, lifted the ban on anti-apartheid political parties like the African National Congress (ANC) in February 1990. That same month, de Klerk ordered the release of political prisoners, most famously ANC leader Nelson Mandela, who had been imprisoned since 1962 on charges of conspiring to overthrow the state.

Because of his leftist sympathies and advocacy of armed revolution, Mandela had long attracted controversy and was officially designated as a "terrorist" by the US government. The CIA had even assisted the

apartheid regime in his 1962 arrest. But because of his more than quar-
ter-century incarceration, by the late 1980s, he had attained almost
legendary status as a living symbol of the anti-apartheid movement.

Only four months after his release, Mandela embarked on a twelve-
day visit to the United States, stopping in eight cities. The tour highlighted the importance of the American labor movement to the cause
of ending apartheid. While in Washington, Mandela addressed a joint
session of Congress and paid a visit to the White House—but also
made a point to meet with the AFL-CIO Executive Council to seek US
labor's continued support in funding and advising South African
unions. "The labor movement in the United States is one of the strongest in the world and has immense experience in the very organization
of trade unions," he told the Council. "You can help tremendously by
making this experience and expertise available to our own trade-union
movement."[10]

The meeting signified the ongoing shift in the AFL-CIO leadership's
approach to South Africa. The Federation had not officially embraced
the divestment and sanctions movement until 1986, and had traditionally been wary of Mandela and the ANC due to their communist connections. "The fact that the AFL-CIO is meeting with the ANC is an incredibly significant event," noted William Lucy, secretary-treasurer of the
American Federation of State, County, and Municipal Employees.

After Washington and a stop in Atlanta, Mandela flew to Miami,
where he addressed 3,000 AFSCME delegates at the union's national
convention. Outside the convention center, about a hundred Cuban
Americans protested the South African visitor because of his professed
admiration for Fidel Castro and earlier visit to Cuba. But inside, Mandela
was hailed as a hero. Lucy presented him with a $275,000 check from
AFSCME to the ANC, which was on top of $500,000 the union had
already donated over the previous decade. "In jail and behind thick
prison walls, we could hear loud and clear your voice calling for our
release," Mandela told the delegates, referencing AFSCME's role in pressuring the South African government to end his imprisonment. "We felt
your impatience with our enslavement."

Immediately after his AFSCME appearance, Mandela got on a plane
to Detroit, where he paid a visit to Ford's River Rouge complex that
same day. Mandela and his wife Winnie were welcomed by UAW president Owen Bieber, and production was temporarily paused while the

distinguished guest addressed about 1,000 rank-and-file UAW members. "It is you who have made the United States of America a superpower, a leader of the world," Mandela told the auto workers.

As the crowd looked on, Bieber—who had been arrested outside the South African Embassy in 1985 and had visited the country in 1986 to advocate against apartheid—handed both of the Mandelas UAW membership cards and informed them that they were now honorary members of the union for life. He then presented them each with a UAW jacket and baseball cap, which they immediately put on to thunderous cheers. A proud Mandela then told the crowd: "Sisters and brothers, friends and comrades, the man who is speaking is not a stranger here. The man who is speaking is a member of the UAW. I am your flesh and blood."[11]

At the end of Mandela's whirlwind visit, he stopped in Oakland, where he was hosted by Congressman Ron Dellums. The proud son of an ILWU Local 10 member, Dellums had been the most committed anti-apartheid voice in Congress for years. Mandela addressed a crowd of 58,000 people at the Oakland Coliseum and called attention to the militant activism of ILWU Local 10. "We salute members of the International Longshore and Warehouse Union Local 10 who refused to unload a South African cargo ship in 1984," Mandela said. "They established themselves as the frontline of the anti-apartheid movement in the Bay area."[12]

Over the next four years, Mandela and de Klerk would negotiate an end to apartheid, both winning the Nobel Peace Prize in the process. In 1994, Mandela was elected South Africa's president in the country's first-ever multiracial elections, and the racist system of white rule finally came to an end.

Shock Therapy

The new geopolitical realities emerging at the start of the 1990s—especially the collapse of Soviet communism—opened the door to drastic global economic change. A week after the Berlin Wall fell, Solidarność leader Lech Wałęsa was in Washington, where he was the guest of honor at the AFL-CIO's biennial convention. Finally able to accept the Meany Human Rights Award in person, he thanked Kirkland and the convention delegates for being "our most steadfast allies in the trade union struggle for human freedom."

Despite high hopes, the electoral victory of Wałęsa's Solidarność in 1989 would lead only to further economic deprivation for Poland's working class. The country still owed $40 billion in debt, and inflation was climbing to as much as 600 percent.

Now in power, Solidarność leaders begged the West for a sorely needed bailout, but the US government, International Monetary Fund, and World Bank would only agree to provide substantial assistance if the new government took dramatic steps to rapidly privatize Poland's state-managed economy. Speaking at the AFL-CIO convention that November, Wałęsa explained that his country was "swimming chained hand and foot, trying to summon all of our energy just to make it safely ashore. And on the shore, there is a cheering crowd of people who offer us their admiration instead of simply throwing a life belt."[13]

Taking advice from Harvard economist Jeffrey Sachs, the Solidarność-led government implemented "shock therapy"—transitioning from a socialist economy to a capitalist one practically overnight. State-run industries like mines, factories, and shipyards were quickly sold off to private firms, resulting in mass layoffs. In exchange for embracing the "free market," the International Monetary Fund provided Poland with some debt relief and the White House promised $1 billion in aid. Sachs predicted the rapid privatizations would lead to temporary pain in the Polish economy, followed by a robust recovery.

But such a recovery never happened. In the years after shock therapy was introduced, unemployment in Poland soared to 20 percent (higher for younger workers), poverty increased, and industrial output declined. Under capitalism, the standard of living for many working-class Poles became worse than it had been under communism.

The same pattern played out in post-Soviet Russia under President Boris Yeltsin, but with an even more extreme version of shock therapy. Virtually in an instant, price controls and trade restrictions were lifted, and hundreds of thousands of state-owned companies were devoured by corrupt businessmen and venture capitalists. In only a year, the Russian middle class was decimated, with millions losing their life savings and a third of the population being pushed into poverty.[14]

For his part, Kirkland called on Washington to initiate a "Marshall Plan" for Eastern Europe and the Soviet Union by providing generous amounts of aid to the former communist countries to transform them into prosperous capitalist democracies. "Karl Marx said it was capitalism that created the working class," Kirkland wrote during a May 1990 visit to Poland. "Now it seems as if Marx has been stood on his head: It is Eastern Europe's working class that is creating capitalism." But the AFL-CIO president warned that this new capitalism must be tempered by social welfare policies, robust business regulations, and strong "free" trade unions to protect the interests of workers—an argument that would fall on deaf ears.[15]

For decades, the US foreign policy establishment had been all too eager to partner with labor officials like Kirkland when they were preaching anticommunism. But now that the Soviets were out of the picture and the time had come to shape a post–Cold War global economy, the AFL-CIO's advice on international affairs was suddenly being ignored.

The foreign policy apparatus, the Treasury Department, and key international financial institutions had come under the control of neoliberal ideologues during the Reagan years. Looking to Pinochet's draconian market reforms in Chile of the 1970s as a model for the rest of the globe, they contended that the implosion of world communism signaled nothing less than the total victory of unfettered capitalism. According to the neoliberal vision, the principles traditionally championed by organized labor—social welfare, corporate regulations, a strong public sector, and collective bargaining itself—were nothing more than pesky economic "inefficiencies" that would need to be done away with at the earliest opportunity.

The US labor movement had already been in decline for at least two decades in the face of unchecked union busting, corporate restructuring, and increased capital mobility. The 1980s had been especially bad, with union density falling from 21 percent to 16 percent while real wages stagnated and income inequality skyrocketed.[16]

Under the presidency of George H. W. Bush—who succeeded Reagan in 1989 after serving as his vice president for eight years—economic conditions for working-class Americans only worsened. Bush focused on matters abroad, famously stating that the end of the Cold War afforded the opportunity to forge a "new world order" based on peace and international law. Meanwhile, the US economy fell into a recession.

Much of the public became disillusioned with the president, believing he cared more about foreign policy than domestic problems. Similar criticisms were lodged against Kirkland by national labor leaders. When Bush went to war with Saddam Hussein to expel Iraqi forces from oil-rich Kuwait in early 1991, Kirkland expressed "full support" on behalf of the US labor movement, even as some AFL-CIO officials thought the war merited further discussion and debate.

Kirkland defended himself from criticisms that he was overly fixated on international affairs, explaining that foreign unionists regularly solicited the Federation for help. "We don't go out shopping for clients and customers," he explained. "Workers around the world—white-collar, blue-collar, artistic and otherwise—they come to us because of our history and because of the work this organization has done over the years and despite what our detractors and critics may say about us at home."[17]

Free Trade

For the US foreign policy establishment, facilitating the rise of hyper-capitalist, market-centered economies around the world and integrating them into a single, globalized market became the major priority of the 1990s. For the AFL-CIO's internationalists, protecting US jobs by safeguarding basic labor standards around the world—in direct response to globalization—became the central focus.

This was particularly true of Central America and the Caribbean, where labor-intensive US industries like garment manufacturing were rapidly moving. "The collapse of state socialism in Central and Eastern Europe has given the conservative forces of this hemisphere the economic and political justification they need to base development policies on 'cheap labor,' " noted AIFLD director Bill Doherty in 1991. Ironically, it was hawkish anticommunists in the AFL-CIO like him who had encouraged and celebrated the demise of state socialism in Europe.[18]

But neoliberalism in Central America and the Caribbean had already begun a few years earlier through Reagan's Caribbean Basin Initiative, a unilateral trade program that went into effect on January 1, 1984. By lifting US import duties for goods coming from Central American and Caribbean nations, it incentivized US companies to invest in manufacturing in these countries and encouraged the governments in the region to expand their export sectors. The Reagan administration touted this as a way to develop "stable, democratic, free market-oriented countries close to our shores," but the AFL-CIO warned it would lead to US job losses.[19]

Although the Federation voiced opposition to the Caribbean Basin Initiative, it still firmly supported Reagan's overall Central America policy of isolating and crushing popular, left-wing movements. Whether AFL-CIO officials would like to admit it or not, "free trade" was simply another facet of anticommunism. Much like "free" trade unionism, free trade was packaged as the hallmark of an open, democratic society and antidote to state domination. The National Labor Committee in Support of Democracy and Human Rights in El Salvador (NLC), which led labor's resistance to Reagan's Central America policy despite the AFL-CIO leadership's wishes, certainly saw the connections between anticommunism and neoliberalism, even if Federation leaders did not.

"Over the past seven years, more and more [rank-and-file] AFL-CIO members have come to view US policy in Central America as a labor issue, primarily because it threatens the economic interests of workers as union members and because it has a devastating impact on Central American trade unionists," wrote Dave Slaney in 1988. President of United Steelworkers Local 2431 in Massachusetts, Slaney was one of many union activists who aligned with the NLC and criticized AIFLD's role in El Salvador. He argued that the US-funded repression of leftist unionists in El Salvador was carried out to mold a docile, exploitable workforce attractive to US capital.

"To the extent that US corporations are able to operate in Central America or elsewhere without such constraints as labor laws, union contracts and health and safety regulations, they are enticed to shut down their US plants and move south of the border," Slaney said, noting that a Minnesota clothing factory paying $7 per hour had recently laid off 500 workers and moved to El Salvador, where it paid only $3 a day. "Labor solidarity resonates with self-interest, because the Central American unions under attack are potentially important allies in US labor's battle with transnational corporations."[20]

The civil war in El Salvador was still raging as the new decade began. President José Napoleón Duarte—whom the State Department, CIA, and AIFLD had backed—was unsuccessful in defeating the FMLN guerillas or reining in the rightist death squads. In 1988 and 1989 elections, Duarte and his Christian Democratic Party were roundly beaten by the conservative ARENA (Nationalist Republican Alliance).

The war then briefly escalated in late 1989, but soon after, leaders of both ARENA and the FMLN recognized they were at a stalemate and were eager to find a way out. Coupled with the end of the Cold War and the resultant shifting calculus in Washington, peace accords were signed in January 1992, finally bringing an end to the bloody Salvadoran conflict.

Now under the leadership of ARENA, the Salvadoran government fully embraced neoliberalism. Free trade zones—where foreign corporations could operate manufacturing facilities with few to no regulations—sprang up in the country's urban centers, while traditionally state-owned enterprises were sold off to private companies. Fundamentally weakened and transformed by over a decade of bloodshed, Salvadoran unions struggled to cope with this rapidly changing political-economic context.

Importantly, the National Labor Committee managed to quickly adapt to the changing times. Throughout the 1980s, the driving force in the NLC had been Amalgamated Clothing and Textile Workers Union (ACTWU) organizer David Dyson, who for many years was the organization's only full-time staff person. But in 1990, he took a step back from the labor movement and returned to the ministry.

Charles Kernaghan, a former photojournalist brought onto the NLC's staff to assist Dyson in 1988, now became the organization's key figure. As both the Cold War and Salvadoran civil war ended in the early 1990s, Kernaghan lobbied the NLC's union patrons to keep the organization going, particularly with the aim of addressing problems of free trade. "Over the years, NLC had built up deep contacts on the ground in Central America," Kernaghan later said. "They were precious, based on real trust and real faith. We were hooked up to labor groups, religious groups, women's organizations, students. We had local chapters all across the United States. It seemed nuts to throw it all away."

ACTWU president Jack Sheinkman and other labor leaders were convinced. Despite the Salvadoran civil war's end, the NLC would continue operating—now becoming a foundation dependent on donations from unions as well as church groups and progressive philanthropies, with Kernaghan as executive director.[21]

"The struggle for worker rights in El Salvador and the other countries in Central and South America has never been more important than it is now to the labor movement in the US and Canada," stated an NLC report in 1991. "In the absence of effective worker rights in the region, increased economic integration will only exacerbate the already fierce wage competition which threatens jobs, wages, and living standards of workers throughout the Americas."[22] Under Kernaghan, the NLC particularly focused its attention on how USAID—the AFL-CIO's long-time government partner and AIFLD's traditional funder—was encouraging the offshoring of US manufacturing jobs to Central America.

In an explosive 1992 report, the NLC showed how, for the previous eight years, USAID had given over $100 million to Salvadoran business interests. The money was used to run ad campaigns targeting US corporations, urging them to move production to El Salvador because of its cheaper labor market. A blatant example was an ad placed in US trade magazines featuring a young Salvadoran woman next to a sewing machine with the message: "You can hire her for 33 cents an hour." USAID had also contributed funds to build factories in Salvadoran free trade zones, as well as offered subsidies to US corporations that chose to move production to Central America.

The NLC found that from 1988 to 1992 alone, 15,000 US manufacturing jobs—particularly in the apparel industry—had been moved to free trade zones in Central America and the Caribbean with help from USAID.[23] The same government agency that for decades had been bankrolling the AFL-CIO's overseas institutes was now facilitating the offshoring of US jobs for the explicit purpose of exploiting foreign workers.

The report was highlighted on *60 Minutes* in late September 1992 and caused an immediate uproar, becoming an issue on the presidential campaign trail as Democrat Bill Clinton sought to unseat Bush. Congress then moved to restrict USAID from funding any overseas project that could result in US job losses—a tangible victory (albeit a late one) for US labor, thanks to the NLC.[24]

As the 1990s continued, Kernaghan and the NLC repeatedly made headlines for exposing horrendous labor conditions inside Central America's free trade zones, allowing US consumers to see that their favorite clothing brands were being produced in sweatshops where workers—typically young women and teenage girls—had virtually no rights. At a Taiwanese-owned clothing factory in El Salvador used by the Gap, an NLC pressure campaign led to the establishment of the very first independent system to monitor labor conditions inside a sweatshop in late 1995, an important tool that would later be replicated in export processing zones around the globe to curb labor abuses. [25]

From NAFTA to New Voice

While the National Labor Committee adapted to changing global economic realities, the AFL-CIO leadership floundered. This was especially evident in the Federation's failure to stop passage of the North American Free Trade Agreement (NAFTA) in 1993. Originally negotiated by the Bush administration, NAFTA would create the world's largest free trade bloc by doing away with tariffs and other trade barriers between the United States, Mexico, and Canada. Naturally, US capitalists loved the idea of having unfettered access to Mexico's cheaper labor market and growing consumer market.

When Bush was defeated in the 1992 presidential election by Bill Clinton, Kirkland and the AFL-CIO pressed the incoming president to renegotiate NAFTA to include side agreements guaranteeing strong labor and environmental protections. Organized labor indeed had high hopes for Clinton. He was the first Democratic president in twelve years, and the AFL-CIO had supported his successful campaign to unseat Bush. Union leaders expected Clinton and the Democratic-controlled Congress to enact a host of historic, pro-worker legislation around healthcare and labor law reform.

But this would not come to pass. Much to the AFL-CIO's dismay, Clinton embraced neoliberalism and was determined to get NAFTA approved by Congress.

To appease progressives and the Federation, the Clinton administration did negotiate side agreements on labor and the environment, but they were generally weak and lacked any real enforceability. By the fall of 1993, as both chambers of Congress geared up to vote on NAFTA, the AFL-CIO spearheaded a national coalition of labor, environmental, consumer, farm, and religious groups to defeat the agreement. The coalition spent nearly $6 million on advertising, lobbying, and grassroots mobilizing. Meanwhile, Wall Street and Corporate America spent an estimated $17 million on their own efforts to convince Congress to pass the trade agreement. In November, both the House and Senate approved NAFTA, with many Democrats following Clinton's lead by voting for it. Kirkland called it a "bitter disappointment and a defeat for millions of working Americans."[26]

NAFTA went into effect on January 1, 1994. In the midterm elections later that year, the Republicans won full control of both chambers of Congress for the first time since 1952. It now became clear that there would be no significant break from the anti-labor politics of the Reagan-Bush era after all.

Among national labor officials, criticism of Kirkland's leadership became increasingly vocal. The seventy-three-year-old AFL-CIO president had been remarkably successful at thwarting world communism during his tenure, but he was unable to do anything about the rise of a global trade regime that was driving down wages and labor standards both at home and abroad. SEIU president John Sweeney and AFSCME president Gerald McEntee—whose respective unions were among the only ones to see significant membership growth in that period—argued that the AFL-CIO needed fresh leadership to promote new workplace organizing.

Alarmed by the midterm election results, in early 1995, Sweeney, McEntee, and nine other national union presidents within the AFL-CIO formed an unprecedented "Committee for Change" calling on Kirkland to step down.[27] The Committee for Change initially asked Kirkland to refrain from seeking re-election at the upcoming AFL-CIO convention in October, hoping that the Federation's secretary-treasurer, Tom Donahue, would replace him. But Kirkland stubbornly refused this request, and Donahue—a Kirkland loyalist—declined to run against his boss for the top job.

By summer, the committee had tapped Sweeney to run for AFL-CIO president, Trumka of the United Mine Workers to run for secretary-treasurer, and AFSCME official Linda Chavez-Thompson to run for the newly created position of AFL-CIO executive vice president. The group was dubbed the "New Voice for American Workers" slate. Meanwhile, another ten unions joined the Committee for Change—meaning that at the upcoming convention, 56 percent of the delegates would be in the "New Voice" camp, guaranteeing Kirkland's ouster.

Faced with this, an embittered Kirkland abruptly resigned on August 1, 1995—an ignominious end to a decades' long career. Donahue, who took the helm as interim Federation president, now decided he would run after all in an attempt to deny victory to Sweeney and the dissidents. But when the convention was held in New York that October, a majority of the over 1,000 delegates elected the "New Voice" slate. Promising to devote substantial Federation resources to union organizing, Sweeney, Trumka, and Chavez-Thompson became the AFL-CIO's new top officers.[28]

In August 1999, four years after resigning, Kirkland died of lung cancer. Buried at Arlington National Cemetery, he was remembered and celebrated more for his anticommunist internationalism than for any particular labor advocacy at home. Among those who eulogized the former AFL-CIO president was his old friend Henry Kissinger. "The cause of freedom was his mission," Kissinger said, "opposition to totalitarianism his vocation."

Bill Clinton, who in recent years had awarded Kirkland with the Presidential Medal of Freedom and offered to make him ambassador to Poland, called him a "great American" and a "catalyst for international democracy." Conservative political commentator Ben Wattenberg referred to Kirkland as a "five-star general of the Cold War" and opined that "during the decades of the Cold War it was the AFL-CIO that was the most stalwart institutional bastion of anticommunism in America."[29]

Sweeney and several of the other labor officials who had pushed Kirkland aside in 1995 had been members of the National Labor Committee and were thus openly dissatisfied with the AFL-CIO's traditional hardline anticommunism abroad. Now that the Cold War was over and they were in charge, many of the union presidents who had earlier been active in the NLC believed they could pursue foreign affairs directly through the Federation itself.

As a result, the NLC's connections to US unions became increasingly distant. By the late 1990s, the organization maintained ties only with UNITE (Union of Needletrades, Industrial, and Textile Employees), the union born of a merger between ACTWU and the ILGWU. Otherwise, the NLC was more of an independent nonprofit supported by academics, religious leaders, think tanks, and foundations.[30]

Meanwhile, the "New Voice" leadership promised to revamp the AFL-CIO's International Affairs Department, which had been the source of controversy for so long. Barbara Shailor—who, as head of foreign programs for the International Association of Machinists, had been active in the NLC—was appointed director of the department. In this role, she was credited with "weeding out" some of the old-line cold warriors, including Bill Doherty, who retired in 1996 after over thirty years at AIFLD.[31]

Under Shailor's direction, in July 1997 AIFLD and the other foreign institutes were consolidated into a single entity called the American Center for International Labor Solidarity—better known as the Solidarity Center. Shailor and Sweeney were well aware that AIFLD, the African American Labor Center, the Asian American Free Labor Institute, and the Free Trade Union Institute had all earned negative reputations.

In rebranding them as the Solidarity Center, the AFL-CIO's new leaders were trying to signal a break with the Federation's past foreign policy. Nevertheless, questions remained about how much of a break this really was. Like its predecessor institutes, the Solidarity Center was funded primarily by USAID and the NED, annually receiving about $15 million from the federal government in its first few years. Indeed, the center simply took the place of the Free Trade Union Institute as the NED's core grantee representing labor.[32]

Before being renamed and restructured, the final public controversy ignited by AIFLD involved the same country where it had first earned infamy some thirty years earlier: Guyana.

In the decades since the Institute had conspired with the Kennedy administration and CIA to successfully destabilize the government of socialist Cheddi Jagan, Guyana had suffered misrule, economic deprivation, and ongoing racial enmity between its Asian and Black populations. It had also hosted notorious US cult leader Jim Jones and his intentional community, where over 900 people died in a mass suicide in 1978. But in 1992, the country held its first genuinely democratic election since independence, which was personally monitored by Jimmy Carter. Jagan, now seventy-four years old, was elected Guyana's president.

Although the US government had once regarded Jagan as a Fidel Castro imitator and worked tirelessly to oust him, there was now little concern about the Guyanese leader in Washington, a reflection of changing geopolitical concerns. In 1994, President Clinton planned to nominate AIFLD director Bill Doherty to serve as US ambassador to Guyana.

On the surface, Doherty seemed like a fine choice. As head of an international nonprofit for three decades, he had contacts across the region, close ties to the US foreign policy establishment, and intimate knowledge of diplomacy and geopolitics. His father had even served as the first US ambassador to independent Jamaica. But when Jagan learned that the AIFLD head had been tapped for the job of top US diplomat in his country, he was "flabbergasted" and let it be known he was "not happy." He had not forgotten the role Doherty and the Institute played in fueling his political opposition and sowing chaos in his country in the early 1960s.

Like much of the American public, Clinton had apparently been unaware of all this. "Everybody in Guyana knows what happened," Jagan said. "Maybe President Clinton doesn't know our history, but the people who advise him should at least know their own history." Clinton soon dropped Doherty from consideration and ordered the CIA and State Department to declassify documents related to their anti-Jagan intrigues from the 1960s.

The venerable historian Arthur Schlesinger Jr.—who, as an advisor to President John F. Kennedy, had participated in the efforts to oust Jagan— admitted that, in retrospect, the United States had been wrong to intervene in Guyana's political affairs. Speaking about the controversy surrounding Doherty's nomination, Schlesinger quoted Oscar Wilde: "The one duty we owe to history is to rewrite it."[33]

Conclusion

This book has attempted to offer new understandings of the fateful decline of US labor in the late twentieth century by examining the AFL-CIO's extensive international activities during the period. Ostensibly the voice of American workers, the Federation was also one of the country's most staunchly anticommunist institutions. Instead of uncompromisingly confronting corporate power, organizing against militarism and war, and encouraging genuine union democracy at home and abroad, top labor officials maintained an unwholesome alliance with Washington's foreign policy apparatus—and occasionally with Corporate America as well—to undermine class-conscious, militant workers' movements around the world. The result of the AFL-CIO-backed Cold War was a world in which workers would have exceedingly little power and an increasingly reckless capitalist class would reign supreme.

In the late 1940s, the onset of the Cold War and the accompanying Red Scare in the United States significantly constrained the labor movement. After several years of dynamic growth and unprecedented success during the New Deal and World War II, US labor was forced back onto the defensive in the more conservative political climate resulting from the Cold War—especially after passage of the anti-union Taft-Hartley Act in 1947.

But it is important to remember that the Cold War did not simply "happen" to organized labor. AFL officials like George Meany were relentlessly demonizing communists and trying to provoke a standoff with the Soviets even before World War II was over, while CIO leaders like Walter Reuther embraced Cold War logic, calculating that it would be most expedient to raid and purge communist-led unions and renounce class struggle in favor of anticommunism and class collaboration. What's more, labor leaders had already wagered that the best path forward for their unions was one of servility toward the state rather than militant shopfloor struggle.

With the World Federation of Trade Unions, communist and noncommunist labor organizations attempted to build the kind of international unity that might have served as a powerful rebuke to the Cold War, but the AFL and CIO sabotaged this vision. Disagreements over the Marshall Plan between Soviet and Western trade unionists might have doomed international labor unity regardless, but it must be noted that the AFL was already determined to split the WFTU years before the Marshall Plan had ever been conceived. Meanwhile, through the machinations of AFL international agents like Jay Lovestone, Irving Brown, and Serafino Romualdi, labor movements across Western Europe, Latin America, and Asia were intentionally divided along the new Cold War battle lines in the late 1940s and 1950s, in full partnership with the State Department and CIA.

As with the WFTU, some of these splits might well have occurred even without US labor's meddling due to internal political dynamics within nations and regions, but the AFL and its government partners propped up otherwise small and insignificant splinter labor organizations like France's Force Ouvrière or Guatemala's Union of Free Workers, ensuring that divisions would continue and grow more bitter.

Rather than being a hapless victim of Cold War politics, then, American labor encouraged and exacerbated the Cold War. Wanting to see the success of the emerging, US-managed international capitalist order because they believed it would economically benefit their members, AFL and CIO officials essentially made the labor movement an appendage of Washington's foreign policy apparatus. Meany, who became president of the newly merged AFL-CIO in 1955, was so enthusiastic about this arrangement that he valued partnering with the US government far more than he did partnering with the world's other anticommunist labor movements in the International Confederation of Free Trade Unions.

In the 1960s, the AFL-CIO further cemented its foreign policy alliance with Washington by creating three USAID-funded "institutes" to bring anticommunism to the labor movements of the Third World. The first, largest, and most consequential of these institutes—AIFLD—trained hundreds of thousands of Latin American unionists in the ways of conservative business unionism, winning their loyalty through development projects like the construction of low-cost worker housing. Under officials like Romualdi and Bill Doherty, AIFLD and its trainees became important instruments of US imperialism in the region, helping see to it that progressive, democratic leaders like Guyana's Cheddi Jagan, Brazil's João Goulart, and the Dominican Republic's Juan Bosch were pushed out and kept out of power.

In Africa, the AFL-CIO's Maida Springer offered a different model of international labor solidarity—one that prioritized anticolonialism above defeating leftists at any cost. But the determined anticommunism of her bosses like Meany and Lovestone, along with the paternalistic racism of the ICFTU's European affiliates, made sure the African labor movement was also divided and thus weakened.

The US war in Vietnam was a crucial turning point in the Cold War. Fought in the name of containing communism and modernizing South Vietnam, the war revealed to much of the American public the brutal and imperial nature of US foreign policy. The war opened new political space to challenge anticommunist orthodoxy in the United States, but Meany and his inner circle would have none of this. Instead of using its economic muscle or close relationship with Washington to call for a swift end to the conflict, the AFL-CIO enthusiastically supported the war, even indirectly participating in it through its aid to South Vietnam's anticommunist labor leader, Tran Quoc Buu. The formal support of what was then one of the country's largest mass membership organizations gave Presidents Johnson and Nixon political cover and helped allow the slaughter in Southeast Asia to continue, even as domestic divisions over the war became ever more intense.

Walter Reuther gradually adopted an antiwar position, breaking with Meany and pulling his United Auto Workers, then the AFL-CIO's largest union, out of the Federation. The AFL-CIO was falling victim to the same type of Cold War fracture it had repeatedly engineered in other countries' labor movements—and just when global economic forces were shifting out of favor for US industrial workers.

In the wake of the Vietnam War, as more and more details about organized labor's partnership with the US foreign policy apparatus came to light, the AFL-CIO plowed ahead with its international intrigues, most notoriously in Chile. This only further alienated a younger generation of more progressive rank-and-file union members who already felt that labor leaders were out of touch, undemocratic, and unwilling to fight the growing power of multinational corporations. Meanwhile, amid increasing foreign competition, technological change, and upheavals in international finance, Corporate America moved to protect its profits in the 1970s by outsourcing jobs and offshoring production, accelerating a process of deindustrialization that would gut much of the AFL-CIO's membership in the proceeding decades.

As new figures like Lane Kirkland and Tom Kahn succeeded Meany and Lovestone, the Federation's major focus in this period was not organizing new workers or listening to younger members, but joining with neoconservatives in reigniting superpower tensions in the face of détente. The AFL-CIO repeatedly demonstrated that it was an instrument for waging the Cold War first, and a vehicle to advance the lot of the working class second.

Partnering with Ronald Reagan—the most anti-labor US president since before the New Deal—the Federation escalated its anticommunist crusade in the 1980s. With additional government funding through the newly created National Endowment for Democracy (NED), Kirkland and Kahn intervened inside the communist world itself by financially supporting Solidarność in Poland. But when AFL-CIO officials went along with Reagan's violent counterinsurgency policy in Central America, dozens of US union presidents and tens of thousands of rank-and-file members loudly protested.

These union dissidents were driven not only by a concern for the human rights of people in countries like El Salvador and Nicaragua, but also by a fear that Reagan's efforts to crush progressive movements in Central America would only make it easier for US corporations to move production there. Indeed, by the end of the decade, Cold War anticommunism had given way to neoliberalism's "race to the bottom," with multinationals emboldened to move operations to wherever they found workers most exploitable. Celebrating the collapse of world communism, AFL-CIO leadership had no real plan for how to respond to this new geopolitical and economic reality.

For decades, American labor officials had been close partners of the US government in waging the Cold War around the world. While Washington's foreign policy goals were often realized thanks to this arrangement, US workers ultimately did not benefit. The same federal government that generously gave the AFL-CIO hundreds of millions of dollars to interfere in foreign labor movements—supposedly in the name of "free" trade unionism—did little to promote union freedom at home. The anti-union Taft-Hartley Act was not repealed, labor law was not reformed to make it easier for workers to join unions, the right to strike was not protected, and union jobs were not safeguarded from elimination. Instead, by the Cold War's conclusion, Washington only made it easier for corporations to exploit workers both at home and abroad by facilitating free trade agreements like NAFTA.

With the creation of the Solidarity Center in place of AIFLD and the other anticommunist foreign institutes in 1997, it appeared to some that the AFL-CIO had finally turned a corner and would now base its international affairs on building genuine working-class unity across the globe. But as political scientist Nelson Bass has pointed out, the idea of combining AIFLD and the other institutes into a single entity seems to have originated not with the AFL-CIO's "New Voice" leadership, but rather with USAID officials for reasons of bureaucratic efficiency.[1]

A 1996 report from the General Accounting Office explained that in response to post–Cold War budget cuts to foreign assistance, "USAID is encouraging the AFL-CIO to consolidate its regional institutes into a new single global institute and to set strategic objectives globally and within specific regions," which would "conform to USAID's own efforts to improve oversight of labor programs as well as to manage and allocate in line with agency priorities."[2] A year later, the Solidarity Center was born.

Three decades later, the Solidarity Center continues to be the AFL-CIO's face overseas. Active in over sixty countries, the center does commendable work like promoting enforceable safety standards in Bangladeshi garment factories, amplifying the voices of South African domestic workers at the International Labor Organization, bringing together hotel housekeepers from the United States and Cambodia to share stories and strategies, and supporting Mexican auto workers challenging the stranglehold of corrupt union bureaucracies.

But like its predecessor institutes, the Solidarity Center is primarily funded by Washington. Of its nearly $42 million in total support and revenue in 2020, $38.8 million came from federal grants, including $22.6 million from the NED and $14.9 million from USAID. Just $300,000 came from the AFL-CIO itself.[3]

It remains one of only four of the NED's core grantees, alongside the respective international wings of the US Chamber of Commerce, Democratic Party, and Republican Party. Funding for the Solidarity Center's programs has tended to mirror US foreign policy priorities. For example, when President George W. Bush invaded Iraq in 2003, the Solidarity Center simultaneously received $860,000 from the NED for its Middle East programs, up from $292,000 the year before. Or when the socialist Hugo Chávez was elected president of Venezuela in 1999 much to the concern of Washington, the NED's annual funding for the Solidarity Center's programs in that country suddenly jumped from $54,289 to $242,926.[4]

At a Washington meeting of union officials to discuss labor internationalism in the late 1990s, AFL-CIO international affairs director Barbara Shailor was confronted by Chris Townsend, political action director of the independent United Electrical Workers (UE). Townsend questioned whether the Solidarity Center was really so different from AIFLD and the other old institutes, given its near total reliance on State Department and NED funds and that its employees are required to pass a national security background check by the US government.

"She wasn't going to argue with a UE guy very long," Townsend recalled, "so in a huff she told me that, 'The State Department controls the [Solidarity Center's] work in the countries that have either oil resources or Islamic insurgencies, and we can have the rest.' This of course was to assert that the work she was doing was legitimate and that I should somehow recognize that and give her a pass." Townsend said the AFL-CIO later stopped inviting him to such meetings.[5]

The Solidarity Center's activities in Venezuela have been particularly disturbing. When Chávez was temporarily ousted in a right-wing coup in April 2002, only to quickly return to power after millions took to the streets, journalists and activists uncovered evidence that implicated the Solidarity Center and its Venezuelan client—the CTV (Venezuelan Workers Confederation)—in the attempted overthrow. Representing the more privileged, professional strata of Venezuelan labor, the CTV partnered with business leaders from the Venezuelan Federation of Chambers of Commerce to destabilize the Chávez government, particularly by calling a general strike during the coup and, after the coup failed, an oil industry lockout.

The Solidarity Center gave NED funds to the CTV in the run-up to the coup, but it disavowed the attempted overthrow and claimed the money had gone only to progressive elements within the CTV. AFL-CIO officials said at the time that although they still took funds from the State Department and NED for foreign labor programs, the money came with "no strings or political attachments" and that the Solidarity Center thus operated independently. In the years after the coup attempt, the center continued supporting anti-Chávez groups with money from the NED.[6]

Given the history related in this book, US unionists today should, at the very least, take an active interest in the Solidarity Center's activities, its dependence on government funding, and its close association with the controversial NED. But there is virtually no current discussion about this within the AFL-CIO or its affiliates. That is not especially surprising, considering that the Federation has yet to formally acknowledge or apologize for the significant role it played during the Cold War in dividing labor movements abroad, undermining foreign democracies, and endorsing militarism.

In 2004, however, delegates at the California Labor Federation's convention—representing 2 million members—passed the "Build Unity and Trust Among Workers Worldwide" resolution. Spearheaded by Fred Hirsch, the unionist who, in the 1970s, had helped expose AIFLD's role in the Chilean coup, the resolution was the result of a rank-and-file effort calling on the AFL-CIO to fully account for its record of hostile overseas interventions and to formally renounce its CIA ties. After passing in California, the resolution was supposed to head to the 2005 national AFL-CIO convention in Chicago, but it was effectively killed by the Resolutions Committee before the convention even began.[7]

Organized labor around the world should be striving toward the creation of a truly unified working-class movement, dependent on its own collective strength, and dedicated to replacing capitalism with socialism and militarism with peace. While this may seem obvious, it historically has not been the official approach of the AFL-CIO and its affiliated unions, which, at their worst, have assisted the US government around the world in dividing workers, suppressing democracy, waging unjust wars, and foiling progressive movements.

Hope for global labor unity ultimately lies in the ability of trade unionists everywhere to put class solidarity above national allegiance, and to act with their fellow workers, whoever and wherever they may be, for their collective liberation and mutual survival. With the US working class now more "international" than it has ever been—composed of people of a multitude of nationalities, ethnicities, races, religions, languages, and cultures—identifying exactly how to achieve and maintain this kind of class unity, and translate it into effective action, can perhaps begin at home.

If they are to be serious vehicles for strengthening and protecting the working class both at home and abroad in this era of overlapping crises, today's AFL-CIO and its affiliated unions must adopt the kind of principled labor internationalism that would inevitably bring them into conflict with US foreign policy instead of reflexively serving it. But a labor movement that places class struggle and anti-imperialism ahead of deference to Washington's international designs will not come into being unless workers, both within and outside the AFL-CIO, build it themselves.

Acknowledgements

First and foremost, I'm indebted to my teacher, advisor, and friend Leon Fink for giving me abundant opportunities to develop my skills as a labor historian. His trust in my abilities gave me the necessary confidence to write this book. I'm also thankful to Jasmine Kerrissey, who has been a reliable advisor and colleague for more than a decade and has been particularly supportive of this project in its many incarnations over the years. Nelson Lichtenstein has been most generous with his time and efforts in reading through multiple versions of this research over several years and consistently providing invaluable feedback.

Rosemary Feurer also kindly took the time to read through an early draft of this manuscript and offered incredibly helpful insights and suggestions. The sections on South Africa benefited greatly from comments by Peter Cole. Ben Mabie provided meticulous, useful notes that tremendously strengthened this manuscript, while Asher Dupuy-Spencer was instrumental in getting it across the finish line. Of course, I alone am responsible for any errors or shortcomings in this book.

I'm grateful to my erstwhile teachers, colleagues, and comrades at the University of Illinois Chicago's History Department for their support and encouragement as I slowly put this project together during my time as a PhD student and adjunct instructor there, including Joaquín Chávez, Kevin Schultz, Jeff Sklansky, Sue Levine, Rama Mantena, Gosia Fidelis, Chris Boyer, Robert Johnston, Adam Goodman, Elizabeth

Todd-Breland, Noah Glaser, Adam Mertz, Jeff Wheeler, Josh Bergeron, Marla McMackin, Stephanie Smith, Carl Ewald, Sharaya Tindal Wiesendanger, Dan Berman, Frankee Lyons, Zukhra Kasimova, Paul Ribera, Sohini Majumdar, Dylan Shearer, Kyran Schnur, and numerous others.

I've also learned much from several teachers and mentors at other universities throughout my academic career, including Eve Weinbaum, Tom Juravich, Christian Appy, Jude Fernando, Dianne Rocheleau, Richard Peet, Anita Fabos, and Tracy Brady. More recently, I've enjoyed learning from my colleagues at the Harry Van Arsdale Jr. School of Labor Studies at SUNY Empire State University, including Maria Figueroa, Richard Wells, Sharon Szymanski, Barrie Cline, Mary Helen Kolisnyk, Moshe Adler, Jessica Rosa, Leetoya Young, Jennifer Morris, Nedelka McLean, and Sophia Mavrogiannis, among others.

This book would never have been possible without the decades of work by dozens of scholars, journalists, researchers, and trade unionists determined to tell the story of American labor's ties to the US foreign policy apparatus. Their books and articles are cited in these pages, and I'm thankful to those who have personally helped me by sharing information or offering feedback on my own work, including Kim Scipes, Thomas Field, Rob McKenzie, Yevette Richards, Ruth Needleman, and Frank Hammer. Similar credit is due to the dedicated and helpful staff at the University of Maryland Special Collections, Kheel Center, Reuther Library, and Tamiment Library.

I owe special thanks to Micah Uetricht for long championing this book and its publication, and to Sarah Lazare, who has also been a strong advocate of this project, source of encouragement, and brilliant collaborator. Thanks also to Miles Kampf-Lassin, Jessica Stites, Ari Bloomekatz, and Shawn Gude for always being interested in and supportive of my writing.

I've benefited from being able to work with and learn from some exceptional trade unionists and labor advocates over the years, including several of the individuals already mentioned above, as well as Carl Rosen, Chris Townsend, Leah Fried, Mark Meinster, Sean Fulkerson, Judy Atkins, Dave Cohen, John Thompson, Dawn Tefft, Anne Kirkner, Marco Rosaire Rossi, Erin O'Callaghan, Veronica Shepp, Sarah Moberg, Jessica Cook-Qurayshi, Kristin Lytie, Alyssa Greenberg, Susan Hurley, Alex Han, Jeff Edwards, Aaron Krall, Sophie Bauerschmidt Sweeney,

Jake Williams, Jocelyn Silverlight, Patrick Burke, Alyssa Goldstein, Jon Weismann, Avery Fuerst, Nina Griecci Woodsum, Darby Frye, Lindsay Jenkelunas, Santiago Vidales, Anna Waltman, Eric Hoyt, Ferd Wulkan, and the late great Janet Smith, among many others.

Finally, for their support, encouragement, and love, I'm grateful to my family, including my late grandparents; my aunts, uncles, and cousins; Jerry, Jo, and Brian Schuhrke; James and Rachel Sloan; Jeff Cousar; and especially my mom, Terri O'Brien Cousar.

Notes

Introduction

1 Neil Sheehan, "CIA Men Aided Strikes in Guiana Against Dr. Jagan," *New York Times*, February 22, 1967; Richard Harwood, "Public Service Union Abroad Aided by CIA," *Washington Post*, February 23, 1967; Robert Waters and Gordon Daniels, "The World's Longest General Strike: The AFL-CIO, the CIA, and British Guiana," *Diplomatic History* 29:2 (2005); Stephen G. Rabe, *US Intervention in British Guiana: A Cold War Story* (Chapel Hill: University of North Carolina Press, 2005), 110–13, 149–50; Joseph E. Hower, "Jerry Wurf, the Rise of AFSCME, and the Fate of Labor Liberalism, 1947–1981" (PhD diss., Georgetown University, 2013), 213–14n9.

2 James A. Wechsler, "CIA and AFL-CIO: The Bigger Story," *New York Post*, February 16, 1967; George Morris, *CIA and American Labor: The Subversion of the AFL-CIO's Foreign Policy* (New York: International Publishers, 1967); Ronald Radosh, *American Labor and United States Foreign Policy* (New York: Random House, 1969).

3 Kim Scipes, *AFL-CIO's Secret War Against Developing Country Workers: Solidarity or Sabotage?* (Lanham, MD: Lexington Books, 2010); Robert Anthony Waters Jr. and Geert Van Goethem, eds., *American Labor's Global Ambassadors: The International History of the AFL-CIO During the Cold War* (New York: Palgrave Macmillan, 2013); Anthony Carew, *American Labour's Cold War Abroad: From Deep Freeze to Détente, 1945–1970* (Edmonton: Athabasca University Press, 2018).

4 Mike Davis, *Prisoners of the American Dream: Politics and Economy in the History of the US Working Class* (London: Verso, 1986), 1–10.

5 Stuart Bruce Kaufman, *Samuel Gompers and the Origins of the American Federation of Labor, 1848–1896* (Westport, CT: Greenwood Press, 1973); Kim Voss, *The Making of American Exceptionalism: The Knights of Labor and Class Formation in the Nineteenth Century* (Ithaca, NY: Cornell University Press, 1994); Julie Greene, *Pure and Simple Politics: The American Federation of Labor and Political Activism, 1881–1917* (New York: Cambridge University Press, 1998); Paul Buhle, *Taking Care of*

   Business: Samuel Gompers, George Meany, Lane Kirkland, and the Tragedy of American Labor (New York: Monthly Review Press, 1999).

6   Elizabeth McKillen, "Labor and US Foreign Relations," *Oxford Research Encyclopedia of American History* (August 2019), 3–5; Steven Parfitt, "Constructing the Global History of the Knights of Labor," *Labor: Studies in Working Class History* 14:1 (2017), 13–38; Philip S. Foner, *May Day: A Short History of the International Workers' Holiday, 1886–1986* (New York: International Publishers, 1986).

7   McKillen, "Labor and US Foreign Relations," 5–8; Philip S. Foner, *History of the Labor Movement in the United States*, vol. 2 (New York: International Publishers 1955), 404–39; Scipes, *AFL-CIO's Secret War*, 9–11; David Montgomery, "Workers' Movements in the United States Confront Imperialism: The Progressive Era Experience," *Journal of the Gilded Age and Progressive Era* 7:1 (2008), 7–42.

8   Elizabeth McKillen, *Making the World Safe for Workers: Labor, the Left, and Wilsonian Internationalism* (Urbana: University of Illinois Press, 2013), 20–50; Sinclair Snow, *The Pan-American Federation of Labor* (Durham, NC: Duke University Press, 1964).

9   David Montgomery, *The Fall of the House of Labor: The Workplace, the State, and American Labor Activism, 1865–1925* (New York: Cambridge University Press, 1987), 370–1; McKillen, *Making the World Safe*, 181–240; Simeon Larson, *Labor and Foreign Policy: Gompers, the AFL, and the First World War, 1914–1918* (Cranbury, NJ: Associated University Presses, 1975); Joseph McCartin, *Labor's Great War: The Struggle for Industrial Democracy and the Origins of Modern American Labor Relations, 1912–1921* (Chapel Hill: University of North Carolina Press, 1997).

10 Samuel Gompers, *Seventy Years of Life and Labor* (New York: E. P. Dutton, 1957 [1925]), 215, 225, 284.

11 Leon Fink, *The Long Gilded Age: American Capitalism and the Lessons of a New World Order* (Philadelphia: University of Pennsylvania Press, 2015), 92, 109.

12 Christopher L. Tomlins, *The State and the Unions: Labor Relations, Law and the Organized Labor Movement in America, 1880–1960* (New York: Cambridge University Press, 1985).

13 Nelson Lichtenstein, *Labor's War at Home: The CIO in World War II* (Philadelphia: Temple University Press, 1982).

1. The Free Trade Union Committee

1   "World Labor View of AFL Affirmed," *New York Times*, April 6, 1945; Joseph C. Goulden, *Meany* (New York: Atheneum, 1972), 125–6.

2   Goulden, *Meany*, 12–16.

3   Archie Robinson, *George Meany and His Times: A Biography* (New York: Simon & Schuster, 1981), 123–5.

4   Quoted in ibid., 52.

5   Quoted in Judith Stepan-Norris and Maurice Zeitlin, *Left Out: Reds and America's Industrial Unions* (New York: Cambridge University Press, 1992), 41.

6   Ibid., 14–15.

7   Anthony Carew, *American Labour's Cold War Abroad: From Deep Freeze to Détente, 1945–1970* (Edmonton: Athabasca University Press, 2018) 19.

8 Goulden, *Meany*, 116–18.

9 "Pickets of A.F.L. to Patrol Fur Area," *New York Times*, June 11, 1927.

10 Sidney Lens, "Lovestone Diplomacy," *Nation*, July 5, 1965; Goulden, *Meany*, 120; Carew, *American Labour*, 22.

11 David Dubinsky and A. H. Raskin, *David Dubinsky: A Life with Labor* (New York: Simon and Schuster, 1977), 56–7; Robert D. Parmet, *The Master of Seventh Avenue: David Dubinsky and the American Labor Movement* (New York: New York University Press, 2005), 31–53.

12 Dubinsky and Raskin, *David Dubinsky*, 68.

13 Irving Bernstein, *The Turbulent Years: A History of the American Worker 1933–1941* (Chicago: Haymarket Books, 2010 [1969]), 84–9, 709–12; Merlyn S. Pitzele, "Can American Labor Defeat the Communists?," *Atlantic*, March 1947.

14 Lens, "Lovestone Diplomacy"; Bernstein, *The Turbulent Years*, 407; Carew, *American Labour*, 19; Nathan Godfried, "Revising Labor History for the Cold War: The ILGWU and the Film, With These Hands," *Historical Journal of Film, Radio, and Television* 28: 3 (2008), 311–33.

15 Quenby Olmsted Hughes, *"In the Interest of Democracy": The Rise and Fall of the Early Cold War Alliance Between the American Federation of Labor and Central Intelligence Agency* (Bern: Peter Lang, 2011), 28–30.

16 Bernstein, *The Turbulent Years*, 556.

17 Quoted in Hughes, *In the Interest of Democracy*, 36.

18 Ted Morgan, *A Covert Life: Jay Lovestone: Communist, Anti-Communist, and Spymaster* (New York: Random House, 1999), 84–104.

19 Ibid., 110–11; Dubinsky and Raskin, *David Dubinsky*, 241.

20 Victor G. Reuther, *The Brothers Reuther and the Story of the UAW* (Boston: Houghton Mifflin, 1976), 183.

21 Roger Keeran, *The Communist Party and the Auto Workers' Unions* (New York: International Publishers, 1980), 178–97.

22 Carew, *American Labour*, 21.

23 Quoted in Morgan, *A Covert Life*, 143.

24 Lens, "Lovestone Diplomacy."

25 Quoted in Goulden, *Meany*, 122.

26 Barret Dower, "The Influence of the American Federation of Labor on the Force Ouvrière, 1944–1955," in *American Labor's Global Ambassadors: The International History of the AFL-CIO During the Cold War*, Robert Anthony Waters Jr. and Geert Van Goethem, eds. (New York: Palgrave Macmillan, 2013), 88; Carew, *American Labour*, 33.

27 James R. Prickett, "Anti-Communism and Labor History," *Industrial Relations* 13:3 (1974), 220.

28 Ben Rathbun, *The Point Man: Irving Brown and the Deadly Post-1945 Struggle for Europe and Africa* (Montreux: Minerva Press, 1995), 44–51; Carew, *American Labour*, 25–7.

29 Carew, *American Labour*, 23–4.

30 Quoted in Ronald Radosh, *American Labor and United States Foreign Policy* (New York: Random House, 1969), 313.

31 Quoted in ibid. 314–15.

32 Dower, "Influence of the American Federation of Labor," 88.

33 Quoted in Radosh, *American Labor and United States Foreign Policy*, 315; Carew, *American Labour*, 31, 36–7.

34 Quoted in Radosh, *American Labor and United States Foreign Policy*, 318.
35 George Hartmann, "Official of AFL Blasts CIO for Reds in Union," *Chicago Daily Tribune*, October 10, 1946.
36 Hartmann, "AFL Denounces Red Control of Europe's Labor," *Chicago Daily Tribune*, October 15, 1946.
37 Carew, *American Labour*, 39–41.
38 Dower, "Influence of the American Federation of Labor," 87; Carew, *American Labour*, 49.
39 Quoted in Dower, "Influence of the American Federation of Labor," 87–8.
40 Ibid., 88–9; Carew, *American Labour*, 49–50.
41 Quoted in Carew, *American Labour*, 50.
42 Herrick Chapman, Mark Kesselman, and Martin A. Schain, *A Century of Organized Labor in France: A Union Movement for the Twenty-First Century?* (New York: St. Martin's Press, 1998), 10–11; Val R. Lorwin, *The French Labor Movement* (Cambridge, MA: Harvard University Press, 1954), 127.
43 Carew, *American Labour*, 49–51.
44 Mike Davis, *Prisoners of the American Dream: Politics and Economy in the History of the US Working Class* (London: Verso, 1986), 194–5.

2. Good Neighbors

1 Greg Grandin, *Empire's Workshop: Latin America, the United States, and the Rise of the New Imperialism* (New York: Henry Holt, 2010), 16–20.
2 Ronald Radosh, *American Labor and United States Foreign Policy* (New York: Random House, 1969), 348–9; Kim Scipes, *AFL-CIO's Secret War Against Developing Country Workers: Solidarity or Sabotage?* (Lanham, MD: Lexington, 2010), 1–26.
3 Camile Nick Buford, "A Biography of Luis N. Morones, Mexican Labor and Political Leader" (PhD diss., Louisiana State University, 1971), 27; Robert J. Alexander and Eldon M. Parker, *International Labor Organizations and Organized Labor in Latin America and the Caribbean: A History* (Santa Barbara: Praeger, 2009), 12–17; Elizabeth McKillen, *Making the World Safe for Workers: Labor, the Left, and Wilsonian Internationalism* (Urbana: University of Illinois Press, 2013), 20–50.
4 Radosh, *American Labor and United States Foreign Policy*, 350–4; Buford, *Luis N. Morones*, 31; Alexander and Parker, *International Labor*, 19; Charles W. Toth, "Samuel Gompers, Communism, and the Pan American Federation of Labor," *The Americas* 23:3 (1967), 275.
5 Quoted in Toth, "Samuel Gompers," 273.
6 Buford, *Luis N. Morones*, 69–70, 85
7 Daniela Spenser, *In Combat: The Life of Lombardo Toledano* (Chicago: Haymarket Books, 2019), 84–97.
8 Robert Paul Millon, *Mexican Marxist: Vicente Lombardo Toledano* (Chapel Hill: University of North Carolina Press, 1966), 119–29; Alexander and Parker, *International Labor*, 58.
9 Millon, *Mexican Marxist*, 129–31; Alexander and Parker, *International Labor*, 60.
10 Quoted in Millon, *Mexican Marxist*, 138–9.

11 Leslie Bethell and Ian Roxborough, "The Impact of the Cold War on Latin America," in *Origins of the Cold War: An International History*, Melvyn Leffler and David Painter, eds. (New York: Routledge, 1994), 299–316; Spenser, *In Combat*, 274–6.

12 Miles E. Galvin, "The Latin American Union Leadership Training Program of the Labor Relations Institute of the University of Puerto Rico" (master's thesis, Cornell University, 1961), 1.

13 Serafino Romualdi, *Presidents and Peons: Recollections of a Labor Ambassador in Latin America* (New York: Funk and Wagnalls, 1967), 11–13; "Serafino Romualdi, Biographical Sketch," n.d., box 128, folder 5, Sidney Lens Papers, Chicago History Museum.

14 Romualdi, *Presidents and Peons*, 15–17.

15 Quoted in ibid., 20 (emphasis added).

16 Ibid., 21–9.

17 Ibid., 37.

18 Ibid., 40–2; Spenser, *In Combat*, 277.

19 Romualdi, *Presidents and Peons*, 40–2; Alexander and Parker, *International Labor*, 99–100.

20 George Hartmann, "Labor Leaders of 2 Americas to Combat Reds," *Chicago Daily Tribune*, October 12, 1946.

21 Quoted in Romualdi, *Presidents and Peons*, 47.

22 "Text of the President's Message," *Washington Post*, March 13, 1947.

23 Quoted in Ernesto Seman, *Ambassadors of the Working Class: Argentina's International Labor Activists and Cold War Democracy in the Americas* (Durham, NC: Duke University Press, 2017), 44.

24 Interview with Daniel Horowitz, May 27, 1994, Association for Diplomatic Studies and Training Foreign Affairs Oral History Project, Labor Series; Romualdi, *Presidents and Peons*, 72–4.

25 Alexander and Parker, *International Labor*, 98.

26 Seman, *Ambassadors of the Working Class*, 46–53.

27 Ibid., 57–8; Romualdi, *Presidents and Peons*, 51–3.

28 A. H. Raskin, "US Unionists Assail Peron for Dictatorial Rule of Labor," *New York Times*, March 10, 1947; Seman, *Ambassadors of the Working Class*, 59.

29 Raskin, "US Unionists Assail Peron."

30 Alexander and Parker, *International Labor*, 99–100; Million, *Mexican Marxist*, 150–1; Magaly Rodriguez Garcia, "The AFL-CIO and ORIT in the Andes," in *American Labor's Global Ambassadors: The International History of the AFL-CIO During the Cold War*, Robert Anthony Waters Jr. and Geert Van Goethem, eds. (New York: Palgrave Macmillan, 2013), 142–3; Bethell and Roxborough, "Impact of the Cold War," 312.

31 Quoted in Romualdi, *Presidents and Peons*, 74–5.

32 Alexander and Parker, *International Labor*, 100.

33 Milton Bracker, "Labor Conference Convenes in Peru," *New York Times*, January 10, 1948; Romualdi, *Presidents and Peons*, 82; Spenser, *In Combat*, 284–5.

34 Buford, *Luis N. Morones*, 225–9; Spenser, *In Combat*, 283–5.

35 Millon, *Mexican Marxist*, 142; Romualdi, *Presidents and Peons*, 79; Spenser, *In Combat*, 244–7.

36 Spenser, *In Combat*, 348–52.

37 Millon, *Mexican Marxist*, 150–2.
38 Quoted in Romualdi, *Presidents and Peons*, 87.

3. A Larger Pie

1   Leo Panitch and Sam Gindin, *The Making of Global Capitalism: The Political Economy of American Empire* (New York: Verso, 2012), 5–11.
2   "Moscow Charges US 'Colonial' Aim," *New York Times*, November 17, 1947.
3   Michael J. Hogan, *The Marshall Plan: America, Britain, and the Reconstruction of Western Europe, 1947–1952* (New York: Cambridge University Press, 1987), 141.
4   Anthony Carew, *American Labour's Cold War Abroad: From Deep Freeze to Détente, 1945–1970* (Edmonton: Athabasca University Press, 2018), 58.
5   "Saillant of WFTU Hits at US Unions," *New York Times*, February 15, 1948; Carew, *American Labour*, 60–3.
6   Quoted in Nelson Lichtenstein, *The Most Dangerous Man in Detroit: Walter Reuther and the Fate of American Labor* (New York: Basic Books, 1995), 44.
7   Ibid., 177.
8   Ibid., 260.
9   Richard O. Boyer and Herbert M. Morais, *Labor's Untold Story* (Pittsburgh: United Electrical, Radio, and Machine Workers of America, 1955), 345.
10 Boyer and Morais, *Labor's Untold Story*, 268–70; Toni Gilpin, *The Long Deep Grudge: A Story of Big Capital, Radical Labor, and Class War in the American Heartland* (Chicago: Haymarket Books, 2020), 143–5; Kim Moody, *An Injury to All: The Decline of American Unionism* (New York: Verso, 1988), 46–7; Judith Stepan-Norris and Maurice Zeitlin, *Left Out: Reds and America's Industrial Unions* (New York: Cambridge University Press, 1992), 172–3, 266–7.
11 "Woll Sounds CIO on Re-Entering the AFL," *New York Times*, May 5, 1948.
12 Hogan, *The Marshall Plan*, 203; Carew, *American Labour*, 68.
13 Gilpin, *The Long Deep Grudge*, 191.
14 Quoted in Lichtenstein, *The Most Dangerous Man*, 309.
15 Stepan-Norris and Zeitlin, *Left Out*, 270–1; Gilpin, *The Long Deep Grudge*, 297; Lichtenstein, *The Most Dangerous Man*, 309–10.
16 Nelson Lichtenstein, *A Contest of Ideas: Capital, Politics, and Labor* (Urbana: University of Illinois Press, 2013), 79–99.
17 Leon Fink, *Undoing the Liberal World Order: Progressive Ideals and Political Realities Since World War II* (New York: Columbia University Press, 2022), 26.
18 Boyer and Morais, *Labor's Untold Story*, 340–70; Daniel Cantor and Juliet Schor, *Tunnel Vision: Labor, the World Economy, and Central America* (Boston: South End Press, 1987), 21–48; Moody, *An Injury to All*, 55–60; Dana Frank, *Buy American: The Untold Story of Economic Nationalism* (Boston: Beacon Press, 1999), 102–14 (Reuther quoted on 109).
19 Katherine V. W. Stone, "The Post-War Paradigm in American Labor Law," *Yale Law Journal* 90: 7 (1987), 1509–80; Christopher L. Tomlins, "The New Deal, Collective Bargaining, and the Triumph of Industrial Pluralism," *Industrial and Labor Relations Review* 39:1 (1985), 19–34.

20 Laura A. Belmonte, *Selling the American Way: US Propaganda and the Cold War* (Philadelphia: University of Pennsylvania Press, 2008), 119–20.

21 Anthony Carew, *Labour Under the Marshall Plan: The Politics of Productivity and the Marketing of Management Science* (Manchester: Manchester University Press, 1987), 56–8, 189–91; Ronald W. Schatz, *The Labor Board Crew: Remaking Worker-Employer Relations from Pearl Harbor to the Reagan Era* (Urbana: University of Illinois Press, 2021).

22 Melvyn Dubofsky and Joseph McCartin, eds., *American Labor: A Documentary Collection* (New York: Palgrave Macmillan, 2004), 294; Nelson Lichtenstein, *State of the Union: A Century of American Labor* (Princeton, NJ: Princeton University Press, 2002), 136; Melvyn Dubofsky, *The State and Labor in Modern America* (Chapel Hill: University of North Carolina Press, 1994), 214; Gabriel Winant, *The Next Shift: The Fall of Industry and the Rise of Health Care in Rust Belt America* (Cambridge, MA: Harvard University Press, 2021), 11–19.

23 Adolf Sturmthal, "The International Confederation of Free Trade Unions," *Industrial and Labor Relations Review* 3:3 (1950), 376–7; Anthony Carew et al., *The International Confederation of Free Trade Unions* (Bern: Peter Lang, 2000), 198.

24 Carew, *American Labour*, 75.

4. Joining the CIA

1   Interview with Morris Weisz, July 30, 1990, Association for Diplomatic Studies and Training Foreign Affairs Oral History Project, Labor Series, 14; Ted Morgan, *A Covert Life: Jay Lovestone: Communist, Anti-Communist, and Spymaster* (New York: Random House, 1999), 144–5.

2   Quenby Olmsted Hughes, *"In The Interest of Democracy": The Rise and Fall of the Early Cold War Alliance Between the American Federation of Labor and Central Intelligence Agency* (Bern: Peter Lang, 2011), 67.

3   Anthony Carew, *American Labour's Cold War Abroad: From Deep Freeze to Détente, 1945–1970* (Edmonton: Athabasca University Press, 2018), 59.

4   Quoted in Hughes, *In the Interest*, 70–3.

5   Hugh Wilford, *The Mighty Wurlitzer: How the CIA Played America* (Cambridge, MA: Harvard University Press, 2009), 54; Carew, *American Labour*, 86; Thomas W. Braden, "I'm Glad the CIA Is 'Immoral,' " *Saturday Evening Post*, May 20, 1967.

6   Wilford, *The Mighty Wurlitzer*, 53; Victor G. Reuther, *The Brothers Reuther and the Story of the UAW* (Boston: Houghton Mifflin, 1976), 412.

7   "LABOR: The Most Dangerous Man," *Time*, March 17, 1952; Irwin M. Wall, *The United States and the Making of Postwar France, 1945–1954* (New York: Cambridge University Press, 1991), 109.

8   Carew, *American Labour*, 90–5; Reuther, *The Brothers Reuther*, 412; C. D. Stelzer, "The CIA's French Connection and Other Footnotes to History," STLREPORTER, 2006, stlreporter.com; Vijay Prashad, *Washington Bullets: A History of the CIA, Coups, and Assassinations* (New York: Monthly Review Press, 2020), 79–80.

9   Quoted in Carew, *American Labour*, 101.

10 Ronald L. Filippelli, *American Labor and Postwar Italy, 1943–1953: A Study of Cold War Politics* (Stanford, CA: Stanford University Press, 1989); Morgan, *A Covert Life*,

190–3; Anthony Carew, "The American Labor Movement in Fizzland: The Free Trade Union Committee and the CIA," *Labor History* 39:1 (1998), 29; Carew, *American Labour*, 100–3; Alessandro Brogi, "The AFL and CIO Between 'Crusade' and Pluralism in Italy, 1944–1963," in *American Labor's Global Ambassadors: The International History of the AFL-CIO during the Cold War*, Robert Anthony Waters Jr. and Geert Van Goethem, eds. (New York: Palgrave Macmillan, 2013), 66–8.

11 Carew, "Fizzland," 27; Patrick J. Iber, "'Who Will Impose Democracy?': Sacha Volman and the Contradictions of CIA Support for the Anticommunist Left in Latin America," *Diplomatic History* 37: 5 (2013), 999; Carew, *American Labour*, 95–7.

12 Quoted in Frances Stonor Saunders, *The Cultural Cold War: The CIA and the World of Arts and Letters* (New York: New Press, 1999), 155–6.

13 Free Trade Union Committee Minutes, Attachment 1, October 31, 1950, box 35, folder 29, RG18-003, George Meany Memorial AFL-CIO Archive (GMMA), University of Maryland, College Park; Morgan, *A Covert Life*, 300–3; Wilford, *The Mighty Wurlitzer*, 55–6; Carew, *American Labour*, 380; John E. Moes, "Trade Unionism in Indonesia," *Far Eastern Survey* 28:2 (1959), 17–24.

14 Harry Goldberg, "Sukarno and 'Guided Democracy,'" *American Federationist*, August 1959.

15 Letter to Mr. Harry Goldberg from C. P. Cabell, August 28, 1959, General CIA Records, CREST, CIA-RDP80R01731R000200110022-8; Letter to Mr. Harry Goldberg from Allen W. Dulles, December 17, 1960, General CIA Records, CREST, CIA-RDP80B01676R003600060006-3.

16 Vincent Bevins, *The Jakarta Method: Washington's Anticommunist Crusade and the Mass Murder Program That Shaped Our World* (New York: Public Affairs, 2020), 140–1, 251–2.

17 Harry Goldberg, "Indonesian Developments: The Holocaust," June 30, 1966, box 43, folder 12, RG18-003, GMMA.

18 Morgan, *A Covert Life*, 202; Wilford, *The Mighty Wurlitzer*, 56.

19 "Secret: Free China Labor League (A preliminary program)," n.d., box 35, folder 14, RG18-003, GMMA.

20 Quoted in Morgan, *A Covert Life*, 204; Wilford, *The Mighty Wurlitzer*, 57-8.

21 Lu Ching-shih to Jay Lovestone, November 14, 1950, box 35, folder 14, RG18-003, GMMA.

22 Morgan, *A Covert Life*, 204–5; Wilford, *The Mighty Wurlitzer*, 56–7.

23 Quoted in Carew, "Fizzland," 28, 32–3.

24 Ibid., 23, 30–2; Wilford, *The Mighty Wurlitzer*, 59–62.

25 David Dubinsky and A. H. Raskin, *David Dubinsky: A Life with Labor* (New York: Simon and Schuster, 1977), 261.

26 Carew, "Fizzland," 31–9.

5. Inter-Americanism

1 Serafino Romualdi, *Presidents and Peons: Recollections of a Labor Ambassador in Latin America* (New York: Funk and Wagnalis, 1967), 112–19; Robert J. Alexander and Eldon M. Parker, *International Labor Organizations and Organized Labor in Latin America and the Caribbean: A History* (Santa Barbara, CA: Praeger, 2009),

117–19; Daniela Spenser, *In Combat: The Life of Lombardo Toledano* (Chicago: Haymarket, 2019), 336–8.

2 Magaly Rodriguez Garcia, *Liberal Workers of the World Unite? The ICFTU and the Defence of Labour Liberalism in Europe and Latin America* (Bern: Peter Lang, 2010), 172, 197–206.

3 Ernesto Seman, *Ambassadors of the Working Class: Argentina's International Labor Activists and Cold War Democracy in the Americas* (Durham, NC: Duke University Press, 2017).

4 Ibid., 147.

5 Alexander and Parker, *International Labor*, 180–93.

6 "Anti-US Drift Seen in Latin America," *New York Times*, September 19, 1952.

7 Alexander and Parker, *International Labor*, 190–3; Stephen G. Rabe, *Eisenhower and Latin America: The Foreign Policy of Anticommunism* (Chapel Hill, NC: University of North Carolina Press, 1988), 37–8.

8 Romualdi, *Presidents and Peons*, 126; Alexander and Parker, *International Labor*, 122.

9 Patrick J. Iber, "'Who Will Impose Democracy?': Sacha Volman and the Contradictions of CIA Support for the Anticommunist Left in Latin America," *Diplomatic History* 37:5 (2013), 998–1001.

10 Harry Fleischman, *Norman Thomas: A Biography* (New York: Norton, 1964), 328–30.

11 John D. French, "The Robert J. Alexander Interview Collection," *Hispanic American Historical Review* 84:2 (2004), 315–26.

12 Iber, "Who Will Impose," 1003–5; Alexander and Parker, *International Labor*, 122.

13 Stephen Kinzer, *Overthrow: America's Century of Regime Change from Hawaii to Iraq* (New York: Times Books, 2006), 133.

14 Piero Gleijeses, *Shattered Hope: The Guatemalan Revolution and the United States, 1944–1954* (Princeton, NJ: Princeton University Press, 1991), 155.

15 Ibid., 130, 186, 240–70; Kinzer, *Overthrow*, 132–4.

16 Romualdi, *Presidents and Peons*, 242–4; Robert J. Alexander and Eldon M. Parker, *A History of Organized Labor in Panama and Central America* (Westport, CT: Praeger, 2008), 232–3.

17 Gleijeses, *Shattered Hope*, 259–60.

18 Quoted in Alexander and Parker, *International Labor*, 125.

19 Serafino Romualdi, "Report and Recommendation on Guatemala," May 20, 1954, box 3, folder 11, Serafino Romualdi Papers, Kheel Center for Labor-Management Documentation and Archives (KC), Cornell University; Deborah Levenson-Estrada, *Trade Unionists Against Terror: Guatemala City, 1954–1985* (Chapel Hill: University of North Carolina Press, 1994), 30.

20 Gleijeses, *Shattered Hope*, 280–300; Kinzer, *Overthrow*, 138–40.

21 Romualdi, "Report and Recommendation on Guatemala."

22 Romualdi, *Presidents and Peons*, 244.

23 Gleijeses, *Shattered Hope*, 320–60; Kinzer, *Overthrow*, 141–7; Levenson-Estrada, *Trade Unionists Against Terror*, 23–4

24 Levenson-Estrada, *Trade Unionists Against Terror*, 25–6.

25 Quoted in Romualdi, *Presidents and Peons*, 240.

26 "ORIT Statement on Guatemala," Mexico City, June 25, 1954, box 3, folder 11, Romualdi Papers, KC; Alexander and Parker, *International Labor*, 126.

27 "Guatemala Labor Being Reshuffled," *New York Times*, July 20, 1954; Romualdi, *Presidents and Peons*, 244; Levenson-Estrada, *Trade Unionists Against Terror*, 29–34; Alexander and Parker, *International Labor Organizations*, 125.

28 Greg Grandin, *The Last Colonial Massacre: Latin America in the Cold War* (Chicago: University of Chicago Press, 2004); Levenson-Estrada, *Trade Unionists Against Terror*.

29 Patrick Iber, *Neither Peace Nor Freedom: The Cultural Cold War in Latin America* (Cambridge, MA: Harvard University Press, 2015), 123.

30 Alexander and Parker, *International Labor*, 117–18; Romualdi, *Presidents and Peons*, 181; Iber, *Neither Peace*, 123–4.

31 Iber, *Neither Peace*, 124; Michelle Chase, *Revolution Within the Revolution: Women and Gender Politics in Cuba, 1952–1962* (Chapel Hill: University of North Carolina Press, 2015), 22, 66–7.

32 Alexander and Parker, *International Labor*, 131–2; Romualdi, *Presidents*, 187–98.

33 Iber, *Neither Peace*, 133.

34 Samuel Farber, *The Origins of the Cuban Revolution Reconsidered* (Chapel Hill: University of North Carolina Press, 2006), 154–7.

35 Robert Alexander to Jay Lovestone, June 8, 1959, box 3, folder 37, Robert Jackson Alexander Papers, Special Collections and University Archives, Rutgers University.

36 Romualdi, *Presidents and Peons*, 202–9.

37 Iber, *Neither Peace*, 133.

38 AFL-CIO Executive Council statement, May 4, 1960, quoted in Romualdi, *Presidents and Peons*, 222–5.

6. Merger

1 A. H. Raskin, "The New Labor Leaders: A Dual Portrait," *New York Times*, December 21, 1952.

2 Nelson Lichtenstein, *The Most Dangerous Man in Detroit: Walter Reuther and the Fate of American Labor* (New York: Basic Books, 1995), 322.

3 Ted Morgan, *A Covert Life: Jay Lovestone: Communist, Anti-Communist, and Spymaster* (New York: Random House, 1999), 231–2, 245; Hugh Wilford, *The Mighty Wurlitzer: How the CIA Played America* (Cambridge, MA: Harvard University Press, 2009), 62–3, 67.

4 Anthony Carew, *American Labour's Cold War Abroad: From Deep Freeze to Détente, 1945–1970* (Edmonton: Athabasca University Press, 2018), 115–18; Victor G. Reuther, *The Brothers Reuther and the Story of the UAW* (Boston: Houghton Mifflin, 1976), 412.

5 Thomas W. Braden, "I'm Glad the CIA Is 'Immoral,' " *Saturday Evening Post*, May 20, 1967; Reuther, *Brothers Reuther*, 425–6.

6 Wilford, *The Mighty Wurlitzer*, 63–4; Carew, *American Labour*, 119–29; Reuther, *Brothers Reuther*, 382–3.

7 Vijay Prashad, *The Darker Nations: A People's History of the Third World* (New York: New Press, 2007), 45.

8 A. H. Raskin, "Meany Says Nehru and Tito Aid Reds," *New York Times*, December 14, 1955; Lichtenstein, *The Most Dangerous Man*, 341; Carew, *American Labour*, 152.

9 Raskin, "Meany Says Nehru and Tito Aid Reds"; Lichtenstein, *The Most Dangerous Man*, 341; David Burgess, *Fighting for Social Justice: The Life Story of David Burgess* (Detroit: Wayne State University Press, 2000), 112.

10 Reuther, *Brothers Reuther*, 388; Lichtenstein, *The Most Dangerous Man*, 341; Burgess, *Fighting for Social Justice*, 112–14; David S. Burgess Interview, The Association for Diplomatic Studies and Training, Foreign Affairs Oral History Project, Labor Series, April 7, 1991.

11 Lichtenstein, *The Most Dangerous Man*, 342; Burgess, *Fighting for Social Justice*, 114–16.

12 Quoted in Philip S. Foner, *US Labor and the Vietnam War* (New York: International Publishers, 1989), 5–6.

13 "Meany Belittles US-Soviet Talks," *New York Times*, January 9, 1959.

14 James Marlow, "US Labor Leaders Give Mikoyan Grilling on Policies and Propaganda," *Washington Post*, January 9, 1959; Drew Pearson, "Labor-Mikoyan Meeting Candid," *Washington Post*, January 23, 1959; Lichtenstein, *The Most Dangerous Man*, 343.

15 A. H. Raskin, "Meany in Attack on Soviet Leader," *New York Times*, September 18, 1959; A. H. Raskin, "Unionists Spurn Views of Premier," *New York Times*, September 22, 1959.

16 "Summary of the Dinner Debate Between US Union Leaders and Khrushchev," *New York Times*, September 22, 1959.

17 Anthony Carew, "The American Labor Movement in Fizzland: The Free Trade Union Committee and the CIA," *Labor History* 39:1 (1998), 38–9; Carew, *American Labour*, 160.

18 Carew, *American Labour*, 175–7.

19 Quoted in ibid., 177.

20 Ibid., 174.

21 Morgan, *A Covert Life*, 247–9, 348; Wilford, *The Mighty Wurlitzer*, 58, 69.

7. Comradely Brainwashing

1 Miles E. Galvin, "The Latin American Union Leadership Training Program of the Labor Relations Institute of the University of Puerto Rico" (master's thesis, Cornell University, 1961), 145–51; Arnold Zack, *Labor Training in Developing Countries: A Challenge in Responsible Democracy* (New York: Praeger, 1964), 115.

2 Jeff Schuhrke, " 'Comradely Brainwashing': International Development, Labor Education, and Industrial Relations in the Cold War," *Labor: Studies in Working-Class History* 16:3 (2019), 39–67.

3 Thomas C. Field Jr., "Transnationalism Meets Empire: The AFL-CIO, Development, and the Private Origins of Kennedy's Latin America Labor Program," *Diplomatic History* 42:2 (2018), 312–14; Serafino Romualdi, *Presidents and Peons: Recollections of a Labor Ambassador in Latin America* (New York: Funk and Wagnalis, 1967), 416.

4 Galvin, *Latin American Union Leadership Training Program*, 215.

5 Proposal by Joseph A. Beirne, April 28, 1960, Joseph Mire to Robert Alexander, June 6, 1960, Joseph Mire to Executive Committee, August 3, 1960, box 18, folder 11,

National Institute for Labor Education Files (NILE), Kheel Center for Labor-Management Documentation and Archives (KC), Cornell University; "A Proposal for a Comprehensive Educational Program for Leaders of South American Trade Unions," August 17, 1960, box 56, folder 27, RG1-038, George Meany Memorial AFL-CIO Archive (GMMA), University of Maryland, College Park; John McCollum to Joseph Mire, September 8, 1960, box 17, folder 8, NILE, KC.

6 Policy and Design Committee of the AFL-CIO, University of Chicago Latin American Trade Union Project, "A Proposal for the Establishment of a Fund or Foundation for Union Leadership Development in Latin America," June 1961, box 20, folder 8, LR002254, Walter P. Reuther Library of Labor and Urban Affairs (Reuther Library), Wayne State University; Policy and Design Committee, Minutes of the Meeting, May 12, 1961, box 16, folder 16, RG18-007, GMMA; McCollum to Board of Trustees, September 26, 1961, and McCollum to Ross, October 17, 1961, box 16, folder 15, RG18-007, GMMA.

7 John McCollum and Joseph Beirne correspondence, August 14 to December 5, 1961, box 25, folder 10, University of Chicago Extension Records, Series VII.

8 McCollum to Board of Trustees, January 8, 1962, box 57, folder 1, RG1-038, GMMA.

9 Interview with Ben Stephansky, Chevy Chase, MD, June 27, 1975, box 10, folder 39, Robert Jackson Alexander Papers, Special Collections and University Archives, Rutgers University.

10 John F. Kennedy, Inaugural Address, January 20, 1961, jfklibrary.org.

11 Field, "Transnationalism Meets Empire," 316–22.

12 Comptroller General of the United States, *How to Improve Management of US-Financed Programs to Develop Free Labor Movements in Less Developed Countries*, Washington, DC, December 29, 1975, 65; Zack, *Labor Training*, 175–6.

13 Romualdi, *Presidents and Peons*, 417–18.

14 Romualdi, "The Communist Threat to Labor in Latin America," Address to the Annual Meeting of the United States Inter-American Council, December 10, 1959, box 11, folder 2, Serafino Romualdi Papers, KC.

15 AFL-CIO News, "Meany to Industry: Aid Latin Progress," Sept. 28, 1963, box 57, folder 7, RG1-038, GMMA.

16 J. Peter Grace, "A Consensus in Action: The AIFLD," Address on the Occasion of Observance of International Trade Week, Sept. 16, 1965, box 319, folder 2, Communications Workers of America Records (CWA), The Tamiment Library and Robert F. Wagner Labor Archives (TL), New York University.

17 "Boldness on Latin America," *New York Times*, February 11, 1961; J. Peter Grace, "United States Business Responds," *Annals of the American Academy of Political and Social Science* no. 331 (March 1961), 143–7.

18 Victor Reuther to Walter Reuther, n.d. (likely August or September 1961), box 20, folder 8, LR002254, Reuther Library.

19 Victor Reuther to Walter Reuther, June 1, 1962, box 20, folder 11, LR002254, Reuther Library; "Amazing Grace: The Story of W. R. Grace and Co.," *NACLA's Latin America and Empire Report* 10:3 (March 1976), 13.

20 Comptroller General of the United States, *How to Improve Management of US-Financed Programs*, 65.

21 *Goal: A Better Mañana, Democratic Labor Schools in the Americas*, 1965, box 16, folder 22, RG18-007, GMMA; Robert J. Alexander and Eldon M. Parker, *A History of Organized Labor in Brazil* (Westport, CT: Praeger, 2003), 163; Robert J. Alexander

and Eldon M. Parker, *A History of Organized Labor in Peru and Ecuador* (Westport, CT: Praeger, 2007), 79–81; Hobart A. Spalding Jr., *Organized Labor in Latin America* (New York: New York University Press, 1977), 261.

22 Romualdi, *Presidents and Peons*, 422.

23 AIFLD Annual Progress Report, 1969, box 17, folder 7, RG18-007, GMMA.

24 Condensed Report of the Second Meeting of AIFLD Field Representatives and Directors of Education, June 1965, box 16, folder 21, RG18-007, GMMA.

25 Romualdi, *Presidents and Peons*, 423.

26 *AIFLD Report*, October 1963, box 57, folder 1, RG1-038, GMMA.

27 Eugene H. Methvin, "Labor's New Weapon for Democracy," *Reader's Digest*, October 1966, 24.

28 Report on Internship Program for Graduates of the First Course, n.d., box 1, folder 7, NILE, KC.

29 Luis Carlos Vasco, August 2010, quoted in Larissa Rosa Corrêa, " 'Democracy and Freedom' in Brazilian Trade Unionism," in *American Labor's Global Ambassadors: The International History of the AFL-CIO During the Cold War*, Robert A. Waters and Geert Van Goethem, eds. (New York: Palgrave Macmillan, 2013), 185.

30 Bermúdez Pose to McLellan, December 15, 1968, box 25, folder 10, RG18-001, GMMA.

31 *AIFLD Report*, January 1965, box 10, folder 1, Romuladi Papers, KC; Larissa Rosa Corrêa, "Looking at the Southern Cone: American Trade Unionism in the Cold War Military Dictatorships of Brazil and Argentina," *International Review of Social History* 62:S25 (2017), 253.

32 Doherty Jr. to Sam Haddad, April 15, 1966, box 17, folder 1, RG18-007, GMMA.

33 "AIFLD Graduate Expresses Views," July–August 1964, US Department of Labor, box 6, folder 9, LR000488_VRLC, Reuther Library.

34 Report on Internship Program for Graduates of the First Course, box 1, folder 7, NILE, KC.

35 George C. Lodge, *Spearheads of Democracy: Labor in Developing Countries* (New York: Harper and Row/Council on Foreign Relations, 1962), 180–1.

36 James Barron, "William C. Doherty, Ex-President of Letter Carriers' Union, Is Dead," *New York Times*, August 12, 1987.

37 Interview with William Doherty Jr., Association for Diplomatic Studies and Training Foreign Affairs, Oral History Project, Labor Series, October 3, 1996.

38 $3.38 million was allocated to the Education Department compared with $2.09 million the Social Projects Department: AIFLD Estimated Budget Overview, 1966, box 17, folder 2, RG18-007, GMMA.

39 Doherty to Meany, February 11, 1964, and ASINCOOP Brochure, 1965, box 57, folders 8 and 9, RG18-038, GMMA; AIFLD Annual Progress Report, 1969, box 17, folder 7, RG18-007, GMMA.

40 AIFLD Report, June 1965, box 10, folder 1, Romualdi Papers, KC; "American Institute for Free Labor Development: A Union to Union Program for the Americas," n.d., 23, box 464, folder 1, Archive Union File #6046, KC.; Jeff Schuhrk⬚e, "Agrarian Reform and the AFL-CIO's Cold War in El Salvador," *Diplomatic History* 44:4 (2020), 527–53.

41 "Impact Projects: The Quick Help, Small-Project Program to Enable Unionists to Help Themselves and Expand Their Community Roles," March 1965, box 57, folder 9, RG1-038, GMMA.

42 Andrew Herod, *Labor Geographies: Workers and the Landscapes of Capitalism: Workers and the Landscapes of Capitalism* (New York: Guilford Press, 2001), 168; AIFLD Annual Progress Report, 1969, box 17, folder 7, RG18-007, and AIFLD Administrator's Monthly Report to the Board of Trustees, December 1965, box 57, folder 9, RG1-038, GMMA.

43 Angelo Verdu to AIFLD, June 7, 1965, box 16, folder 21, RG18-007, GMMA; "Brother to Brother, Worker to Worker: The John F. Kennedy Memorial Housing Project," AIFLD, n.d., box 68, folder 4, Archive Union File #6046, KC; "AFL-CIO Loan Has Alliance for Progress Booming in Mexico," AIFLD Report, December 1963, box 128, folder 1, Lens Papers, CHM; Susana Collin Moya, "Cuando gringos construyeron departamentos en Balbuena," *El Universal*, September 29, 2018, eluniversal.com.

44 Dan Kurzman, "Lovestone's Aid Program Bolsters US Foreign Policy," *Washington Post*, January 2, 1966; Robert J. Alexander and Eldon M. Parker, *A History of Organized Labor in Uruguay and Paraguay* (Westport, CT, 2005), 56–8.

45 NACLA and Carlos Diaz, "AIFLD Losing Its Grip," *NACLA's Latin America and Empire Report* 8:9 (November 1974), 11.

46 US Congressional Record, Senate, September 25, 1968, 28192, 28203; Herod, *Labor Geographies*, 191.

8. Intervenors

1 John D. Pomfret, "Lovestone Gets High Labor Post," *New York Times*, December 21, 1963; Dan Kurzman, "Lovestone's Cold War," *New Republic*, June 25, 1966; Mike Davis, *Prisoners of the American Dream: Politics and Economy in the History of the US Working Class* (London: Verso, 1986), 132–3.

2 Thomas C. Field Jr., *From Development to Dictatorship: Bolivia and the Alliance for Progress in the Kennedy Era* (Ithaca, NY: Cornell University Press, 2014).

3 Stephen G. Rabe, *US Intervention in British Guiana: A Cold War Story* (Chapel Hill: University of North Carolina Press, 2005), 93–4; National Security Action Memoranda (NSAM): NSAM 135, British Guiana, March 8, 1962, JFKNSF-335-014-p0005, Papers of John F. Kennedy. Presidential Papers. National Security Files, jfklibrary.org.

4 Stanley Meisler, "Meddling in Latin America," *The Nation*, February 10, 1964, 134; "Note on the Trade Union Movement in British Guiana Showing How It is Under the Dominance of the United States Trade Union Movement, Whose Aim Is to Overthrow the Government of British Guiana," June 1964, box 136, folder 5, Sidney Lens Papers, Chicago History Museum.

5 Serafino Romualdi, *Presidents and Peons: Recollections of a Labor Ambassador in Latin America* (New York: Funk and Wagnalis, 1967), 352.

6 Neil Sheehan, "CIA Men Aided Strikes in Guiana Against Dr. Jagan," *New York Times*, February 22, 1967; Rabe, *US Intervention in British Guiana*, 110–12; Robert Waters and Gordon Daniels, "The World's Longest General Strike: The AFL-CIO, the CIA, and British Guiana," *Diplomatic History* 29:2 (2005), 297.

7 Cheddi Jagan, "Jagan Defends Labor Bill," *New York Times*, June 28, 1963.

8 Romualdi, *Presidents and Peons*, 351; Rabe, *US Intervention in British Guiana*, 111.

9 Rabe, *US Intervention in British Guiana*, 127–38; Romualdi, *Presidents and Peons*, 345–6.

10 Andrew Herod, *Labor Geographies: Workers and the Landscapes of Capitalism* (New York: Guilford Press, 2001), 189–90.

11 Report on Brazil prepared by the AFL-CIO Department of International Affairs, May 4, 1964, box 16, folder 10, RG18-001, George Meany Memorial AFL-CIO Archive (GMMA), University of Maryland, College Park.

12 Cliff Welch, "Labor Internationalism: US Involvement in Brazilian Unions, 1945–1965," *Latin American Research Review* 30:2 (1995), 81; Romualdi, *Presidents and Peons*, 286–8.

13 "Academic Program: Third Training Group," January–May 1963, box 1, folder 7, National Institute for Labor Education Papers, Kheel Center for Labor-Management Documentation and Archives (KC), Cornell University.

14 Romualdi, *Presidents and Peons*, 289.

15 "Washington Participants: Union Affiliation, Position, and Activities: Brazil," December 1965, box 319, folder 14, Communications Workers of America Records (CWA), The Tamiment Library and Robert F. Wagner Labor Archives (TL), New York University; Eugene H. Methvin, "Labor's New Weapon for Democracy," *Reader's Digest*, October 1966, 28.

16 Thomas E. Skidmore, *The Politics of Military Rule in Brazil, 1964–85* (New York: Oxford University Press, 1988), 24–5.

17 Serafino Romualdi, July 8, 1964, box 2, folder 5, Serafino Romualdi Papers, KC; AIFLD, *Goal: A Better Mañana, Democratic Labor Schools in the Americas*, 1965, box 16, folder 22, RG18-007, GMMA.

18 Labor News Conference, Mutual Broadcasting System, "Building Free Trade Unionism in Latin America," July 13, 1964, box 16, folder 11, RG18-001, GMMA; Victor Reuther to Walter Reuther, July 29, 1964, box 6, folder 9, LR000488_VRLC, Walter P. Reuther Library of Labor and Urban Affairs, (Reuther Library), Wayne State University; *On Company Business*, directed by Allan Francovich, released April 15, 1980.

19 Larissa Rosa Corrêa, "'Democracy and Freedom' in Brazilian Trade Unionism," in *American Labor's Global Ambassadors: The International History of the AFL-CIO during the Cold War*, Robert A. Waters and Geert Van Goethem, eds. (New York: Palgrave Macmillan, 2013), 187–8.

20 Labor News Conference (emphasis added), July 13, 1964, box 16, folder 11, RG18-001, GMMA.

21 Victor Reuther to Walter Reuther, July 29, 1964, box 6, folder 9, LR000488_VRLC, Reuther Library.

22 Andrew McLellan, Aide Mémoire, November 8, 1966, box 16, folder 11, RG18-001, GMMA.

23 *AIFLD Report*, September 1964, box 10, folder 1, Romualdi Papers, KC.

24 McLellan to Herbert Baker, June 15, 1966, box 16, folder 4, RG18-001, GMMA.

25 Robert J. Alexander and Eldon M. Parker, *A History of Organized Labor in Brazil* (Westport, CT: Praeger, 2003), 165.

26 Dan Kurzman, "Use of Marines Irked Lovestone," *Washington Post*, January 1, 1966.

27 Interview with John Crimmins, Brasilia, August 8, 1975, box 5, folder 1, Robert Jackson Alexander Papers, Special Collections and University Archives, Rutgers University; Alexander and Parker, *A History of Organized Labor in Brazil*, 163–4.

28 Piero Gleijeses, *The Dominican Crisis: The 1965 Constitutionalist Revolt and American Intervention* (Baltimore: Johns Hopkins University Press, 1978), 304–7.

29 Howard J. Wiarda, "The Aftermath of the Trujillo Dictatorship: The Emergence of a Pluralist Political System in the Dominican Republic" (PhD diss. University of Florida, 1965), 70.

30 Susanne Bodenheimer, "The AFL-CIO in Latin America: The Dominican Republic, a Case Study," *Viet Report* (September/October 1967), 17.

31 Ibid., 18.

32 Patrick J. Iber, " 'Who Will Impose Democracy?': Sacha Volman and the Contradictions of CIA Support for the Anticommunist Left in Latin America," *Diplomatic History* 37: 5 (2013), 1011–12, 1016–17.

33 Ibid., 1010–13.

34 Bodenheimer, "The AFL-CIO in Latin America," 18.

35 Ibid., 27–8; Iber, "Who Will Impose," 1013.

36 Romualdi, *Presidents and Peons*, 402–3.

37 Gleijeses, *The Dominican Crisis*, 253–8.

38 Bodenheimer, "The AFL-CIO in Latin America," 28; Iber, "Who Will Impose," 1023.

39 "The CIA at Bay," *Columbus Citizens-Journal*, September 2, 1964; "Public Has Right to Expect Somebody to Keep Tabs on CIA," *Evansville Press*, September 1, 1964.

40 Iber, "Who Will Impose," 1024–6.

41 Bodenheimer, "The AFL-CIO in Latin America," 18, 27.

42 AIFLD, Washington Participants: Union Affiliation, Position, and Activities, Dominican Republic, December 1965, box 319, folder 14, CWA, TL.

43 Bodenheimer, "The AFL-CIO in Latin America," 9; Herod, *Labor Geographies*, 173; Dan Kurzman, "Lovestone's Aid Program Bolsters US Foreign Policy," *Washington Post*, January 2, 1966.

44 Memorandum from Joe Bermudez, AIFLD Country Program Director, to Alexander Firfer, USAID Mission Director, December 1, 1967 and AIFLD, report on Dominican Republic programs, 1969, RG18-001, box 20, folder 11, GMMA.

9. Mama Maida

1 Memorandum of Conversation with AID Director David Bell, Oct. 2, 1963, box 65, folder 1, RG1-038, George Meany Memorial AFL-CIO Archive (GMMA), University of Maryland, College Park; Labor Advisory Committee, Meeting Minutes, January 7, 1964, March 3, 1964, and August 17, 1964, box 327, folder 6, Communications Workers of America Records (CWA), The Tamiment Library and Robert F. Wagner Labor Archives (TL), New York University.

2 "Women Labor Leaders Are Going to England in Good-Will Exchange with 4 from There," *New York Times*, January 10, 1945.

3 Yevette Richards, *Maida Springer: Pan-Africanist and International Labor Leader* (Pittsburgh: University of Pittsburgh Press, 2000), 36–7, 77–8, 95.

4 Ibid., 41–3.

5 Ibid., 8, 100–3.

6 Frederick Cooper, *Decolonization and African Society: The Labor Question in French and British Africa* (Cambridge: Cambridge University Press, 1996), 273–4; Opoku Agyeman, *The Failure of Grassroots Pan-Africanism: The Case of the All-African Trade Union Federation* (Lanham, MD: Lexington Books, 2003), 52–4.

7   Frederick Cooper, *Africa Since 1940: The Past of the Present* (New York: Cambridge University Press, 2002), 52, 70–1; Cooper, *Decolonization and African Society*, 285–386.

8   Richards, *Maida Springer*, 101, 114–17, 133–5.

9   "Tunisian Nationalist in Plea over 'Voice'; French Not Consulted, Ponder A.F.L. Role," *New York Times*, September 4, 1951; Ted Morgan, *A Covert Life: Jay Lovestone: Communist, Anti-Communist, and Spymaster* (New York: Random House, 1999), 256; Anthony Carew, *American Labour's Cold War Abroad: From Deep Freeze to Détente, 1945–1970* (Edmonton: Athabasca University Press, 2018), 168–9.

10 Richards, *Maida Springer*, 106–7, 118–21; "World 'New Deal' Urged by African," *New York Times*, May 15, 1959; Elana Schor, "The Other Obama-Kennedy Connection," *The Guardian*, January 10, 2008.

11 Richards, *Maida Springer*, 130–48; Carew, *American Labour*, 178.

12 Richards, Maida Springer, 153–5; John C. Stoner, "'We Will Follow a Nationalist Policy, But We Will Never Be Neutral': American Labor and Neutralism in Cold War Africa, 1957–1962," in *American Labor's Global Ambassadors: The International History of the AFL-CIO during the Cold War*, Robert A. Waters and Geert Van Goethem, eds. (New York: Palgrave Macmillan, 2013), 241.

13 Agyeman, *The Failure*, 126, 145–7; Richards, *Maida Springer*, 195–7.

14 Richards, *Maida Springer*, 178–80; Agyeman, *The Failure*, 125–6.

15 Gary K. Busch, *The Political Role of International Trade Unions* (New York: St. Martin's Press, 1983), 94; Richards, *Maida Springer*, 209–10.

16 Richards, *Maida Springer*, 179–80; Stoner, "We Will Follow," 247; Carew, *American Labour*, 180–1.

17 Emmanuel Gerard and Bruce Kuklick, *Death in the Congo: Murdering Patrice Lumumba* (Cambridge, MA: Harvard University Press, 2015).

18 "Unionists in Africa Reject Outside Ties," *New York Times*, May 31, 1961.

19 Agyeman, *The Failure*, 131–7; Richards, *Maida Springer*, 213–15, 221.

20 Richards, *Maida Springer*, 198.

21 Ibid., 247–52.

22 Maida Springer to Jay Lovestone, April 10, 1962, box 10, folder 19, RG18-001, GMMA.

23 Tailors and Textile Workers Union to ILGWU, June 26, 1961, box 10, folder 20, RG18-001, GMMA.

24 Richards, *Maida Springer*, 239–40; Springer to Lovestone, March 16, 1965, box 11, folder 22, RG18-001, GMMA.

25 Agyeman, *The Failure*, 129–31, 234–5.

26 Ibid., 198–203; Richards, *Maida Springer*, 254–5.

27 Omer Becu to Irving Brown, March 25, 1965, box 1, folder 23, Jay Lovestone Papers, Kheel Center for Labor-Management Documentation and Archives (KC), Cornell University.

28 Quoted in Stoner, "We Will Follow," 245.

29 American Federation of Labor-Congress of Industrial Organizations, *Proceedings of the Seventh Convention*, vol. 2, Bal Harbour, FL, December 7–12, 1967, 100.

30 AALC Board of Directors Meeting, January 19, 1965, box 2, folder 10, RG18-003, GMMA.

31 "Preamble," 1964, box 15, folder 19, RG18-007, GMMA.

32 Irving Brown, Basic Aims of the African-American Labor Center, 1965, box 15, folder 18, RG18-007, GMMA

33 Comptroller General of the United States, *How to Improve Management of US-Financed Programs to Develop Free Labor Movements in Less Developed Countries*, Washington, DC, December 29, 1975, 67; AALC Fiscal and Program Report, April 1967, box 16, folder 1, RG18-007, GMMA.

34 Nathaniel Godfried, "Spreading American Corporatism: Trade Union Education for Third World Labour," *Review of African Political Economy* 39 (September 1987), 55.

35 African-American Labor Center, March 1967, box 15, folder 22, RG18-007, GMMA.

36 Rozell Nesbitt, "Belaboring Liberation in South Africa/AFL-CIO in Africa," Rozell 'Prexy' Nesbitt Writings and Speeches 37 (1986), digitalcommons.colum.edu; Godfried, "Spreading American Corporatism," 57.

37 "AATUF and African Unity: Neo-Colonialist Intrigues Will Fail," *Ghana Evening News*, February 9, 1965, box 11, folder 22, RG18-001, GMMA.

38 Seymour Hersh, "CIA Said to Have Aided Plotters Who Overthrew Nkrumah in Ghana," *New York Times*, May 9, 1978.

39 Lovestone to Ernest Lee, January 23, 1967, box 15, folder 22, RG18-007, GMMA [emphasis added].

40 AFL-CIO, *Proceedings of the Seventh Convention*, vol. 2, 101.

41 Ukandi Damachi, *The Role of Trade Unions in the Development Process: With a Case Study of Ghana* (New York: Praeger, 1974), 85–6.

42 Lester Trachtman to Franklin H. Williams, May 17, 1967, box 16, folder 1, RG18-007, GMMA; Agyeman, *The Failure*, 241–2.

43 Agyeman, *The Failure*, 304–5; Richards, *Maida Springer*, 258–9.

10. Vietnam

1 Edmund Wehrle, *Between a River and a Mountain: The AFL-CIO and the Vietnam War* (Ann Arbor: University of Michigan Press, 2005), 36–54.

2 Ibid., 56–8.

3 Ibid., 66–70, 80–3.

4 Ibid., 89–96.

5 Ibid., 102–7.

6 Local 1199 would become an independent union in the 1980s before merging with the Service Employees International Union in 1998.

7 Philip S. Foner, *US Labor and the Vietnam War* (New York: International Publishers, 1989), 12, 17.

8 Leon Fink and Brian Greenberg, *Upheaval in the Quiet Zone: A History of Hospital Workers' Union, Local 1199* (Urbana: University of Illinois Press, 1989), 23.

9 Foner, *US Labor*, 23.

10 Frank Koscielski, *Divided Loyalties: American Unions and the Vietnam War* (New York: Garland Publishing, 1999), 59.

11 Foner, *US Labor*, 23–31.

12 Ibid., 29–31.

13 STEP budget, grants, November 22, 1968, box 24, folder 24, LR000488_VRLC, Walter P. Reuther Library of Labor and Urban Affairs, Wayne State University.

14 Victor G. Reuther, *The Brothers Reuther and the Story of the UAW* (Boston: Houghton Mifflin, 1976), 411; STEP budget, grants, November 22, 1968, box 24, folder 24, LR000488_VRLC, Reuther Library; William C. Doherty Jr. to Joseph Beirne, July 21, 1966, box 319, folder 1, Communications Workers of America Records (CWA), The Tamiment Library and Robert F. Wagner Labor Archives (TL), New York University.

15 Harry Bernstein, "AFL-CIO Unit Accused of 'Snooping' Abroad," *Los Angeles Times*, May 22, 1966.

16 AFL-CIO Executive Council statement on Victor Reuther, n.d. (August 1966), box 319, folder 19, CWA, TL.

17 Foner, *US Labor*, 36–40.

18 "US Labor Shunning Conference of I.L.O.," *New York Times*, June 4, 1966; John P. Windmuller, "The Foreign Policy Conflict in American Labor," *Political Science Quarterly* 82:2 (1967), 206–14; Reuther, *Brothers Reuther*, 376; George Morris, *CIA and American Labor: The Subversion of the AFL-CIO's Foreign Policy* (New York: International Publishers, 1967), 117.

19 Foner, *US Labor*, 41–2

20 Windmuller, "The Foreign Policy Conflict," 220–1; Anthony Carew, *American Labour's Cold War Abroad: From Deep Freeze to Détente, 1945–1970* (Edmonton: Athabasca University Press, 2018), 272–3.

21 UAW Administration Letter, December 28, 1966, box 319, folder 1, CWA TL.

22 UAW officers' resignation notice, February 3, 1967, box 4, folder 7, Jay Lovestone Papers, Kheel Center for Labor-Management Documentation and Archives (KC), Cornell University; Reuther, *Brothers Reuther*, 378.

23 Nelson Lichtenstein, *The Most Dangerous Man in Detroit: Walter Reuther and the Fate of American Labor* (New York: Basic Books, 1995), 421.

24 Koscielski, *Divided Loyalties*, 72–3.

25 Foner, *US Labor*, 50–1, 54–5, 64; John Bennet Sears, "Peace Work: The Antiwar Tradition in American Labor from the Cold War to the Iraq War," *Diplomatic History* 34:4 (2010), 710.

26 Quoted in Foner, *US Labor*, 52–3.

27 Ibid., 58–61.

28 "Labor on Vietnam," *New York Times*, January 5, 1968.

29 Reuther, *Brothers Reuther*, 378.

30 Wehrle, *Between a River*, 131–3.

31 AFL-CIO Press Release, March 29, 1968, box 18, folder 2, RG18-007, George Meany Memorial AFL-CIO Archive (GMMA), University of Maryland, College Park.

32 Wehrle, *Between a River*, 143–5.

33 Memorandum of AAFLI Activities, June 19, 1969, box 17, folder 6, RG18-007, GMMA.

34 Comptroller General of the United States, *How to Improve Management of US-Financed Programs to Develop Free Labor Movements in Less Developed Countries*, Washington, DC, December 29, 1975, 66.

35 Richard M. Nixon to J. Peter Grace, February 18, 1969, box 320, folder 10, CWA, TL.

36 Wehrle, *Between a River*, 149–51

37 Greg Grandin, *Kissinger's Shadow: The Long Reach of America's Most Controversial Statesman* (New York: Metropolitan Books, 2015), 55–65.

38 Koscielski, *Divided Loyalties*, 17–18.
39 Juan de Onis, "Nixon Puts 'Bums' Label On Some College Radicals," *New York Times*, May 2, 1970.
40 Koscielski, *Divided Loyalties*, 18.
41 Foner, *US Labor*, 100–2.
42 Quoted in ibid., 166–7.
43 Some, including Victor Reuther, have openly questioned whether the plane crash was an accident or the result of foul play. See Michael Parenti and Peggy Noton, "The Wonderful Life and Strange Death of Walter Reuther," *CovertAction* 54 (Fall 1995), 37–43.
44 Les Leopold, *The Man Who Hated Work and Loved Labor: The Life and Times of Tony Mazzocchi* (White River Junction, VT: Chelsea Green Publishing Company, 2007), 277–8.
45 Christian G. Appy, *American Reckoning: The Vietnam War and Our National Identity* (New York: Viking, 2015), 193–5; Koscielski, *Divided Loyalties*, 19; Foner, *US Labor*, 104–5.
46 Edmund F. Wehrle, " 'Partisan for the Hard Hats': Charles Colson, George Meany, and the Failed Blue-Collar Strategy," *Labor: Studies in Working-Class History of the Americas* 5:3 (2010), 45–55.
47 Quoted in Appy, *American Reckoning*, 195.
48 Koscielski, *Divided Loyalties*, 20.
49 Quoted in Appy, *American Reckoning*, 200.
50 Koscielski, *Divided Loyalties*, 21.
51 Wehrle, "Partisan for the Hard Hats," 58–65.
52 Penny Lewis, *Hardhats, Hippies, and Hawks: The Vietnam Antiwar Movement as Myth and Memory* (Ithaca, NY: Cornell University Press, 2013).
53 Wehrle, *Between a River*, 179–85.
54 Ibid., 187–91.
55 Quoted in Foner, *US Labor*, 152.

11. Exposed

1 Dan Georgakas and Marvin Surkin, *Detroit: I Do Mind Dying* (Cambridge, MA: South End Press, 1975).
2 "The CIA's Campus Capers," *New York Post*, February 15, 1967; Juan de Onis, "Ramparts Says CIA Received Student Report," *New York Times*, February 16, 1967.
3 Don Irwin and Vincent J. Burke, "21 Foundations, Union Got Money from CIA," *Los Angeles Times*, February 26, 1967; "Public Has Right to Expect Somebody to Keep Tabs on CIA," *Evansville Press*, September 1, 1964; "Misuse of Foundations," *Minneapolis Star*, September 16, 1964.
4 James A. Wechsler, "CIA and AFL-CIO: The Bigger Story," *New York Post*, February 16, 1967; Jim Crellin, "Vic Reuther Says CIA Has AFL-CIO Tie," *Detroit News*, February 17, 1967.
5 William H. Rudy, "The CIA Dispute Heats Up," *New York Post*, February 18, 1967; Richard Harwood, "Public Service Union Abroad Aided by CIA," *Washington Post*, February 23, 1967; Joseph E. Hower, "Jerry Wurf, the Rise of AFSCME, and the Fate

of Labor Liberalism, 1947–1981" (PhD diss., Georgetown University, 2013), 213–14n9; Stephen G. Rabe, *US Intervention in British Guiana: A Cold War Story* (Chapel Hill: University of North Carolina Press, 2005), 149–50.

6   Harwood, "Public Service Union Abroad Aided by CIA"; Brandon Kirk Williams, "Labor's Cold War Missionaries: The IFPCW's Transnational Mission for the Third World's Petroleum and Chemical Workers, 1954–1975," *Labor: Studies in Working-Class History of the Americas* 7:4 (2010), 57; Victor G. Reuther, *The Brothers Reuther and the Story of the UAW* (Boston: Houghton Mifflin, 1976), 413; Les Leopold, *The Man Who Hated Work and Loved Labor: The Life and Times of Tony Mazzocchi* (White River Junction, VT: Chelsea Green Publishing Company, 2007), 164–96.

7   Dan Kurzman, "Labor Group Got $1 Million from CIA," *Washington Post*, February 21, 1967.

8   Thomas W. Braden, "I'm Glad the CIA Is 'Immoral,' " *Saturday Evening Post*, May 20, 1967.

9   James D. Selk, "No Spy Work, UAW Official Says," *Wisconsin State Journal*. June 27, 1967.

10 Damon Stetson, "Meany Opposes CIA Aid to Labor," *New York Times*, February 21, 1967; Ted Morgan, *A Covert Life: Jay Lovestone: Communist, Anti-Communist, and Spymaster* (New York: Random House, 1999), 350.

11 Meany to National Press Club, June 27, 1967, box 68, folder 5, Archive Union Files, Kheel Center for Labor-Management Documentation and Archives, Cornell University.

12 Joseph J. Palisi, "CIA Front Groups," *Washington Post*, January 2, 1967, box 31, folder 28, Victor G. Reuther Papers, Walter P. Reuther Library of Labor and Urban Affairs (Reuther Library), Wayne State University.

13 Ernest Lee to Rutherford Poats, May 15, 1968, box 19, folder 26, LR000488_VRLC, Reuther Library; Richard Dudman, "Agent Meany," *New Republic*, May 3, 1969.

14 Reuther, *Brothers Reuther*, 423.

15 George Morris, *CIA and American Labor: The Subversion of the AFL-CIO's Foreign Policy* (New York: International Publishers, 1967); Ronald Radosh, *American Labor and United States Foreign Policy* (New York: Random House, 1969).

16 Radosh, *American Labor and United States Foreign Policy*, 25.

17 Quoted in Philip S. Foner, *US Labor and the Vietnam War* (New York: International Publishers, 1989), 86–7.

18 "Senate Study Criticizes US Latin-Labor Unit," *Washington Post*, July 15, 1968.

19 Statement by J. William Fulbright Concerning a Report by the GAO on the American Institute for Free Labor Development, 1970, box 57, folder 17, RG1-038, GMMA; Felix Belair Jr., "Meany Clashes with Fulbright," *New York Times*, August 2, 1969.

20 Statement by J. William Fulbright Concerning a Report by the GAO on the American Institute for Free Labor Development, 1970, box 57, folder 17, RG1-038, GMMA; Belair, "Meany Clashes with Fulbright."

21 Statement by J. William Fulbright Concerning a Report by the GAO on the American Institute for Free Labor Development, 1970, box 57, folder 17, RG1-038, GMMA.

22 Dan Kurzman, "Lovestone Now at Odds with Free Trade Unions," *Washington Post*, December 31, 1965.

23 John P. Windmuller, "Internationalism in Eclipse: The ICFTU after Two Decades," *ILR Review* 23:4 (1970), 512–21; Radosh, *American Labor and United States Foreign Policy*, 449.

12. Crisis

1 Kim Moody, *An Injury to All: The Decline of American Unionism* (London: Verso, 1988), 96; Leo Panitch and Sam Gindin, *The Making of Global Capitalism: The Political Economy of American Empire* (New York: Verso, 2012), 135.

2 Mike Davis, *Prisoners of the American Dream: Politics and Economy in the History of the US Working Class* (London: Verso, 1986), 132.

3 Aaron Brenner, Robert Brenner, and Cal Winslow, eds., *Rebel Rank and File: Labor Militancy and Revolt from Below During the Long 1970s* (London: Verso, 2010).

4 Lane Windham, *Knocking on Labor's Door: Union Organizing in the 1970s and the Roots of a New Economic Divide* (Chapel Hill: University of North Carolina Press, 2017).

5 Michael Latham, *The Right Kind of Revolution: Modernization, Development, and US Foreign Policy from the Cold War to the Present* (Ithaca, NY: Cornell University Press, 2011), 166–74.

6 Vijay Prashad, *The Darker Nations: A People's History of the Third World* (New York: New Press, 2007), 132, 189–90.

7 AIFLD, "American Institute for Free Labor Development: A Union to Union Program," Archive Union Files #6046, n.d., box 464, folder 1, Kheel Center for Labor-Management Documentation and Archives (KC), Cornell University.

8 Comptroller General of the United States, *How to Improve Management of US-Financed Programs to Develop Free Labor Movements in Less Developed Countries*, Washington, DC, December 29, 1975, 65–7.

9 AIFLD, "American Institute for Free Labor Development: A Union to Union Program," n.d., box 464, folder 1, Archive Union Files #6046, KC.

10 Peter Winn, "The Pinochet Era," in *Victims of the Chilean Miracle: Workers and Neoliberalism in the Pinochet Era, 1973–2002*, Peter Winn, ed. (Durham, NC: Duke University Press, 2004), 17.

11 Quoted in Tim Shorrock, "Labor's Cold War," *Nation*, May 1, 2003.

12 Fred Hirsch, *An Analysis of Our AFL-CIO Role in Latin America: or, Under the Covers with the CIA* (San Jose: self-published, 1974), 33.

13 Rob McKenzie and Patrick Dunne, *El Golpe: US Labor, the CIA, and the Coup at Ford in Mexico* (London: Pluto Press, 2022), 45.

14 Hirsch, *An Analysis*, 38.

15 McKenzie and Dunne, *El Golpe*, 48–52; Rudolph Rauch, "The Bloody End of a Marxist Dream," *Time*, September 24, 1973; Hirsch, *An Analysis*, 36–8; Gary K. Busch, *The Political Role of International Trade Unions* (New York: St. Martin's Press, 1983), 174–6; Hobart A. Spalding Jr., *Organized Labor in Latin America* (New York: New York University Press, 1977), 266; Kim Scipes, *AFL-CIO's Secret War Against Developing Country Workers: Solidarity or Sabotage?* (Lanham, MD: Lexington Books, 2010), 40–8; Don Thompson and Rodney Larson, *Where Were You, Brother? An Account of Trade Union Imperialism* (London: War on Want, 1979), 47.

16 Hirsch, *An Analysis*, 35–7.

17 Vincent Bevins, *The Jakarta Method: Washington's Anticommunist Crusade and the Mass Murder Program that Shaped Our World* (New York: Public Affairs, 2020), 301n56.

18 Winn, "The Pinochet Era," 19.

19 Robert J. Alexander and Eldon M. Parker, *International Labor Organizations and Organized Labor in Latin America and the Caribbean: A History* (Santa Barbara, CA: Praeger, 2009), 276, 280–1.

20 Seymour Hersh, "CIA Is Linked to Strikes in Chile That Beset Allende," *New York Times*, September 20, 1974.

21 David Bacon, "Fred Hirsch: Doing the Work That Needed to Be Done," *Convergence*, December 28, 2020; Rodney Larson, "CIA Using AFL-CIO Unions to Topple Governments," *Capital Times*, September 24, 1974, box 328, folder 3, CWA, TL.

22 Hirsch, *An Analysis*; "AFL-CIO Role in Latin America Quizzed," *Northern California Labor* 22:12 (April 12, 1974) and "AFL-CIO Speaker Due Here," *Northern California Labor* 23:2 (June 14, 1974), box 328, folder 3, CWA, TL; Fred Hirsch, *The AIFLD, International Trade Secretariats, and Fascism in Chile: An Open Letter to the Labor Movement* (San Jose, CA, self-published, 1975); McKenzie and Dunne, *El Golpe*, 54–6.

23 Quoted in Tim Shorrock, "Labor's Cold War," *Nation*, May 1, 2003.

24 Peter B. Levy, *The New Left and Labor in the 1960s* (Urbana: University of Illinois Press, 1994), 160; Resolution to Suspend American Institute for Free Labor Development, Montgomery County Federation of Teachers, n.d., box 328, folder 3, CWA, TL.

25 Bill Boyarsky and Larry Pryor, "AFL-CIO Conclave: It All Centers on Meany," *Los Angeles Times*, December 11, 1977.

26 George N. Schmidt, *The American Federation of Teachers and the CIA* (Chicago: Substitutes United for Better Schools, 1978).

27 Carlos Diaz, "AIFLD Losing Its Grip," *NACLA Latin America and Empire Report* 8:9 (1974); Thompson and Larson, *Where Were You, Brother*; "Research Associates International," n.d., box 328, folder 3, CWA, TL.

28 Philip Agee, *Inside the Company: CIA Diary* (New York: Bantam Books, 1975); "Union Federation Wins Damages from Penguin," *The Times*, July 22, 1975, box 328, folder 3, CWA, TL.

29 "CIA and CWA," letter to Senator Frank Church from San Diego CWA members, June 1, 1975, box 328, folder 3, TL.

30 Dana Frank, *Buy American: The Untold Story of Economic Nationalism* (Boston: Beacon Press, 1999), 132–3, 150.

31 Damon Stetson, "Meany Criticizes Policies on Freeze and China," *New York Times*, October 1, 1971; William Serrin, "Leonard Woodcock, 89, Ex-U.A.W. Chief Who Was an Ambassador to China, Is Dead," *New York Times*, January 18, 2001.

32 George Meany, "The Shambles of Detente," April 8, 1975, box 18, folder 42, RG34-002, GMMA; Dan Morgan, "Labor's Hierarchy Rejects United States Policy of Detente," *Washington Post*, December 9, 1973.

33 Bernard Gwertzman, "Detente Scored by Solzhenitsyn," *New York Times*, July 1, 1975.

34 Beth Sims, *Workers of the World Undermined: American Labor's Role in US Foreign Affairs* (Boston: South End Press, 1992), 54; George Morris, "Meany Creates Another Channel for CIA-Type Subversion," *Daily World*, December 15, 1977.

35 Comptroller General of the United States. *How to Improve Management of US-Financed Programs*, 61.

13. New Blood

1 Ted Morgan, *A Covert Life: Jay Lovestone: Communist, Anti-Communist, and Spymaster* (New York: Random House, 1999), 350–1.
2 Jimmy Carter, "Statement on the Death of the Former President of the American Federation of Labor and Congress of Industrial Organizations George Meany," January 11, 1980, online by Gerhard Peters and John T. Woolley, The American Presidency Project, presidency.ucsb.edu.
3 Timothy J. Minchin, *Labor Under Fire: A History of the AFL-CIO Since 1979* (Chapel Hill: University of North Carolina Press, 2017), 51.
4 Elaine Sciolino, "Kirkland Wins Acclaim for Success Abroad, but Faces Criticism at Home," *New York Times*, December 15, 1989.
5 Joe Holley, "Rights Activist Irena Kirkland," *Washington Post*, January 25, 2007.
6 Henry Kissinger, Lane Kirkland Eulogy, September 23, 1999, box 735, folder 11, Henry A. Kissinger Papers, part II, Manuscripts and Archives, Yale University Library, findit.library.yale.edu.
7 Minchin, *Labor Under Fire*, 48–50
8 Ibid., 51–4; Sciolino, "Kirkland Wins Acclaim for Success Abroad."
9 "Auto Workers Rejoin AFL-CIO," *UPI*, July 2, 1981.
10 Sciolino, "Kirkland Wins Acclaim for Success Abroad."
11 Beth Sims, *Workers of the World Undermined: American Labor's Role in US Foreign Affairs* (Boston: South End Press, 1992), 11; Interview with William Doherty, October 3, 1996, Association for Diplomatic Studies and Training Foreign Affairs Oral History Project, Labor Series, 5–6.
12 Rachelle Horowitz, "Tom Kahn and the Fight for Democracy: A Political Portrait and Personal Recollection," *Democratiya* 11 (Winter 2007), 234.
13 Ibid., 207–12.
14 John D'Emilio, *Lost Prophet: The Life and Times of Bayard Rustin* (New York: Free Press, 2003), 276–8.
15 Horowitz, "Tom Kahn," 215–25.
16 Richard D. Kahlenberg, *Tough Liberal: Albert Shanker and the Battles over Schools, Unions, Race, and Democracy* (New York: Columbia University Press, 2007), 62, 93–111.
17 Quoted in Kahlenberg, *Tough Liberal*, 148.
18 Ibid., 172–4.
19 Horowitz, "Tom Kahn," 215–25; *A "Freedom Budget" for All Americans* (Washington, DC: A. Philip Randolph Institute, January 1967).
20 Quoted in D'Emilio, *Lost Prophet*, 438–9.
21 Ibid., 458–9.
22 Quoted in Horowitz, "Tom Kahn," 228–9.
23 James Creegan, "The Rebel Who Came in From the Cold: The Tainted Career of Bayard Rustin," *Portside*, March 17, 2016.
24 Quoted in "Socialist Party Is Now Social Democrats, USA," *New York Times*, December 31, 1972.
25 Democratic Socialist Organizing Committee, "You're Us" pamphlet, n.d., box 39, folder 10, LP000002_VGR, Walter P. Reuther Library of Labor and Urban Affairs, Wayne State University.

26 James Kirkchick, "Odd Man Out," *New Republic*, August 26, 2007; Michael Massing, "Trotsky's Orphans: From Bolshevism to Reaganism," *New Republic*, June 22, 1987.

27 Justin Vaïsse, *Neoconservatism: The Biography of a Movement* (Cambridge, MA: Harvard University Press, 2010); Shanker quoted in Kahlenberg, *Tough Liberal*, 258.

28 Jack Clark, "The Ex Syndrome," *NACLA Report on the Americas* (May/June 1988), 26; George Morris, *"Social Democrats-USA": In the Service of Reaction* (New York: New Outlook Publishers, 1976); Sims, *Workers of the World Undermined*, 47; Kahlenberg, *Tough Liberal*, 269–70.

29 Horowitz, "Tom Kahn," 231–4.

14. Endowing Democracy

1 Timothy J. Minchin, *Labor Under Fire: A History of the AFL-CIO Since 1979* (Chapel Hill: University of North Carolina Press, 2017), 118.

2 Rachelle Horowitz, "Tom Kahn and the Fight for Democracy: A Political Portrait and Personal Recollection," *Democratiya* 11 (Winter 2007), 234–6; Gregory F. Domber, "The AFL-CIO, the Reagan Administration and Solidarność," *Polish Review* 52:3 (2007), 278; Eric Chenoweth, "AFL-CIO Support for Solidarity: Moral, Political, Financial," in *American Labor's Global Ambassadors: The International History of the AFL-CIO during the Cold War*, Robert Anthony Waters Jr. and Geert Van Goethem, eds. (New York: Palgrave Macmillan, 2013), 105–6.

3 Quoted in Chenoweth, "AFL-CIO-Support for Solidarity," 106–8.

4 Horowitz, "Tom Kahn," 236–7; Chenoweth, "AFL-CIO Support for Solidarity," 107.

5 Naomi Klein, *The Shock Doctrine: The Rise of Disaster Capitalism* (New York: Picador, 2007), 218–19.

6 Minchin, *Labor Under Fire*, 120.

7 Quoted in ibid., 75–6.

8 Ibid., 77.

9 Quoted in Domber, "The AFL-CIO, the Reagan Administration and Solidarność," 280.

10 Ibid., 282; Chenoweth, "AFL-CIO Support for Solidarity," 111–12.

11 Chenoweth, "AFL-CIO Support for Solidarity," 112.

12 Quoted in Domber, "The AFL-CIO, the Reagan Administration and Solidarność," 283.

13 Chenoweth, "AFL-CIO Support for Solidarity," 108.

14 Domber, "The AFL-CIO, the Reagan Administration and Solidarność," 288, 292–3.

15 Ibid., 284–5.

16 Quoted in Gregory F. Domber, *Empowering Revolution: America, Poland, and the End of the Cold War* (Chapel Hill: University of North Carolina Press, 2014), 109.

17 Ibid., 109–10.

18 Robert Pee, *Democracy Promotion, National Security and Strategy: Foreign Policy Under the Reagan Administration* (London: Routledge, 2015).

19 Bernard Gwertzman, "Skeptics Pelt Shultz with Queries on Reagan's 'Project Democracy,'" *New York Times*, February 24, 1983; Ben A. Franklin, "Project Democracy Takes Wing," *New York Times*, May 29, 1984.

20 Kathy Sawyer, "The AFL-CIO Toils in Foreign Vineyards," *Washington Post*, November 19, 1983.

21 Fay Hansen, "International Labor: The AFL-CIO and Endowment for Democracy," May–June 1985, box 1, folder 14, AFSCME Office of the President Jack Howard Records, Walter P. Reuther Library of Labor and Urban Affair, (Reuther Library), Wayne State University; Beth Sims, *Workers of the World Undermined: American Labor's Role in US Foreign Affairs* (Boston: South End Press, 1992), 43.

22 David K. Shipler, "Missionaries for Democracy: US Aid for Global Pluralism," *New York Times*, June 1, 1986.

23 Domber, "The AFL-CIO, the Reagan Administration and Solidarność," 296; Domber, *Empowering Revolution*, 268.

24 Ben A. Franklin, "Project Democracy Takes Wing"; Seymour Hersh, "Panama General Said to Have Told Army to Rig Vote," *New York Times*, June 22, 1986.

25 Ben A. Franklin, "Democracy Project Facing New Criticisms," *New York Times*, December 4, 1985.

26 Tim Shorrock and Kathy Selvaggio, "Which Side Are You On, AAFLI?", *Nation*, February 15, 1986.

27 Kim Scipes, *AFL-CIO's Secret War against Developing Country Workers: Solidarity or Sabotage?* (Lanham, MD: Lexington Books, 2010), 51–2; Sims, *Workers of the World Undermined*, 14–15.

28 Quoted in Shorrock and Selvaggio, "Which Side Are You On, AAFLI?"

29 AFL-CIO, *Proceedings of the Sixteenth Constitutional Convention of the AFL-CIO, Daily Proceedings and Executive Council Reports*, Anaheim, CA, October 28–31, 1985, 180.

30 "AFL-CIO Units Emerge as Key Organizations in National Endowment for Democracy's Varied Overseas Activities," November 10, 1986, box 1, folder 14, Howard Records, Reuther Library.

31 Seth Mydans, "Major Leftist Leader Is Found Slain in Philippines," *New York Times*, November 14, 1986.

32 Kim Scipes, *KMU: Building Genuine Trade Unionism in the Philippines, 1980–1994* (Quezon City: New Day Publishers, 1996), 116–25; Scipes, *AFL-CIO's Secret War*, 52–5.

33 Piero Gleijeses, *Conflicting Missions: Havana, Washington, and Africa, 1959–1976* (Chapel Hill: University of North Carolina Press, 2011).

34 "AFL-CIO Opposes South Africa," *Vincennes Sun-Commercial*, February 26, 1978.

35 Nathaniel Godfried, "Spreading American Corporatism: Trade Union Education for Third World Labour," *Review of African Political Economy* 39 (September 1987), 57.

36 Godfried, "Spreading American Corporatism," 57–8; Yevette Richards, *Maida Springer: Pan-Africanist and International Labor Leader* (Pittsburgh: University of Pittsburgh Press, 2000), 279–281.

37 Godfried, "Spreading American Corporatism," 58–9; Rozell Nesbitt, "Belaboring Liberation in South Africa/AFL-CIO in Africa," *Rozell 'Prexy' Nesbitt Writings and Speeches* 37 (January 15, 1986), 3; Jim Shevis, "Black S. African, in US Exile, Works to Help Unions Back Home," *Christian Science Monitor*, October 10, 1986.

38 Godfried, "Spreading American Corporatism," 59.

39 AALC, "Report of the AFL-CIO Delegation to South Africa," *South Africa Labor News* (January/February 1983).

40 Nesbitt, "Belaboring Liberation," 9; AALC, "Report of the AFL-CIO Delegation to South Africa."

41 Richards, *Maida Springer*, 280–1

42 Steve Mufson, "Dissent Splits South Africa's Black Unions," *Wall Street Journal*, May 2, 1986; Nesbitt, "Belaboring Liberation," 8.

43 Truth and Reconciliation Commission, *Truth and Reconciliation Commission of South Africa Report, Volume Two* (1998), 469; "Inkathagate: How Buthelezi's Cover Was Blown," *Mail and Guardian*, April 21, 2010.

44 Quoted in Nesbitt, "Belaboring Liberation," 10.

45 Godfried, "Spreading American Corporatism," 59–60; Nesbitt, "Belaboring Liberation," 10.

46 Manning Marable, *Speaking Truth to Power: Essays on Race, Resistance and Radicalism* (Boulder, CO: Westview Press, 1996), 194.

47 Ibid., 191–2.

48 Marable, *Speaking Truth to Power*, 192; Joan Walsh, "Free South Africa Movement Must Cope with Sudden Success," *In These Times*, April 10, 1985.

49 Quoted in Marable, *Speaking Truth to Power*, 195.

50 Peter Cole, *Dockworker Power: Race and Activism in Durban and the San Francisco Bay Area* (Urbana: University of Illinois Press, 2018), 193–200; Marable, *Speaking Truth to Power*, 195.

51 Don Shannon, "Unionist Is 'Outraged' by S. African Actions, Calls for Labor Protest," *Los Angeles Times*, December 1, 1984; Peter Perl and Karlyn Barker, "Unions Join Protests of Apartheid," *Washington Post*, December 5, 1984; Peter Perl, "Labor Urged to Pressure South Africa: Effort to Pull Out Key Firms Discussed," *Washington Post*, January 11, 1985.

52 Marable, *Speaking Truth to Power*, 193; Walsh, "Free South Africa Movement"; Karlyn Barker, "UMW to Escalate Protests Against South Africa," *Washington Post*, July 26, 1985; Frank Swoboda, "Mandela Thanks US Unions for Support, Seeks More Aid," *Washington Post*, June 29, 1990.

53 Richards, *Maida Springer*, 281–2.

54 "Labor Chief Calls for South African Sanctions," *Reno Gazette-Journal*, August 1, 1986.

15. Civil War

1 Greg Grandin, *Empire's Workshop: Latin America, the United States, and the Rise of the New Imperialism* (New York: Henry Holt, 2010), 71.

2 Hobart A. Spalding Jr., "AIFLD Amok," *NACLA Report on the Americas* (May/June 1988), 24; Carlos Al Santiago Rivera, "Labor Relations During the Sandinista Government," *Caribbean Studies* 24:3–4 (1991), 245; G. Nelson Bass, "Organized Labor and US Foreign Policy: The Solidarity Center in Historical Context," PhD diss., Florida International University, 2012), 64–5.

3 Christian G. Appy, *American Reckoning: The Vietnam War and Our National Identity* (New York: Viking, 2015), 290–1.

4 Donald Robinson, "Bill Doherty's Blue-Collar Freedom Fighters," *Reader's Digest*, September 1985, 141.

5 Spalding, "AIFLD Amok," 25; Hobart A. Spalding Jr., "The Two Latin American Foreign Policies of the US Labor Movement: The AFL-CIO Top Brass vs. Rank-and-File," *Science*

and Society 56:4 (1992), 425; Beth Sims, *Workers of the World Undermined: American Labor's Role in US Foreign Affairs* (Boston: South End Press, 1992), 51; Ken I. Boodhoo, "The Grenada Revolution: Rationale for Failure and Lessons for the Caribbean", LACC Occasional Papers Series, Dialogue #61, 1986, digitalcommons.fiu.edu, 21–2; Bass, "Organized Labor and US Foreign Policy", 68–9.

6 Jeff Schuhrke, "Agrarian Reform and the AFL-CIO's Cold War in El Salvador", *Diplomatic History* 44:4 (2020), 535–6.

7 Jeffrey L. Gould and Aldo Lauria-Santiago, *To Rise in Darkness: Revolution, Repression, and Memory in El Salvador, 1920–1932* (Durham, NC: Duke University Press, 2008).

8 Confidential Cables, American Embassy El Salvador to Secretary of State Washington, DC, June 22 and 26, 1973, Electronic Telegrams, 1973, Central Foreign Policy Files, created, 7/1/1973–12/31/1979, documenting the period ca. 1973–12/31/1979 (hereafter CFPF), National Archives at College Park, College Park (hereafter USNA) [retrieved from the Access to Archival Databases at archives.gov, June 5, 2018].

9 Schuhrke, "Agrarian Reform", 542.

10 Ibid., 545–6.

11 Christopher Dickey, "2 US Aides, Salvadoran Assassinated", *Washington Post*, January 5, 1981.

12 Schuhrke, "Agrarian Reform", 549–53; J. Michael Luhan, "AIFLD's Salvadoran Civil Wars", *Dissent* (Summer 1986), 341; Spalding, "AIFLD Amok", 23.

13 Luhan, "AIFLD's Salvadoran Civil Wars", 342–5; Spalding, "The Two Latin American Foreign Policies of the US Labor Movement", 428.

14 Kitty Krupat, "From War Zone to Free Trade Zone", in *No Sweat: Fashion, Free Trade, and the Rights of Garment Workers*, Andrew Ross, ed. (London: Verso, 1997), 64; Dave Slaney, "Solidarity and Self-Interest", *NACLA Reports* (May/June 1988), 29.

15 Krupat, "From War Zone", 65; Slaney, "Solidarity and Self-Interest", 29; Dyson quoted in Andrew Battista, "Unions and Cold War Foreign Policy in the 1980s: The National Labor Committee, the AFL-CIO, and Central America", *Diplomatic History* 26:3 (2002), 423.

16 National Labor Committee, *El Salvador: Labor, Terror, and Peace: A Special Fact-Finding Report by the National Labor Committee in Support of Democracy and Human Rights in El Salvador* (New York, 1984).

17 Ibid.

18 Battista, "Unions and Cold War Foreign Policy", 441–2.

19 Slaney, "Solidarity and Self Interest", 31; Battista, "Unions and Cold War Foreign Policy", 439–40.

20 Battista, "Unions and Cold War Foreign Policy", 424.

21 National Labor Committee, *The Search for Peace in Central America: A Special Report by the National Labor Committee in Support of Democracy and Human Rights in El Salvador* (New York, 1985).

22 AFL-CIO, *Proceedings of the Sixteenth Constitutional Convention of the AFL-CIO: Daily Proceedings and Executive Council Reports*, Anaheim, CA, October 28–31, 1985, 216–17.

23 Ibid., 222.

24 Ibid., 225–7.

25 Leslie Berger, "The Actor as Activist," *Washington Post*, February 16, 1982; Eleanor Blau, "Asner Calls 'Lou Grant' Censored," *New York Times*, May 18, 1982.
26 AFL-CIO, *Proceedings of the Sixteenth Constitutional Convention of the AFL-CIO*, 223–4.
27 Ibid., 234–6
28 William Serrin, "Reagan Bid Stirring Longstanding Labor Debate," *New York Times*, March 4, 1986; Slaney, "Solidarity and Self-Interest," 33–4.
29 Battista, "Unions and Cold War Foreign Policy," 423–4.
30 Slaney, "Solidarity and Self-Interest," 36; Battista, "Unions and Cold War Foreign Policy," 439–40.
31 Slaney, "Solidarity and Self-Interest," 36; Wayne King, "Thousands Protest US Policy in Central America," *New York Times*, April 26, 1987.
32 Quoted in Slaney, "Solidarity and Self-Interest," 35.

16. Hollow Victory

1 Eric Chenoweth, "AFL-CIO Support for Solidarity: Moral, Political, Financial," in *American Labor's Global Ambassadors: The International History of the AFL-CIO During the Cold War*, Robert Anthony Waters Jr. and Geert Van Goethem, eds. (New York: Palgrave Macmillan, 2013), 110–14.
2 Gregory F. Domber, *Empowering Revolution: America, Poland, and the End of the Cold War* (Chapel Hill: University of North Carolina Press, 2014), 210.
3 Ibid., 210.
4 Elaine Sciolino, "Kirkland Wins Acclaim for Success Abroad, but Faces Criticism at Home," *New York Times*, December 15, 1989.
5 "Remarks at the Presentation Ceremony for the Presidential Medal of Freedom," October 17, 1988, The American Presidency Project, presidency.ucsb.edu; AFL-CIO press release, February 10, 1989, box 17, folder 5, ILGWU International Relations Department files #5780/062, Kheel Center for Labor-Management Documentation and Archives (KC), Cornell University; Ted Morgan, *A Covert Life: Jay Lovestone: Communist, Anti-Communist, and Spymaster* (New York: Random House, 1999), 369.
6 Theodore H. Friedgut and Lewis H. Siegelbaum, "The Soviet Miners' Strike, July 1989: Perestroika from Below," The Carl Beck Papers (University of Pittsburgh Center for Russian and Eastern European Studies, 1990); Esther B. Fein, "Soviet Miners Strike in Defiance of Ban," *New York Times*, October 26, 1989; Francis X. Clines, "Soviet Miners' Strike Spreads, Testing Walkout Ban," *New York Times*, November 3, 1989; Frank Swoboda, "AFL-CIO to Aid Labor Groups In Soviet Union," *Washington Post*, December 20 1989; Swoboda, "Organizing Labor and Testing Glasnost," *Washington Post*, January 11, 1990.
7 Quoted in John Lewis Gaddis, *The Cold War: A New History* (New York: Penguin, 2005), 257.
8 Kate Geoghegan, "A Policy in Tension: The National Endowment for Democracy and the US Response to the Collapse of the Soviet Union," *Diplomatic History* (42:5, 2018), 791.
9 David Ignatius, "Innocence Abroad: The New World of Spyless Coups," *Washington Post*, September 22, 1991.

10 Frank Swoboda, "Mandela Thanks US Unions for Support, Seeks More Aid," *Washington Post*, June 29, 1990.

11 Scott Kraft and Barry Bearak, "After Miami, Mandela Finds Hero's Welcome in Detroit," *Los Angeles Times*, June 29, 1990; Swoboda, "Mandela Thanks US Unions for Support, Seeks More Aid"; John Nichols, "Nelson Mandela: Union Man," *The Nation*, December 6, 2013.

12 John Kifner, "Mandela Ends Tour of US with Oakland Appearance," *New York Times*, July 1, 1990; Peter Cole, *Dockworker Power: Race and Activism in Durban and the San Francisco Bay Area* (Urbana: University of Illinois Press, 2018), 200.

13 Frank Swoboda, "Walesa Makes Passionate Plea for US Investment in Poland," *Washington Post*, November 15, 1989.

14 Naomi Klein, *The Shock Doctrine: The Rise of Disaster Capitalism* (New York: Picador, 2007), 220–42, 275–83; Elizabeth C. Dunn, *Privatizing Poland: Baby Food, Big Business, and the Remaking of the Polish Working Class* (Ithaca, NY: Cornell University Press, 2004).

15 Lane Kirkland, "Creating Capitalism in Eastern Europe," *Indianapolis Star*, May 13, 1990.

16 "Walesa the Latest Star in 'Union Yes' Ad Campaign," *Associated Press*, November 16, 1989; Sciolino, "Kirkland Wins Acclaim for Success Abroad, but Faces Criticism at Home."

17 Timothy J. Minchin, *Labor Under Fire: A History of the AFL-CIO Since 1979* (Chapel Hill: University of North Carolina Press, 2017), 180; Steven Greenhouse, "Labor, Breaking Tradition, Criticizes War Preparations," *New York Times*, February 28, 2003; Sciolino, "Kirkland Wins Acclaim for Success Abroad, but Faces Criticism at Home."

18 Rudolph A. Oswald and William C. Doherty, "Latin American Labor and Structural Adjustment in the 90s: A Union View of Open Markets and a Worker-Ownership Response," AFL-CIO/AIFLD, January 1991, box 464, folder 1, Archive Union Files #6046, KC.

19 George Bush, quoted in NLC, "Paying to Lose Our Jobs," in *No Sweat: Fashion, Free Trade, and the Rights of Garment Workers,* Andrew Ross, ed. (London: Verso, 1997), 81; Clyde N. Farnsworth, "Battles Seem Likely over Caribbean Aid Proposal," *New York Times*, February 25, 1982.

20 Dave Slaney, "Solidarity and Self-Interest," *NACLA Reports* (May/June 1988), 29.

21 Quoted in Kitty Krupat, "From War Zone to Free Trade Zone," in *No Sweat*, 71; Andrew Battista, "Unions and Cold War Foreign Policy in the 1980s: The National Labor Committee, the AFL-CIO, and Central America," *Diplomatic History* 26:3 (2002), 447.

22 Quoted in Battista, "Unions and Cold War Foreign Policy," 447.

23 National Labor Committee, "Paying to Lose Our Jobs," 79–93.

24 Michael DeCourcy Hinds, "Workers Say US Program Took Their Jobs," *New York Times*, October 19, 1992; Keith Bradsher, "Congress Set to Rein in Foreign Aid Agency," *New York Times*, October 4, 1992.

25 Krupat, "From War Zone," 54–62; Bob Herbert, "A Sweatshop Victory," *New York Times*, December 22, 1995.

26 Jefferson Cowie, "National Struggles in a Transnational Economy: A Critical Analysis of US Labor's Campaign Against NAFTA," *Labor Studies Journal* 21:1 (1997), 23–5; Minchin, *Labor Under Fire*, 200–2.

27 Minchin, *Labor Under Fire*, 214–18.

28 Ibid., 220–36.

29 J. Y. Smith, "AFL-CIO's Kirkland Dies at 77," *Washington Post*, August 15, 1999; Henry Kissinger, Lane Kirkland Eulogy, September 23, 1999, box 735, folder 11, Henry A. Kissinger Papers, part II, Manuscripts and Archives, Yale University Library, findit.library.yale.edu; Ben Wattenberg, "Five-Star Cold War General," *Paris News*, August 25, 1999.

30 Battista, "Unions and Cold War Foreign Policy," 448.

31 Simon Rodberg, "The CIO without the CIA: Inside the AFL-CIO's Solidarity Center," *American Prospect*, December 19, 2001; Cowie, "National Struggles in a Transnational Economy," 29; Bart Barnes, "Barbara Shailor Borosage, Labor Activist for Union and in Government, Dies at 72," *Washington Post*, August 8, 2019.

32 Rodberg, "The CIO without the CIA."
    Tim Weiner, "A Kennedy-CIA Plot Returns to Haunt Clinton," *New York Times*, October 30, 1994; Al Kamen, "Labor Aide's Past Clouds His Future", *Washington Post*, September 19, 1994; Robert Waters and Gordon Olivier Daniels, "'When You're Handed Money on a Platter, It's Very Hard to Say, "Where Did You Get This?"' The AFL-CIO, the CIA, and British Guiana," *Revue Belge de Philologie et d'Histoire* 84:4 (2006), 1078.

Conclusion

1 G. Nelson Bass, "Organized Labor and US Foreign Policy: The Solidarity Center in Historical Context" (PhD diss., Florida International University, 2012), 101–9.

2 Jess T. Ford to Senator David Pryor, April 30, 1996, GAO/NSIAD-96-142R, AIFLD Funding and Programs.

3 ProPublica, Nonprofit Explorer, American Center for International Labor Solidarity, projects.propublica.org.

4 G. Nelson Bass, "Organized Labor and US Foreign Policy: The Solidarity Center in Historical Context" (PhD diss., Florida International University, 2012), 121, 149.

5 Chris Townsend, email to the author, August 17, 2022.

6 Christopher Marquis, "US Bankrolling Is Under Scrutiny for Ties to Chávez Ouster," *New York Times*, April 25, 2002; Tim Shorrock, "Toeing the Line? Sweeney and US Foreign Policy," *New Labor Forum* (Fall/Winter 2002); Kim Scipes, *AFL-CIO's Secret War Against Developing Country Workers: Solidarity or Sabotage?* (Lanham, MD: Lexington Books, 2010), 56–66; Eva Golinger, *The Chávez Code: Cracking US Intervention in Venezuela* (London: Pluto Press, 2007); George Ciccariello-Maher, *We Created Chávez: A People's History of the Venezuelan Revolution* (Durham, NC: Duke University Press, 2013), 167–70, 180–8; Tim Gill, "Newly Revealed Documents Show How the AFL-CIO Aided US Interference in Venezuela," *Jacobin*, August 5, 2020.

7 Scipes, *AFL-CIO's Secret War*, 74–6.

Index

Hammer, Frank, 259
Hammer, Michael, 251, 253, 259, 262
Hannah, John, 198
Hannah, Philip, 58
"Hard Hat Riot," 185–7
Harrington, Michael, 224, 227
Hatch, Orrin, 235, 236, 240, 261, 262
Haymarket Square affair, 10, 12
Herling, John, 53
Herrera, Ernesto, 239
Hindustan Times, on W. Reuther's visit to
    India, 108
Hirsch, Fred, 213, 214, 289
Hoffmann, Abbie, 263
Homestead strike, 13
Hoover, J. Edgar, 104
Horowitz, Rachelle, 228, 229
housing projects
    by AIFLD, 131–2, 149–50
    in the Philippines, 239
Humphrey, Hubert, 173, 181, 182
Hussein, Saddam, 274

Ibáñez, Bernardo, 49, 50, 53, 57, 58–9
ICFTU (International Confederation of
    Free Trade Unions). *See*
    International Confederation of Free
    Trade Unions (ICFTU)
IFPCW (International Federation of
    Petroleum and Chemical Workers),
    194, 196
Iglesias, Santiago, 44
Ignatius, David, 269
ILGWU (International Ladies' Garment
    Workers' Union), 17, 29–30, 32, 152,
    218–19, 280
ILO (International Labor Organization),
    15, 89, 158, 175
ILWU (International Longshore and
    Warehouse Union), 27, 68, 172,
    246–7, 259
IMF (International Monetary Fund), 61,
    217, 218, 272
Indian National Trade Union Congress,
    107–8, 109
Indonesia, US intrigues in, 79–81
industrial pluralism, 68–72, 218
Industrial Workers of the World (IWW),
    14, 16, 44
informal empire, use of term, 4
Inside the Company (Agee), 215, 216
Institute of International Labor Research,
    89, 90, 144, 152, 194

Inter-American Confederation of
    Workers (CIT), 58–9, 71, 86
Inter-American Labor Congress (Lima,
    1948), 57–9
International Affairs Department (AFL),
    39
International Affairs Department
    (AFL-CIO), 114, 152, 161, 179, 196,
    229, 258, 281
International Association of Machinists,
    175, 281
International Brotherhood of Teamsters, 180
International Center for Free Trade
    Unionists in Exile (Exile Center), 78,
    89
International Confederation of Free
    Trade Unions (ICFTU)
    and AFL-CIO, break with, 200–1
    and AFL-CIO, bringing back into, 223
    in Africa, 155, 157, 158–61, 162, 163,
        164, 166
    anticommunist labor movements in,
        284
    conducting foreign policy through, 106
    education initiatives of, 120–2
    founding of, 71, 72, 77, 86, 113
International Solidarity Fund, 114
International Cooperation
    Administration, 124
International Federation of Petroleum
    and Chemical Workers (IFPCW),
    194, 196
International Federation of Plantation,
    Agricultural, and Allied Workers,
    215
International Federation of Trade Unions
    (AKA Amsterdam International), 17
International Labor Organization (ILO),
    15, 89, 158, 175
International Labor Relations Committee
    (AFL), 29
International Ladies' Garment Workers'
    Union (ILGWU), 17, 29–30, 32, 152,
    218–19, 280
International Longshore and Warehouse
    Union (ILWU), 27, 68, 172, 246–7,
    259
International Metalworkers Federation,
    138, 174
International Monetary Fund (IMF), 61,
    217, 218, 272
International Organization of Masters,
    Mates and Pilots, 222

Cold War intrigues of, 5–6
communists in, 27
decline of, 273, 283
as fighting for larger pie, 69
during Grenada invasion, 250
history of, 9–20
impact of Cold War on decline of, 6–7
impact of détente on, 219–20
imperialism of, 196–7
interaction with Soviet Bloc, 109–12
membership in (1940), 20
membership in (1946), 20, 63
membership in (1947), 6
membership in (1991), 7
support for Cold War by, 15–16, 20
support for World War I by, 14–15, 18
support for World War II by, 15–16, 19–20
support of trade liberalization by, 68–9
and Vietnam War, 171–90
youth-led renaissance in, 4
labor movements (Europe), rift between socialist and communist unionists in, 17–18
labor unions. *See* foreign unions; *specific unions*
Lacerda, Carlos, 138, 140
La Matanza (the massacre), 252
Lane, Tom, 76, 77
Lansdale, Edward, 170
Larson, Rodney, 215
Latin America. *See also specific countries*
labor education in, 121–2. *See also* American Institute for Free Labor Development (AIFLD)
labor movement in, 43–59
unions in, 43–59
Latinos
as entering ranks of organized labor, 206
organizing campaigns targeting, 191
Law of Salary Compression (Brazil), 141
LCGIL (Free General Confederation of Italian Labor), 77
League for Industrial Democracy (LID), 224–5, 228, 233
League of Nations, ILO as part of, 15
League of Revolutionary Black Workers, 192, 206
Lee, Ernest, 34, 221
Levenson-Estrada, Deborah, 95
Lewis, John L., 26, 27, 30, 46, 66
Lichtenstein, Nelson, 20, 63

Liebstein, Jacob. *See* Lovestone, Jay (born Jacob Liebstein)
Lindsay, John, 185
Lipset, Seymour Martin, 228
Loan, Nguyen Ngoc, 181
Lombardo Toledano, Vicente, 45, 46, 47, 50, 58, 59
López, Robinson Ruiz, 146
Lovestone, Jay (born Jacob Liebstein), 31–4, 36, 39, 40–1, 62, 72, 73, 74, 75, 77, 78, 79, 81, 83, 84, 85, 99, 100, 104, 105–6, 107, 109, 113, 114, 115, 138, 143, 145, 152, 155, 160–1, 163, 164, 166, 169, 174, 181, 186, 187, 188, 193, 195, 221, 224, 229, 267, 284, 285
Lu Ching-shih, 83
Lucy, William, 248, 270
Lumumba, Patrice, 160
Lynch, Leon, 247

Machinists, 256
Magdalena, 80–1
Mahomo, Nelson ("Nana"), 243
Mandela, Nelson, 269–71
Mandela, Winnie, 270, 271
Mao Zedong, 67, 219
Marable, Manning, 246–7
Marcos, Ferdinand, 238, 239, 240
Marinho, Rômulo Teixeira, 140
Maritime Confederation of Chile, 210, 212
Marshall, George, 39, 41, 60
Marshall Plan, 40–1, 60–2, 66, 68, 73–4, 75, 105, 124, 284
Martin, Homer, 32, 33, 36
Marx, Karl, 12, 120, 273
May 1 (May Day), as International Workers' Day, 12
May First Movement (KMU). *See* KMU (May First Movement)
Mazey, Emil, 172, 173, 178, 179, 180
Mazzini Society, 48
Mazzocchi, Tony, 185
Mboya, Tom, 156, 159, 161, 162, 167
McCabe, William Howard, 136, 194
McCarthy, Eugene, 178, 181
McCollum, John, 121–2, 123
McCray, George, 157, 158, 159, 163
McEntee, Gerald, 279
McGovern, George, 187, 227
McLellan, Andrew, 142, 143–4, 145, 215
Meakins, Gene, 137, 193